THAT USED
TO BE US

D1235580

ALSO BY THOMAS L. FRIEDMAN

From Beirut to Jerusalem (1989)
The Lexus and the Olive Tree (1999)
Longitudes and Attitudes (2002)
The World Is Flat (2005)
Hot, Flat, and Crowded (2008)

ALSO BY MICHAEL MANDELBAUM

The Nuclear Question (1979)
The Nuclear Revolution (1981)
The Nuclear Future (1983)
Reagan and Gorbachev (co-author, 1987)
The Fate of Nations (1988)
The Global Rivals (co-author, 1988)
The Dawn of Peace in Europe (1996)
The Ideas That Conquered the World (2002)
The Meaning of Sports (2004)
The Case for Goliath (2006)
Democracy's Good Name (2007)
The Frugal Superpower (2010)

THAT USED TO BE US

What Went Wrong with America – and How It Can Come Back

Thomas L. Friedman

AND

Michael Mandelbaum

Little, Brown

LITTLE, BROWN

First published in the USA in 2011 by Farrar, Straus and Giroux
First published in Great Britain in 2011 by Little, Brown
Reprinted 2011

Copyright © Thomas L. Friedman and Michael Mandelbaum 2011

The right of Thomas L. Friedman and Michael Mandelbaum to be identified
as the Authors of this Work has been asserted by them in accordance with
the Copyright, Designs and Patents Act 1988.

All rights reserved.
No part of this publication may be reproduced, stored in a
retrieval system, or transmitted, in any form or by any means, without
the prior permission in writing of the publisher, nor be otherwise circulated
in any form of binding or cover other than that in which it is published
and without a similar condition including this condition being
imposed on the subsequent purchaser.

Grateful permission is made to reprint the following material: Graph on page 129 courtesy of
The New York Times, Copyright © 2010 The New York Times. Graph on page 230 courtesy
of The Washington Post, © April 30, 2011 The Washington Post. Maps on page 251 courtesy
of 'Zombie', an Xpress Blogger for Pajamas Media at www.pajamasmedia.com. Lyrics from
'Fallin' and Flyin", words and music by Stephen Bruton and Gary Nicholson, Copyright
© 2009, 2010 Stephen Bruton/Brutunes/administered by Bug Music, Sony/ATV Music
Publishing LLC and Gary Nicholson Music LLC. Lyrics reproduced with kind permission
of Publishers and Writers. Lyrics from 'Of Thee I Sing', music and lyrics by George
Gershwin and Ira Gershwin, Copyright © 1931 (Renewed) WB Music Corp.

A CIP catalogue record for this book
is available from the British Library.

Hardback ISBN 978-1-4087-0358-8
C format ISBN 978-1-4087-0359-5

Printed and bound in Great Britain by
Clays Ltd, St Ives plc

Papers used by Little, Brown are from well-managed forests
and other responsible sources.

MIX
Paper from
responsible sources
FSC
www.fsc.org   FSC® C104740

Little, Brown
An imprint of
Little, Brown Book Group
100 Victoria Embankment
London EC4Y 0DY

An Hachette UK Company
www.hachette.co.uk

www.littlebrown.co.uk

To Ann Friedman and Anne Mandelbaum

It makes no sense for China to have better rail systems than us, and Singapore having better airports than us. And we just learned that China now has the fastest supercomputer on Earth—that used to be us.

—President Barack Obama, November 3, 2010

Contents

Preface: Growing Up in America

A reader might ask why two people who have devoted their careers to writing about foreign affairs—one of us as a foreign correspondent and columnist at *The New York Times* and the other as a professor of American foreign policy at The Johns Hopkins University School of Advanced International Studies—have collaborated on a book about the American condition today. The answer is simple. We have been friends for more than twenty years, and in that time hardly a week has gone by without our discussing some aspect of international relations and American foreign policy. But in the last couple of years, we started to notice something: Every conversation would begin with foreign policy but end with domestic policy—what was happening, or not happening, in the United States. Try as we might to redirect them, the conversations kept coming back to America and our seeming inability today to rise to our greatest challenges.

This situation, of course, has enormous foreign policy implications. America plays a huge and, more often than not, constructive role in the world today. But that role depends on the country's social, political, and economic health. And America today is not healthy—economically or politically. This book is our effort to explain how we got into that state and how we get out of it.

We beg the reader's indulgence with one style issue. At times, we include stories, anecdotes, and interviews that involve only one of us. To make clear who is involved, we must, in effect, quote ourselves: "As Tom recalled . . ." "As Michael wrote . . ." You can't simply say "I said" or "I saw" when you have a co-authored book with a lot of reporting in it.

Readers familiar with our work know us mainly as authors and commentators, but we are also both, well, Americans. That is important, because that identity drives the book as much as our policy interests do. So here are just a few words of introduction from each of us—not as experts but as citizens.

Tom: I was born in Minneapolis, Minnesota, and was raised in a small suburb called St. Louis Park—made famous by the brothers Ethan and Joel Coen in their movie *A Serious Man*, which was set in our neighborhood. Senator Al Franken, the Coen brothers, the Harvard political philosopher Michael J. Sandel, the political scientist Norman Ornstein, the longtime NFL football coach Marc Trestman, and I all grew up in and around that little suburb within a few years of one another, and it surely had a big impact on all of us. In my case, it bred a deep optimism about America and the notion that we really can act collectively for the common good.

In 1971, the year I graduated from high school, *Time* magazine had a cover featuring then Minnesota governor Wendell Anderson holding up a fish he had just caught, under the headline "The Good Life in Minnesota." It was all about "the state that works." When the senators from your childhood were the Democrats Hubert Humphrey, Walter Mondale, and Eugene McCarthy, your congressmen were the moderate Republicans Clark MacGregor and Bill Frenzel, and the leading corporations in your state—Dayton's, Target, General Mills, and 3M—were pioneers in corporate social responsibility and believed that it was part of their mission to help build things like the Tyrone Guthrie Theater, you wound up with a deep conviction that politics really can work and that there is a viable political center in American life.

I attended public school with the same group of kids from K through 12. In those days in Minnesota, private schools were for kids in trouble. Private school was pretty much unheard of for middle-class St. Louis Park kids, and pretty much everyone was middle-class. My mom enlisted in the U.S. Navy in World War II, and my parents actually bought our home thanks to the loan she got through the GI Bill. My dad, who never went to college, was vice president of a company that sold ball bearings. My wife, Ann Bucksbaum, was born in Marshalltown, Iowa, and was raised in Des Moines. To this day, my best friends are still those kids I grew up with in St. Louis Park, and I still carry around a mental image—no doubt idealized—of Minnesota that anchors and informs a lot of my political choices. No matter where I go—London, Beirut, Jerusalem, Washington, Beijing, or Bangalore—I'm always looking to rediscover that land of ten thousand lakes where politics actually worked to make people's lives better, not pull them apart. *That used to be us.* In fact, it used to be my neighborhood.

Michael: While Tom and his wife come from the middle of the country, my wife, Anne Mandelbaum, and I grew up on the two coasts—she in Manhattan and I in Berkeley, California. My father was a professor of anthropology at the University of California, and my mother, after my two siblings and I reached high school age, became a public school teacher and then joined the education faculty at the university that we called, simply, Cal.

Although Berkeley has a reputation for political radicalism, during my childhood in the 1950s it had more in common with Tom's Minneapolis than with the Berkeley the world has come to know. It was more a slice of Middle America than a hotbed of revolution. As amazing as it may seem today, for part of my boyhood it had a Republican mayor and was represented by a Republican congressman.

One episode from those years is particularly relevant to this book. It occurred in the wake of the Soviet Union's 1957 launching of Sputnik, the first Earth-orbiting satellite. The event was a shock to the United States, and the shock waves reached Garfield Junior High School (since renamed after Martin Luther King Jr.), where I was in seventh grade. The entire student body was summoned to an assembly at which the principal solemnly informed us that in the future we all would have to study harder, and that mathematics and science would be crucial.

Given my parents' commitment to education, I did not need to be told that school and studying were important. But I was impressed by the gravity of the moment. I understood that the United States faced a national challenge and that everyone would have to contribute to meeting it. I did not doubt that America, and Americans, would meet it. There is no going back to the 1950s, and there are many reasons to be glad that that is so, but the kind of seriousness the country was capable of then is just as necessary now.

We now live and work in the nation's capital, where we have seen first-hand the government's failure to come to terms with the major challenges the country faces. But although this book's perspective on the present is gloomy, its hopes and expectations for the future are high. We know that America can meet its challenges. After all, that's the America where we grew up.

Thomas L. Friedman
Michael Mandelbaum
Bethesda, Maryland, June 2011

PART I
THE DIAGNOSIS

ONE

If You See Something, Say Something

This is a book about America that begins in China.

In September 2010, Tom attended the World Economic Forum's summer conference in Tianjin, China. Five years earlier, getting to Tianjin had involved a three-and-a-half-hour car ride from Beijing to a polluted, crowded Chinese version of Detroit, but things had changed. Now, to get to Tianjin, you head to the Beijing South Railway Station—an ultramodern flying saucer of a building with glass walls and an oval roof covered with 3,246 solar panels—buy a ticket from an electronic kiosk offering choices in Chinese and English, and board a world-class high-speed train that goes right to another roomy, modern train station in downtown Tianjin. Said to be the fastest in the world when it began operating in 2008, the Chinese bullet train covers 115 kilometers, or 72 miles, in a mere twenty-nine minutes.

The conference itself took place at the Tianjin Meijiang Convention and Exhibition Center—a massive, beautifully appointed structure, the like of which exists in few American cities. As if the convention center wasn't impressive enough, the conference's co-sponsors in Tianjin gave some facts and figures about it (www.tj-summerdavos.cn). They noted that it contained a total floor area of 230,000 square meters (almost 2.5 million square feet) and that "construction of the Meijiang Convention Center started on September 15, 2009, and was completed in May, 2010." Reading that line, Tom started counting on his fingers: Let's see—September, October, November, December, January . . .

Eight months.

Returning home to Maryland from that trip, Tom was describing the Tianjin complex and how quickly it was built to Michael and his wife, Anne. At one point Anne asked: "Excuse me, Tom. Have you been to our subway stop lately?" We all live in Bethesda and often use the Washington Metrorail subway to get to work in downtown Washington, D.C. Tom had just been at the Bethesda station and knew exactly what Anne was talking about: The two short escalators had been under repair for nearly six months. While the one being fixed was closed, the other had to be shut off and converted into a two-way staircase. At rush hour, this was creating a huge mess. Everyone trying to get on or off the platform had to squeeze single file up and down one frozen escalator. It sometimes took ten minutes just to get out of the station. A sign on the closed escalator said that its repairs were part of a massive escalator "modernization" project.

What was taking this "modernization" project so long? We investigated. Cathy Asato, a spokeswoman for the Washington Metropolitan Transit Authority, had told the *Maryland Community News* (October 20, 2010) that "the repairs were scheduled to take about six months and are on schedule. Mechanics need 10 to 12 weeks to fix each escalator."

A simple comparison made a startling point: It took China's Teda Construction Group thirty-two weeks to build a world-class convention center from the ground up—including giant escalators in every corner— and it was taking the Washington Metro crew twenty-four weeks to repair two tiny escalators of twenty-one steps each. We searched a little further and found that WTOP, a local news radio station, had interviewed the Metro interim general manager, Richard Sarles, on July 20, 2010. Sure, these escalators are old, he said, but "they have not been kept in a state of good repair. We're behind the curve on that, so we have to catch up . . . Just last week, smoke began pouring out of the escalators at the Dupont Circle station during rush hour."

On November 14, 2010, *The Washington Post* ran a letter to the editor from Mark Thompson of Kensington, Maryland, who wrote:

> I have noted with interest your reporting on the $225,000 study that Metro hired Vertical Transportation Excellence to conduct into the sorry state of the system's escalators and elevators . . . I am sure that the study has merit. But as someone who has ridden Metro for more than 30 years, I can think of an easier way

to assess the health of the escalators. For decades they ran silently and efficiently. But over the past several years—when the escalators are running—aging or ill-fitting parts have generated horrific noises that sound to me like a Tyrannosaurus Rex trapped in a tar pit screeching its dying screams.

The quote we found most disturbing, though, came from a *Maryland Community News* story about the long lines at rush hour caused by the seemingly endless Metro repairs: " 'My impression, standing on line there, is people have sort of gotten used to it,' said Benjamin Ross, who lives in Bethesda and commutes every day from the downtown station."

The National Watercooler

People have sort of gotten used to it. Indeed, that sense of resignation, that sense that, well, this is just how things are in America today, that sense that America's best days are behind it and China's best days are ahead of it, have become the subject of watercooler, dinner-party, grocery-line, and classroom conversations all across America today. We hear the doubts from children, who haven't been to China. Tom took part in the September 2010 Council of Educational Facility Planners International (CEFPI) meeting in San Jose, California. As part of the program, there was a "School of the Future Design Competition," which called for junior high school students to design their own ideal green school. He met with the finalists on the last morning of the convention, and they talked about global trends. At one point, Tom asked them what they thought about China. A young blond-haired junior high school student, Isabelle Foster, from Old Lyme Middle School in Connecticut, remarked, "It seems like they have more ambition and will than we do." Tom asked her, "Where did you get that thought?" She couldn't really explain it, she said. She had never visited China. But it was just how she felt. It's in the air.

We heard the doubts about America from Pennsylvania governor Ed Rendell, in his angry reaction after the National Football League postponed for two days a game scheduled in Philadelphia between the

Philadelphia Eagles and the Minnesota Vikings—because of a severe snowstorm. The NFL ordered the games postponed because it didn't want fans driving on icy, snow-covered roads. But Rendell saw it as an indicator of something more troubling—that Americans had gone soft. "It goes against everything that football is all about," Rendell said in an interview with the sports radio station 97.5 The Fanatic in Philadelphia (December 27, 2010). "We've become a nation of wusses. The Chinese are kicking our butt in everything. If this was in China, do you think the Chinese would have called off the game? People would have been marching down to the stadium, they would have walked, and they would have been doing calculus on the way down."

We read the doubts in letters to the editor, such as this impassioned post by Eric R. on *The New York Times* comments page under a column Tom wrote about China (December 1, 2010):

> We are nearly complete in our evolution from Lewis and Clark into Elmer Fudd and Yosemite Sam. We used to embrace challenges, endure privation, throttle our fear and strike out into the (unknown) wilderness. In this mode we rallied to span the continent with railroads, construct a national highway system, defeated monstrous dictators, cured polio and landed men on the moon. Now we text and put on makeup as we drive, spend more on video games than books, forswear exercise, demonize hunting, and are rapidly succumbing to obesity and diabetes. So much for the pioneering spirit that made us (once) the greatest nation on earth, one that others looked up to and called "exceptional."

Sometimes the doubts hit us where we least expect them. A few weeks after returning from China, Tom went to the White House to conduct an interview. He passed through the Secret Service checkpoint on Pennsylvania Avenue, and after putting his bags through the X-ray machine and collecting them, he grabbed the metal door handle to enter the White House driveway. The handle came off in his hand. "Oh, it does that sometimes," the Secret Service agent at the door said nonchalantly, as Tom tried to fit the wobbly handle back into the socket.

And often now we hear those doubts from visitors here—as when a neighbor in Bethesda mentions that over the years he has hired several young women from Germany to help with his child care, and they always remark on two things: how many squirrels there are in Washington, and how rutted the streets are. They just can't believe that America's capital would have such potholed streets.

Frustrated Optimists

So, do we buy the idea, increasingly popular in some circles, that Britain owned the nineteenth century, America dominated the twentieth century, and China will inevitably reign supreme in the twenty-first century—and that all you have to do is fly from Tianjin or Shanghai to Washington, D.C., and take the subway to know that?

No, we do not. And we have written this book to explain why no American, young or old, should resign himself or herself to that view either. The two of us are not pessimists when it comes to America and its future. We are optimists, but we are also frustrated. We are frustrated optimists. In our view, the two attitudes go together. We are optimists because American society, with its freewheeling spirit, its diversity of opinions and talents, its flexible economy, its work ethic and penchant for innovation, is in fact ideally suited to thrive in the tremendously challenging world we are living in. We are optimists because the American political and economic systems, when functioning properly, can harness the nation's talents and energy to meet the challenges the country faces. We are optimists because Americans have plenty of experience in doing big, hard things together. And we are optimists because our track record of national achievement gives ample grounds for believing we can overcome our present difficulties.

But that's also why we're frustrated. Optimism or pessimism about America's future cannot simply be a function of our capacity to do great things or our history of having done great things. It also has to be a function of our will actually to do those things again. So many Americans are doing great things today, but on a small scale. Philanthropy, volunteerism, individual initiative: they're all impressive, but what the country needs most is collective action on a large scale.

We cannot be pessimists about America when we know that it is home to so many creative, talented, hardworking people, but we cannot help but be frustrated when we discover how many of those people feel that our country is not educating the workforce they need, or admitting the energetic immigrants they seek, or investing in the infrastructure they require, or funding the research they envision, or putting in place the intelligent tax laws and incentives that our competitors have installed.

Hence the title of this opening chapter: "If you see something, say something." That is the mantra that the Department of Homeland Security plays over and over on loudspeakers in airports and railroad stations around the country. Well, we have seen and heard something, and millions of Americans have, too. What we've seen is not a suspicious package left under a stairwell. What we've seen is hiding in plain sight. We've seen something that poses a greater threat to our national security and well-being than al-Qaeda does. We've seen a country with enormous potential falling into disrepair, political disarray, and palpable discomfort about its present condition and future prospects.

This book is our way of saying something—about what is wrong, why things have gone wrong, and what we can and must do to make them right.

Why say it now, though, and why the urgency?

"Why now?" is easy to answer: because our country is in a slow decline, just slow enough for us to be able to pretend—or believe—that a decline is not taking place. As the ever-optimistic Timothy Shriver, chairman of the Special Olympics, son of Peace Corps founder Sargent Shriver, and nephew of President John F. Kennedy, responded when we told him about our book: "It's as though we just slip a little each year and shrug it off to circumstances beyond our control—an economic downturn here, a social problem there, the political mess this year. We're losing a step a day and no one's saying, Stop!" No doubt, Shriver added, most Americans "would still love to be the country of great ideals and achievements, but no one seems willing to pay the price." Or, as Jeffrey Immelt, the CEO of General Electric, put it to us: "What we lack in the U.S. today is the confidence that is generated by solving one big, hard problem—together." It has been a long time now since we did something big and hard together.

We will argue that this slow-motion decline has four broad causes. First, since the end of the Cold War, we, and especially our political leaders, have stopped starting each day by asking the two questions that are crucial for determining public policy: What world are we living in, and what exactly do we need to do to thrive in this world? The U.S. Air Force has a strategic doctrine originally designed by one of its officers, John Boyd, called the OODA loop. It stands for "observe, orient, decide, act." Boyd argued that when you are a fighter pilot, if your OODA loop is faster than the other guy's, you will always win the dogfight. Today, America's OODA loop is far too slow and often discombobulated. In American political discourse today, there is far too little observing, orienting, deciding, and acting and far too much shouting, asserting, dividing, and postponing. When the world gets really fast, the speed with which a country can effectively observe, orient, decide, and act matters more than ever.

Second, over the last twenty years, we as a country have failed to address some of our biggest problems—particularly education, deficits and debt, and energy and climate change—and now they have all worsened to a point where they cannot be ignored but they also cannot be effectively addressed without collective action and collective sacrifice. Third, to make matters worse, we have stopped investing in our country's traditional formula for greatness, a formula that goes back to the founding of the country. Fourth, as we will explain, we have not been able to fix our problems or reinvest in our strengths because our political system has become paralyzed and our system of values has suffered serious erosion. But finally, being optimists, we will offer our own strategy for overcoming these problems.

"Why the urgency?" is also easy to answer. In part the urgency stems from the fact that as a country we do not have the resources or the time to waste that we had twenty years ago, when our budget deficit was under control and all of our biggest challenges seemed at least manageable. In the last decade especially, we have spent so much of our time and energy—and the next generation's money—fighting terrorism and indulging ourselves with tax cuts and cheap credit that we now have no reserves. We are driving now without a bumper, without a spare tire, and with the gas gauge nearing empty. Should the market or Mother Nature make a sudden disruptive move in the wrong direction, we would not have the resources to shield ourselves from the worst effects, as we had in the past. Winston Churchill was fond of saying that "America will always do the right thing, but only after exhausting all other options." America simply doesn't have time anymore for exhausting any options other than the right ones.

Our sense of urgency also derives from the fact that our political system is not properly framing, let alone addressing, our ultimate challenge. Our goal should not be merely to solve America's debt and deficit problems. That is far too narrow. Coping with these problems is important—indeed necessary and urgent—but it is only a means to an end. The goal is for America to remain a great country. This means that while reducing our deficits, we must also invest in education, infrastructure, and research and development, as well as open our society more widely to talented immigrants and fix the regulations that govern our economy. Immigration, education, and sensible regulation are traditional ingredients of the American formula for greatness. They are more vital than ever if we hope to realize the full potential of the American people in the coming decades, to generate the resources to sustain our prosperity, and to remain the global leader that we have been and that the world needs us to be. We, the authors of this book, don't want simply to restore American solvency. We want to maintain American greatness. We are not green-eyeshade guys. We're Fourth of July guys.

China, Again

And to maintain American greatness, the right option for us is not to become more like China. It is to become more like ourselves. Certainly, China has made extraordinary strides in lifting tens of millions of its people out of poverty and in modernizing its infrastructure—from convention centers, to highways, to airports, to housing. China's relentless focus on economic development and its willingness to search the world for the best practices, experiment with them, and then scale those that work is truly impressive.

But the Chinese still suffer from large and potentially debilitating problems: a lack of freedom, rampant corruption, horrible pollution, and an education system that historically has stifled creativity. China does not have better political or economic systems than the United States. In order to sustain its remarkable economic progress, we believe,

China will ultimately have to adopt more features of the American system, particularly the political and economic liberty that are fundamental to our success. China cannot go on relying heavily on its ability to mobilize cheap labor and cheap capital and on copying and assembling the innovations of others.

Still, right now, we believe that China is getting 90 percent of the potential benefits from its second-rate political system. It is getting the most out of its authoritarianism. But here is the shortcoming that Americans should be focused on: We are getting only 50 percent of the potential benefits from our first-rate system. We are getting so much less than we can, should, and must get out of our democracy.

In short, our biggest problem is not that we're failing to keep up with China's best practices but that we've strayed so far from our own best practices. America's future depends not on our adopting features of the Chinese system, but on our making our own democratic system work with the kind of focus, moral authority, seriousness, collective action, and stick-to-itiveness that China has managed to generate by authoritarian means for the last several decades.

In our view, all of the comparisons between China and the United States that you hear around American watercoolers these days aren't about China at all. They are about us. China is just a mirror. We're really talking about ourselves and our own loss of self-confidence. We see in the Chinese some character traits that we once had—that once defined us as a nation—but that we seem to have lost.

Orville Schell heads up the Asia Society's Center on U.S.-China Relations in New York City. He is one of America's most experienced China-watchers. He also attended the Tianjin conference, and one afternoon, after a particularly powerful presentation there about China's latest economic leap forward, Tom asked Schell why he thought China's rise has come to unnerve and obsess Americans.

"Because we have recently begun to find ourselves so unable to get things done, we tend to look with a certain over-idealistic yearning when it comes to China," Schell answered. "We see what they have done and project onto them something we miss, fearfully miss, in ourselves"—that "can-do, get-it-done, everyone-pull-together, whatever-it-takes" attitude that built our highways and dams and put a man on the moon. "These were hallmarks of our childhood culture," said Schell. "But now we view our country turning into the opposite, even as we see China becoming animated by these same kinds of energies . . . China desperately wants to prove itself to the world, while at the same time America seems to be losing its hunger to demonstrate its excellence." The Chinese are motivated, Schell continued, by a "deep yearning to restore China to greatness, and, sadly, one all too often feels that we are losing that very motor force in America."

The two of us do feel that, but we do not advocate policies and practices to sustain American greatness out of arrogance or a spirit of chauvinism. We do it out of a love for our country and a powerful belief in what a force for good America can be—for its own citizens and for the world—at its best. We are well aware of America's imperfections, past and present. We know that every week in America a politician takes a bribe; someone gets convicted of a crime he or she did not commit; public money gets wasted that should have gone for a new bridge, a new school, or pathbreaking research; many young people drop out of school; young women get pregnant without committed fathers; and people unfairly lose their jobs or their houses. The cynic says, "Look at the gap between our ideals and our reality. Any talk of American greatness is a lie." The partisan says, "Ignore the gap. We're still 'exceptional.'" Our view is that the gaps do matter, and this book will have a lot to say about them. But America is not defined by its gaps. Our greatness as a country— what truly defines us—is and always has been our never-ending effort to close these gaps, our constant struggle to form a more perfect union. The gaps simply show us the work we still have to do.

To repeat: Our problem is not China, and our solution is not China. Our problem is us—what we are doing and not doing, how our political system is functioning and not functioning, which values we are and are not living by. And our solution is us—the people, the society, and the government that we used to be, and can be again. That is why this book is meant as both a wake-up call and a pep talk—unstinting in its critique of where we are and unwavering in its optimism about what we can achieve if we act together.

TWO

Ignoring Our Problems

It is not the strongest of the species that survives, nor the most intelligent that survives. It is the one that is the most adaptable to change.
—Evolutionary theory

We are going to do a terrible thing to you. We are going to deprive you of an enemy.   —Georgi Arbatov, Soviet expert on the United States, speaking at the end of the Cold War

It all seems so obvious now, but on the historic day when the Berlin Wall was cracked open—November 11, 1989—no one would have guessed that America was about to make the most dangerous mistake a country can make: We were about to misread our environment. We should have remembered Oscar Wilde's admonition: "In this world there are only two tragedies. One is not getting what one wants, and the other is getting it." America was about to experience the second tragedy. We had achieved a long-sought goal: the end of the Cold War on Western terms. But that very achievement ushered in a new world, with unprecedented challenges to the United States. No one warned us—neither Oscar Wilde nor someone like the statesman who had done precisely that for America four decades earlier: George Kennan.

On the evening of February 22, 1946, Kennan, then the forty-two-year-old deputy chief of mission at the U.S. embassy in Moscow, dispatched an 8,000-word cable to the State Department in Washington. The "Long Telegram," as it was later known, became the most famous diplomatic communication in the history of the United States. A condensed version, which ran under the byline "X" in *Foreign Affairs* the next year, became perhaps the most influential journal article in American history.

Kennan's cable earned its renown because it served as the charter for American foreign policy during the Cold War. It called for the "containment" of the military power of the Soviet Union and political resistance to its communist ideology. It led to the Marshall Plan for aid to war-torn Europe; to NATO—the first peacetime military alliance in American history—and the stationing of an American army in Europe; to America's wars in Korea and Vietnam; to the nuclear arms race; to a dangerous brush with nuclear war over Cuba; and to a political rivalry waged in every corner of the world through military assistance, espionage, public relations, and economic aid.

The Cold War came to an end with the overthrow of the communist regimes of Eastern Europe in 1989 and the collapse of the Soviet Union in 1991. But the broad message of the Long Telegram is one we need to hear today: "Wake up! Pay attention! The world you are living in has fundamentally changed. It is not the world you think it is. You need to adapt, because the health, security, and future of the country depend upon it."

It is hard to realize today what a shock that message was to many Americans. The world Kennan's cable described was *not* the one in which most Americans believed they were living in or wanted to live in. Most of them assumed that, with the end of World War II, the United States could look forward to good relations with its wartime Soviet ally and the end of the kind of huge national exertion that winning the war had required. The message of the Long Telegram was that both of these happy assumptions were wrong. The nation's leaders eventually accepted Kennan's analysis and adopted his prescription. Before long the American people knew they had to be vigilant, creative, and united. They knew they had to foster economic growth, technological innovation, and social mobility in order to avoid losing the global geopolitical competition with their great rival. The Cold War had its ugly excesses and its fiascos—Vietnam and the Bay of Pigs, for example—but it also set certain limits on American politics and society. We just had to look across at the Iron Curtain and the evil empire behind it—or take part in one of those nuclear bomb drills in the basements of our elementary schools—to know that we were living in a world defined by the struggle for supremacy between two nuclear-armed superpowers. That fact shaped both the content of our politics and the prevailing attitude of our leaders and citizens, which was one of constant vigilance. We didn't always read the world correctly, but we paid close attention to every major trend beyond our borders.

Americans had just seen totalitarian powers conquer large swaths of the world, threatening free societies with a return to the Dark Ages. The nation had had to sacrifice mightily to reverse these conquests. The Cold War that followed imposed its own special form of discipline. If we flinched, we risked being overwhelmed by communism; if we became trigger-happy, we risked a nuclear war. For all these reasons, it was a serious, sober time.

Anybody Around Here Know How to Write a Telegram?

Then that wall in Berlin came down. And like flowers in spring, up sprouted a garden full of rosy American assumptions about the future. Is it any wonder? The outcome of the global conflict eliminated what had loomed for two generations as by far the most menacing challenge the country had faced: the economic, political, and military threat from the Soviet Union and international communism. Though no formal ceremony of surrender took place and there was no joyous ticker-tape parade for returning servicemen and women as after World War II, it felt like a huge military victory for the United States and its allies. In some ways, it was. Like Germany after the two world wars of the twentieth century, the losing power, the Soviet Union, gave up territory and changed its form of government to bring it in line with the governments of the victors. So, watching on CNN as people in the formerly communist states toppled statues of Lenin, it was natural for us to relax, to be less serious, and to assume that the need for urgent and sustained collective action had passed.

We could have used another Long Telegram. While the end of the Cold War was certainly a victory, it also presented us with *a huge new challenge*. But at the time we just didn't see it.

By helping to destroy communism, we helped open the way for two billion more people to live like us: two billion more people with their own versions of the American dream, two billion more people practicing capitalism, two billion more people with half a century of pent-up aspirations to live like Americans and work like Americans and drive like Americans and consume like Americans. The rest of the world looked at the victors in the Cold War and said, "We want to live the way they do." In this sense, the world we are now living in is a world that we invented.

The end of communism dramatically accelerated the process of globalization, which removed many of the barriers to economic competition. Globalization would turn out to be a blessing for international stability and global growth. But it enabled so many more of those "new Americans" to compete for capital and jobs with the Americans living in America. In economic terms, this meant that Americans had to run even faster—that is, work harder—just to stay in place. At the end of the Cold War, America resembled a cross-country runner who had won his national championship year after year, but this time the judge handed him the trophy and said, "Congratulations. You will never compete in our national championship again. From now on you will have to race in the Olympics, against the best in the world—every day, forever."

We didn't fully grasp what was happening, so we did not respond appropriately. Over time we relaxed, underinvested, and lived in the moment just when we needed to study harder, save more, rebuild our infrastructure, and make our country more open and attractive to foreign talent. Losing one's primary competitor can be problematic. What would the New York Yankees be without the Boston Red Sox, or Alabama without Auburn? When the West won the Cold War, America lost the rival that had kept us sharp, outwardly focused, and serious about nation-building at home—because offering a successful alternative to communism for the whole world to see was crucial to our Cold War strategy.

In coastal China, India, and Brazil, meanwhile, the economic barriers had begun coming down a decade earlier. The Chinese were not like citizens of the old Soviet Union, where, as the saying went, the people pretended to work and the government pretended to pay them. No, they were like us. They had a powerful work ethic and huge pent-up aspirations for prosperity—like a champagne bottle that had been shaken for fifty years and now was about to have its cork removed. You didn't want to be in the way of that cork. Moreover, in parallel with the end of the Cold War, technology was flattening the global economic playing field, reducing the advantages of the people in developed countries such as the United States, while empowering those in the developing ones. The pace of global change accelerated to a speed faster than any we had seen before. It took us Americans some time to appreciate that while many of our new competitors were low-wage, low-skilled workers, for the first time a growing number, particularly those in Asia, were low-wage, *high*-skilled workers. We knew all about cheap labor, but we had never had to deal with *cheap genius*—at scale. Our historical reference point had always been Europe. The failure to understand that we were living in a new world and to adapt to it was a colossal and costly American mistake.

To be sure, the two decades following the Cold War were an extraordinarily productive period for some Americans and some sectors of the American economy. This was the era of the revolution in information technology, which began in the United States and spread around the world. It made some Americans wealthy and gave all Americans greater access to information, entertainment, and one another—and to the rest of the world as well—than ever before. It really was revolutionary. But it posed a formidable challenge to Americans and contributed to our failure as a country to cope effectively with its consequences. That failure had its roots in what we can now see as American overconfidence.

"It was a totally lethal combination of cockiness and complacency," Secretary of Education Arne Duncan told us. "We were the king of the world. But we lost our way. We rested on our laurels . . . we kept telling ourselves all about what we did yesterday and living in the past. We have been slumbering and living off our reputation. We are like the forty-year-old who keeps talking about what a great high school football player he was." It is this dangerous complacency that produced the potholes, loose door handles, and protracted escalator outages of twenty-first-century America. Unfortunately, America's difficulties with infrastructure are the least of our problems.

The Big Four

And that brings us to the core argument of this book. The end of the Cold War, in fact, ushered in a new era that poses four major challenges for America. These are: how to adapt to globalization, how to adjust to the information technology (IT) revolution, how to cope with the large and soaring budget deficits stemming from the growing demands on government at every level, and how to manage a world of both rising energy consumption and rising climate threats. These four challenges, and how we meet them, will define America's future.

The essence of globalization is the free movement of people, goods, services, and capital across national borders. It expanded dramatically because of the remarkable economic success of the free-market economies of the West, states that traded and invested heavily among themselves. Other countries, observing this success, decided to follow the Western pattern. China, other countries in East and Southeast Asia, India, Latin America, and formerly communist Europe all entered the globalized economy. Americans did not fully grasp the implications of globalization becoming—if we can put it this way—even more global, in part because we thought we had seen it all before.

All the talk about China is likely to give any American over the age of forty a sense of déjà vu. After all, we faced a similar challenge from Japan in the 1980s. It ended with America still rising and Japan declining. It is tempting to believe that China today is just a big Japan.

Unfortunately for us, China and the expansion of globalization, to which its remarkable growth is partly due, are far more disruptive than that. Japan threatened one American city, Detroit, and two American industries: cars and consumer electronics. China—and globalization more broadly—challenges every town in America and every industry. China, India, Brazil, Israel, Singapore, Vietnam, Taiwan, Korea, Chile, and Switzerland (and the list could go on and on) pose a huge challenge to America because of the integration of computing, telecommunications, the World Wide Web, and free markets. Japan was a tornado that blew through during the Cold War. China and globalization are a category-5 hurricane that will never move out to sea in the post–Cold War world.

Charles Vest, the former president of MIT, observed that back in the 1970s and 1980s, once we realized the formidable challenge posed by Japan, "we took the painful steps that were required to get back in the game. We analyzed, repositioned, persevered, and emerged stronger. We did it. In that case, the 'we' who achieved this was U.S. industry." But now something much more comprehensive is required.

"This time around," said Vest, "it requires a public awakening, establishment of political will, resetting of priorities, sacrifice for the future, and an alliance of governments, businesses, and citizens. It requires truth-telling, sensible investment, a rebirth of civility, and a cessation by both political and corporate leaders of pandering to our baser instincts. Engineering, education, science, and technology are clearly within the core of what has to be done. After all, this is the knowledge age. The United States cannot prosper based on low wages, geographic isolation, or military might. We can prosper only based on brainpower: properly prepared and properly applied brainpower."

If globalization has put virtually every American job under pressure, the IT revolution has changed the composition of work—as computers, cell phones, the Internet, and all their social-media offshoots have spread. It has eliminated old jobs and spawned new ones—and whole new industries—faster than ever. Moreover, by making almost all work more complex and more demanding of critical-thinking skills, it requires every American to be better educated than ever to secure and keep a well-paying job. The days when you could go directly from high school to a job that supported a middle-class lifestyle, the era memorably depicted in two of the most popular of all American situation comedies—*The Honeymooners* of the 1950s, with Jackie Gleason as the bus driver Ralph Kramden, and *All in the Family* of the 1970s, starring Carroll O'Connor as Archie Bunker, the colorful denizen of Queens, New York—are long gone. The days when you could graduate from college and do the same job, with the same skills, for four decades before sliding into a comfortable retirement are disappearing as well. The IT revolution poses an educational challenge—to expand the analytical and innovative skills of Americans—that is no less profound than those created by the transition from plow horses to tractors or from sailing ships to steamships.

The third great challenge for America's future is the rising national debt and annual deficits, which have both expanded to dangerous levels since the Cold War through our habit of not raising enough money through taxation to pay for what the federal government spends, and then borrowing to bridge the gap. The American government has been able to borrow several trillion dollars—a good chunk of it from China and other countries—because of confidence in the American economy and because of the special international role of the dollar, a role that dates from the days of American global economic supremacy.

In effect, America has its own version of oil wealth: dollar wealth. Because its currency became the world's de facto currency after World War II, the United States can print money and issue debt to a degree that no other country can. Countries that are rich in oil tend to be fiscally undisciplined; a country that can essentially print its own dollar-denominated wealth can fall into the same trap. Sure enough, since the end of the Cold War, and particularly since 2001, America has suffered a greater loss of fiscal discipline than ever before in its history. And it has come at exactly the wrong time: just when the baby boomer generation is about to retire and draw on its promised entitlements of Social Security and Medicare.

The accumulation of annual deficits is the national debt, and here the widely cited numbers, hair-raising though they are, actually understate what is likely to be the extent of American taxpayers' obligations. The figures do not take account of the huge and in some cases probably unpayable debts of states and cities. By one estimate, states have $3 trillion in unfunded pension-related obligations. The gaps between what New York, Illinois, and California in particular will owe in the coming years and the taxes their governments can reasonably expect to collect are very large indeed.

Vallejo, California, a city of about 117,000 people, which declared bankruptcy in May 2008, was devoting about 80 percent of its budget to salaries and benefits for its unionized policemen, firefighters, and other public safety officials. Tracy, California, made news when it announced in 2010 that citizens were henceforth being asked to pay for 911 emergency services—$48 per household per year, $36 for low-income households. The fee rises automatically to $300 if the household actually calls 911 and the first responder administers medical treatment. The federal government will surely be called upon to take responsibility for some of these obligations. It will also come under pressure to rescue some of the private pension plans that are essentially bankrupt. And most estimates assume that the country will have to pay only modest interest costs for the borrowing it undertakes to finance its budget deficits. Doubts about the U.S. government's creditworthiness could, however, raise the interest rates the Treasury Department has to offer in order to find enough purchasers for its securities. This could increase the total debt significantly—depending on how high future interest rates are. In short, our overall fiscal condition is even worse than we think. There is a website that tracks the "Outstanding Public Debt of the United States," and as of June 15, 2011, the national debt was $14,344,566,636,826.26. (Maybe China will forgive us the 26 cents?)

As for the fourth challenge, the threat of fossil fuels to the planet's biosphere, it is a direct result of the surge in energy consumption, which, in turn, is a direct result of the growth that has come about through globalization and the adoption (especially in Asia) of free-market economics. If we do not find a new source of abundant, cheap, clean, and reliable energy to power the future of all these "new Americans," we run the risk of burning up, choking up, heating up, and smoking up our planet far faster than even Al Gore predicted.

This means, however, that the technologies that can supply abundant, cheap, clean, and reliable energy will be the next new global industry. Energy technology—ET—will be the new IT. A country with a thriving ET industry will enjoy energy security, will enhance its own national security, and will contribute to global environmental security. It also will be home to innovative companies, because companies cannot make products greener without inventing smarter materials, smarter software, and smarter designs. It is hard to imagine how America will be able to sustain a rising standard of living if it does not have a leading role in this next great global industry.

What all four of these challenges have in common is that they require a collective response. They are too big to be addressed by one party alone, or by one segment of the public. Each is a national challenge; only the nation as a whole can deal adequately with it. Of course, a successful response in each case depends on individuals doing the right things. Workers must equip themselves with the skills to win the well-paying jobs, and entrepreneurs must create these jobs. Americans must spend less and save more and accept higher taxes. Individuals, firms, and industries must use less fossil fuel. But to produce the appropriate individual behavior in each case, we need to put in place the incentives, regulations, and institutions that will encourage it, and putting them in place is a collective task.

Because these are challenges that the nation as a whole must address, because addressing them will require exertion and sacrifice, and because they have an international dimension, it seems natural to discuss them in the language of international competition and conflict. The challenge that Kennan identified in his Long Telegram really was a war of sorts. The four major challenges the country confronts today have to be understood in a different framework. It seems to us that the appropriate framework is provided by the great engine of change in the natural world, evolution. The driving force of evolution is adaptation. Where Kennan was urging Americans to oppose a new enemy, we are calling on Americans to adapt to a new environment.

Over hundreds of millions of years, many thousands of species (plants and animals, including humans) have survived when their biological features have allowed them to adapt to their environment—that is, allowed them to reproduce successfully and so perpetuate their genes. If gray-colored herons are better disguised from their predators than white ones, more and more grays and fewer and fewer whites will survive and reproduce in every generation until all herons are gray. (The phrase "survival of the fittest" that is often used to describe evolution means survival of the best adapted.)

Adaptation becomes particularly urgent when a species' environment changes. Birds may fly to an island far from their previous habitat. Whether these birds survive will depend on how well adapted they happen to be to their new home, and whether the species as a whole survives there will depend on how successfully those adaptations are passed down to subsequent generations.

Sixty-five million years ago, scientists believe, a large meteor or a series of them struck the Earth, igniting firestorms and shrouding the planet in a cloud of dust. This caused the extinction of three-quarters of all then existing species, including the creatures that at the time dominated the Earth, the dinosaurs.

The end of the Cold War and the challenges that followed brought on a fundamental change in our environment. Only the individuals, the companies, and the nations that adapt to the new global environment will thrive in the coming decades. The end of the Cold War should have been an occasion not for relaxation and self-congratulation but for collective efforts to adapt to the new world that we invented.

We thought of ourselves as the lion that, having just vanquished the leader of the competing pride of lions on the savanna, reigns as the undisputed king of all he surveys. Instead we were, and are, running the risk of becoming dinosaurs.

The analogy between the effects of evolution on particular species and the impact of social, economic, and political change on sovereign states breaks down in a couple of crucial ways, though. For one, adaptation in biology takes place across hundreds of generations, while the adaptation we are talking about will have to happen within a few years. And whether or not a species is well adapted to its environment is the product of uncontrollable genetic coding. Individuals, groups, and nations, by contrast, can understand their circumstances and deliberately make the adjustments necessary to flourish in them. The dinosaurs could do nothing to avoid extinction. The United States can choose to meet the challenges it faces and adopt the appropriate policies for doing so.

The country is not facing extinction, but the stakes involved are very high indeed.

The Stakes

Our success in meeting the four challenges will determine the rate and the shape of U.S. economic growth, and how widely the benefits of such growth are shared. For most of its history the United States achieved impressive annual increases in GDP, which lifted the incomes of most of its citizens. That economic growth served as the foundation for almost everything we associate with America: its politics, its social life, its role in the world, and its national character. Fifty-five years ago the historian David Potter, in *People of Plenty*, argued that affluence has shaped the American character. The performance of the U.S. economy has generally made it possible for most Americans who worked hard to enjoy at least a modest rise in their material circumstances during their lifetimes—and enabled them to be confident that their children would do the same. Economic growth created opportunity for each generation of Americans, and over time most Americans came to expect that the future would be better than the past, that hard work would be rewarded, and that each generation would be wealthier than the previous one. That expectation came to have a name: "the American dream." The American dream depends on sustained, robust economic growth, which now depends on the country meeting the four major challenges it faces.

As Senator Lindsey Graham, a South Carolina Republican, put it to us: "America needs to think long term just at a time when long-term thinking has never been more difficult to achieve. I hope it is just more difficult, not impossible." He added: "Those who do not think the American dream is being jeopardized are living in a dark corner somewhere . . . It is my hope that the Tea Party, Wall Street, labor unions, and soccer moms will all rally around the idea that 'I don't want to lose the American dream on my watch.'"

More and more Americans, though, fear that the American dream is slipping away. A poll published by Rasmussen Reports (November 19, 2010) found that while 37 percent of the Americans polled believed that the country's best days lay ahead, many more, 47 percent of those polled, thought that the country's best days had already passed. Failing to take collective action to solve the problems that globalization, IT, debt, and energy and global warming have created risks proving the pessimists right.

"Lots of things in life are more important than money," goes the old saying, "and they all cost money." In his 2005 book, *The Moral Consequences of Economic Growth*, the Harvard economist Benjamin M. Friedman shows how periods of economic prosperity were also periods of social, political, and religious tolerance that saw the expansion of rights and liberties and were marked by broad social harmony. By contrast, when the American economy did poorly, as after the crash of 1929, conflict of all kinds increased. The American dream is the glue that has held together a diverse, highly competitive, and often fractious society.

The manager of the Liverpool, England, soccer team once observed of his sport, which everyone except Americans calls football: "Some people say that football is a matter of life and death. They are wrong. It's much more important than that." Similarly, while America's success or failure in mastering the challenges of globalization, IT, debt, energy, and global warming will define the country's future, more than the American future is at stake. Because America plays such a vital role in world affairs, the way things turn out in the United States will have effects on the people of the next generations all over the world.

As Michael argued in his 2006 book, *The Case for Goliath: How America Acts as the World's Government in the Twenty-first Century*, since 1945, and especially since the end of the Cold War, the United

States has provided to the world many of the services that governments generally furnish to the societies they govern. World leaders appreciate this role even when they do not publicly acknowledge it. America has acted as the architect, policeman, and banker of the international institutions and practices it established after World War II and in which the whole world now participates. While maintaining the world's major currency, the dollar, it has served as a market for the exports that have fueled remarkable economic growth in Asia and elsewhere. America's navy safeguards the sea-lanes along which much of the world's trade passes, and its military deployments in Europe and East Asia underwrite security in those regions. Our military also guarantees the world's access to the oil of the Persian Gulf, on which so much of the global economy depends. American intelligence assets, diplomatic muscle, and occasionally military force do most to resist the most dangerous trend in modern international politics—the proliferation of nuclear weapons.

Over and above all of this, there is America's visible demonstration of the connections between freedom, economic growth, and human fulfillment. The power of example is a hugely potent social force, and the American example, with its remarkable record of economic success, has had a particularly strong global impact. Of course, other countries are democratic, prosperous, powerful, and influential. The political and economic principles on which the United States is based originated in the British Isles. After the collapse of communism, the countries of Central and Eastern Europe were inspired to follow the capitalist and democratic paths by the democratic, capitalist example of Western Europe. The increasingly prosperous countries of Asia adopted their versions of free-market economies from Japan.

Still, it was the United States that helped to establish and protect democracy and free-market economies in Western Europe and Japan after World War II, and it is the United States that has been, over the past hundred years, the most consistently democratic, prosperous, and powerful—and therefore the most influential—country in the world. It is the American example that deserves the most credit for the global spread of democratic politics and free-market economies. In this sense, too, the world of today is a world that we invented.

Alas, no country is prepared to step in to replace the United States as the world's government, the way we stepped in when Great Britain went into decline. Nor will our economically pressed allies in Europe and Asia shoulder the costs of these global services. Therefore, a weaker America would leave the world a nastier, poorer, more dangerous place.

In sum, America's future—and the future of the world beyond America—depends on how well we deal with all four of our challenges. Because they are so important to the United States, and because the United States is so important to the rest of the world, it is not an exaggeration to say that the course of the rest of the century depends on how we respond collectively to them.

There is every reason to think that the United States can rise to meet them. Our optimism rests on our country's history of rising to great challenges. America is a nation that won its independence through a daring, violent break with the richest country and the greatest maritime power in the world. Americans then settled a vast and wild continent and waged a bloody civil war from which they recovered so rapidly that they built the largest economy on the planet within a few decades. Our armed forces tipped the balance in Europe in the first great war of the twentieth century; and our tanks, ships, and airplanes, as well as the efforts of our fighting men and women, were central to the defeat of Germany and Japan in the second one.

Winston Churchill once said to his British compatriots that "we have not journeyed across the centuries, across the oceans, across the mountains, across the prairies, because we are made of sugar candy." The same could be said of Americans. Yet faced with era-defining challenges, the country has responded with all the vigor and determination of a lollipop. It has no concerted, serious, well-designed, and broadly supported policies to prepare Americans for the jobs of the future, or to put the nation's fiscal affairs in order, or to hedge against dangerous changes in the planet's climate. How to explain our failure of will? Our political system has gone awry, and so cannot produce the big, ambitious policies the country needs. And the American people have not demanded that our leaders tackle the challenges we face because they still have not fully understood the world we are living in.

What world *are* we living in? What do we need to do to thrive in this world? Do we have the requisite policies and are we carrying them out effectively? How do we adjust them to work better?

In Singapore, the political and business leaders ask these questions obsessively, as Tom saw during a visit to the country in the winter of

2011. The Singaporean economist Tan Kong Yam pinpointed the reason: Because of its small size and big neighbors, Singapore, he said, is "like someone living in a hut without any insulation. We feel every change in the wind or the temperature and have to adapt. You Americans are still living in a brick house with central heating and don't have to be so responsive."

Tom saw the result of Singapore's obsessive attention to what it must do in order to thrive when he visited a fifth-grade science class in an elementary school in a middle-class neighborhood. All the eleven-year-old boys and girls were wearing white lab coats with their names monogrammed on them. Outside in the hall, yellow police tape had blocked off a "crime scene." Lying on a floor, bloodied, was a fake body that had been "murdered." The class was learning about DNA through the use of fingerprints and evidence-collecting, and their science teacher had turned each one into a junior *CSI* investigator. All of them had to collect fingerprints and other evidence from the scene and then analyze them. Asked whether this was part of the national curriculum, the school's principal said that it was not. But she had a very capable science teacher interested in DNA, the principal explained, and the principal was also aware that Singapore was making a big push to expand its biotech industries, so she thought it would be a good idea to expose her students to the subject.

A couple of them took Tom's fingerprints. He was innocent—but impressed.

Curtis Carlson, the CEO of SRI International, a Silicon Valley innovation laboratory, has worked with both General Motors and Singapore's government, and he had this to say: "Being inside General Motors, this huge company, it felt a lot like being inside America today. Adaptation is the key to survival, and the people and companies who adapt the best, survive the best. When you are the biggest company in the world, you become arrogant, and your mind-set is such that no one can convince you that Toyota has anything to teach you. You are focused inward and not outward; you are focused on the politics inside your company rather than on the outside and what your competition is doing. If you become arrogant, you become blind. That was General Motors, and that is, unfortunately, America today . . . You cannot adapt unless you are constantly monitoring what is happening in your environment. Countries that do that well, such as Singapore, are all about looking out."

Singapore has no natural resources, and even has to import sand for building. But today its per capita income is just below U.S. levels, built entirely with advanced manufacturing, services, and exports. The country's economy grew in 2010 at 14.7 percent, led by exports of pharmaceuticals and biomedical equipment. The United States is not Singapore, and it is certainly not about to adopt the more authoritarian features of Singapore's political system. Nor, like Singapore, are we likely to link the pay of high-level bureaucrats and cabinet ministers to the top private-sector wages (all top government officials in Singapore make more than $1 million a year) or give them annual bonuses tied to the country's annual GDP growth rate. But we do have something to learn from the seriousness and creativity the Singaporeans bring to elementary education and economic development, and from their attention to the requirements for success in the post–Cold War world. Carlson told us he once met with a senior Singaporean economic minister whom he complimented on the country's educational and economic achievements. Carlson said the minister "would not accept the compliment." "Rather, he said, 'We are not good enough. We must never think we are good enough. We must continuously improve.' Exactly right—there is no alternative: adapt or die."

To be sure, countries don't compete directly with one another in economic terms. When Singapore or China gets richer, America does not become poorer. To the contrary, Asia's surging economic growth has made Americans better off. But individuals do compete against one another for good jobs, and those with the best skills will get the highest-paying ones. In today's world, more and more people around the world are able to compete with Americans in this way.

Another reason that Americans have not recognized the magnitude of the challenges they face is that these challenges are all the products of American *success*. For years, the United States was the world's most vigorous champion of free trade and investment—the essence of globalization. Globalization spread due to the remarkable productivity of the free-market economies of the West, which traded and invested heavily among themselves. By contrast, the communist countries were discredited by their dismal record in achieving economic growth. So they embraced free markets and globalization.

Likewise, the IT revolution was started in the United States. The transistor, communications satellites, the personal computer, the cell phone, and the Internet, not to mention the PalmPilot, the iPad, the iPhone, and the Kindle, were all invented in the United States and then were brought to the world market by American-based companies. That gave more people than ever the tool kit to compete with us and remove the barriers erected by their own governments.

Similarly, the American government has been able to borrow several trillion dollars because of confidence, both at home and abroad, in the American economy and because of the special international role of the dollar, which dates from the days of American global economic supremacy. And the global population uses so much fossil fuel that it threatens to disrupt the climate precisely because economic growth, which is expanding rapidly, goes hand in hand with a rise in fuel consumption. The surge in growth over the last two decades has come about because of the expansion of American-sponsored globalization and the adoption, especially in Asia, of the American and Western system of free-market economics.

In sum, the world to which the United States must adapt is, to a very great extent, "Made in America." But in this case familiarity and pride of authorship have bred complacency. We are dangerously complacent about this new world precisely because it is a world that we invented.

Another feature of the four challenges America confronts is the fact that they will require sacrifice, which makes generating collective action much more difficult. This is most obvious in the case of the federal deficits. Americans will have to pay more in taxes and accept less in benefits. Paying more for less is the reverse of what most people want out of life, so it is no wonder that deficits have grown so large. Similarly, Americans won't begin to use less fossil fuel and industry won't invest in nonfossil sources of energy unless the prices of coal, oil, and natural gas rise significantly to reflect the true cost to society of our use of them. Higher American fuel bills will ultimately be good for the country and for the planet because they will stimulate the development of renewable energy sources, but they will be hard on household budgets in the short term. To meet the challenge of globalization and the IT revolution and to achieve the steadily rising standard of living U.S. citizens have come to expect, Americans will have to save more, consume less, study longer, and work harder than they have become accustomed to doing in recent decades.

Ours is "no longer a question of sacrificing or not sacrificing—we gave up that choice a long time ago," notes Michael Maniates, a professor of political science and environmental science at Allegheny College in Pennsylvania, who writes on this theme. We cannot choose whether or not Americans will sacrifice, but only who will bear the brunt of it. The more the present generation shrinks from the nation's challenges now, the longer sacrifice is deferred, the higher will be the cost to the next generation of the decline in America's power and Americans' wealth.

Fifty years ago, at his inauguration, John F. Kennedy urged his fellow citizens, "Ask not what your country can do for you. Ask what you can do for your country." That idea resonated with most of the Americans to whom he spoke because they had personal memories of an era of supreme and successful sacrifice, which earned them the name "the Greatest Generation."

Unfortunately, today's challenges differ in an important way from those of the last century. The problems the Greatest Generation faced were inescapable, immediate, and existential: the Great Depression, German and Japanese fascism, and Soviet communism. The enemies they had to confront were terrifying, tangible, and obvious: long unemployment lines, soup kitchens, heartless bankers evicting families from their homes, the twisted wreckage of Pearl Harbor, the maniacal countenance and braying voice of Adolf Hitler, the ballistic missiles decorating the May Day parades in Red Square in Moscow—missiles that one day were dispatched to Cuba, just ninety miles from America's shores. When the Soviets weren't putting up a wall topped with barbed wire, slicing through the heart of Berlin like a jagged knife, they were invading Hungary and Czechoslovakia to stomp out a few wildflowers of freedom that had broken through the asphalt layer of communism the Soviet Union had laid down on those two countries. These challenges were impossible to ignore.

Whether or not the public and the politicians all agreed on the strategies for dealing with those challenges—and often they didn't—they recognized that decisions had to be made, endless wrangling had to stop, and denying the existence of such threats or postponing dealing with them was unthinkable. Most Americans understood the world they were living in. They understood, too, that in confronting these problems they had to pull together—they had to act collectively—in a unified, serious, and determined way. Confronting those challenges meant bringing to bear the full weight and power of the American people. It also meant that leaders could not avoid asking for sacrifice. Kennedy also summoned his countrymen to "pay any price, bear any burden, meet any hardship, support any friend, oppose any foe." Everyone had to contribute something—time, money, energy, and, in many cases, lives. Losing was not an option, nor were delay, denial, dithering, or despair.

Today's major challenges are different. All four—globalization, the IT revolution, out-of-control deficits and debt, and rising energy demand and climate change—are occurring incrementally. Some of their most troubling features are difficult to detect, at least until they have reached crisis proportions. Save for the occasional category-5 hurricane or major oil spill, these challenges offer up no Hitler or Pearl Harbor to shock the nation into action. They provide no Berlin Wall to symbolize the threat to America and the world, no Sputnik circling the Earth proclaiming with every cricket-like chirp of its orbiting signal that we are falling behind in a crucial arena of geopolitical competition. We don't see the rushing river of dollars we send abroad every month—about $28 billion— to sustain our oil addiction. The carbon dioxide that mankind has been pumping into the atmosphere since the Industrial Revolution, and at rising rates over the past two decades, is a gas that cannot be seen, touched, or smelled.

To be sure, the four great challenges have scarcely gone unnoticed. But in the last few years the country was distracted, indeed preoccupied, by the worst economic crisis in eight decades. It is no wonder that Americans became fixated on their immediate economic circumstances. Those circumstances were grim: American households lost an estimated $10 trillion in the crisis. For more than a year the American economy contracted. Unemployment rose to 9 percent (and if people too discouraged to seek jobs were included, the figure would be significantly higher).

There is an important difference between the challenge of the economic crisis and the four long-term challenges that America faces. The deep recession of late 2007 to 2009 was what economists call a "cyclical event." A recession reduces economic growth to a point below its potential level. But the economy, and the country, eventually recover. By contrast, the four great challenges will determine our overall economic potential. A recession is like an illness, which can ruin a person's week, month, or even year. The four challenges we face are more like chronic conditions. Ultimately, these determine the length and the quality of a person's life. Similarly, how we respond to these major challenges will determine the quality of American life for decades to come. And it is later than we think.

A few years ago, fans of the Chicago Cubs baseball team, which last won the World Series in 1908, took to wearing T-shirts bearing the slogan "Any team can have a bad century." Countries, too, can have bad centuries. China had three of them between 1644 and 1980. If we do not master the four major challenges we now face, we risk a bad twenty-first century.

Failure is by no means inevitable. Coming back, thriving in this century, preserving the American dream and the American role in the world, will require adopting policies appropriate to confronting the four great challenges. For this there are two preconditions. One is recognizing those challenges—which we have clearly been slow to do. The other is remembering how we developed the strength to face similar challenges in the past. As Bill Gates put it to us: "What was all that good stuff we had that other people copied?" That is the subject of the next chapter.

THREE

Ignoring Our History

On January 5, 2011, the opening day of the 112th Congress, the House of Representatives began its activities with a reading of the Constitution of the United States. The idea originated with the Tea Party, a grassroots movement whose support for Republican candidates in the 2010 elections had helped sweep them to victory, giving the GOP control of the House. The members of the new majority wanted to drive home the point that they had come to Washington to enforce limits on both the spending and the general powers of the federal government—which they believed had gone far beyond the powers granted to it in the Constitution. Historians said it was the first time the Constitution, completed in 1787, was read in its entirety on the House floor.

The Constitution has served as the framework of American political and economic life for nearly 225 years, a span of time in which the United States has grown from a series of small cities, towns, villages, and farms along the eastern seaboard to a superpower of continental dimensions with the largest economy in the world. For America's remarkable history, the Constitution deserves a large share of the credit.

But even reverence for the Constitution can be taken too far. Former congressman Bob Inglis, a conservative Republican from South Carolina who lost his party's 2010 primary to a Tea Party–sponsored opponent, told us about an experience he had speaking to members of that group at the main branch of the Greenville, South Carolina, county library several weeks before the primary. "About halfway into the hour and a half program, a middle-aged fellow stood up to ask his question," Inglis said. "He identified himself as a night watchman/security guard. Pulling a copy of the Constitution out of his shirt pocket and waving it in the air, he asked me, 'yes or no,' if I would vote to eliminate all case law and go back to just 'this'—the Constitution."

"'No,' I replied. The crowd hissed and the night watchman shook his head in disgust. 'Well, think about it.' Pulling my cell phone out of its holster, I held it up and said, 'The Constitution says nothing about cell phones, but there are lots of cases and some statutes that govern the use of these things. If we eliminated all case law, we wouldn't have these cell phones.' I went on to explain that without Judge Green's decisions in the AT&T breakup we might not have any cell phones, and we'd still be paying outrageous rates for long-distance calls." Inglis said that his questioner clearly was not impressed or persuaded.

The Constitution's framers themselves knew that the document they had produced—through protracted and sometimes bitter negotiation—was necessary but not sufficient to secure the future of the country they had founded. And it certainly hasn't been the only shaper of America's destiny. We have always relied on something more: not a single document but a set of practices for prosperity that began with our founding and has been updated and applied over and over again. We call it "the American formula." Although we think its importance should be obvious, it is not obvious today. America has lost sight of this traditional source of strength precisely when we should have been upgrading it. There is no chance—none—that America can address the great challenges it now faces without renewing, refreshing, and reinvesting in its formula. And yet this formula has been allowed to erode in almost every aspect for the last two decades.

It is in particular jeopardy now because America will have to reduce public expenditure sharply in the years ahead to address the government's soaring deficits. In an era of retrenchment it will be all too easy to underinvest in our traditional, time-tested formula. We will do this at our peril. A brief history of the American formula makes clear why this is so.

The Five Pillars of Prosperity

There is a business adage that says, "You win in the turns." That is, when there are big shifts in the marketplace, the best companies gain market share and put distance between themselves and their competitors because they have the vision and flexibility to spot tectonic change and leap ahead when it occurs, while others are simply overwhelmed. They have, that is, a formula for success. Countries face similar challenges. If America were a company, Wall Street analysts would say that it has a remarkable track record. It has thrived at every turning point in its history—with every change in technology and social norms. America built the world's most vibrant economy and democracy precisely because, in every historical turn since its founding, it has applied its own particular formula for prosperity.

That formula consists of five pillars that together constitute the country's own version of a partnership between the public and private sectors to foster economic growth. The first pillar is providing public education for more and more Americans. As technology has improved, the country has prepared people to exploit new inventions—from cotton gins, to steamships, to assembly lines, to laptops, to the Internet.

The second pillar is the building and continual modernizing of our infrastructure—roads, bridges, ports, airports, bandwidth, fiber-optic lines, and wireless networks—so that American workers and firms can communicate and collaborate effectively and deliver their goods and services swiftly and cheaply to their destinations. Since the building of the Erie Canal between 1817 and 1825, governments at every level in the United States have financed the infrastructure necessary for commerce to flourish.

The third pillar involves, with a few periods of exception, keeping America's doors to immigration open so that we are constantly adding both the low-skilled but high-aspiring immigrants who keep American society energized and the best minds in the world to enrich our universities, start new companies, and engineer new breakthroughs from medicine to manufacturing.

The fourth pillar is government support for basic research and development, which not only increases the store of human knowledge by pushing out the frontiers of basic chemistry, biology, and physics but also spawns new products and processes that have enriched American entrepreneurs and workers. For the American economy to keep growing in an information age in which innovation will have a greater economic importance than ever before, research on every front will be more vital than ever before.

The fifth pillar is the implementation of necessary regulations on private economic activity. This includes safeguards against financial collapse and environmental destruction, as well as regulations and incentives that encourage capital to flow to America, lead innovators to flock to this country to lodge their patents and intellectual property—because they know these things will be protected—and inspire small businesses and venture capitalists to start up in America.

Throughout our history, these five pillars have made it possible for Americans to apply their individual energies, their talents, and their entrepreneurial drive to make themselves, and their country, richer and more powerful. Taken together, the five make up a uniquely American formula for prosperity, one in which the government creates the foundations for the risk-taking and innovation delivered by the private sector. This formula has made possible America's two centuries of increases in living standards. It is what has made America the world's greatest magnet for dreamers everywhere.

The Formula Builders

For nearly 235 years, America has managed to produce leaders who could sense that we were in a major turn, frame the challenges involved so that people could understand what was happening, and then rally the public to adopt the policies needed to upgrade the American formula to meet the challenges. Here is a sampler of our leading formula builders.

The father of America's public-private partnership was the nation's first secretary of the Treasury, Alexander Hamilton. Hamilton saw the need for a strong and active although limited government. We now reside, as the biographer Ron Chernow, put it, "in the bustling world of trade, industry, stock markets, and banks that Hamilton envisioned." He established a budget and tax system, a funded debt, a customs service, and a coast guard. He encouraged manufacturing and, out of office, drew up plans for the kind of peacetime army that the United States did not field until after World War II. Although he did not live to see it develop, the five-part formula for a public-private partnership that has evolved in the United States over the years descends directly from Hamilton's vision, at the end of the eighteenth century, of both the character of the country and the role of its government as an enabler of prosperity.

Starting with the founding fathers, government has supported public education. Before he died on July 4, 1826, Thomas Jefferson asked that three of his achievements be engraved on his tombstone—that he wrote the Declaration of Independence, that he authored the Virginia Statute for Religious Freedom, and that he was the father of the University of Virginia. Unlike other major industrial countries, though, the federal government in the United States never has had the primary authority over K–12 public education. That has fallen to individual states and local school districts, which are funded through a combination of local property taxes, state tax receipts, and federal dollars. This combination of government support has transformed education in America from an elite privilege to a universal entitlement. In their book *The Race Between Education and Technology,* Harvard University's Claudia Goldin and Lawrence Katz noted that thanks to the steady expansion of primary education, then the high school movement, and then the expansion of two- and four-year colleges and universities, "each generation of Americans achieved a level of education that greatly exceeded that of the previous one, with typical adults having considerably more years of schooling than their parents." As a result, racial and regional differences in educational resources, educational attainment, and economic outcomes had narrowed substantially.

At the dawn of the twentieth century only about 6 percent of teenagers graduated from high school. By the end of the century that was up to 85 percent. At the beginning of the century about 2 percent of Americans age eighteen to twenty-four were enrolled in a two- or four-year college; by the end of the century 63 percent were going right from high school to some postsecondary institution, according to Department of Education statistics. Goldin and Katz argue that this American investment in mass education paid huge dividends: It both reduced income gaps and ensured that American workers could handle each new advance in technology.

Abraham Lincoln is best known, of course, for presiding over the federal government during the Civil War, but during that conflict his administration passed several landmark pieces of legislation that spurred America's transition from an agrarian to an industrial society. One was the Homestead Act of 1862, which opened up the West for settlement by anyone who had not fought against the Union. Another was the Pacific Railway Acts of 1862 and 1864, which connected the eastern to the western part of the country and so laid the basis for a truly national economy. A third was the Morrill Act of 1862, which established a system of land-grant colleges, giving rise to institutions of higher education from Georgia to California and from Minnesota to Texas. States received federal land to establish colleges or vocational schools for educating students in agriculture, science, engineering, and other skills the country as a whole needed. Lincoln signed the National Academy of Sciences into being on March 3, 1863, to bring together America's best researchers to "investigate, examine, experiment, and report upon any subject of science or art" whenever called upon to do so by any department of the government. Remarkably, all of this happened while we were fighting a civil war.

Theodore Roosevelt secured his place on Mount Rushmore chiefly through his contributions to the American formula. His experience as a reformist police commissioner in New York City, leader of the Civil Service Commission, and governor of New York taught him that for business to thrive it required consistent and transparent rules, as well as regulators authorized to prevent abuses and hold businesses accountable. As president, he took on large business monopolies in order to foster the free competition on which economic growth depends. American business was often unhappy with the rules and regulations that Roosevelt championed, but the competition, the transparency, and the public confidence that his handiwork helped to foster probably benefited business and investors more than any other group in the country. His concept of the vital role government had to play to regulate markets, as well as to protect public health and safety, not to mention to safeguard our nation's wilderness, laid the basis for America's Progressive era.

In 1907, the next-to-last full year of Roosevelt's presidency, 1,285,349 people came to the United States from other countries, the largest single annual intake in American history to that point. The United States has always been a nation of immigrants, descended as it is from the earliest European settlements in North America in what became Virginia and Massachusetts. In the first half of the nineteenth century, most immigrants came from northern Europe. In the second half and the early decades of the twentieth, a great many originated in southern and eastern Europe. America became a great industrial power after the Civil War by capitalizing on the rapid population growth due to immigration. Many of the people who manned the factories that entrepreneurs built and dug the coal that powered these factories came originally from Europe.

Franklin D. Roosevelt's New Deal built dams, levees, roads, parks, airports, power stations, reservoirs, tunnels, auditoriums, schools, and public libraries. These public investments in infrastructure and education gave a huge boost to the American economy during the Great Depression, during World War II, and in the years that followed. With the Securities Act of 1933, often referred to as the "truth in securities" law, and the re-regulation of the banking system, FDR stabilized the country's finances, and these measures may well have saved capitalism in the United States. Moreover, with the introduction of the Social Security and unemployment insurance programs in a 1935 Fireside Chat, he founded the American social safety net, which is itself an indirect guarantor of capitalism. The competition that is central to a free-market economy produces losers as well as winners. This process of "creative destruction" so central to capitalism is just that—creative and destructive—and we cannot sustain the destruction without the social safety net that affords some protection to the losers. Without it, they might seek to bring down the very system that has made Americans wealthy. As America enters a necessary debate about how generous unemployment insurance, Social Security, and Medicare should be, it is well to remember that this social safety net ensures the legitimacy and stability of the free-market economy.

While FDR did not significantly expand immigration, which had been curtailed in the 1920s, thousands of Europeans, many of them Jews, made their way to America as refugees from Nazi Germany in the middle to late 1930s. Many were elite scientists, physicists, writers, artists, musicians, historians, and intellectuals. This "brain wave," epitomized by Albert Einstein, played a critical role in shifting the world's intellectual leadership from Europe to the United States.

The administration of FDR's successor, Harry Truman, saw the enactment of the Servicemen's Readjustment Act of 1944, known as the GI Bill of Rights, which provided college tuition and vocational training to returning World War II veterans. (After World War I, most discharged veterans got little more than a $60 stipend and a train ticket home.) According to the Department of Veterans Affairs website,

Thanks to the GI Bill, millions who would have flooded the job market instead opted for education. In the peak year of 1947, veterans accounted for 49 percent of college admissions. By the time the original GI Bill ended on July 25, 1956, 7.8 million of 16 million World War II veterans had participated in an education or training program. Millions also took advantage of the GI Bill's home loan guaranty. From 1944 to 1952, VA backed nearly 2.4 million home loans for World War II veterans.

Also in the Truman administration came the establishment of the National Science Foundation, in 1950, through which the federal government distributed, over the years, billions of dollars for scientific research. Truman's successor, Dwight Eisenhower, is often caricatured as a retired general more interested in golf than in legislation. In fact, he made huge contributions to America's growth-promoting formula. He built on the government's partnership with science during World War II, which had produced the first atomic bombs. He also capitalized on the national alarm over the Soviet Union's launch of the first Earth-orbiting satellite, Sputnik 1, in 1957. We forget today how Sputnik both electrified and challenged Americans and why it prompted us to update our formula so energetically.

Within a year of Sputnik's launch, Congress passed the National Defense Education Act, which supported the study of science, foreign languages, and the history, politics, and economics of foreign countries. To improve defense research and innovation, the government established the Advanced Research Projects Agency, later the Defense Advanced Research Projects Agency, which over the years made concrete contributions to the Saturn V rocket, the one that propelled the Apollo astronauts to the moon; the world's first surveillance satellites; the research network that was the precursor to today's Internet; new materials now used in high-speed integrated circuits; and the computer mouse.

Eisenhower, who had been impressed by the German autobahn system, also made a monumental contribution to America's infrastructure. He won support for the creation of the interstate highway system on the grounds that it was necessary to move around military equipment, troops, and supplies more efficiently in the event of a war with the Soviet Union. Today there is a ringtone you can download on the Internet of a song called "Eisenhower Is the Father of the Interstate Highway System."

Eisenhower was a forceful defender of immigration, more out of a sense of duty to those fleeing oppression than as a strategy to import more brainpower. Nevertheless, it had both effects. In his January 12, 1961, State of the Union speech, he noted that

> over 32,000 victims of communist tyranny in Hungary were brought to our shores, and at this time our country is working to assist refugees from tyranny in Cuba. Since 1953, the waiting period for naturalization applicants has been reduced from 18 months to 45 days. The Administration also has made legislative recommendations to liberalize existing restrictions upon immigration while still safeguarding the national interest. It is imperative that our immigration policy be in the finest American tradition of providing a haven for oppressed peoples and fully in accord with our obligation as a leader of the free world.

A few years later, under President Lyndon Johnson, the immigration pillar of our formula was further expanded when Congress liberalized laws that had severely restricted Asian immigration. The Immigration and Nationality Act of 1965 opened the doors for the massive immigration of brainpower from India. Today there are nearly three million Indian immigrants, many of them scientists, doctors, and academics, greatly enriching America's talent pool. "In the 1970s something on the order of 80 percent of the engineering graduates of the Indian Institutes of Technology (IITs) came to America to do graduate studies and research, and the vast majority of them became permanent residents and citizens," said Subra Suresh, the current director of the National Science Foundation, who was one of them. A large number of them became leaders in academia, industry, government labs, and start-ups in the United States. In 2009, only about 16 percent of the graduates of the IITs came to the United States for graduate studies and research. "If this trend is sustained from IITs and other similar institutions in other countries, it could have a huge impact for our research enterprise. More than 40 percent of the 375 faculty members in the School of Engineering at the Massachusetts Institute of Technology (MIT) are foreign-born," added Suresh, who served previously as MIT's dean of engineering.

The government has provided three of the five parts of the American formula—education, infrastructure, and research and development—through the use of taxpayers' money. A fourth, immigration, is governed by laws Congress passes. The fifth part of that formula involves the use not of the government's money but of its power.

Government regulation of the economy seems to contradict the fundamental principle of free-market economics. Like the social safety net, the proper extent of regulation is the subject of ongoing debate; and just as Social Security and Medicare have grown too expensive in their present form for the country to afford, so regulations have become more complicated than may be good for the health of the American economy.

President Obama admitted as much when he declared in *The Wall Street Journal* (January 18, 2011) that he was ordering "a government-wide review of the rules already on the books to remove outdated regulations that stifle job creation and make our economy less competitive." As with the social safety net, however, while it is sensible to prune the thicket of regulations within which American business operates, it would be utterly foolish to do away with government regulation altogether.

Markets are not just wild gardens that can be left untended. They need to be shaped by regulations that promote risk-taking but prevent recklessness on a scale that can harm everyone. The need for regulations arises from an unavoidable feature of any free-market economy, one that economists call "externalities." These are the costs of free-market activities that are not captured by prices, for which, therefore, nobody pays, and that can injure the society as a whole. To correct this market failure, government has to step in to make sure that something closer to the full costs of the activity do somehow get paid. It can do this either by regulating the activity or by taxing it. A common and familiar externality is the pollution that industrial activity generates and that finds its way into the air that people breathe and the water that they drink. In recognition of the breadth of the problem that pollution presents, an entire federal agency was created to deal with it: the Environmental Protection Agency, established in 1970, during the administration of Richard Nixon.

Intelligent regulations and standards, often drawn up in consultation with business, also promote innovation and investment. When the U.S. government sets high energy-efficiency standards for air conditioners, for example, and every American manufacturer has to innovate in order to meet them, those companies can then compete effectively in every other market in the world. By contrast, when we lower our standards, we invite competition from every low-cost manufacturer around the world.

At the same time, regulations and regulatory bodies provide the vital foundation of trust that fosters innovation and risk-taking. The creation of the Securities and Exchange Commission in 1934 increased the importance of the New York Stock Exchange by making it a less risky place. The Federal Deposit Insurance Corporation, created by the Banking Act of 1933, substantially reduced the chance of bank runs, and the stability of the FDIC helped attract capital from around the world. The North American Free Trade Agreement, which went into effect in 1994, created a regulatory framework that has triggered massive cross-border investments and trade between the United States and both Mexico and Canada. America's patent laws, which protect the intellectual property of innovators, encourage even foreigners to register their patents in America, where they know their ideas will not be stolen—unlike in China. In 2010, more than 500,000 patents were filed with the United States Patent and Trademark Office, thousands of them by non-Americans.

The country's first Patent Act was signed into law by President George Washington, and over the next two hundred years successive presidents enlarged protections for all kinds of intellectual property— in the form of copyrights, trademarks, and patents. Today, the United States Patent and Trademark Office proudly boasts that over the last two hundred years it has granted patents for "Thomas Edison's electric lamp, Alexander Graham Bell's telegraphy, Orville and Wilbur Wright's flying machine, John Deere's steel plow, George Washington Carver's use of legume oils to produce cosmetics and paint, and Edwin Land's Polaroid camera." America's patent process has created a huge bank of scientific and technical knowledge in the form of roughly eight million issued patents and more than two million trademarks since its founding.

One reason America became a nation of starter-uppers is that failure did not carry the permanent stigma that it carried in old Europe. This was a cultural difference, but also one that was enshrined in our formula through steadily evolving regulations that made it possible to get a fresh start.

One of those regulations was the bankruptcy law. Beginning in the nineteenth century, the United States enacted laws to allow companies and individuals to declare bankruptcy and start over relatively easily. The banks could liquidate your assets or force you to reorganize, but then you could try again. Yes, there would be a black mark on your credit record for a few years, but then it would disappear. While no one wants to encourage bankruptcy, there was not a lot of stigma attached to bankruptcy in America—at least compared to Europe, where a single bankruptcy was a mark of Cain that usually meant the end of your business life. American bankruptcy laws emphasized rehabilitating debtors rather than punishing them. Europeans have long marveled at how easy it is for entrepreneurs in Silicon Valley to try something, fail, declare bankruptcy, try again, fail again, try again, and then strike it rich. The easier it is to go under, the easier it is to start over.

All these regulations, notes the Stanford University historian David Kennedy, "were not about creating more state control and less private ownership. They were about creating the right synergy between the two." When you undergird markets with the right government rules, regulations, and incentives, "you set the stage for more risk-taking," said Kennedy. "Predictability actually creates the opportunity and more incentives to innovate."

The country's economy would scarcely be what it is today without highly motivated risk takers such as Warren Buffett, Bill Gates, and Steve Jobs. But their achievements would not have been possible without the public side of America's unique public-private partnership for success.

And that is why we are worried.

The Secret of Our Success Is Too Secret

While it is true that in driver education class one of the first things a student learns is not to pass on the turns, in economic history classes students learn that turns are where you *get* passed. So in a high-speed turn, a country has to drive with much more determination than on a straightaway. The end of the Cold War has coincided with the fastest turn America has ever faced. It is driven by the merger of two major trends: globalization and the IT revolution. We need to win in this turn. So we need to upgrade and improve our American formula—now more than ever. Unfortunately, our politics have moved in the opposite direction.

Again, former representative Bob Inglis, the South Carolina Republican, can testify to this. He recalled a vivid example from a town hall meeting on health care that he held in Simpsonville, South Carolina, during the 2010 campaign. "I was talking about health-care issues and an elderly man stands up and says, 'Keep your government hands off my Medicare.'

"I said to him, 'Well, sir, of course Medicare is a government program.' 'Yes,' he says, 'but I am paying for it.' And I say, 'Yes, you are. You *are* paying—25 percent of the premium—and the government is picking up 75 percent' through Medicare Part B. Now he is threatened, and he says, 'Yes, but I paid for it while I was working.' And I say, 'Yes, 1.45 percent you, and 1.45 percent your employers, paid a Medicare tax on your payroll.' I was trying to be as diplomatic as I could be. He looked to be about seventy-five years old, a man in okay health. So I added: 'And I have to say, if you had one or two hospital admissions you have used up all that you and your employer have ever paid in.' He sat down, angry. That man's self-conception was that he rode out onto the prairie on his own horse and tamed this country and got what he has entirely by his own effort. Deep down, though, he knew that he had not gotten this on his own. He was dependent on other people and that threatened his identity.

"What I needed to say to win him over and win my election," Inglis said, "was that 'I am going to prevent that socialist in the White House, who is probably not even an American citizen and who is illegitimately in the White House, from getting his hands on your Medicare.' Then I would have been a political hero—but I would have left them in ignorance. What is tragic right now is that we have people—leading people—who choose to leave audiences in ignorance or even encourage stupidity."

That same ignorance can be found in sectors of the business

community, where scorn for the government and regulation has become the norm. Who can ever forget Ronald Reagan's famous campaign line: "The nine most terrifying words in the English language are, 'I'm from the government and I'm here to help.'" Of course, every businessperson in America wants lower taxes and less regulation. Most Americans do. But every one of us also benefits from, indeed depends upon, the five pillars of the American formula. Failing to recognize that fact endangers one of the major sources of our strength.

Fortunately, at least some of America's most prominent investors and entrepreneurs do fully appreciate how much our formula enables the American economy to create more wealth from fewer and fewer inputs. "You always have to renew your lead," Bill Gates remarked to us. "But we have to ask: Where did this lead come from in the first place? It was that we educated more people than the other guys, and we attracted more talent," and we built better infrastructure. We need to get back to work in "renewing the sources of our advantage," he said.

Jeffrey Immelt, the chairman and CEO of General Electric, one of the largest private companies in the world, noted the dangers to America of the mistaken belief that the government has no constructive role at all to play in the economy: "We worship false idols in terms of the power of the free market. The U.S. government has been the catalyst for change for generations. The National Institutes of Health shaped a generation of leading-edge health-care technology. And all of the defense spending has spawned the nuclear power industry and the Internet.

"I'm a free-market guy," Immelt added. "I believe in the endless possibilities of individual choice and private initiative. But there's a long history in this country of government spending that prepares the way for new industries that thrive for generations."

Warren Buffett likes to make this point about his own spectacularly successful career, explaining that the billions of dollars he has made as an investor have been due in large part to the fact that his career unfolded in America, with this country's vibrant institutions, free markets, rule of law, and formula for prosperity.

"I was born in the right country at the right time," Buffett said in an interview on ABC (November 28, 2010). "Bill Gates has always told me if I had been born, you know, many thousands of years ago, I'd have been some animal's lunch because I can't run very fast, I can't climb trees, and some animal would be chasing me and I would say, Well, I allocate capital. The animal would say, Those are the kind that taste the best."

John Doerr, one of America's premier venture capitalists—an early backer of Netscape, Google, and Amazon.com—puts it this way: "You have to take risks when you are in a high-speed turn. Sometimes you're going so fast and the turn is so sharp, your car's riding on only two wheels. But without risk-taking nothing big happens." It is the American formula, Doerr added, that provides the underpinnings—in support for basic research that spins out new breakthroughs in physics, biology, and chemistry—that have made America's venture capital firms so productive in these turns.

It is worth noting that the American formula has been, in no small part, a Republican creation, which means that twenty-first-century Republicans who deny any economic role for the federal government are at odds with their own tradition. Alexander Hamilton belonged to the Federalist Party, a distant ancestor of the Republicans and the opponent of Thomas Jefferson's Democratic-Republicans (they later renamed themselves Democrats), from which the Democratic Party of today is descended. The Republican presidents Abraham Lincoln, Theodore Roosevelt, and Dwight Eisenhower all significantly expanded and updated the formula. The Republican Party has traditionally favored limited government, but also strong and effective government where it is required.

Lincoln, Roosevelt, and Eisenhower, along with their Democratic counterparts, understood that the challenges of the world they were living in compelled the United States to enhance its national strength and prosperity, and at critical moments they articulated a vision of American greatness that persuaded the public to support, and Congress to authorize, measures appropriate for reinvigorating the formula. That is surely a common denominator among our greatest presidents—the ability to summon the nation to renew its traditional formula at each critical turn in our history.

Alas, the historical record also shows that the formula has expanded fastest and farthest in wartime. When a country is engaged in a war, especially a war considered essential to its survival, large numbers of its people will support almost any measure that can help it win. The Civil

War era, for example, was also the occasion for authorizing the first federal income tax.

From Benjamin Franklin and his lightning rod onward, America produced gifted inventors, but government-sponsored research and development only began in a major way during World War II with the Manhattan Project. The effort to build an atomic bomb came about because FDR and his advisers feared that, without it, Nazi Germany would get the bomb first. After the war, as scientific research became crucial for technical advance and the scale and complexity of that research could no longer be adequately sustained by private companies alone, the United States led the way. The low-hanging fruit had already been plucked by tinkerers in garages, and scientific progress now required national laboratories and partnerships between government, universities, and private companies. The programs that Eisenhower added to the nation's formula for prosperity had the common goal of assisting in the global struggle against the Soviet Union and international communism. Seventy-five years after World War II and two decades after the Cold War, America's oldest national laboratory, the Argonne National Laboratory in Illinois, is doing basic research into solar energy, the smart electric grid, and electric cars. Examples of this public-private partnership make the news pages every day. For instance, as AOL's DailyFinance.com noted (January 7, 2011), General Motors has licensed a technology from Argonne "that will boost the performance of lithium-ion battery cells that power electric cars" such as GM's Volt, creating "safer, cheaper batteries with longer operating lives that can also go further between charges."

Our big challenges today require the kind of national responses that wars have evoked, but without a major ongoing conflict it will be difficult to mobilize the American people to make the difficult policy choices needed to meet them. In seeking to rally support for such policies when he assumed office, President Obama referred to a "Sputnik moment" for the United States. The original "Sputnik moment" spurred thousands of Americans to take up careers in science and engineering, and related businesses, and galvanized the country as a whole to invest in mathematics, science, and technology, as well as to improve the nation's infrastructure. The purpose was to avoid falling behind the Soviet Union, but one of the by-products was to update the traditional American formula for prosperity, which made the American economy even more creative and productive.

Today the United States has no such rival; but we have to find a way to do now what Sputnik spurred us to do then: update our formula to match the needs of the moment. After all, we are driving on roads and bridges built in the 1950s and even the 1930s. We are cutting back on the very universities that were chartered by Lincoln. We are learning from breakthroughs made by scientists who were inspired by Kennedy's moon shot or who immigrated to America in the 1970s, spurred by Kennedy's vision. In short, we are living off upgrades to our formula made a long time ago. While the $787 billion economic stimulus package Congress approved in February 2009 included some investments in infrastructure and research and development, much of the spending undertaken to fight the recession went to tax cuts, to unemployment insurance, and to such minuscule improvements as the new lighting on the train platforms in Penn Station in New York City, which makes it easier to see just how grimy, undersized, and outdated they are. The formula has a long lead time; it involves one generation investing on behalf of another. So when we opt for deferring maintenance on the formula rather than making farsighted investments in it, we are denying the next generation the tools it will need to maintain the American dream.

Unfortunately, the political debate in America has strayed absurdly from the virtues of our public-private formula. Liberals blame all of America's problems on Wall Street and big business while advocating a more equal distribution of an ever shrinking economic pie. Conservatives assert that the key to our economic future is simple: close our eyes, click our heels three times, and say "tax cuts," and the pie will miraculously grow.

We need to get back to basics, and fast. We need to upgrade and invest in our formula the way that every generation that came before us has done. We are entering a new economic turn, one that America did more to generate than any other country. Now we have to make sure that every American citizen and company has the skills and tools to navigate it.

PART II

THE EDUCATION CHALLENGE

FOUR

Up in the Air

In 2009, a movie appeared that vividly reflected the impact of two of America's four major challenges—globalization and the revolution in information technology. The film was *Up in the Air*, which starred George Clooney as a "career transition counselor" who flies around the country firing redundant white-collar workers at the behest of their bosses. His life is an endless and lonely montage of airport hotels, frequent-flier lounges, TSA patdowns, and in-flight magazines. Along the way, Clooney meets his female clone, played by Vera Farmiga, another lonely road warrior armed with multiple credit cards, wrinkle-free clothing, and carry-on luggage that fits perfectly above the seat. Their affair reminds us that everybody, even a loner, needs somebody to love.

The real co-star, though, is Clooney's new protégée, played by Anna Kendrick, a hyper-confident, twenty-three-year-old, freshly minted efficiency expert, who comes up with an even better idea for firing people than Clooney's fly-by pink-slips shtick: handle all the firings from a central office using computers and the Internet, and eliminate the travel and all that I-feel-your-pain-face-to-face stuff that the Clooney character does so well. As Anthony Lane noted in his review in *The New Yorker* (December 7, 2009), "The film begins with a sequence of talking heads—the faces and expostulations of the newly sacked, as they respond to the life-draining news. If you're wondering why they seem so artless and sincere in their dismay, that's because they are; far from being Hollywood bit players, these are real victims of job loss, found in St. Louis and Detroit." They stare into the camera, responding to the news that a Clooney-like grim reaper has just delivered, with emotions ranging from "This is what I get for thirty years at this company?" to "Who the fuck are you?"

That's a very good question. It is the raw version of a very basic question many Americans are asking.

While one of the movie's themes is that even the professionally lonely don't really want to be alone, its larger point is that the same forces of technology, automation, and outsourcing that are destroying the jobs of the people that Clooney is firing will get him in the end as well, through Kendrick and her techno solution for the mass delivery of pink slips. So while the romantic theme of this film is that no one wants to be alone, the bigger message is that *no one is safe*—not even the guy whose job is firing people. The convergence of globalization and technology will eventually touch everyone. These forces are far larger than any individual. They are ferocious, impersonal, and inescapable. They are leaving a whole class of American workers up in the air. It is incumbent on all of us to understand how these two forces are shaping American lives and what we need to do, individually and as a country, to harness them rather than be steamrolled by them.

The Merger

Let's start with a simple declarative sentence: The merger of globalization and the IT revolution that coincided with the transition from the twentieth to the twenty-first century is changing everything—every job, every industry, every service, every hierarchical institution. It is creating new markets and new economic and political realities practically overnight. This merger has raised the level of skill a person needs to obtain and retain any good job, while at the same time increasing the global competition for every one of those jobs. It has made politics more transparent, the world more connected, dictators more vulnerable, and both individuals and small groups more empowered.

Here are three random news items that sum up what has happened.

The first comes from the Asian subcontinent. An Indian newspaper, the *Hindustan Times*, ran a news item (October 30, 2010) reporting that a Nepali telecommunications firm had just started providing third-generation mobile network service (3G) at the summit of Mount Everest, the world's tallest mountain. This, the story noted, would "allow thousands of climbers access to high-speed Internet and video calls using their mobile phones." Following up this story, the BBC observed that this was a far cry from 1953, when Edmund Hillary first climbed to the Everest summit and "used runners to carry messages from his expedition to the nearest telegraph office."

You can imagine the phone calls being made: "Hi, Mom! You'll never guess where I'm calling you from . . ."

The same month that story appeared, the business pages of American newspapers reported that Applied Materials, the Silicon Valley–headquartered company that makes machines that produce sophisticated, thin-film solar panels, had opened the world's largest commercial solar research-and-development center in Xi'an, China. Initially, Applied Materials sought applicants for 260 scientist/technologist jobs in Xi'an. Howard Clabo, a company spokesman, said that the Xi'an center received some 26,000 Chinese applications and hired 330 people—31 percent with master's or Ph.D. degrees. "Roughly 50 percent of the solar panels in the world were made in China last year," explained Clabo. "We need to be where the customers are."

Our last item comes from Manama, Bahrain, the tiny Persian Gulf state off the east coast of Saudi Arabia. In the run-up to parliamentary elections, *The Washington Post* ran a story (November 27, 2006) about disaffected Shiite voters there, which turned out to be a harbinger of revolutions to come. "Mahmood, who lives in a house with his parents, four siblings and their children," the paper reported, "said he became even more frustrated when he looked up Bahrain on Google Earth and saw vast tracts of empty land, while tens of thousands of mainly poor Shiites were squashed together in small, dense areas. 'We are 17 people crowded in one small house, like many people in the southern district,' he said. 'And you see on Google how many palaces there are and how the al-Khalifas [the Sunni ruling family] have the rest of the country to themselves.' Bahraini activists have encouraged people to take a look at the country on Google Earth, and they have set up a special user group whose members have access to more than 40 images of royal palaces." Nearly five years later, Google Earth images helped to fuel a revolution in Bahrain and other repressive Arab states.

The first story tells us how fast and far the network of information technologies that are driving globalization has expanded, just in the last five years. Every day the world's citizens, governments, businesses, terrorists—and now mountaintops—are being woven together into an ever tightening web, giving more and more people in more and more places access to cheap tools of connectivity, creativity, and collaboration.

The second story tells us that all this connectivity is enabling a whole new category of workers to join the global marketplace. In the process it is exposing Americans to competition from a category of workers we have not seen before on a large scale: *the low-wage, high-skilled worker.* We have gotten used to low-wage, low-skilled workers in large numbers. But the low-wage, high-skilled worker is a whole new species, to which we will have to adapt.

The third story tells us that these technologies are now empowering individuals to level hierarchies—from Arab tyrannies, to mainstream-media companies, to traditional retail outlets, to the United States of America itself. As a result, many of the structural advantages that America had in the Cold War decades are being erased. Yes, America still has an abundance of land for agriculture, a ring of port cities like no other country, and huge domestic natural resources. But these alone are not enough to drive our GDP anymore, especially when you think about what we no longer have: overwhelming dominance. America emerged from World War II as the only major economy with its industrial base intact. Europe and Japan eventually caught up, but other major countries didn't really compete. China was all but closed, its energies diverted by Maoism and a cultural revolution. India was less closed, but its leaders were content with 2 percent per capita net annual growth. Brazil was partly closed, and handicapped by populist economic policies. Manufacturers in Korea and Taiwan concentrated on cheap plastics, consumer electronics, and textiles, although they later entered the semiconductor business. The United States was able to vacuum up the best minds from India, China, the Arab world, and Latin America, where there were few opportunities for unfettered innovation or academic research. Wall Street firms dominated global markets and America had the world's only developed venture capital system. It wasn't that Americans were not hard workers or that our rising living standard was some fluke of history. We did work hard. Our success was based on real innovation, real education, real research, real industries, real markets, and real growth—*but* the playing field was also tilted in our direction. Now we have to try to sustain all those good things without all those structural advantages. Your children will only know that world when everything was tilted America's way from reading history books. The merger of globalization and the IT revolution can make us either better off or worse off—richer or poorer. It depends on us—on how well we understand this new world that we invented and how effectively we respond to it.

Flat World 1.0

Globalization and the IT revolution are totally intertwined, each being spurred on by the other. New technologies erase boundaries, break down walls, and connect the previously disconnected. Then those connected people and firms and governments build up webs of trade, commerce, investment, innovation, and collaboration that create markets for, and demand for, more technologies to connect more people at even lower costs.

It all happened so fast, but it is clear that sometime around the year 2000 many people in many places realized that they were engaging with people with whom they had never engaged before—whether it was Tom's mom and her new online bridge partner in Siberia or the local gas station owner discovering through the Internet a new supplier of cheaper tires in Panama. At the same time, these same people in these same places discovered that they were being touched *by* people who had never touched them before—whether it was a young Indian voice on the phone from a Bangalore call center trying to sign them up for a new Visa card or a young Chinese student in Shanghai who had just taken the place they had hoped to have at Harvard.

What they were all feeling was that *the world is flat* (the title of Tom's 2005 book)—meaning that more people could suddenly compete, connect, and collaborate with more other people from more different places for less money with greater ease than ever before in the history of humankind. That flattening, which would eventually affect businesses, schools, armies, terrorist groups, governments, and—most of all—individual workers across the globe, was the product of three powerful forces that came together between the late 1980s and the new millennium.

The first was the personal computer, which enabled more and more people to create their own content—words, books, algorithms, programs, photos, data, spreadsheets, music, applications, and videos—in digital form. Men and women have been creating what we now call "content" ever since cavemen and cavewomen started drawing figures on cave walls. But with the PC they could suddenly create content in digital form and, once it was in bits and bytes, they could manipulate it in many more ways.

Second, the Internet and the World Wide Web that spread across the globe in the late 1990s suddenly gave people the ability to send their digital content to so many more places and to share it, and work together on it, with so many more people for the low costs associated with gaining access to a PC and an Internet connection.

Finally, and contemporaneous with that, a quiet revolution, but a hugely important one, was taking place. It was a revolution in software programming languages and transmission protocols that go by names such as HTML, HTTP, XML, SOAP, AJAX, EDI, FTP, SSH, SFTP, VAN, SMTP, and AS2. You don't really need to know what they all stand for; you just need to know that together this alphabet soup has made everyone's desktop computer, laptop, BlackBerry, iPhone, iPad, and no-name Chinese or Indian cell phone interoperable with everyone else's. Call it the "workflow revolution" because it has made digital content flow securely in all directions. As a result, anyone could get on his or her computer or cell phone and dispatch a PDF, e-mail a friend, text a colleague, or transmit a picture and know that whatever was said, posted, texted, videoed, PowerPointed, or e-mailed could go anywhere in the world and be accessed from anywhere in the world—no matter what computer or software was being used to send and receive it. That all feels totally natural today, but it was truly revolutionary at the time, when so many people were running different machines using different operating systems and software.

Put these three innovations all together and the result was that in the span of a decade, people in Boston, Bangkok, and Bangalore, Mumbai, Manhattan, and Moscow, all became virtual next-door neighbors. Probably two billion new people suddenly found themselves with new powers to communicate, compete, and collaborate globally—*as individuals*. Whereas previously it was largely only countries and companies who could act globally in this way, when the world got flat, individuals could act globally—as individuals—and more and more of them every day.

Flat World 2.0

According to the International Telecommunications Union (ITU), an agency of the United Nations, as of 2010 there were about 4.6 billion cell phones in use worldwide. There are 6.8 billion people on the planet, so the number of cell phones in circulation now equals roughly two-thirds of the world's total population. Since there were only about one billion cell-phone subscribers worldwide in 2002, it is clear that the rate of growth is staggering—with most of it now coming from the developing world: India, for example, is adding 15 to 18 *million* cell-phone users a month. According to the ITU, about 23 percent of the global population uses the Internet today, up from 12 percent in 2002. Every day now there are millions of free or dirt-cheap interactions and collaborations happening in places and among people who were not connected just five years ago. We know where this eventually goes—to universal connectivity to the Internet via cell phone, smartphone, or traditional computer, probably within a decade.

"I call my mother in Karachi every day. I use Skype and she uses her regular phone. It costs so little, it's almost free," Raziuddin Syed, a senior IT engineer based in Tampa, Florida, told the Pakistani newspaper *Dawn* (February 20, 2011). Syed "works for an international accounting firm, thanks to internet-connected laptop computer and the Voice over Internet Protocol technology. 'Five years ago the cost of phone calls, especially those using VOIP, was much higher than it is today. Calls between members of services like Skype are always free but calls to other phones, landlines or mobiles, carry a very small per minute charge,' Syed says."

In other words, since *The World Is Flat* was published in 2005, the world has only gotten, well, flatter. How far and how fast have we come? When Tom wrote *The World Is Flat*, Facebook wasn't even in it. It had just started up and was still a minor phenomenon. Indeed, in 2005 Facebook didn't exist for most people, "Twitter" was still a sound, the "cloud" was something in the sky, "3G" was a parking space, "applications" were what you sent to colleges, and "Skype" was a typo.

That is how much has changed in just the last six years. In fact, so many new technologies and services have been introduced that we would argue that sometime around the year 2010 we entered Flat

World 2.0—a difference of degree that deserves its own designation. That is because Flat World 2.0 is everything Flat World 1.0 was, but with so many more people able to connect to the Flat World platform, so many more people able to communicate with others who are also connected, and so many more people now empowered to find other people of like mind to collaborate with—whether to support a politician, follow a rock group, invent a product, or launch a revolution—based on shared values, interests, and ideals.

We look at it this way: Flat World 1.0 was built around the PC-server relationship. In order to participate, most everyone had to use a laptop or a desktop computer—usually connected by landline or fiber-optic cable to an Internet Web server somewhere. It was not very mobile, and the cost of participating still excluded some people. You had to have enough money to buy a desktop or a laptop, rent one at an Internet café, or use one at the office where you worked. The penetration was global, and in that sense it really did flatten the world, thanks to the rapid diffusion of landlines and fiber cable on land and undersea, but it tended to connect people living in cities and towns—less so villages and countryside—who were of a certain minimum income level.

Flat World 1.0 was particularly strong not only at enabling individuals to take part in a global conversation via e-mail, but also at enabling people to work together to make stuff, sell stuff, and buy stuff—from more places than ever before. It was great at enabling Boeing to make part of its 777 jetliner with a team that included designers in Moscow, wing manufacturers in China, and control electronics producers in Wichita. It was great at enabling the outsourcing of everything from the reading of X-rays to the tracing of lost luggage on Delta flights. It was great for empowering powerful breakthroughs in online education, entertainment, publishing, and commerce, and actually enhancing the cultural diversity of the world, not squashing it. And it was great for promoting global collaboration among individuals, so that "the crowd" could write and then upload everything from an encyclopedia (Wikipedia) to a new operating system for PCs (Linux).

Flat World 2.0 is doing all that still—and more—because it is being driven by the diffusion of more PCs (more than 350 million were sold in 2010), as well as by smartphones enabled with text messaging, Web browsers, and cameras, as well as by wireless connectivity in place of landlines to reach more remote communities, as well as by new social networks that enable collaboration on more and more things. And all of these activities are now increasingly being supported by a vast new array of software applications stored on huge interlinked server farms known collectively as "the cloud."

The cloud really is a "new, new thing." It holds every imaginable software program and every imaginable application—from bird-watching guides for southern Africa to investing guides for Wall Street—and it is being updated seamlessly every moment. The beauty of the cloud, and the reason that it is driving the flattening further and faster, is that it can turn any desktop, laptop, or simple handheld device with a browser into an information-creation or -consumption powerhouse by serving as a central location for those myriad applications, which run on individual user's devices.

Amazon.com, for example, is now selling not only books and chain saws but business facilities in the cloud. Andy Jassy is Amazon's senior vice president in charge of Amazon Web Services, *Bloomberg Business-Week* explained (March 3, 2011), which means that his job is to rent space to individual innovators, or companies, on Amazon's rent-a-cloud.

> Although all shoppers are welcome, this Amazon, [Jassy] explains, is for business customers and isn't well marked on the home page. It's called Amazon Web Services, or AWS . . . , which rents out computing power for pennies an hour. "This completely levels the playing field," Jassy boasts. AWS makes it possible for anyone with an Internet connection and a credit card to access the same kind of world-class computing systems that Amazon uses to run its $34 billion-a-year retail operation . . . AWS is growing like crazy. Although he won't cite exact numbers, Jassy claims "hundreds of thousands of customers" already use the service, and analysts at UBS estimate Amazon will do about $750 million of business on AWS this year. In fact, a whole generation of Internet companies couldn't exist without it. Netflix's movie-streaming empire runs on it; Zynga, the social gaming company, uses it to handle sudden spikes in usage. AWS has become such a fact of life for Silicon Valley startups that ven-

ture capitalists actually hand out Amazon gift cards to entrepreneurs. Keeping up with the demand requires frantic expansion: Each day, Jassy's operation adds enough computing muscle to power one whole Amazon.com circa 2000, when it was a $2.8 billion business. The physical expansion of all that data takes place in Amazon's huge, specially designed buildings—the biggest can reach 700,000 square feet, or the equivalent of roughly 16 football fields. These interconnected facilities, scattered all over the world, are where AWS conducts its business: cloud computing. The "cloud" refers to the amorphous, out-of-sight, out-of-mind mess of computer tasks that happen on someone else's equipment.

Though the cloud is still in its infancy, in 2009 alone global data flows grew by 50 percent thanks in part to its emergence, along with wireless connectivity. "The more people are connected, the more people connect," said Hewlett-Packard's CEO, Léo Apotheker, "so you get these network effects, and that is just flattening the world even more every day."

Indeed, every day more and more of the features that defined the personal computer are finding their way into the phone and the tablet. True, the majority of the world's people still don't have smartphones. But you can see the future, and it will be smart; there will be Web- and video-enabled phones everywhere for everyone—and sooner than you think. As a result, *another two billion people* are joining the daily global conversation, with more and cheaper tools they can use to connect, compete, and collaborate on the global playing field. Many of them can just dive right in and start texting on their phones, without having to buy or rent a PC or learn any software-writing program.

To summarize: Flat World 1.0, from roughly 1995 to 2005, made Boston and Bangalore next-door neighbors. Flat World 2.0, from 2005 to the present, is making Boston, Bangalore, and Sirsi next-door neighbors. Where is Sirsi? Sirsi is an agricultural trading center of 90,000 people some 275 miles from Bangalore in the Indian countryside. And this is happening everywhere in every country.

In Flat World 1.0, said Alan Cohen, Vice President of Mobility Solutions at Cisco Systems, "everyone was a consumer of goods and information in what has become the ultimate consumer marketplace. You could buy anything from anyone anywhere." Some people also became producers of goods and information (people who had never dreamed of being able to do so in the past), starting their own websites or uploading and sharing their opinions, music, pictures, software programs, or encyclopedia entries. This new Flat World 2.0 platform for connectivity, being so cheap and mobile, continues and broadens that phenomenon into the most remote areas, bringing a whole new swath of humanity into the game. It can only lead to more innovation of all sorts much faster. "Imagine what they are going to produce," said Cohen. "The cloud is like this huge shared factory, where anyone who wants to produce something can come and rent the tools for almost nothing."

If Flat World 1.0 was about producing goods and services on this new global platform, Flat World 2.0 is about all that—but also about generating and sharing ideas on this platform. As Craig Mundie, Chief Strategy and Research Officer for Microsoft, put it to us, what the PC plus the Internet plus the search engine did for Web pages "was enable anyone with connectivity to find *anything* that interests them," and what the PC and smartphone plus the Internet plus Facebook is doing "is enabling anyone to find *anyone*" who interests them—or at least any of the 500 million people already using social networks. They can find anyone who shares their special interest in knitting, Ethiopian cooking, the New York Yankees, kids with Down syndrome, cancer research, launching a jihad against America, or toppling the government in Egypt, Tunisia, or Syria.

When so many people can find anything and anyone and more easily than ever, and can stay in touch more easily than ever to collaborate to make products, encyclopedias, or revolutions, you are into Flat World 2.0—a *hyper-connected* world. And that has profound implications.

"The people now have not only their own information access system to understand what is going on better inside their own countries or abroad, not only to discuss that with one another, but also the command-and-control mechanism to organize themselves to do something about it," adds Mundie. "In the past, only governments and armies had these kinds of high-scale command-and-control systems. Now the people do. And the more these tools penetrate at great volumes, the more the price of making and using them goes down, then the more they penetrate and diffuse farther. And the more they diffuse the more impossible it becomes to control anything from the center." The more impossible it also becomes to keep anything "local" anymore. Everything now flows instantly from the most remote corners of any country onto this global platform where it gets shared.

One big indication of this move from Flat World 1.0 to 2.0 can be found in the uprisings across the Arab world in 2011. Flat World 1.0 connected Detroit and Damascus. Flat World 2.0, though, connected Detroit, Damascus, and Dara'a. Where is Dara'a? It is a small, dusty town on the Syrian border with Jordan where the revolution in Syria began and from which a stream of pictures, video, and words about what was happening inside Syria have been pumped out to the world. The people of Dara'a had so many cell phones and wireless connections that the Syrian regime could not suppress information about its own brutality. Think about it: the Syrian regime refused to permit any foreign TV networks into the country—no CNN, no BBC—so it thought that no one outside Syria would know of its brutal crackdown. Out of nowhere, someone inside or outside Syria created a website called "Sham News Network" or SNN, where Syrians in Dara'a and then elsewhere began posting their cell-phone videos of the regime killing its own people. They did the same on YouTube. Suddenly, big global networks like al-Jazeera and CNN were running video and crediting SNN—a site that probably cost only a few hundred dollars to create and operate and that no one knows who runs. The people were telling their own story. In the old days, the Syrian government would have just shut down a TV or radio station broadcasting opinions it did not like. But today the Syrian regime can no more afford to shut down its cell-phone network than it can afford to shut down its electricity grid.

It is for all of these reasons that we would argue that Flat Worlds 1.0 and 2.0 together constitute the most profound inflection point for communication, innovation, and commerce since the Gutenberg printing press. In a relatively short time, virtually everyone will have both the tools and the networks to participate in this hyper-connected world. The effects of the printing press, though, took hundreds of years to percolate through society. This is happening in a few decades, which is much more challenging in terms of adaptation.

This change will affect America and Americans in many ways—

from politics to commerce to the workplace to education. What interests us most in this chapter is how these forces are helping to reshape the workplace and the skills that the individual will need in order to get and hold a job. We can already see that this hyper-connecting of the world is altering everyone's business and forcing everyone who is in business to learn how to take advantage of these new tools to become more productive, no matter how big or small their company is. We can see that when so many people have so many tools to compete, connect, and both pull and push new innovations and information, the speed with which companies need to update their own products or invent new ones before competitors overtake them just gets faster. We can also see that this hyper-connected world is empowering more individuals and small groups to start up their own companies and create new jobs with greater ease and for less money than ever before. And, finally, we can see that it is challenging every worker who wants to hold a job for any length of time at any company—large or small, new or old—to develop the skills needed to keep up.

Let's look at all of these changes.

Everyone Is Feeling the Pressure

Michael Barber, the chief education officer for the Pearson publishing group and formerly the top education adviser to British prime minister Tony Blair, told us that whenever he lectures on globalization today he begins by telling this story: "I was at friend's fiftieth birthday party in Wales. The morning after the party another guest and I agreed to take a walk up a nearby hill. We had not met before. To make conversation as we set out, I asked him, 'What do you do?' He said, 'I am a monumental stonemason,' which in British English means he carves gravestones. I immediately said to him, 'It must be great to be in a line of work not affected by globalization.' And he looks at me with this question mark in his eyes, and says, 'What do you mean? If I didn't buy my stone over the Internet from India, I'd be out of business.' Everything had changed for him in the previous two or three years. If a stonemason [in Wales] has to get his best stone from India to stay competitive, there is no job left not affected by globalization."

Barber's story is not unusual these days. Whether you are talking to stonemasons or global corporate titans, all of them will tell you this: Changes in technology that affect their core enterprise are coming faster than they ever imagined, challenges are coming from places they never imagined, and opportunities are being opened in places they never imagined. Therefore every business executive large and small has to scour the world every day and take advantage of every way to access talent, develop new markets, and lower production costs—because if they don't do it, it will be done to them.

Tom has interviewed Victor Fung, the group chairman of Li & Fung, one of Hong Kong's oldest and most respected textile manufacturers, several times over the last decade. Fung grew up in the industry and for many years it operated on the same basic rules. As he explained: "You sourced in Asia, and you sold in America and Europe." When Tom spoke with him in early 2011, Fung had a different message. In today's hyper-connected world, he said, his whole business model has been flattened. Asia is becoming a huge market on its own, as are other areas of the developing world, and new manufacturing and design possibilities are opening up in places where they were never imaginable before. Said Fung, "Now our motto is 'Source everywhere, manufacture everywhere, sell everywhere.' The whole notion of an 'export' is really disappearing."

Mike Splinter, the CEO of Applied Materials, echoes this point. "Outsourcing was ten years ago, where you'd say, 'Let's send some software generation overseas,'" he explained. "This is not outsourcing we're doing today. This is just where I am going to get something done. Now you say, 'Hey, half my Ph.D.'s in my R-and-D department would rather live in Singapore, Taiwan, or China because that is their hometown and they can go there and still work for my company.' This is the next evolution. I have more options, many more options, to do more things than I had five or ten years ago."

From St. Louis to New Delhi

But so, too, do the little guys in this world! Every year now it takes less money to start a more ambitious company with greater reach and higher aspirations. Consider two companies: one founded by Americans in

St. Louis that operates virtually to make a medical device, and the other in a garage in South Delhi that provides banking services to India's poor. Their stories tell you about the vast new opportunities every American entrepreneur has in this new world—and also the powerful new competitors those Americans will have in this world.

You've heard the saying "As goes General Motors, so goes America." Fortunately, that is no longer true. We wish the new GM well, but thanks to the hyper-connecting of the world our economic future is no longer tied to its fate. The days of the single factory providing 10,000 jobs for one town are fast disappearing. What we need are start-ups of every variety, size, and shape. That is why our motto is "As EndoStim goes, so goes America."

EndoStim is a St. Louis, Missouri, company that is developing a proprietary implantable medical device to treat acid reflux. We have no idea whether the product will make it to the marketplace, but we were fascinated by how EndoStim was formed and does business. It is the epitome of the new kind of start-up that can propel the American economy: new immigrants using old money to innovate in a flatter world. EndoStim was inspired by Cuban and Indian immigrants to America and funded by St. Louis venture capitalists. Its device is being manufactured in Uruguay, with the help of Israeli engineers and with constant feedback from doctors in India, the United States, Europe, and Chile. Oh, and the CEO is a South African, who was educated at the Sorbonne but lives in Missouri and California. His head office is an iPad. While rescuing General Motors will save some old jobs, only by spawning thousands of EndoStims—and we do mean thousands—will we generate the good new jobs we need to keep raising the country's standard of living.

EndoStim started up by accident. Dr. Raul Perez, an obstetrician and gynecologist, immigrated to America from Cuba in the 1960s and came to St. Louis, where he met Dan Burkhardt, a local investor. "Raul had a real nose for medical investing and what could be profitable in a clinical environment," Burkhardt recalled. "So we started investing together." In 1997, they created a medical venture fund, Oakwood Medical Investors. Perez had a problem with acid reflux and went for treatment to the Mayo Clinic in Arizona, where he was helped by an Indian American doctor, Virender K. Sharma. During his follow-ups,

Dr. Sharma said the four words every venture capitalist wants to hear: "I have an idea"—to use a pacemaker-like device to control the muscle that would choke off acid reflux. Burkhardt, Perez, and Sharma were joined by Bevil Hogg (a South African and a founder of the Trek Bicycle Corporation), who became the CEO, to raise the initial funds to develop the technology. Two Israelis, Shai Policker, a medical engineer, and Dr. Edy Soffer, a prominent gastroenterologist, joined a Seattle-based engineering team (led by an Australian) to help with the design. A company in Uruguay specializing in pacemakers built the prototype.

This is the latest in venture investing: a lean start-up whose principals are rarely in the same place at the same time and which takes advantage of all the tools of the connected world—teleconferencing, e-mail, the Internet, Facebook, Twitter, and faxes—to make use of the best expertise and low-cost, high-quality manufacturing. We've described cloud computing. This is cloud manufacturing.

The early clinical trials for EndoStim were conducted in India and Chile and are now being expanded into Europe. "What they have in common," said Hogg, "is superb surgeons with high levels of skill, enthusiasm for the project, an interest in research, and reasonable costs." What's in it for America? As long as the venture money, core innovation, and key management comes from this country—a lot. If EndoStim works out, its tiny headquarters in St. Louis will grow much larger. The United States is where the best jobs—top management, marketing, design—and the main shareholders will be, said Hogg. Where innovation occurs and capital is raised still matters.

To go from EndoStim to Eko India Financial Services—humming away in a garage in South Delhi—is to go from the most virtual of start-ups to the most conventional, but it is still striking how much they have in common. Eko's founders, Abhishek Sinha and his brother Abhinav, started with the simplest observation: Low-wage Indian migrant workers flocking to Delhi from poorer regions had no place to put their savings and no secure way to send money home to their families. India has relatively few bank branches for a country its size, so many migrants stuffed money in their mattresses or sent cash home through traditional *hawala*, hand-to-hand networks.

This gave the brothers an idea. In most Indian neighborhoods and villages, there's a mom-and-pop kiosk that sells drinks, cigarettes, candy, and a few groceries. Why not turn each one into a virtual bank? they asked themselves. To do so, they created a software program whereby a migrant worker in Delhi, using his cell phone and proof of identity, could open a bank account registered on his cell-phone text system. Mom-and-pop shopkeepers would act as the friendly neighborhood banker and do the same, so no new bricks and mortar were needed. Then the worker living in his shantytown around Delhi could give his kiosk owner 1,000 rupees (about $20) and the shopkeeper would record it on his phone and text the receipt of the deposit to the system's mother bank, the State Bank of India. The worker's wife back in Bihar could then just go to the mom-and-pop kiosk in her village, also tied in to the system, and make a withdrawal using her cell phone. The shopkeeper there would give her the 1,000 rupees sent by her husband. Each shopkeeper would earn a small fee from each transaction, as would the State Bank of India. Besides money transfers, workers could also use the system to bank their savings.

Eighteen months after opening for business in 2008, this virtual bank had 180,000 users doing more than 7,000 transactions a day through 500 "branches"—those mom-and-pop kiosks—in Delhi, and 200 more in Bihar and Jharkhand, from where many maids and other internal migrants come. Eko gets a modest commission from the Bank of India for each transaction and was already showing a small profit in 2010. Abhishek, who was inspired by a similar program in Brazil, said the kiosk owners "are already trusted people in each community" and routinely extend credit to their poor customers. "So we said, 'Why not leverage them?' We are the agents of the bank, and these retailers are our subagents."

Why not, indeed? The cheapest Indian-made cell phone today has enough computing power to become a digital "mattress" and digital bank for the poor. The whole system is being run out of a little house and garage with a dozen employees, a bunch of laptops, and cheap Internet connectivity. Not surprisingly, the Sinha team began building its own core software with some free, open source code downloaded from the cloud. Realizing that they did not have the capital themselves to invest in large-scale hardware, they run their whole business on cloud-computing servers hosted at a data center in Noida, a suburb of Delhi.

The core idea of the business, says Abhishek, is "to close the last mile—the gap where government services end and the consumer begins." There is a huge business in closing that last mile for millions of poor Indians, who, without it, can't get proper health care, education, or insurance. Eko, Abhishek added, "leveraged existing telecom networks and existing distribution networks" and with relatively little capital invested is now able to serve more than 700,000 low-income customers across eight Indian states. By early 2011, Eko was processing more than 20,000 transactions daily, worth $2.5 million.

It was telling that the small Eko team included graduates from India's most prestigious institutes of technology, who were working in America but decided to return to Delhi to join this start-up. Jishnu Kinwar, who earned a master's in computer science from Lamar University in Texas and an MBA from the University of Alabama, worked for ten years in the United States before he and his wife left their plum jobs to head back to Delhi, where Kinwar now works in the Eko garage. The chief operating officer, Matteo Chiampo, is an Italian technologist who left a good job in Boston to work in India because, as he put it, this is "where the excitement is."

The same forces empowering EndoStim and Eko are also empowering one- and two-person firms that can go global from anywhere. We can see this in the multibillion-dollar come-out-of-nowhere "apps" industry. Apple released the iPhone in June 2007 and the iPad in April 2010. A 2011 report produced by Forrester Research estimated that the revenue generated through the sales of smartphone and tablet applications will reach $38 billion annually by 2015. Think about that: An industry that did not exist in 2006 will be generating $38 billion in revenues within a decade, with a slew of new online stores—Google's Android Market, Microsoft's Marketplace, BlackBerry's App World, and Hewlett-Packard's Palm App Catalog. Apple's iPhone, iPod Touch, and iPad alone already had generated some 350,000 apps when we wrote this book in the winter of 2011, and the company had paid more than $2 billion to developers of programs sold at its App Store. The potential for individuals today to globalize their talents, hobbies, and passions into applications with a worldwide market is without precedent in history and unbounded in potential.

That's the good news. The bad news, or, as we prefer to call it, "the challenging news," is this: The emerging apps industry combines software, art, math, creativity, writing, gaming, education, composing, and marketing—everything that goes into different applications. In other words, it requires combining the skills of MIT, MTV, and Madison Avenue. These skills, in turn, require a lot more training and creativity than just writing software code.

Within a few years, virtually everyone on the planet will have the tools and network connections to participate in the hyper-connected flat world. As that happens, all of these instruments of innovation and connectivity will become what electricity is for most of the world. "You will just presume they are there—they will actually just disappear into the background," argues Joel Cawley, the vice president for strategy at IBM. And as that happens, two things will differentiate companies, countries, and individuals from one another, Cawley says. One is analytics. Once everyone is connected, your prosperity will depend on how well you or your company or country can "analyze and apply" all the data pouring through these networks to optimize your ability to provide better health care, education, e-commerce, innovation, customer service, and government services to everyone on the network. After all, the tools your company uses to perform all of this analysis will be sitting there in the cloud for every other company to use as well.

Also, once all the technology is a given, Cawley predicts, "all the old-fashioned stuff will start to matter even more." Then "the only advantage you can have is in the human stuff." How good is your school system? How well have you trained your workers? What kind of creativity, inspiration, and imagination do they bring to this platform? How good is your rule of law and your national governance, and how smart are your regulatory, patent, and tax policies? "These," said Cawley, "will be the real differentiators. The technology everyone will have."

Dov Seidman, the CEO of LRN, a company that helps other companies create sustainable business cultures, and the author of *How: Why How We Do Anything Means Everything*, summarizes the change from Flat World 1.0 to 2.0 this way: "We have gone from connected to interconnected to interdependent. All the links are getting so much tighter. So many more people can now connect, collaborate, and partner in much deeper ways. When the world is tied together this intimately, everyone's values and behavior matter more than ever, because they impact so many more people than ever."

Creators and Servers

And that brings us back to America.

All these dramatic changes in the workplace, coming in rapid-fire succession, have left a lot of people feeling up in the air and asking, "Where do I fit in? How do I stay relevant in my job? And what kind of skills do I need to learn at school?" The short answer is that the workplace is undergoing a fundamental restructuring that every educator, parent, and worker needs to understand.

The pressure on workers starts with the fact that the combination of the Great Recession and the hyper-flattening and hyper-connecting of the global marketplace is spurring every company to become more productive—to produce more goods and services for less money and with fewer workers. This explains why, despite the recession, U.S. productivity has gone up, corporate profits have gone up, and unemployment has gone up all at the same time. Companies are learning to do more with less, so more and more old jobs are never coming back and more and more new jobs are being done by machines and microchips.

"There is a big tectonic change happening, driven by technology," said Raghuram Rajan, a professor of finance at the University of Chicago's Booth School of Business and the author of *Fault Lines*. Throughout the post–World War II period, until 1991, "it typically took on average eight months for jobs that were lost at the trough of a recession to come back to the old peak," said Rajan. But with the introduction of all these new technologies and networks over the last two decades, that is no longer the case. With each recession and with each new hyper-flattening and hyper-connecting of the global marketplace, more and more jobs are being automated, digitized, or outsourced.

"Look at the last three recessions," said Rajan. "After 1991, it took twenty-three months for the jobs to come back to prerecession levels. After 2001, it took thirty-eight months. And after 2007, it is expected to take up to five years or more." A key reason is that in the old cyclical recovery people got laid off and were rather quickly hired back into the workforce once demand rose again. The nature of the work did not change that radically from one recession to the next, so workers did not have to adjust that much. Today, said Rajan, under the pressure of globalization and the IT revolution, industries are becoming far more focused on productivity. And "once they have started letting people go, they have realized why not go whole hog and rethink entirely how we do things and where we do things?"

Byron Auguste, a managing director at the McKinsey & Company consulting firm, who has worked on this subject, said a 2011 McKinsey study indicates that historically in a downturn, when there is a drop in demand, companies restructure. In past recessions, they would make up for lost business through a combination of laying off workers and accepting lower profits or even losses. So those companies would retain 60 to 70 percent of the workers in order to preserve their core base of employee expertise, while letting 30 to 40 percent go. Then, when the economy started to recover and demand rose again, they would hire back the workers that were laid off. With each recession over the last two decades, though, this pattern has been less and less pronounced. In the recession of 2008, said Auguste, citing McKinsey's research, companies made up for roughly 98 percent of their lost revenue by laying off workers and then replacing their work with more automation and outsourcing. "When demand comes back," said Auguste, "firms won't hire back as many workers [as in the past], because they have now fundamentally restructured their operations to do their business with fewer people."

Did employers do this because they have gotten meaner over the last twenty years? No. They did it because the hyper-connecting of the world both enabled them to do it and required them to do it before their competitors did.

Over the past decade this process eliminated a lot of American jobs, but the booming economy both disguised it and cushioned us from its effects, argues Rajan. How so? "By creating a huge housing bubble and a huge credit bubble to artificially sustain people's standards of living," he explained. "In effect, we created an industry—housing construction—to absorb all the unskilled labor" that would otherwise struggle to find jobs in a super-competitive marketplace. Once the housing and credit bubbles blew up, though, many workers found themselves literally up in the air. The bursting of the housing bubble wiped out a whole swath of low-skilled blue-collar jobs (many of the people who were building the houses) just when the intensification of globalization wiped out a whole swath of low- and mid-level white-collar jobs (many of the people who were buying the houses).

There is no question that stimulating the economy with short-term measures meant to increase demand (tax cuts, low interest rates, and increased government spending) would help revive some of these jobs. We do have a serious demand problem. But we also have a new structural challenge in the labor market that can only be addressed by more education and more innovation.

Here is a simple example of what is happening across the economy. For twenty years, Colorado ski resorts sold lift tickets that you clipped to your jacket for a lift operator to punch each morning when you took your first ride to the top of the mountain. These were relatively unskilled jobs that attracted mostly young people from around the world who came to America on temporary visas for the winter season. Their ID badges would often say what country they were from, and it was always fun for skiers to engage them: "Hey, you're from Argentina. We were just there last year." Then, with automation and digitization, the lift tickets were made with bar codes and the hole-punch tools were retired and replaced by handheld scanners, but the resorts still needed crews of unskilled workers to scan the tag on each skier's jacket. In 2010, the Snowmass resort adopted a different system. Your lift ticket is now a credit-card-size piece of plastic with a microchip embedded in it. You slip the card into a jacket pocket. At the lift-line entrance, instead of stopping to get your ticket punched, you walk through a turnstile equipped with a sensor that automatically reads your card and, after picking up the signal, lets you pass through with a green light—an E-ZPass for skiers. There is no one from Argentina or Colorado checking your ticket with a welcoming smile. Instead of four lift employees, one at each gate, there is just one person, standing to the side, operating the whole system from a computer screen. One more highly skilled and no doubt better-paid employee and a computer have replaced four lesser-skilled, lesser-paid employees.

This shift is happening all through the workplace—improving productivity for every company, wiping out whole categories of jobs, and raising the bar for higher-skilled ones.

Who Ate My Job?

In September 2010, Harvard University's Lawrence Katz and MIT's David Autor, two labor economists, produced a paper for the National

Science Foundation entitled *Grand Challenges in the Study of Employment and Technological Change,* which helps explain how this phenomenon is playing out today.

The big change wrought by the merger of globalization and the IT revolution, argue Katz and Autor, was the creation of "a labor market that greatly rewards workers with college and graduate degrees but is unfavorable to the particularly less-educated males." This trend is called "employment polarization," or skill-biased technological change. It means that a computer or a robot makes an educated person more productive and able to sell his or her goods and services in more markets around the world, but often makes a less-educated person less employable. When globalization and IT converge, the best-educated workers get raises and the least-educated get pink slips—or don't get jobs in the first place. Tom's *New York Times* colleague David Leonhardt makes the point with a few grim statistics (April 11, 2011): "In the worst economic times of the 1950s and '60s, about 9 percent of men in the prime of their working lives (twenty-five to fifty-four years old) were not working. At the depth of the severe recession in the early 1980s, about 15 percent of prime-age men were not working. Today, more than 18 percent of such men aren't working. That's a depressing statistic: nearly one out of every five men between twenty-five and fifty-four is not employed. Yes, some of them are happily retired. Some are going to school. And some are taking care of their children. But most don't fall into any of these categories. They simply aren't working. They're managing to get by some other way."

Broadly speaking, today's job market can be divided into three segments, which are steadily collapsing into two. The first includes what are known as nonroutine high-skilled jobs. A nonroutine job is one whose function cannot be reduced to an algorithm that can then be programmed into a computer or robot, or easily digitized and outsourced abroad. These jobs involve critical thinking and reasoning, abstract analytical skills, imagination, judgment, creativity, and often math. They require the ability to read a situation, to extrapolate from it, and to create something new—a new product, a new insight, a new service, a new investment, a new way of doing old things, or new things to do in new ways in an existing company. Nonroutine high-skilled work is generally the province of engineers, programmers, designers, financiers, senior executives, stock and bond traders, accountants, performers, athletes, scientists, doctors, lawyers, artists, authors, college professors, architects, contractors, chefs, specialized journalists, editors, sophisticated machine-tool operators, and innovators.

Far from supplanting these nonroutine jobs, the merger of global-ization and the IT revolution has made those who do them even more productive. These workers use Google to do their own research; they use Windows to produce their own PowerPoints; they use Macs to de-sign their own online ads, posters, and apps, as well as to edit their own films and to design their own buildings. They use laptops to create their own spreadsheets and crunch their own numbers, and cell phones to make their own trades and gather their own information. They can do all these things anywhere and do them faster and more cheaply by them-selves than any secretary, clerk, or assistant can. If you fall into this non-routine high-skilled category of work, then globalization and the IT revolution have been your friends, making you individually more pro-ductive, globally more attractive, and most likely better paid.

In the second category are routine middle-skilled jobs, involving a lot of standardized repetitive tasks, of either the white-collar or blue-collar variety. They include factory assembly-line work, number-crunching and filing in the back room of a bank or brokerage house, routine report-ing for a newspaper, transcribing interviews or doctor's notes, producing a PowerPoint presentation for the boss, making routine sales calls, or tracing lost luggage. This routine middle-skilled work has been devas-tated by the merger of globalization and the IT revolution. White-collar routine work—someone managing files in a bank or brokerage, for in-stance—which could be reduced to algorithms either got digitized and computerized or outsourced via the Internet to much cheaper labor markets. Even some high-skilled work that could be routinized fell into this category, such as reading X-rays or filing tax returns. Thanks to glob-alization and the IT revolution, those tasks could be turned into bits and bytes and transmitted overnight via fiber-optic cable to India, where lower-paid radiologists or accountants could perform them and send the results right back over the same cable by the next morning. Globaliza-tion and the IT revolution have not been kind to any kind of routine work, whether white-collar or blue-collar.

"Eventually we will all pump our own gas," adds Curtis Carlson, the

CEO of SRI International. "By that, I mean that services that can be automated and modified to allow us to do the task ourselves will go that way—online services, bag our own groceries, phone operators, your assistant, etc. Mainly it is for cost but we often like it more because it gives us more control." Indeed, remind us again why you need a salesclerk to check you out at the drugstore? You don't, which is why CVS pharmacies have been automating all their checkouts, so now you do it yourself while one better-trained employee watches over you and the computer-checkout machines.

Katz and Autor quote the Yale economist William Nordhaus as estimating that "the real cost of performing a standardized set of computational tasks fell at least 1.7 trillionfold between 1850 and 2006, with the bulk of this decline occurring in the last three decades . . . The consequence," they write, "has been a sharp decline in the share of U.S. employment in traditional 'middle-skill' jobs. The four 'middle-skill' occupations—sales, office workers, production workers, and operatives—accounted for 57 percent of employment in 1979 but only 46 percent in 2009," and the trend is clearly downward.

The third segment of the job market involves workers doing nonroutine low-skilled jobs that have to be done in person or manually—in an office, a hospital, a shopping center or restaurant, or at a specific construction site, factory, or locale. These jobs do not require a lot of critical thinking or an advanced degree. They include dental assistant, hairstylist, barber, waitress, truck driver, cook, baker, policeman, fireman, construction worker, deliveryman, plumber, electrician, maid, taxi driver, masseuse, salesclerk, nurse, and health-care aide at a nursing home. No robot or computer can replace these jobs, and no one in India or China can take them away, either. They will always exist, but how many such jobs there are and how much they pay will depend on the overall state of the economy and local supply and demand.

Putting all three categories together makes clear why the experts speak of job market "polarization." Nonroutine high-skilled work becomes, if anything, more lucrative, depending on the overall economy. Nonroutine low-skilled work can pay decently, depending on the local economy and how well that worker performs. But white- and blue-collar routine work shrinks, gets squeezed on pay, or just vanishes. The net result of the "rising demand for highly educated workers performing abstract tasks and for less-educated workers performing 'manual' or service tasks is the partial hollowing out or polarization of employment opportunities," conclude Katz and Autor.

Andy Kessler, a former hedge fund manager and the author of *Eat People: And Other Unapologetic Rules for Game-Changing Entrepreneurs*, published a piece in *The Wall Street Journal* (February 17, 2011) proposing an even simpler and more evocative typology of the new labor market:

> Forget blue-collar and white-collar. There are two types of workers in our economy: creators and servers. Creators are the ones driving productivity—writing code, designing chips, creating drugs, running search engines. Servers, on the other hand, service these creators (and other servers) by building homes, providing food, offering legal advice, and working at the Department of Motor Vehicles. Many servers will be replaced by machines, by computers and by changes in how business operates.

This dichotomy between "creators" and "servers" focuses attention on the most important question every worker will have to ask himself or herself: Am I adding value by doing something unique and irreplaceable? Am I putting some extra chocolate sauce, whipped cream, and a cherry on top of whatever I do?

We think the best way to understand today's labor market is to blend Katz, Autor, and Kessler. That yields four types of jobs. The first are "creative creators," people who do their nonroutine work in a distinctively nonroutine way—the best lawyers, the best accountants, the best doctors, the best entertainers, the best writers, the best professors, and the best scientists. Second are "routine creators," who do their nonroutine work in a routine way—average lawyers, average accountants, average radiologists, average professors, and average scientists. The third are what we would call "creative servers," nonroutine low-skilled workers who do their jobs in inspired ways—whether it is the baker who comes up with a special cake recipe and design or the nurse with extraordinary interpersonal bedside skills in a nursing home or the wine steward who dazzles you with his expertise on Australian cabernets. And the fourth are "routine servers," who do routine serving work in a routine way, offering nothing extra.

Attention: Just because you are doing a "nonroutine" job—as, say, a doctor, lawyer, journalist, accountant, teacher, or professor—doesn't mean that you are safe. If you do a nonroutine high-skilled job in a routine way—if you are what we would call a "routine creator"—you will be vulnerable to outsourcing, automation, or digitization, or you will be the first to be fired in an economic squeeze. And just because you are a server, doing some face-to-face job, doesn't mean you are safe. You, too, will be vulnerable to outsourcing, automation, foreign labor digitization—or you will be the first to be fired in an economic squeeze.

Remember George Clooney. *No one is safe.*

On March 4, 2011, lawyers in America woke up to this headline in *The New York Times*: "Armies of Expensive Lawyers, Replaced by Cheaper Software." The story explained:

> When five television studios became entangled in a Justice Department antitrust lawsuit against CBS, the cost was immense. As part of the obscure task of "discovery"—providing documents relevant to a lawsuit—the studios examined six million documents at a cost of more than $2.2 million, much of it to pay for a platoon of lawyers and paralegals who worked for months at high hourly rates. But that was in 1978. Now, thanks to advances in artificial intelligence, "e-discovery" software can analyze documents in a fraction of the time for a fraction of the cost. In January, for example, Blackstone Discovery of Palo Alto, Calif., helped analyze 1.5 million documents for less than $100,000. Some programs go beyond just finding documents with relevant terms at computer speeds. They can extract relevant concepts . . . even in the absence of specific terms, and deduce patterns of behavior that would have eluded lawyers examining millions of documents. "From a legal staffing viewpoint, it means that a lot of people who used to be allocated to conduct document review are no longer able to be billed out," said Bill Herr, who as a lawyer at a major chemical company used to muster auditoriums of lawyers to read documents for weeks on end. "People get bored, people get headaches. Computers don't."

So this is the world we are in. This is where every conversation about how we must fix our economy and transform our schools has to start. In this world, America must have companies that are more productive—that are using the tools of hyperconnectivity in every way possible to produce more goods and services with fewer people—and we must have more and more companies that spawn decent-paying jobs.

There is only one way to square this circle: more innovation powered by better education for every American. A healthy economy is one driven not just by greater efficiency and productivity but also by innovation. That is, more people inventing more goods and services that make others more comfortable, more productive, better educated, more entertained, healthier, and more secure—and finding ways to make these goods and deliver these services in America. American cities and towns cannot just sit around hoping Ford, Boeing, or Intel will come and build a five-thousand-worker factory there. Those big plants are scarce already, and they are going to be even scarcer in the age of robotics. What a town needs to thrive today is a hundred people starting companies that employ twenty-five people each, and twenty people starting companies that employ fifty people each, and five people starting companies that employ three hundred people each.

In short, we need as many people as possible to be creative creators and creative servers. Some can do that by inventing a new product, others by reinventing an existing job, and others by delivering a routine service with some extra passion, a personal touch, or a new insight. This is what every employer is now looking for. If you have any doubts about that, just ask them. Or just turn the page.

FIVE

Help Wanted

What are you looking for in an employee today?"

We put that question to four employers: one who employs low-skilled white-collar workers in India; one who employs high-skilled white-collar lawyers in Washington, D.C.; one who employs green-collar workers all over Afghanistan and Iraq (the U.S. Army); and one who employs blue-collar workers all over the world (DuPont). No matter what color the collar, all four employers gave nearly identical answers. They are looking for workers who can think critically, who can tackle nonroutine complex tasks, and who can work collaboratively with teams located in their office or globally.

And that's just to get a job interview.

That's right. The employers we interviewed consider all those skills "table stakes" today—merely the conditions of entry for a new job. Now they also expect all the workers they hire to think of themselves along the lines of what we've called "creative creators" or "creative servers"—people who not only can do their assigned complex tasks but can enhance them, refine them, and even reinvent them by bringing something extra. By listening to what these employers say, and what they are seeking in employees, we can understand the urgency of the need to adapt our education system to compete and thrive in the hyper-connected world.

"We have never asked so much from people as we are going to now—leaders and led," argues Dov Seidman, whose company, LRN, advises executives on leadership. "Today, we are asking every American to climb his own Mount Everest and make that cell-phone call from

the peak: 'Mom, guess where I am.' In today's hyper-connected marketplace, to be a leading company, now a company has to be a company
of leaders—every individual has to contribute significant value and
impact."

Herewith, the new help-wanted section.

White-Collar Indian

In February 2004 Tom went to Bangalore, India, to make a documentary program on outsourcing for the New York Times–Discovery Channel. Part of the documentary was filmed at the outsourcing company
24/7 Customer and its call center, manned by hundreds of Indians doing what were then relatively low-wage white-collar service jobs via long-
distance phone lines. Late at night—daytime in America—the room was
a cacophony of voices, with young Indian men and women trying to fix
someone's Dell computer or straighten out a credit card account or sell
a new phone contract. It was a cross between a coed college dormitory
and a phone bank raising money for the local public TV station. There
were 2,500 twentysomethings, some with college degrees, some just out
of high school, working either as "outbound" operators, selling credit
cards or phone minutes, or "inbound" operators, tracing someone's lost
luggage or dealing with computer glitches.

Seven years later, the company's founder, PV Kannan, told us that
we would not recognize his office today. "To begin with, it's a lot less
noisy," he explained. That is because much of the voice work once done
over long-distance fiber-optic phone lines or via satellite has now shifted
to text messaging over the Internet. Moreover, 24/7 Customer no longer
just waits to receive calls about problems. "It's all proactive now," explained Kannan. "Now, when a customer goes online and, say, opens his
phone bill or cable bill from the company we are working for, we know
about it. Today most of the customer questions revolve around bills that
they are looking at online. We know from our software that it is the first
bill you have been sent by this cable or phone company. You thought
you signed up for a $99.99-a-month cable package and the bill is for
$278.00. We can track when you opened your bill online, and if you
keep it open for more than two minutes a little dialogue box will pop up

and say, 'Would you like to discuss your bill?' One of our operators will then interact with you online. This requires a very different kind of operator. So now when we recruit people they have to have the savvy to link things together, and they have to be able to multitask—to know what you are looking at, be sensitive to the context of the dialogue, and then pull up all the relevant information quickly and resolve the problem. So the way we recruit now is that we invite candidates to take an online test where all of this is simulated."

Seven years ago, when Tom visited the 24/7 Customer office in India, most of the employees there "were entry level," said Kannan, whose company is actually headquartered in Campbell, California. "They had to stick to a written script, and they were afraid the minute someone got them off of it. A supervisor would randomly listen to the calls of agents and then give them feedback or help them with a customer . . . Now the software we have is predicting what the consumer is doing, so we don't need so many supervisors, because technology is now following what our operators are texting, while they are texting! Today what I am most interested in knowing is what else did the customer have issues with, what services did they seem to be looking for. So we ended up transitioning many of our supervisors into new jobs that we created that revolved around analyzing data. These are better-paying jobs, but they require more skill. So we picked out the supervisors who had the science and math degrees to make the transition, and the others we kept as supervisors.

"A call center never employed Ph.D.'s—now I have an army of them, trying to analyze all this data," said Kannan. "We started doing this about four years ago, but 2010 was the big crossover year." Now, instead of looking just for people whose jobs will involve answering the phone or making phone calls—of which Kannan still employs many—he's also looking for statisticians, psychologists, and Ph.D.'s.

"What we ultimately are hoping to do is combine in the same person the technical talent to understand what the data is telling them and the service skills to deliver the new services that the data says people want," Kannan explained. "If we learn from the data that 80 percent of consumers who receive their first bill from a mobile company or cable are going to pick up the phone and call, we also now know exactly how to service them. It means the agent who deals with them is much better prepared."

Kannan said, "Everyone in the chain makes more money now because we are able to charge more money, because we are delivering more value to our clients. And people are also much more satisfied with their work. You're not just calling people hour after hour, trying to sell them a credit card. Now we look for employees who have their own Facebook profiles, who are adept at writing little blogs and have real comfort living and interacting in that online world. The old workers who showed up and just read off a script—a lot of them are gone.

"We want people who have a completely open mind," he added, "and then the ability to learn constantly and challenge the status quo— no matter what the level of the company where they are employed. Challenging the status quo is the most critical thing, because if your employees don't challenge your status quo, someone else's employees will and they will disrupt the status quo before you do.

"There is really no such thing as a low-end job anymore," said Kannan. "If it were really routine, it would have been automated. Every two or three years the skilled thing you are doing is going to get scrapped. The question is whether you are going to scrap it and own the next job, or let someone else do that."

Although he is describing a service business, Kannan's observation points to one of the most important reasons that America needs to keep high-skilled manufacturing at home. So many innovations come from engineers and workers who are actually handling the product, seeing what goes wrong, and anticipating the next breakthrough improvement. "If none of the work is being done in America any longer, that is dangerous," explained Kannan. "Sometimes my clients say to me, 'PV, I don't understand why you are still in the call-center business, a bunch of entry-level jobs. The value we get from you is all these data and analytics. Why don't you carve that out as a separate business and list it on the stock exchange?' My answer is that if I don't do the customer-facing part of the business, I lose touch with reality, and then I am really in the cloud."

Kannan explained that though many of his workers are in India, his whole technology platform is run out of the United States on servers based in America; some of the data analytics are done in America, and his experts who help clients interpret that data and what it means for their businesses actually sit in the offices with those clients, side by side.

"So, in many ways, the best jobs are here in California, but they also demand the most skill," said Kannan.

Obviously we cannot keep every factory in America. But we need to understand that, particularly for the high end of manufacturing, when a factory moves offshore now it takes with it not just the jobs of today but also, perhaps, the jobs of tomorrow. "If all the manufacturing and then more and more of the engineering moves to India and China," Kannan warned, "it is only a matter of time before the next Google or Facebook comes out there."

White-Collar American

At the worst point of the subprime crisis, Tom asked his friend Jeff Lesk, the managing partner of the Washington office of the international law firm Nixon Peabody, how the legal business was being affected by it. "Heavily," Lesk said. Everyone was laying off lawyers. Out of curiosity, Tom asked him who was laid off first. The answer was surprising. Lesk explained that it was not necessarily last in, first out anymore. Rather, the lawyers who were getting laid off by most big law firms were those who, when work was booming during the credit and real estate bubbles, took the work, did it, and then handed it back when finished. Some of them were now gone. These were people who were doing nonroutine work but doing it in a routine way—uncreative creators. Those keeping their jobs were the ones who were finding new, more efficient ways to do the old work, with new technologies and processes, or were coming up with entirely new work to do in new ways.

This is indicative of the new labor trends in the hyper-connected world. While the jobs of lawyers—and others like them—may in theory fall into the category of nonroutine creators, that does not make them immune from the pressures of globalization and the IT revolution. Sure, at the height of the credit bubble, firms signed up whoever came out of the best law schools and were generous with bonuses. But today globalization, IT, and the tight economy are prompting more and more big companies to put their legal work out to bid whenever they can—treating it as a commodity. So law firms that want to continue to pay high bonuses need to offer something extra to justify high fees.

That is why, in the winter of 2011, Nixon Peabody created a new position: chief innovation officer.

Say what? A chief innovation officer? Why would a law firm need a chief innovation officer?

"We are in business to help other businesses," explained Lesk, an expert in putting together real estate transactions involving tax credits to generate financing for community-oriented developments, such as low-income housing. "And what we are finding is that the core of American business is changing—the repeat deals, involving similar structures, are fewer and farther between. There is more competition, barriers to entry are lower, our clients are reaching out to us for new ideas now much more frequently." His law firm therefore has to be more creative and nimble in every way.

For instance, says Lesk, his firm was a pioneer in putting together low-income housing credits with solar-energy credits in order to finance affordable housing for low-income people that would also come with solar-powered energy.

"A few experienced practitioners in the industry were looking at the base product that we had used for years—the Low-Income Housing Tax Credit—and at the same time we were learning about renewable-energy tax credits," explained Lesk. "We wondered what would happen if we combined the two. So together with some clients and colleagues we put these financing tools side by side, looking at the rules and requirements and conflicts between these two complex government programs, and then we thought about how to overcome those conflicts." Then they did some financial modeling, made some assumptions on pricing, and came up with a model that showed "we could build an affordable housing project with solar panels that would utilize tax credits for both of these important programs—and at a minimal or negligible cost," said Lesk. "So you end up with people having affordable housing with lower energy bills, financed by private investors who can use those tax credits. We were among the first to work through all the issues and come up with a product that could meet governmental requirements, attract private capital, and, most important, scale."

But no sooner did Nixon Peabody help to open that path than competing law firms and accounting firms followed suit, turning it into a commodity. As a result, said Lesk, "we constantly have to find ways to improve and adapt our products. Now we're putting together affordable housing with geothermal energy and drafting projects utilizing fuel cells. How about a community wind project? You have to look for original combinations and approaches to stay one step ahead of the competition."

Lesk continued: "Necessity is the mother of invention and we are in the age of great necessity because little that was given in the past is given today—whether it is fees, types of projects, the structure of deals, or availability of financing. I have worked with tax credits and affordable housing for twenty-five years. It was a specialized field and for a long time it had a reasonably limited number of players. Today it changes frequently and the barriers to entry are so low that we have all kinds of new competitors, and not only law firms."

His firm's new chief innovation officer will lead a program to recruit, coach, and inspire lawyers so that they will not only do today's standard legal work but also invent tomorrow's. Those qualifications are already being taken into consideration when the firm determines annual pay and bonuses for its lawyers.

"For this year's partner reviews," said Lesk, who also heads the firm's tax-credit finance practice group, "I asked each partner in my group specifically what was his or her best innovative idea for the past year and what does he or she have on the drawing board to invent this year . . . We are a partnership and we have to share the profits in a way that recognizes past contributions and predicts future performance, and in a way that fairly compensates each partner." The best predictor of the future is not necessarily just how someone has performed in the past, he said. It's also how much the person has adapted, created, and innovated. "If I have to make tough compensation choices between lawyers, a significant factor now for me is their ability to invent," said Lesk. "And my challenge, for the lawyers who don't come by those skills naturally, is to find ways to teach them."

Critical thinking alone just doesn't buy what it used to buy, Lesk concluded. "Critical thinking has become the basic price of admission. If I had to choose who else I would elect to help assure the continued success of this law firm, one of the most important qualities I would be looking for is proven ability to innovate, because with change coming this fast, that is the only thing that will save us."

Green-Collar American

General Martin Dempsey is the Chairman of the Joint Chiefs of Staff—
America's top military officer—but earlier in his career he commanded
the First Armored Division in the Iraq war that took Baghdad from
Saddam Hussein in 2003; served as acting CENTCOM commander, in
charge of all American forces throughout the Middle East; and from
2008 to 2011 was commanding general of the U.S. Army Training and
Doctrine Command, where he oversaw boot camp—the training and
education of American soldiers for twenty-first-century warfare. He re-
members the exact moment when the light started flashing in his head,
saying, "We need to train and educate our soldiers and leaders
differently."

"When I was acting commander at CENTCOM," said Dempsey, "I
went to visit a young U.S. Army captain stationed on the border with
Pakistan, inside Afghanistan. It was the summer of 2008. Out at his base
he described to me his task and purpose there and the recent engage-
ments he had had with Taliban trying to infiltrate. I think he was twenty-
five kilometers from any other base. Yet from his little forward base he
had access to intelligence and information from the lowest tactical level
right up to the national level and he had the authority to order joint fire
from air and artillery. I am guessing he was probably twenty-six years
old. At one point I said to him, 'You have more capability at your finger-
tips than I had as division commander in Baghdad in 2003.' The technology had improved that much . . . The type of threats we face today
are decentralized, networked, and syndicated. They are not massed
threats but threats at the edge. To confront a network you have to be a
network, and to confront a decentralized foe your power needs to be
decentralized."

Dempsey returned from Afghanistan to Central Command headquarters in Tampa, Florida, saying to himself, "We have empowered our
soldiers to be effective in this new kind of battle. We have given them
the capability and authority and responsibility to function in distributed
operations, semiautonomously. But we have not changed the way we
trained them to accept this responsibility."

As soon as he took over the army's training and education systems,
that became his primary focus. "We say that a leader's responsibility is to

visualize, understand, decide, and direct," said Dempsey. "And yet we used to spend the vast majority of our time providing the knowledge skills and attributes to allow a commander to decide and direct and almost no time on how to visualize and understand."

The changes the U.S. military is undertaking now start with recruitment. Thirty years ago, said Dempsey, "we would have said we want men who are physically fit, educated, and disciplined. Now, what we say is that we want someone who wants to belong to a values-based group, who can communicate, who is inquisitive, and who has an instinct to collaborate—and we will take care of the rest."

Dempsey began reforming army training by asking that all-important question: What world are we living in? The military, he concluded, was living in what he called "a competitive learning environment." By that he meant a world in which military capability is diffusing into the hands of non-state actors, terrorists, and criminals. Nation-states no longer have a monopoly on competitive military capabilities.

"It is a fool's errand," Dempsey said, to chase every new capability emerging from your adversary—whether it is new roadside bombs or devices that confuse GPS signals. "We cannot be oblivious to these things, but we cannot be consumed by them in isolation. What we should be consumed by is developing leaders in our own military who can adapt to whatever future they will find and innovate to create a future that is more favorable to us." You need people who can constantly adapt and innovate because the technology and how the enemy is using it are constantly changing.

Thirty years ago, noted Dempsey, the experiences a person had in the local high school, the experience in basic training, the experience in the army unit to which the new recruit was assigned, and the experience a soldier had on the battlefield "were not so different." That made training easy, but it simply isn't true anymore. Now, even traditional armies will confront America on the battlefield in a "hybrid" decentralized manner. So the army has to train its soldiers to reflect that prospect. It has to empower them to respond to the unpredictable experiences they will have in a village in Iraq or Afghanistan.

Fighting decentralized enemies, said Dempsey, is like "dropping a bowling ball into mercury." So sometimes you need to inject chaos deliberately into the classroom. "When I say we want to inject chaos, foster creativity, and leverage technology to create a different learning model," explained Dempsey, he means that drill instructors have to change, too. "What we have right now in many cases are instructors who want to be the sage on the stage: 'I have the knowledge and you know nothing, so pay attention to my PowerPoint presentation and take notes. And then on the last day maybe we will get around to problem-solving exercises.' The new model is for the classroom to provide a kind of warehouse of tools and applications that the students can download and deliver themselves."

Army manuals are changing accordingly. "We have roughly four to five hundred doctrinal manuals that we are migrating to a Wiki format," said Dempsey. "We have done about fifty already—how do you operate a forward base, a manual for bridge crossings, how to manage IEDs [improvised explosive devices], how to conduct a key-leader engagement in Iraq or Afghanistan, how to make best use of an unmanned aerial system. Let's say you had a manual on how to organize a forward operating base in Afghanistan. In the past, the community responsible for doctrine would publish it. That would take three or four years to do, with a steering committee or review boards, and then it would take five to seven years to permeate the army schoolhouse. Now we are putting that all up in a Wiki that allows the community of practice to edit it constantly and contribute to it from their battlefield experiences. So it is always up-to-date, self-correcting, and adaptable in real time by the soldiers in the field. It is a living doctrinal textbook, with officers assigned to watch over and manage each doctrinal Wiki site." (Don't worry, they are protected so al-Qaeda cannot read them as well!)

The new recruits coming into the military today, said Dempsey, have an almost insatiable appetite for information, access, and connectivity. "They want to be by themselves sitting in the middle of the football field but connected to the rest of the world," Dempsey said, adding: "They come in much less physically fit than previous generations because of lack of exercise. They come in with a mixed bag of values." That is, he explained, they come with a genuine sense of purpose and patriotism and general desire to belong to something, but it is often not much more developed than that. "So we have made major changes to the physical-fitness training and we have made major changes in how we inculcate values," he said. "I am not suggesting they have bad values, but among all the values that define our profession, first and most important is trust. If we could only do one thing with new soldiers, it would be to instill in them trust for one another, for the chain of command, and for the nation."

A decade ago, the army was still trying to instill knowledge through rote memorization, especially in basic training. "We still have that, but now we balance it with outcomes-based training," said Dempsey. "So the task might be to evacuate a casualty. In the past we might do that with a PowerPoint in a classroom and then take the kids out and demonstrate it in the field. Now we start in the field because we not only want to develop the proficiency [in handling] of the task but we want to develop trust, we want trust to be one of the outcomes. We also have peer-to-peer instruction. Before, the drill sergeant was God. If he said it, it was to be believed. And if he didn't, it wasn't important. Now the sergeants are alive to the idea that there are young men and women in the ranks who have leadership skills. Now they nurture them. They will tell some of the basic trainees, 'You are responsible for this task: Here is an iPhone with an app on it. You learn about it and collaborate on it, and on Friday you teach the class.' We find that the students are more attentive to their peers than to us. It requires a soldier not only to master the skill he is teaching but to be able to add value by teaching it to his peers."

The bottom line: "Collaboration is important on the battlefield and trust is the cement of collaboration," said Dempsey. "And trust is the prerequisite for creativity. You will never be creative if you think that what you have to say will be discounted. So creativity cannot happen without trust, communication cannot happen without trust, and collaboration cannot happen without trust. It is the essential driver. And that is why you build authority now from the bottom up and not the top down."

Not so long ago, Dempsey explained, a junior officer would get the intelligence and information from above and then execute on the basis of that information. No one held that officer accountable for understanding or contributing significantly to higher headquarters' understanding. "Now, in the kind of environments in which we find ourselves, the more important information comes from the bottom up, not the top down," he said. That means lower-ranking personnel are as responsible for creating and understanding the context in which they are operating as the most senior leader on the field. "We are issuing iPhones to basic trainees so that they can pull down applications and collaborate on coursework," said Dempsey. "I like to think of us as getting more and more adaptable—learning from what we experience as fast as possible and reacting to it. We have to do that fast and smart . . . I want this [U.S. Army] to be an adaptable learning organization."

Dempsey's former colleague in Iraq, General Stanley McChrystal, witnessed this evolution in the battlefield at the very cutting edge when he commanded the Special Forces operations in Iraq that fought an underground war with al-Qaeda and Baathist elements and helped the surge succeed. They fought that war with a combination of unorthodox, innovative methods and modern technologies. Here is how McChrystal described his evolution to us:

"My grandfather was a soldier. My father was a soldier. From the time my grandfather, at the end of World War I, went from lieutenant to colonel, there was a change in technology. But it was not so fast or so great that his experience did not provide him with a body of expertise that made him legitimate and credible with his men. The reality today is that when a general officer speaks to a captain, that general officer has almost never used any of the communications systems, intelligence assets, or weapons systems that the captain has. So when the general or colonel goes down there and tries to be the leader and the captain looks at him, [that captain knows] that this guy has never done the job he is doing, nothing close. So the reality is: How does the leader retain his legitimacy in his big organization? What is the basis for his credibility? Is it his good looks? This is a really big deal. Things go so fast now it is very difficult for people to be experts and still be leading."

One way to do both is to be more of an orchestrator and inspirer than a traditional hard-charging, follow-me-up-the-hill commander. As an example of this, McChrystal described special operations commanders in Iraq who adapted their units, turning them from just "shooters"— the people who go out on missions and kill or capture the enemy—into intelligence analysts who are always looking for targets and thinking about targets when they are not in the field. "In the past, when they were not going on the target, the shooters would just have been working out or sleeping," McChrystal said. Instead, the commanders put them behind desks to analyze and sift through and argue over all the raw intelligence about potential targets. "As a consequence, [those commanders] probably increased their field capacity tenfold. They created guys who were entrepreneurial and always fighting for more information. *They owned the mission much more*—because they were actually assembling and analyzing the information and selecting priorities . . . They were careful not to waste intelligence assets, because it affected their productivity, [and] they did not send the assault force on a stupid mission, because they *were* the assault force that was going on that mission. When we captured people, they would sit in on the interrogations. It made them so much more effective."

Blue-Collar American

DuPont makes a lot of things. To survive for 208 years a company has to be good at making a lot of things. In fact, DuPont makes so many things that if you go to its website and click on "Products & Services," it shows you the alphabet. If you click on any letter—except J, Q, or X—there is something DuPont makes that starts with that letter. Hit "H" and you get directed to "Harmony® Extra XP herbicide." Hit "Z" and you get directed to "Zenite® LCP liquid crystal polymer resin." Given how many products DuPont makes, and the number of blue-collar workers it employs all over the world, there are few executives who can better describe the kind of blue-collar workers needed for the twenty-first century than Ellen Kullman, who became DuPont's nineteenth CEO in 2009.

In an interview at company headquarters in Wilmington, Delaware, Kullman summarized in a single word what she looks for in every employee today, from senior vice presidents to production line employees: "presence." "We want every employee to be present in the room. What I mean by that is that all the rote jobs today are gone—they are done by machines. Now you have to have people who can think and interact and collaborate. But to do that they have to be engaged and paying attention—*they have to be present*—so that they are additive, and not just taking up space. Whatever job you have in the company, you need to understand how your job adds value wherever you are [in the chain]. Because if you know that, then you *can* add value. But you will not be successful here if you just come to work and say, 'When do I arrive and when do I get to leave?'"

Production-line workers at today's DuPont plants, she added, have to "collaborate and work in teams, they have to be able to communicate with engineers and tell them everything that they are seeing on the line every day. They have to bring their thinking into what they do—they can't just go into their little zone and punch buttons all day. It is just a much more integrative and collaborative environment."

A line worker who is engaged can save a company millions of dollars with just one insight, as Kullman explained with an example. DuPont invests a huge amount of money every year in factories and equipment, and one key to making profits is having those machines working twenty-four hours a day, seven days a week. "So we are constantly measuring uptime and yields on every piece of equipment," said Kullman. The company has a big plant in Spruance, Virginia, and on a particular production line of spinning cells that put out Kevlar fibers the machines kept prematurely failing, bringing the whole line down. "So the engineers are sitting there trying to solve the problem in one area of the line," Kullman recalled, "and one of the line operators broke in and said to them, 'You know what is strange is that the machines that fail sound different.' So they started to work with the guy and isolated the problem, which had to do with new units. It immediately increased the utilization of the whole plant. Now, the engineers don't live there like the line operators do. They are not listening every day . . . It is why you need every employee to have the mind-set of how they help us make every product better."

DuPont recently installed a company-wide production-management system that is based on inviting every employee to help improve a product or manufacturing process. "Every worker has to be engaged," she explained, "so we now spend a lot of time thinking about how we as leaders create a better environment for that—so we can get the best out of our employees, our equipment and plants, and our company."

Kevlar, a synthetic fabric used to make protective vests, is one of DuPont's signature products. Only by using the assets of the whole company has DuPont been able to maintain its lead in that product area. According to Kullman, "The Kevlar we make today is vastly different from two decades ago in terms of tenacity and how lightweight it is. It took researchers working with engineers and with production employees to make the whole system better. We had to. The world doesn't wait for you. We have competitors who are very aggressive. I was recently down in one of our plants in Texas and you had a cross section of maintenance workers, operators, and engineers all in one room—ten of them—working on a real problem: How did they reduce the turnaround time for the maintenance of one of their machines and get more production time out of every day? To see them all work together, each getting up at the drawing board and talking about it, trying to solve the problem together, is something to watch."

DuPont does not operate with cheap labor. "Our plants are made up of big equipment," explained Kullman. "One of the big factors we look at in locating a plant is the availability of an educated workforce. Our plant in Spruance that makes Kevlar has three criteria for hiring a line operator: You need to have more than a high school degree, either a community-college degree or a vocational-college degree; or you have to have had experience at another company; or you have to be a military veteran. You have to have two out of those three. And we partner with community colleges to make sure that we have the right opportunities to get that training. [Also], we interview them differently than we did decades ago. They have to be able to communicate with engineers. They have to be able to bring their thinking into the job."

Carlson's Law

If we step back and take all these stories together, some very important trends in today's workplace become clear: the people on the bottom rung of the workplace are becoming more and more empowered, which means more innovation will come from the bottom up, rather than just from the top down. Therefore it is vital that we retain as much manufacturing in America as possible, so our workers can take part in this innovation.

"People think innovation is the idea you have in the shower," said Ernie Moniz, the physicist who heads MIT's Energy Initiative. "More often it comes from seeing the problem. It comes out of working with the materials." To be sure, there is some pure innovation—coming up with a product or service no one had thought of before. But a lot more innovation comes from working on the line, seeing a problem, and de-

vising a solution that itself becomes a new product. That is why if we
don't retain at least part of the manufacturing process in America, particularly the high-end manufacturing, we will lose touch with an important source of innovation: the experience of working directly with a
product and figuring out how to improve it—or how to replace it with
something even better.

"A lot of innovation now happens on the shop floor," said Hewlett-
Packard's CEO, Léo Apotheker. Indeed, if you open a factory, and are
doing things right, "it will be more productive a year later because the
workers themselves on the factory floor are critical thinkers and can improve processes along the way," said Byron Auguste, the McKinsey director. In any factory or call center, he noted, "there is often dramatic
variation in productivity in different parts of the system. If you have continuous learners on the shop floor or in the call center, there is a constant
opportunity to learn and spread the word, and then everyone improves.
If you are doing that in every node of your production, design, and after-
sales service, you will have a system that delivers three percent productivity growth every year and is not dependent on new inventions coming
out of Carnegie Mellon University or Silicon Valley."

In the past, companies had "innovation centers" off in the woods,
where big-thinking R&D teams devised new things that were then produced on the assembly line. Some companies still have such centers,
but others are opting instead for continuous innovation that includes
frontline workers as well as top management. Now every employee is
part of the process, often using social networking tools such as Twitter
and Facebook. The assembly-line worker today not only has more information than ever before, but also the capacity to communicate what he
or she is learning instantly to upper management and throughout the
company.

Continuous innovation is not a luxury anymore—it is becoming a
necessity. In the hyper-connected world, whatever can be done, will be
done. The only question for a company is whether it will be done by it
or to it: but it will be done. A breakthrough product, such as the iPhone,
instantly generates competition—the Android. Within months, the iPad
had multiple competitors. So a company that does not practice constant
innovation by taking advantage of every ounce of brainpower at every
level will fall behind farther and faster than ever before.

Before the world became hyper-connected, American companies moved jobs around the world—that is, they outsourced parts of their business process—to save money that they then reinvested in new products, services, and people in the United States, because they could. Now companies move jobs around the world to do "crowdsourcing" and distributed innovation, because they must. They find the most creative brainpower, the most productive workforce, the most inviting tax rules, and the best infrastructure in or near the fastest-growing markets, *because they must*. They must use the whole global "crowd" to invent, design, manufacture, improve, and sell their products. If they don't, their competition will. We repeat: In the hyper-connected world, whatever can be done, will be done. The only question is, will it be done by you or to you?

Ask Curtis Carlson, the CEO of SRI International, which serves as an innovation factory for governments and companies on topics ranging from education to clean energy to homeland security. Government agencies and private companies come to Carlson and his teams of scientists, engineers, and educators; they describe what they want—often blue-sky wish lists or solutions to seemingly insoluble problems—and ask SRI to invent it for them. When he gets a request, Carlson's first step is to assemble a team of SRI scientists, engineers, and designers, along with outside experts—fitting the people to the problem as best he can.

"There are few problems left today where one person with one skill can solve them," he explained. "That means you had better assemble the best team. Not a good team—the best team. You don't want to be 'world class.' That just means there are a lot of others like you. You want your team to be best in the world."

Given the rising innovative power and knowledge that can so easily move from the bottom up now—the power to invent, design, manufacture, improve, and sell products—and not just from the top down, Carlson sees the following mega-trend barreling down the highway: "More and more, innovation that happens from the top down tends to be orderly but dumb. Innovation that happens from the bottom up tends to be chaotic but smart." Therefore, "the sweet spot for innovation today is moving down."

We call this Carlson's Law: *Innovation that happens from the top down tends to be orderly but dumb. Innovation that happens from the bottom up tends to be chaotic but smart.* This makes it all the more important for every worker to be a creative creator or creative server and for every boss to understand that the boss's job is to take advantage of Carlson's Law—to find ways to inspire, enable, and unleash innovation from the bottom up, and then to edit, manage, and merge that innovation from the top down to produce goods, services, and concepts.

"We had a group visiting SRI from Japan the other day," Carlson told us in March 2011, "and one of them asked me: 'How many big decisions do you make every day?' I said, 'My goal is to make none of them. I am not the one interacting daily with the customer or the technology. My employees are the ones interacting, so if [moving ahead on a project] has to wait for me to decide, that is too slow. That does not mean I don't have a job. My job is to help create an environment where those decisions can happen where they should happen—and to support them and reward them and inspire them.'"

Carlson said he thinks of himself more as "the mayor" of his company, orchestrating all the departments and listening to his constituencies, rather than as a classic top-down CEO.

So there it is: This is not your grandparents' labor market anymore. It is not even your parents'. Each and every one of us has to be "present" now, all the time, in whatever we do, so that we can be either creative creators or creative servers. That's where the jobs will be. This is why our schools need to prepare all students for careers in which they not only do their assigned tasks but offer something extra. For everyone to find his or her "extra" will require both more education and better education. The next two chapters are about how we can deliver this so every American can adapt to the merger of globalization and the IT revolution.

SIX

Homework x 2 = The American Dream

ORLANDO, Fla., May 31, 2011 /PRNewswire/—Students from Zhejiang University have been crowned World Champions of the 2011 Association for Computing Machinery International Collegiate Programming Contest. Sponsored by IBM, the competition, also known as the "Battle of the Brains," challenged 105 university teams to solve some of the most challenging computer programming problems in just five hours. Mastering both speed and skill, Zhejiang University successfully solved eight problems in five hours. The World Champions will return home with the "world's smartest" trophy as well as IBM prizes, scholarships and a guaranteed offer of employment or internship with IBM. This year's top twelve teams that received medals are:

- Zhejiang University (Gold, World Champion, China)
- University of Michigan at Ann Arbor (Gold, 2nd Place, USA)
- Tsinghua University (Gold, 3rd Place, China)
- St. Petersburg State University (Gold, 4th Place, Russia)
- Nizhny Novgorod State University (Silver, 5th Place, Russia)
- Saratov State University (Silver, 6th Place, Russia)
- Friedrich-Alexander-University Erlangen-Nuremberg (Silver, 7th Place, Germany)
- Donetsk National University (Silver, 8th Place, Ukraine)
- Jagiellonian University in Krakow (Bronze, 9th Place, Poland)
- Moscow State University (Bronze, 10th Place, Russia)
- Ural State University (Bronze, 11th Place, Russia)
- University of Waterloo (Bronze, 12th Place, Canada)

Hillary Clinton never asked us for career advice. Had she done so, we would have told her this: When President Barack Obama came to you and offered the job of secretary of state, you should have said, "No, thank you. I prefer to hold the top national security job. Mr. President, it would have been wonderful to have been secretary of state during the Cold War, when that job was crucial. True, some things haven't changed. Now, as in the past, the secretary of state spends all his or her time talking to and negotiating with other governments. Now, as in the past, success depends far less on his or her eloquence than on how much leverage the secretary brings to the table. Now, as in the past, that depends first and foremost on America's economic vigor. Today, however, more than ever before, our national security depends on the quality of our educational system. That is why I don't want to be secretary of state, Mr. President. Instead, I want to be at the heart of national security policy. I want to be secretary of education."

We are well aware of the limits of the power of even the secretary of education when it comes to raising national educational attainment levels. Indeed, we believe that this responsibility belongs to all of us— the whole society. But symbolically the point is correct. Because of the merger of globalization and the IT revolution, raising math, science, reading, and creativity levels in American schools is the key determinant of economic growth, and economic growth is the key to national power and influence as well as individual well-being. In today's hyper-connected world, the rewards for countries and individuals that can raise their educational achievement levels will be bigger than ever, while the penalties for countries and individuals that don't will be harsher than ever. There will be no personal security without it. There will be no national security without it. That is why it is no accident that President Obama has declared that "the country that out-educates us today will out-compete us tomorrow." That is why it is no accident that the executive search firm Heidrick & Struggles, in partnership with *The Economist*'s intelligence unit, has created a Global Talent Index, ranking different countries, under the motto "Talent is the new oil and just like oil, demand far outstrips supply."

As a country we have not yet adapted to this new reality. We don't think of education as an investment in national growth and national security because throughout our history it has been a localized, decentralized issue, not a national one. Today, however, what matters is not how your local school ranks in its county or state but how America's schools rank in the world.

Michelle Rhee, the former chancellor of the Washington, D.C., school system, put it this way in an interview in *Washingtonian* magazine immediately after stepping down from the job (December 2010):

> This country is in a significant crisis in education, and we don't know it. If you look at other countries, like Singapore— Singapore's knocking it out of the box. Why? Because the number-one strategy in their economic plan is education. We treat education as a social issue. And I'll tell you what happens with social issues: When the budget crunch comes, they get swept under the rug, they get pushed aside. We have to start treating education as an economic issue.

She is right. Fifty years ago, "education was a choice not a necessity—I can choose to be educated or not, but either way I can get a decent job and live a decent life," said Andreas Schleicher, the senior education officer at the Organisation for Economic Co-operation and Development (OECD) in Paris. "Today, education is not an option"—it is a necessity for a middle-class standard of living.

Wage statistics make this obvious. The polarization of employment opportunities in the last three decades "has been accompanied by a substantial secular rise in the earnings of those who complete post-secondary education," noted Lawrence Katz and David Autor. "The hourly wage of the typical college graduate in the U.S. was approximately 1.5 times the hourly wage of the typical high school graduate in 1979. By 2009, this ratio stood at 1.95. This enormous growth in the earnings differential between college- and high school–educated workers reflects the cumulative effect of three decades of more or less continuous increase." In November 2010, the Brookings Institution released a study entitled *Degrees of Separation: Education, Employment, and the Great Recession in Metropolitan America*. The study found that "during the Great Recession, employment dropped much less steeply among college-educated workers than other workers. The employment-to-population ratio dropped by more than 2 percentage points from 2007 to 2009 for working-age adults without a bachelor's degree, but fell by only half a percentage point for college-educated individuals." All in all, according to Brookings, while there were some regional discrepancies, "education appeared to act as a pretty good insurance policy for workers during the Great Recession."

Historically, America has educated its people up to and beyond the technological demands of every era. Lawrence Katz and Claudia Goldin demonstrate in their book *The Race Between Education and Technology* that as long as our educational system kept up with the rate of technology change, as it did until around 1970, our economic growth was widely shared. And when it stopped keeping up, income inequality began widening as job opportunities for high school dropouts shrunk while employers bid for a too-small pool of highly skilled workers. Today's hyper-connected world poses yet another new educational challenge: To prosper, America has to educate its young people up to and beyond the new levels of technology.

Not only does everyone today need *more* education to build the critical thinking and problem-solving skills that are now necessary for any good job; students also need *better* education. We define "better education" as an education that nurtures young people to be creative creators and creative servers. That is, we need our education system not only to strengthen everyone's basics—reading, writing, and arithmetic—but to teach and inspire all Americans to start something new, to add something extra, or to adapt something old in whatever job they are doing.

With the world getting more hyper-connected all the time, *maintaining the American dream will require learning, working, producing, relearning, and innovating twice as hard, twice as fast, twice as often, and twice as much.* Hence the title of this chapter and the new equation for the American middle class: Homework x 2 = the American Dream.

Since this educational challenge is so important, we will divide our discussion of it into two parts. The rest of this chapter will explore what we mean by "more" education. The next chapter will explain what is required for "better" education.

We Have a "More" Problem

America needs to close two education gaps at once. We need to close the gap between black, Hispanic, and other minority students and the average for white students on standardized reading, writing, and math tests. But we have an equally dangerous gap between the average American student and the average students in many industrial countries that we consider collaborators and competitors, including Singapore, Korea, Taiwan, Finland, and those in the most developed parts of China.

Some contend that the results of these tests don't tell the whole story, and that our top students and schools are still as good as any in the world. They are wrong. A study produced for the National Governors Association, entitled "Myths and Realities About International Comparisons," concluded that the notion that other countries test a more select, elite group of students is wrong. Comparison tests now include a sampling of the whole population in each country. The study, published in *The Learning System* (Spring 2011), also dispelled the notion that the United States performs poorly in these tests because of poverty and other family factors. In fact, our students are quite similar in socioeconomic conditions to those tested in peer countries. As for the myth that U.S. student attainment cannot be compared to that of other countries because the United States tries to educate many more students, the report noted that the United States does rank above average in access to higher education, but this does not explain the fact that "significantly more U.S. students enter college than the OECD average, but our college 'survival rate' is 17 points below the average." It also doesn't explain how a country such as Finland, which is not at all diverse, managed to go from the back of the global pack in education to the top. Finland was not diverse when it was mediocre and it was not diverse when it excelled. Diversity was never the issue. Finland vaulted ahead because of specific educational policies. That's why these tests matter.

And standardized international math and reading tests consistently show that American fourth graders compare well with their peers in countries such as Finland, Korea, and Singapore. But our high school students lag, which means that "the longer American children are in school, the worse they perform compared to their international peers," the McKinsey & Company consulting firm concluded in an April 2009 report entitled *The Economic Impact of the Achievement Gap in America's Schools*. There are millions of students in modern American suburban schools "who don't realize how far behind they are," said Matt Miller, one of the report's authors. "They are being prepared for $12-an-hour jobs—not $40 to $50 an hour."

Every three years the OECD Programme for International Student Assessment (PISA) measures how fifteen-year-old students in several dozen industrial countries are being prepared for the jobs of the future by asking them to use their knowledge of math and science to solve real-world problems and to use their reading skills to "construct, extend and reflect on the meaning of what they have read."

Here is a sample PISA science question. Test yourself: "Ray's bus is, like most buses, powered by a petrol engine. These buses contribute to environmental pollution. Some cities have trolley buses: they are powered by an electric engine. The voltage needed for such an electric engine is provided by overhead lines (like electric trains). The electricity is supplied by a power station using fossil fuels. Supporters for the use of trolley buses in a city say that these buses don't contribute to environmental pollution. Are these supporters right? Explain your answer."

Here is a sample math question: "A pizzeria serves two round pizzas of the same thickness in different sizes. The smaller one has a diameter of 30 cm and costs 30 zeds. The larger one has a diameter of 40 cm and costs 40 zeds. Which pizza is better value for the money? Show your reasoning."

Precisely because the PISA test is designed by the OECD to nurture and measure critical thinking and other twenty-first-century workplace skills, the showing of American students in 2009 is troubling. In reading, Shanghai, Korea, Finland, Hong Kong, Singapore, Canada, New Zealand, Japan, and Australia posted the highest scores. American students were in the middle of the pack, tied with those in Iceland and Poland. In math, the American fifteen-year-olds scored below the international average, more or less even with Ireland and Portugal, but lagging far behind Korea, Shanghai, Singapore, Hong Kong, Finland, and Switzerland. In science literacy, the U.S. students again were the middle of the pack, and again lagging behind the likes of Shanghai, Singapore, and Finland. It's notable that Shanghai, the only city tested in China, did better in math, science, and reading than any of the other sixty-five countries.

Of Shanghai's performance, Chester E. Finn Jr., who served in the Department of Education during the Reagan administration, told *The*

New York Times (December 7, 2010), "Wow, I'm kind of stunned, I'm thinking Sputnik . . . I've seen how relentless the Chinese are at accomplishing goals, and if they can do this in Shanghai in 2009, they can do it in 10 cities in 2019, and in 50 cities by 2029." That is the Chinese way: experiment, identify what works, and then scale it. Marc Tucker, the president of the National Center on Education and the Economy, has noted that "while many Americans believe that other countries get better results because those countries educate only a few, while the United States educates everyone, that turns out not to be true." Compared to the United States, most top-performing countries do a better job of educating students from low-income families, he said.

As they say in football, "You are what your record says you are." Our record says that we are a country whose educational performance is at best undistinguished. Secretary of Education Arne Duncan made no excuses for the results. The day the 2009 PISA results were published (December 7, 2010), he issued a statement, saying, "Being average in reading and science—and below average in math—is not nearly good enough in a knowledge economy where scientific and technological literacy is so central to sustaining innovation and international competitiveness."

The PISA test results got some fleeting newspaper coverage and then disappeared. No radio or television station interrupted its programming to tell us how poorly we had done; neither party picked up the issue and used it in the 2010 midterms. Partial-birth abortion received more attention. The president did not make a prime-time address. The twenty-first-century equivalent of Sputnik went up—and yet very few Americans seemed to hear the signal it was sending.

Susan Engel, a senior lecturer in psychology and director of the teaching program at Williams College and the author of *Red Flags or Red Herrings? Predicting Who Your Child Will Become*, frames our challenge this way: "There are two basic problems with education in America. The first glaring problem, the one getting lots of attention, is that too many kids have no choice but to go to schools that are dangerous, badly staffed, educationally indifferent, and underfunded. If you take those kids and put them in a school with reasonable funding, a school board and an administration that are excited about what is happening, and with energetic teachers, it's a huge improvement over what those kids have had. So, problem one: too many kids in America go to schools that don't even begin to offer them the hope of getting to average."

Selected countries' performance in mathematics, reading, and science, 2009

Mathematics		Reading		Science	
Shanghai-China	600	Shanghai-China	556	Shanghai-China	556
Singapore	562	Korea	539	Finland	539
Hong Kong-China	555	Finland	536	Hong Kong-China	536
Korea	546	Hong Kong-China	533	Singapore	533
Chinese Taipei	543	Singapore	526	Japan	526
Finland	541	Canada	524	Korea	524
Liechtenstein	536	New Zealand	521	New Zealand	521
Switzerland	534	Japan	520	Canada	520
Japan	529	Australia	515	Estonia	515
Canada	527	Netherlands	508	Australia	508
Netherlands	526	Belgium	506	Netherlands	506
Macao-China	525	Norway	503	Chinese Taipei	503
New Zealand	519	Estonia	501	Germany	501
Belgium	515	Switzerland	501	Liechtenstein	501
Australia	514	Poland	500	Switzerland	500
Germany	513	Iceland	500	United Kingdom	500
Estonia	512	**United States**	500	Slovenia	500
Iceland	507	Liechtenstein	499	Macao-China	499
Denmark	503	Sweden	497	Poland	497
Slovenia	501	Germany	497	Ireland	497
Norway	498	Ireland	496	Belgium	496
France	497	France	496	Hungary	496
Slovak Republic	497	Chinese Taipei	495	**United States**	495
Austria	496	Denmark	495	Czech Republic	495
Poland	495	United Kingdom	494	Norway	494
Sweden	494	Hungary	494	Denmark	494
Czech Republic	493	Portugal	489	France	489
United Kingdom	492	Macao-China	487	Iceland	487
Hungary	490	Italy	486	Sweden	486
Luxembourg	489	Latvia	484	Austria	484
United States	487	Slovenia	483	Latvia	483
Ireland	487	Greece	483	Portugal	483
Portugal	487	Spain	481	Lithuania	481

Significantly above the OECD average   OECD average   Significantly below the OECD average

PISA focuses on young people's ability to use their knowledge and skills to meet real-life challenges. This orientation reflects a change in the goals and objectives of curricula themselves, which are increasingly concerned with what students can do with what they learn at school and not merely with whether they have mastered specific curricular content.

Source: OECD PISA 2009 database

Our second problem, explains Engel, is just as big, if not bigger. It's that "even the 'nice' schools aren't good enough. These schools have decent facilities, adequate class sizes, a good number of teachers who like their job and/or like kids, and a majority of students who can read, who can pass standardized state tests. These schools are often okay, but not really good. Too many teachers are not that well educated, not that on fire to be teachers, and not that challenged within the system to be terrific. Such schools often lack any coherent or compelling idea about what a good education consists of, what high schools should emphasize, how to be really vibrant learning communities. These 'okay' schools may send kids like yours and mine on a good path—good colleges, good job options—but even in these schools, too many kids are not living up to their intellectual or personal potential. They're not engaged, and not headed to become the inventors, entrepreneurs, and stewards of the Earth that we're going to need."

According to the Department of Education, about a third of first-year students entering college had taken at least one remedial course in reading, writing, or math. The number is even higher for black and Hispanic students. At public two-year colleges, that average number rises to above 40 percent. And having to take just one remedial course is highly correlated with failure to graduate from college.

Engel's point cannot be emphasized enough: We must close the gap between minorities and average whites, because there are virtually no jobs that will provide a decent standard of living anymore for those who can't get some form of post–high school education, let alone a decent high school education that imparts critical thinking, reading, and basic math skills. But we also have to raise the whole American average, because even if the achievement levels of black and Hispanic young people can rise to the level of average white students but our average is in the middle of the world pack, we will not have the critical mass of workers necessary to do the best jobs, let alone invent new ones. Making a Harlem school perform as well as a Scarsdale school is necessary, but only getting both schools to perform as well as or better than a school in Shanghai is insufficient. We need to close the gap between our achievement and our potential today, but our long-term economic vitality depends on raising the potential of our entire society tomorrow. We need to lift the bottom faster and the top higher.

We also need more routes to the top. Many of the good jobs opening up in this country do not require four years of college, but they do require high-quality vocational training. Learning to repair the engine of an electric car, or a robotic cutting tool, or a new gas-powered vehicle that has more computing power in it than the Apollo space capsule— these are not skills you can pick up in a semester of high school shop class. It is vital that high schools and community colleges offer vigorous vocational tracks and that we treat them with the same esteem as we do the liberal arts or "college" tracks. Maybe we don't have to channel students as formally as do Singapore, Finland, and Germany—where early in high school students move either onto a track for four-year college or into vocational training of two or more years—but we do need to make clear that everyone needs postsecondary education, that there is a range of opportunities, that students need to start preparing for those different opportunities in high school, and, ultimately, that learning how to deconstruct a laptop computer in the local community college is as valuable as learning how to deconstruct *The Catcher in the Rye* at the state university.

A high school education today, says Duncan, should prepare a student to attend a university or a vocational college "without remediation," because that is the ticket to a decent job. Until now the goal has just been "to get people to graduate" from high school, he added. But graduation alone is not enough. There are too few decent jobs for such people anymore, and few or none for the young person without a high school degree. A high school education must prepare students for the next step of education or skill-building. "That's the fundamental shift," said Duncan. "We should have made that shift twenty-five years ago. But we didn't, so we have to catch up."

We do not know the exact mix of policies that is needed for "more" education, a subject on which there are many views. That is, we don't know if we need more charter schools or just more effective public schools. We don't know if we need a longer school day or a longer school year, or both or neither. We do not know which technologies or software programs are best at training students so that we see a rise in math abilities and test scores. We don't know to what extent teachers' unions are the problem, by protecting the jobs of mediocre teachers, and to what extent they are part of the solution, in rewarding great teaching. We leave to the educational experts the definition of what is *sufficient* in all these areas to produce more education for all.

We do, though, think we know what is *necessary* to produce what the country needs. We believe that six things are necessary: better teachers and better principals; parents who are more involved in and demanding of their children's education; politicians who push to raise educational standards, not dumb them down; neighbors who are ready to invest in schools even though their children do not attend them; business leaders committed to raising educational standards in their communities; and—last but certainly not least—students who come to school prepared to learn, not to text.

If that list strikes you as including everyone in society, you've gotten the point. Our education challenge is too demanding for the burden to be borne by teachers and principals alone. Let's look at each group.

Teachers and Principals

While teachers and principals cannot be expected to overcome our education deficits alone, outstanding teachers and principals can make a huge difference in student achievement. So we need to do everything we can as a society to recruit, mentor, and develop the best cadre of teachers and principals that we can. Bill Gates, whose Bill and Melinda Gates Foundation invests heavily in studying and improving K–12 public school education, says its research shows that "of all the variables under a school's control, the single most decisive factor in student achievement is excellent teaching. It's astonishing what great teachers can do for their students. Unfortunately, compared to the countries that outperform us in education, we do very little to measure, develop, and reward excellent teaching. We need to build exceptional teacher personnel systems that identify great teaching, reward it, and help every teacher get better. It's the one thing we've been missing, and it can turn our schools around . . . But the remarkable thing about great teachers today is that in most cases nobody taught them how to be great. They figured it out on their own."

Eric A. Hanushek, a senior fellow at Stanford University's Hoover Institution, summarized some of the findings of his research on the importance of quality of teaching in *Education Week* (April 6, 2011):

Studies examining data from a wide range of states and school districts have found extraordinarily consistent results about the importance of differences in teacher effectiveness. The research has focused on how much learning goes on in different classrooms. The results would not surprise any parent. The teacher matters a lot, and there are big differences among teachers. What would surprise many parents is the magnitude of the impact of a good or bad teacher. My analysis indicates that a year with a teacher in the top 15 percent for performance (based on student achievement) can move an average student from the middle of the distribution (the 50th percentile) to the 58th percentile or more. But that implies that a year with a teacher in the bottom 15 percent can push the same child below the 42nd percentile . . . Obviously, a string of good teachers, or a string of bad teachers, can dramatically change the schooling path of a child . . . The results apply to suburban schools and rural schools, as well as schools serving our disadvantaged population.

Why doesn't this issue get more attention? "First," answers Hanushek, "it is likely that ineffective teachers are generally hidden, in the sense that few kids get a string of bad teachers. Principals know very well who the ineffective teachers are, so they can balance a bad teacher one year with a good teacher the next. This implicit averaging process also means that it does not look like schools can do much to alter family background and what the child brings to school. Second, parents do not quite know how to interpret results on achievement tests. The teachers' unions have, since the advent of the No Child Left Behind Act in 2002, conducted a campaign to convince people that these scores do not really matter very much. Here they are flatly contradicted by the evidence."

Achievement in school matters, and it matters for a lifetime. "Somebody who graduates at the 85th percentile on the achievement distribution can be expected to earn 13 percent to 20 percent more than the average student," writes Hanushek. "This applies every year throughout a person's working life, yielding a difference in present value of earnings of $150,000 to $230,000 on average . . . By conservative estimates, the teacher in the top 15 percent of quality can, in one year, add more than $20,000 to a student's lifetime earnings, my research found . . . For a class of 20 students, we see that this very good teacher is adding some

$400,000 in value to the economy each year." A bad teacher in the bottom 15 percent is subtracting the same amount.

What are the best school systems in the world doing to attract and retain the best teachers and principals, and how do we introduce similar reforms here? To answer the question, McKinsey produced a study entitled *How the World's Best-Performing School Systems Come Out on Top* (September 2007). It looked at the world's ten best-performing school systems, such as Finland's and Singapore's, and compared them to less accomplished ones. The study's key findings are these: Most people who become teachers in these successful countries come from among the top 10 percent of their high school or college graduating classes; university students see the teaching profession as one of the top three career choices; the ratio of applications to available places in initial teacher-education courses in these countries is roughly ten to one; starting salaries for teachers in the successful countries are in line with other graduate salaries; teachers in these successful countries spend about 10 percent of their time on professional development—far higher than in America—and these same teachers regularly invite one another into their classrooms to observe and coach; finally, there are clear standards for what students should know, should understand, and should be able to do at each grade level.

The report's conclusions: The quality of an education system cannot exceed the quality of the teachers. The only way to improve outcomes is to improve instruction. Achieving universally high outcomes is only possible by putting in place mechanisms to ensure that schools deliver high-quality instruction to every child.

The McKinsey report did not evaluate principals, but they, too, are vitally important to student achievement. And finding ways to evaluate principals has to be part of any educational reform program. A principal's ability to recruit and retain great teachers, improve the effectiveness of all teachers, and, most important, to serve as an inspirational leader to bring out the best in teachers and students must be part of any evaluation process for any school system. As any teacher can tell you, the difference that a good or bad principal can make for an entire school is enormous. Tony Wagner, the Innovation Education Fellow at the Technology and Entrepreneurship Center at Harvard, argues that America should create a West Point for would-be teachers and principals: "We need a new National Education Academy, modeled after our military academies, to raise the status of the profession and to support the R and D that is essential for reinventing teaching, learning, and assessment in the twenty-first century."

Colorado, Here We Come

America cannot introduce needed reforms with one wave of the wand from Washington—not with our decentralized system of public education, which is composed of some 14,000 independent school districts. We can, however, produce successful local and regional models for education that can be imitated nationwide, models that can overcome the tension between teachers' unions, school administrators, and politicians to raise students' educational attainment. One such reform model is Colorado's.

To learn more about public education in Colorado, we interviewed Michael Johnston, the state senator who helped to found New Leaders for New Schools, an organization dedicated to training and recruiting leaders for urban schools, and who played a leading role in his state's reform initiative. In 2005, he co-founded Mapleton Expeditionary School of the Arts, a public school for disadvantaged youth in Thornton, Colorado. As the school's principal, he oversaw substantial progress in the school's performance, taking a school with a dropout rate of 50 percent and turning it into the first public high school in Colorado to have 100 percent of seniors admitted to four-year colleges. In a state that has a 25 percent dropout rate—50 percent among blacks and Hispanics—every little bit helps, but the need to scale the programs that work is urgent.

A unique feature of Johnston's public school was that the district gave him a free hand to put together his own teaching staff. In 2010, after being appointed to the Colorado state senate, he sought to build on that experience and teamed up with the governor, community leaders, and some members of the teachers' union to shepherd through a pathbreaking teacher quality act (SB 10-191), known as the Great Teachers and Leaders Bill. While many social and economic factors shape student performance, Johnston's approach begins with the conviction that within the schools themselves, nothing is more important than the quality of the teachers and principals.

"When I am talking to teachers," Johnston says, "I always begin by saying, 'First, we all share the same mission: We all want to close the achievement gap, graduate all of our students, and send them to college or a career without the need for remediation.' But we know that we're talking about a problem, an education deficit, of massive proportion. If you're going to solve a problem that big, you need a lever as big as the problem. And what we now know is that the single most important variable determining the success of any student is the effectiveness of the teacher in that classroom. That impact is so significant that when you talk about curriculum, professional development, or even class size, those changes are literally rounding errors compared to the impact of a great teacher." He goes on to say: "If you take our lowest-performing quartile of students and you put them in the classroom of a highly effective teacher, we know that in three years you have nearly closed the achievement gap. And we know that the opposite is true. If you take the lowest quartile of students and put them in the classroom of our least effective teachers and principals, you will blow that achievement gap open so wide you'll never close it.

"As in all professions, we know there are real differences in the effectiveness of teachers from classroom to classroom," Johnston says. "We know that people spend endless hours in the real estate market shopping for houses based on the school their kids might attend. But what actually matters is not what school you walk into but what classroom you walk into. Because we know that the difference in performance between teachers in any given school is twice as large as the difference in performance between schools. You could buy a house in the worst neighborhood in Denver and have a highly effective teacher for your child and you would be much better off than someone who bought a house in the wealthiest neighborhood of Denver and their kid was assigned to an ineffective teacher."

We now have the data to identify teachers who are making three years of gains in the classroom in one year's time. But we don't have a pipeline—from college, to school placement, to teacher evaluation, to pay and promotion systems—that delivers anything like the number of good teachers that we need. The superb ones we have, says Johnston, "are more like flowers that have willed their way up through concrete," rather than flowers grown in abundance in "hothouses" designed to produce them at that scale.

That is hardly surprising, he added, when you think of what we have asked teachers to do. "When I was twenty-one years old, I was a first-year high school teacher, and I taught six sections of *Julius Caesar* to ninth graders each day," said Johnston. "In the room across the hall was a teacher who was sixty-two years old and she taught six sections of *Julius Caesar* each day. That was the career path that I was being offered. This is why we lose 50 percent of teachers in the first three to five years."

Teachers come in loving the idea of sharing literature with young minds, said Johnston, and then they discover that there is no real potential for job growth unless they leave the classroom, very little ongoing professional development, inconsistent evaluation or feedback, and limited opportunities to interact with colleagues who are serious about reflecting on and improving their practice.

The same is true with principals. Other than the classroom teacher, the principal is the most important person in that school building. "What we see around the country," said Johnston, "is that great principals attract and retain great teachers. Terrible principals drive out great teachers. What is amazing is that the system retains as many good teachers as it does," given the uneven quality of principals.

"We are not focusing on teachers because teachers are the problem," said Johnston. "It's because they are the solution." When you look at the data on the difference that great teachers can make "you realize that they are such high-leverage instruments that a small move of the lever produces exponential results in student achievement." That means building systems that attract and retain more of the top teachers and improve or weed out more of the weaker teachers, which could thereby lead to a system-wide change in the quality of teaching. The Great Teachers and Leaders Bill, signed into law by Colorado governor Bill Ritter on May 20, 2010, aims to accomplish just that goal and is built on five principles.

First, explains Johnston, "we make 50 percent of every teacher's and principal's performance evaluation based on demonstrated student growth—and 'growth' is the key word. It doesn't matter what level the kids start at on September 1, we want to see that they know substantially more when they walk out the door on May 30. We are now developing, in consultation with teachers and principals, the metrics for these assessments. This is not meant as 'gotcha!'"

Indeed, it is vitally important to have a teacher-evaluation system, but also a system that teachers help to design and believe is fair. The Colorado evaluation process will include some combination of student survey data, principal reviews, and test results, and could include master-teacher reviews or peer-educator reviews, along with a chance for teachers to show themselves at their best—not just on surprise visits by inspectors.

Second, said Johnston, "we establish career ladders for teachers and principals who are identified as highly effective. We say to them, 'We want to learn what you are doing, and we will pay you a stipend on top of your salary to document and share with other teachers what you are doing that is making you successful.' So we might identify the twenty best math teachers in the state and would then pay them a stipend to video their classrooms when they are teaching a lesson and to upload their lesson plans onto a website. Then, if I am a new seventh-grade teacher, I can go on to the Web, click on 'seventh-grade math,' click on a specific standard, and see how our most effective teachers teach that particular standard. Or I can use the same website to identify master teachers and sign up to actually go visit their classrooms, where I can sit in the back and watch them practice in real time in front of students."

This not only gives all teachers a chance to learn from their best colleagues but also, added Johnston, creates "an incentive for our best teachers to stay in the classroom. Right now, as a teacher, the only way to get substantially more pay is to leave the classroom and become a principal. Now you have another career ladder."

In China, for instance, there are four levels of proficiency in the teaching profession, and in order to move up a level, teachers have to demonstrate their excellence in front of a panel of reviewers. The highest level is called "Famous Teacher." It is a hugely prestigious position in China.

Third, tenure in Colorado will be based on performance rather than seniority. That is, tenure, while not eliminated, will have to be earned and re-earned. Rather than being granted permanent tenure on the first day of his or her fourth year, now a teacher will have to earn tenure by producing three consecutive years of being rated an "effective" teacher. That teacher will then have to continue performing effectively to keep that status. If you are rated "ineffective" for two years, you lose your tenure. That does not mean you lose your job; it just means you are on a one-year contract.

That leads to the fourth principle: In Colorado the old law for teachers stipulated that in the event of cutbacks, the last hired were first to be fired, even if that was not in the best interest of the school or the students. Not anymore. "Now," explains Johnston, "the law says that whenever principals have to make reductions in force, the first criterion is 'teacher effectiveness.' You have to keep your most effective teachers. And only in the event of a tie does seniority kick in. An effective second-year teacher trumps an ineffective twentieth-year teacher."

The fifth principle gives principals the power to hire their own teachers. That is, the school district cannot take ineffective teachers, whom no school wants to hire, and force them on a school. Teachers who are not hired by any school on their merits after one year get released.

How in the world did they get this bill passed, given all the oxen it gored? "We made the case to all the groups involved as to why this was really in their interest," said Johnston. He and his political allies showed the NAACP how school systems were dumping their worst teachers in predominantly black and Hispanic schools. They showed business leaders and the chamber of commerce how subpar students were leading to subpar employees. They went to the two big teachers' unions in Colorado, said Johnston, "and we said, 'You all know that you have some great colleagues and colleagues that you have been carrying for years. There is no reason to do that anymore.'"

The key breakthrough for Johnston, though, was getting the American Federation of Teachers (AFT), led by Randi Weingarten, to support the legislation. Weingarten staked out a gutsy position. The National Education Association, the other big teachers' union, opposed the law, although a number of NEA union representatives in Colorado broke ranks and testified for the bill.

Weingarten, the president of the 1.5 million–member AFT, explained to us why her union supported the Colorado reform. For her and her union members, she said, the key question was how teachers get evaluated. They understood that the old system of granting automatic tenure was not sustainable. But some of the new systems—in which, for example, a teacher has five unannounced evaluations of thirty minutes each by a master teacher or principal, and virtually their entire evaluation is based on those brief visits and the students' standardized test scores—are too limited, she argued.

"We need evaluation systems based on multiple measures of both teacher practice and what students are learning," said Weingarten. In Colorado, she added, teachers and administrators "spent a lot of time talking to each other about how to make this evaluation system about continuous improvement, and that was why at the end of the day we supported the legislation." In that Colorado bill, "there was a teacher voice in how to make schools better," she added. "There was a lot of flexibility in what constituted acquisition of student learning—so it was not just test scores—and there was a lot more due process ensuring that teachers had a fair shake put into that law."

As Johnston put it: "What we got is a bill that requires multiple measures of student growth, that allows teachers multiple opportunities to improve, and doesn't ever force-fire anyone but always leaves that decision to principals and superintendents."

Johnston said that when he thinks about the change that he and others are trying to effect in education, he thinks back to attending President Obama's inauguration in Washington. What impressed him most was seeing a platoon of wheelchairs parting the crowd on the Mall after the president took the oath. Sitting in them were the surviving Tuskegee Airmen, the first African American aviators in the United States armed forces, who flew many successful missions in World War II.

"What I realized was that they lived in a moment when people didn't believe it was possible—they didn't believe that a black man had the courage or intelligence or stamina to fly one of America's most expensive warplanes," Johnson recalled. "So they said, 'Put me up in the air and let me show you,' and they became one of the only air squadrons in World War II who never lost a bomber." And of course they could and did become successful pilots. "And when they did, the world changed— because the argument about whether or not we were all created equal was once and for all over, and nothing else could have happened but that Truman would eventually integrate the air force, or that Johnson would sign the Civil Rights Act, or that sixty years later we would inaugurate the first black president.

"Education needs its own Tuskegee moment. One reason we have not been able to galvanize the whole community for educational reform," Johnston concluded, "is that some people still don't believe that every one of our kids can compete with the smartest kids from Singapore and China. It's our responsibility to get up in the air and prove them wrong. Then the whole world changes."

No Teacher Is an Island

As we noted earlier, if we want to make every teacher more effective, the rest of us need to be more supportive. This is not an argument for going easy on teachers. It is an argument for not going easy on everyone else. We must not do to teachers and principals what we did to the soldiers and officers in Iraq and Afghanistan after 9/11: put the whole effort on their backs while the rest of us do nothing except applaud or criticize from the sidelines. Here is how everyone has to contribute.

Communities: If we want teachers to raise their effectiveness, communities not only have to create an effective reform process that all the key players want to own; they also have to find ways to reward teachers through nonmonetary means. Teaching is a hard job. Unions or no unions, we'd bet that most teachers work more hours for no pay than any other professionals. No one goes into teaching for the money, and thousands of teachers every year dig into their own pockets to buy classroom materials. If teachers are so important—and great teachers are—how about recognizing and celebrating the best of them regularly in your community with something more than a $50 gift certificate from the PTA?

How? Here's an example. On November 1, 2010, the D.C. Public Education Fund, the nonprofit fund-raising arm of the Washington, D.C., public school system, organized "A Standing Ovation for D.C. Teachers" to honor the 662 instructors judged "highly effective" under the city's new IMPACT evaluation system, to which teachers had agreed. The tribute was produced by George Stevens Jr., producer of the annual Kennedy Center Honors, and had all the glitz of an Academy Award ceremony for teachers. Those 662 teachers had been singled out from their schools as highly effective. It was clearly a special evening for all of them. Before he sang, one of the performers, Dave Grohl of Nirvana and the Foo Fighters, recalled the teacher who had most influenced his life: his mother, who had taught in a Virginia public school for thirty-five years. "She was up before the sun every day, grading papers, and every night when it went down," said Grohl. Seven teachers, nominated by their principals, were singled out as All-Stars. Each came onstage to receive a plaque and a $10,000 award (all 662 got performance bonuses), and to deliver an acceptance speech. Kennedy Center chairman David Rubenstein was so moved by the event that he donated twenty more $5,000 awards on the spot. Not every community has access to the Kennedy Center, but every community can do more to make teachers feel appreciated and to inspire excellence.

For instance, every year, in addition to granting honorary degrees, Williams College in Massachusetts honors four high school teachers. But not just any high school teachers. Williams asks the five hundred or so members of its senior class to nominate the high school teacher who had the most profound impact on their lives. Then each year a committee goes through the roughly fifty student nominations, does its own research with the high schools involved, and chooses the four teachers who most inspired a graduating Williams student. Each of the four teachers is given $3,000, plus a $2,500 donation to his or her high school. The winners and their families are then flown to Williams, located in the lush Berkshires, and honored as part of the college's graduation weekend. On the day before graduation, all four of the high school teachers, and the students who nominated them, sit onstage at a campus-wide event, and the dean of the college talks about how and why each teacher influenced that Williams student, reading from the students' nominating letters. Afterward, the four teachers are introduced at a dinner along with the honorary-degree recipients. Morton Owen Schapiro, now the president of Northwestern but formerly the president of Williams, recalled that every time he got to preside over these events one of the high school teachers would say to him, "This is one of the great weekends of my life." When you get to work at a place like Williams, Schapiro added, "and you are able to benefit from these wonderful kids, sometimes you take it for granted. You think we produce these kids. But as faculty members, we should always be reminded that we stand on the shoulders of great high school teachers, that we get great material to work with: well educated, well trained, with a thirst for learning."

A variation on this theme that has been running since 1978 is the Yale–New Haven Teachers Institute, directed by James R. Vivian. It brings together Yale faculty members and New Haven public school teachers for seminars in the faculty members' subjects of expertise. In the seminars, which meet regularly for several months, the teachers work with a faculty member to prepare curricula on the subject they are studying, which they then teach in their schools during the following school year. The seminars thus give the teachers the opportunity both to learn more about a subject of interest—chemistry, mathematics, litera-ture, American history, or another of many different offerings—and to prepare strategies to teach it to their elementary or secondary school students. They also receive a modest honorarium for participating. The program has enjoyed such success that twenty-one different school dis-tricts in eleven states are now participating in the Yale National Initia-tive to strengthen teaching in public schools, which the Institute launched in 2004. The Initiative is a long-term effort to establish similar Institutes around the country and to influence public policy on the pro-fessional development of teachers.

Teachers' institutes differ from most of the programs of professional development that school districts provide and from outreach and contin-uing education programs that universities typically offer in that school-teachers and university faculty members work together as professional colleagues, in a program that is led in crucial respects by the teachers themselves. This not only improves the teachers' classroom performance; it also serves a purpose as important as recruiting and training good teachers: keeping them.

At the Annual Conference held at Yale on October 29, 2010, James Toltz, who teaches English at Middletown High School in Delaware, said this about participating in the Institute: "Recently my wife asked me, 'How long do you think you can keep teaching?' If she had asked me this one year ago, my answer might have been a few more years, maybe five at the most. My answer is just a little bit different now, and it extends from my experience here at Yale . . . We talk all the time about how we need to inspire our students, and we do, but once in a while we forget that we also need to inspire our teachers."

By the way, very few people go into teaching for the money, but many people leave teaching because of the money—especially men. If we really want to show our appreciation for teachers, we need to find innovative ways to pay them more.

Politicians: If we want better teachers, politicians will have to become better educators. They have to educate the country about the world in which we're living, about the vital role education now plays for our economy and our national security, about why raising standards is imperative, and about the skills that students need to acquire. They need to understand that part of their job is traveling around the country, and even the world, to understand the best practices in education so that they can both lead and inform the debate about these issues in their communities. It is vital to our economic growth.

State officials should be competing with one another to raise their educational standards and to demonstrate creativity in using education dollars. For a while, just the opposite was going on. When Congress passed the No Child Left Behind Act of 2002, it mandated that students had to achieve certain standards each year for their schools to benefit from federal funding, but it left it to each state to determine those standards. In recent years, as those standards remained unmet, many states simply lowered them to make it easier for students to pass tests and for schools to avoid the penalty of lost funding or being labeled a "failing school." Nothing could be more dangerous in today's world.

In response, in 2009 the National Governors Association and the Council of Chief State School Officers initiated a nationwide effort to set common standards, enlisting experts in English and math from the College Board and the ACT, and from Achieve, Inc., a group that has long pushed to firm up high school graduation standards. This effort was reinforced by the Department of Education's Race to the Top initiative, in which states were invited to compete for a share of $4 billion in school improvement money by showing a path to raising academic achievement. States competing in Race to the Top earned extra points for participating in the common effort to establish national standards and then adopting them.

Arne Duncan often complains that one of his biggest challenges as secretary of education is that too many Americans believe that their local schools are basically fine and that it is someone else's school that needs fixing. One reason people feel this way is that they are comparing their school with the one in the neighborhood or district next door. The relevant comparison is between their school and P.S. 21 in south Taipei or north Seoul or west Shanghai. This will become apparent when their children apply to college and find themselves competing with the graduates of those schools. Good enough is just not good enough anymore.

"One thing that has been missing is honesty," said Jack Markell, the governor of Delaware, which was one of the first two states to win Race to the Top funds (Tennessee was the other) and has been a leader in the national standards-writing initiative. "When you tell the kids they are proficient based on a test that is administered within their state borders, while in the real world they have to compete for college and for jobs with kids who are not within their state borders, you are not being honest with them. In our old test, 76 percent of Delaware fourth graders were judged to be proficient in reading. With our new test and scoring, that will be 48 percent, because we are being more honest with the kids about what it means to be more proficient."

How does he sell this reform to skeptical Delaware residents? He does it by connecting education with jobs. "I went to Taiwan a month ago," Markell told us in January 2010. "We have two Taiwanese companies in Delaware with 250 employees between them. One of the companies makes solar panels. At the same time that they started in Delaware, they started a factory in China. There is only one thing I am asking myself: 'Where are they going to invest their next dollars?' And you have to put yourself in their shoes. It is going to go where it will have the best return." And part of that, added Markell, will depend on where they find the most productive workers. This is not just about cheap labor. It is about skilled labor.

Neighbors: The role of neighbors today is to appreciate the importance of the public school down the street, even if their own children have long graduated or they have no children at all. Good schools are the foundation of good neighborhoods and communities. Money may be saved in the short term by voting down tax increases to fund schools. But if that results in higher dropout rates and higher unemployment, the overall cost to the community will certainly be higher. When the performance of local schools drops, it usually is not long before the value of nearby houses drops as well. In March 2010, Tom attended the Intel Science Talent Search, a national contest for high school students designed to identify and support the nation's next generation of scientists. "My favorite chat was with Amanda Alonzo, a thirty-year-old biology teacher at Lynbrook High School in San Jose, California," he wrote at the time. "She had taught *two* of the [Intel] finalists. When I asked her the secret, she said it was the resources provided by her school, extremely 'supportive parents,' and a grant from Intel that let her spend part of each day inspiring and preparing students to enter this contest. Then she told me this: Local San Jose Realtors are running ads in newspapers in China and India telling potential immigrants to 'buy a home' in her Lynbrook school district because it produced 'two Intel science winners.'" While every child's educational experience should matter to everyone as a matter of principle, good education is also good economics—for everybody.

McKinsey & Company made that very point in its report entitled *The Economic Impact of the Achievement Gap in America's Schools* (April 2009). The report asked what would have happened if in the fifteen years after the 1983 report *A Nation at Risk* sounded the alarm about the "rising tide of mediocrity" in American education, the United States had lifted lagging student achievement. The answer: If black and Latino student performance had caught up with that of white students by 1998, GDP in 2008 would have been between $310 billion and $525 billion higher. If the gap between low-income students and the rest had been narrowed, GDP in 2008 would have been $400 billion to $670 billion higher.

"We simply don't have the capacity to carry large pockets of our population, whom we know are unskilled and have a life that has a ceiling on it, and think that the United States can still soar and be unique and be the number-one source of good in the world," Kasim Reed, the mayor of Atlanta, told us.

Parents: In January 2011, Yale University law professor Amy Chua set off a firestorm of debate across America when *The Wall Street Journal* published an excerpt from her book *Battle Hymn of the Tiger Mother*. While Chua's child-rearing strategy was extreme and her book evoked a sharp backlash from many parents and educators, we think she ignited a useful debate. It was a wake-up call. Whatever you think of Chua's ironfisted parenting style, we urge you to keep this in mind: She is not alone in her parenting methods, and her approach is not at all rare in Asian culture. It is the norm.

"A lot of people wonder how Chinese parents raise such stereo-typically successful kids," wrote Chua.

> Well, I can tell them, because I've done it. Here are some things my daughters, Sophia and Louisa, were never allowed to do: attend a sleepover, have a playdate, be in a school play, complain about not being in a school play, watch TV or play computer games, choose their own extracurricular activities, get any grade less than an A, not be the No. 1 student in every subject except gym and drama, play any instrument other than the piano or violin, not play the piano or violin . . . Even when Western parents think they're being strict, they usually don't come close to being Chinese mothers . . . Studies indicate that compared to Western parents, Chinese parents spend approximately 10 times as long every day drilling academic activities with their children . . . The Chinese believe that the best way to protect their children is by preparing them for the future, letting them see what they're capable of, and arming them with skills, work habits and inner confidence that no one can ever take away.

We would not expect every parent to mimic Chua in the tough-love department; there is a fine line between involved parenting and making your kid neurotic, which even Chua acknowledges. In general, though, we believe Chua is right about two things: the need to hold children to the highest standards that push them out of their comfort zones, and the need to be involved in their schooling. When children come to school knowing that their parents have high expectations, it makes everything a teacher is trying to do easier and more effective. Self-esteem is important, but it is not an entitlement. It has to be earned.

Arne Duncan tells a story from President Obama's 2009 trip to South Korea to drive home that point to American parents: "President Obama sat down to a working lunch with South Korean president Lee in Seoul. In the space of little more than a generation, South Korea had developed one of the world's best-educated workforces and fastest-growing economies. President Obama was curious about how South Korea had done it. So he asked President Lee, 'What is the biggest education challenge you have?'

"Without hesitating, President Lee replied, 'The biggest challenge I have is that my parents are too demanding.'"

That anecdote usually makes Americans chuckle, says Duncan—and then wince. The president of Korea's parents are complaining that he hasn't done enough with his life.

"I wish my biggest challenge—that America's biggest educational challenge—was too many parents demanding academic rigor," said Duncan. "I wish parents were beating down my doors, demanding a better education for their children, now. President Lee, by the way, wasn't trying to rib President Obama. He explained to President Obama that his biggest problem was that Korean parents, even his poorest families, were insisting on importing thousands of English teachers so their children could learn English in first grade—instead of having to wait until second grade."

American young people have got to understand from an early age *that the world pays off on results, not on effort.* Not everyone should win a prize no matter where he or she finishes. Indeed, America today reminds us a little too much of that scene in *Alice's Adventures in Wonderland* in which the Dodo is organizing a race:

> First it marked out a race-course, in a sort of circle, ("the exact shape doesn't matter," it said), and then all the party were placed along the course, here and there. There was no "One, two, three, and away," but they began running when they liked, and left off when they liked, so that it was not easy to know when the race was over. However, when they had been running half an hour or so, and were quite dry again, the Dodo suddenly called out "The race is over!" and they all crowded round it, panting, and asking "But who has won?"
>
> This question the Dodo could not answer without a great deal of thought, and it sat for a long time with one finger pressed upon its forehead (the position in which you usually see Shake-

speare, in the pictures of him), while the rest waited in silence. At last the Dodo said "*Everybody* has won, and all must have prizes."

All must have prizes! Krista Taubert is the Washington-based correspondent for Finnish Broadcasting Company. She has two children in the Washington, D.C., school system, a nine-year-old and a five-year-old. Since Finland has one of the highest-rated school systems in the world and Tom met her at a movie about Finland's schools, he could not resist asking her to compare her daughters' educational experiences in America and in Finland.

In America, Taubert remarked, "I noticed sometimes in talking to other parents that they reward their kids for effort, not for excellence. My daughter plays soccer and as a nine-year-old she already has these huge trophies, and she actually hasn't won anything. My brother played professional hockey in Finland for a number of years, and he doesn't have any trophies as big as the trophies my daughter has."

Andreas Schleicher oversees the Program for International Student Assessment (PISA), to which we referred above. The program is administered by the Organization for Economic Cooperation and Development, a Paris-based group that includes the world's thirty-four major industrial countries. Schleicher said in an interview that one of the things that the program tested in 2009 for the first time was the impact of parental involvement. "We interviewed between three thousand and five thousand parents of the fifteen-year-olds that we tested in sixteen different countries," said Schleicher. "There was a clear connection between parental involvement in their children's education and their PISA scores. Those young people whose parents were involved with their education—doing as little as asking them each day 'How was school?' or 'What did you do in school today?'—or read books to them clearly performed better on the PISA test than those whose parents were not involved. In some countries it was also clear that the involvement of parents was more important than many traditional school factors." Public policy in education tends to be all focused on institutions, Schleicher added, "but what we have seen in our work is that schools that are really open to parents, that are really community centers that invite parental involvement, like those in Scandinavia," generate more parental involvement in their children's education, and that translates into better performance on tests. "You cannot just call for more parental involvement," said Schleicher. "Parents don't want to be involved in a closed institution. Schools have to be part of the community. People have to feel that. The trick is to get the parents from the less-well-educated backgrounds involved in the school and their children's learning." In Finland, up to high school, said Schleicher, "students meet with their teacher and parents together at the end of the year" and "discuss what they have accomplished and what they should have accomplished and set their goals for the next year."

A December 2005 study by four researchers in the United States and Australia entitled *Scholarly Culture and Educational Success in 27 Nations*, based on twenty years' worth of data, found that

> children growing up in homes with many books get 3 years more schooling than children from bookless homes, independent of their parents' education, occupation, and class. This is as great an advantage as having university-educated rather than unschooled parents, and twice the advantage of having a professional rather than an unskilled father. It holds equally in rich nations and in poor; in the past and in the present; under Communism, capitalism, and Apartheid; and most strongly in China.

The study went on to say that Chinese children who had five hundred or more books at home got 6.6 years more schooling than Chinese children without books. As few as twenty books in a home made an appreciable difference.

Students: We cannot exempt young people themselves, particularly by the time they are in junior or senior high school, from responsibility for understanding the world in which they are living and what it will take to thrive in that world. On November 21, 2010, *The New York Times* ran a story questioning whether American young people have become too distracted by technology. It contained this anecdote:

> Allison Miller, 14, sends and receives 27,000 texts in a month, her fingers clicking at a blistering pace as she carries on as many as seven text conversations at a time. She texts between classes,

at the moment soccer practice ends, while being driven to and from school and, often, while studying. But this proficiency comes at a cost: She blames multitasking for the three B's on her recent progress report. "I'll be reading a book for homework and I'll get a text message and pause my reading and put down the book, pick up the phone to reply to the text message, and then 20 minutes later realize, 'Oh, I forgot to do my homework.'"

We wish the figure of 27,000 texts a month came out of *Ripley's Believe It Not*. In fact, it is the new normal. On January 10, 2010, the Kaiser Family Foundation released the results of a lengthy study entitled *Daily Media Use Among Children and Teens Up Dramatically from Five Years Ago*:

> With technology allowing nearly 24-hour media access as children and teens go about their daily lives, the amount of time young people spend with entertainment media has risen dramatically, especially among minority youth, according to a study released today by the Kaiser Family Foundation. Today, 8–18-year-olds devote an average of 7 hours and 38 minutes (7:38) to using entertainment media across a typical day (more than 53 hours a week). And because they spend so much of that time "media multitasking" (using more than one medium at a time), they actually manage to pack a total of 10 hours and 45 minutes (10:45) worth of media content into those 7½ hours. The amount of time spent with media increased by an hour and seventeen minutes a day over the past five years, from 6:21 in 2004 to 7:38 today . . . While the study cannot establish a cause and effect relationship between media use and grades, there are differences between heavy and light media users in this regard. About half (47%) of heavy media users say they usually get fair or poor grades (mostly Cs or lower), compared to about a quarter (23%) of light users . . . Over the past 5 years, time spent reading books remained steady at about :25 a day, but time with magazines and newspapers dropped (from :14 to :09 for magazines, and from :06 to :03 for newspapers). The proportion of young people who read a newspaper in a typical day dropped from 42% in 1999 to 23% in 2009.

One quote in the study captured the trend: "The amount of time young people spend with electronic media has grown to where it's even more than a full-time workweek," said Drew Altman, Ph.D., the president and CEO of the Kaiser Family Foundation.

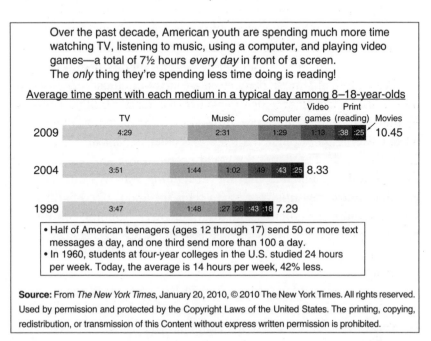

Over the past decade, American youth are spending much more time watching TV, listening to music, using a computer, and playing video games—a total of 7½ hours *every day* in front of a screen.
The *only* thing they're spending less time doing is reading!

Average time spent with each medium in a typical day among 8–18-year-olds

	TV	Music	Computer	Video games	Print (reading)	Movies	
2009	4:29	2:31	1:29	1:13	:38	:25	10.45
2004	3:51	1:44	1:02	:49	:43	:25	8.33
1999	3:47	1:48	:27	:26	:43	:18	7.29

• Half of American teenagers (ages 12 through 17) send 50 or more text messages a day, and one third send more than 100 a day.
• In 1960, students at four-year colleges in the U.S. studied 24 hours per week. Today, the average is 14 hours per week, 42% less.

Source: From *The New York Times*, January 20, 2010, © 2010 The New York Times. All rights reserved. Used by permission and protected by the Copyright Laws of the United States. The printing, copying, redistribution, or transmission of this Content without express written permission is prohibited.

At precisely the moment when we need more education to bring the bottom up to the average and the American average up to the global peaks, our students are spending more time texting and gaming and less time than ever studying and doing homework. Unless we get them to spend the time needed to master a subject, all the teacher training in the world will go for naught.

Business: One of the most unfortunate features of American politics today is that, with a few notable exceptions, the people who know the global labor market best and are most familiar with the skills needed to prosper in it—the members of the business community—have increasingly dropped out of the national debate. Historically, groups such as the Business Roundtable and individual leaders of industry considered it their responsibility to defend, indeed to speak out in favor of, the traditional American formula for greatness. They could be counted upon to go to Washington and lobby, not just on behalf of their own businesses but more broadly for better education, infrastructure, immigration, free trade, and rules to promote constructive risk-taking. That has become less and less true in the last decade. Business leaders are less and less interested in the whole pie and more and more interested in their own slice.

With the merger of globalization and the IT revolution, when American-based multinational firms meet resistance from Washington, D.C., today—arguing in favor of more visas for high-skilled workers, for example—they just move their research facilities abroad or outsource their work to foreign subsidiaries. When Microsoft couldn't get more visas for high-skilled immigrants to work in its headquarters outside Seattle, Washington, it opened a research center in Vancouver, Canada, 115 miles north. The flatter the world becomes, the less interested the most powerful companies become in fighting with Washington over visas, or almost anything other than their specific tax and antitrust issues. The standard approach of the American business community toward Washington today is, as medieval maps put it, "Here Be Dragons." You go there, you lobby for your particular tax break, and then you leave—quickly.

The turning point may have come in January 2004, when a consortium of eight leading information-technology company executives, known as the Computer Systems Policy Project, gathered in Washington to lobby Congress against legislation designed to restrict the movement of jobs overseas, where labor costs are lower. As part of their public outreach, the then CEO of Hewlett-Packard, Carly Fiorina, declared that "there is no job that is America's God-given right anymore." At the same time CSPP issued a report explaining that America's lead in high technology was in serious jeopardy due to competition from other nations.

In an article about the event, the *San Francisco Chronicle* noted (January 9, 2004) that CSPP offered a long-term proposal to improve grade school and high school education, double federal spending on basic research in the physical sciences, and implement a national policy to promote high-speed broadband communications networks, as Japan and Korea have done. It was exactly the kind of brutally honest intervention from business—here is the world we're living in and what we need to thrive in it—that we should welcome. Unfortunately, rather than calling for a serious national debate on this broad issue, the subsequent coverage focused almost entirely on Fiorina's blunt declaration about jobs not being an American right. She got hammered across the country.

One CEO who was at the meeting, but asked not to be identified, told us seven years later that as soon as the words were out of Fiorina's mouth, he and his colleagues wanted to tiptoe out of the press conference and out of town because they knew the backlash was coming. And come it did. "We have another idea," the *Seattle Post-Intelligencer* wrote in a January 9, 2004, editorial that was typical of the backlash. "Why not export a few chief executives' suites? We're certain there's qualified folks somewhere in a far-off land who might run a company for far less than what CEOs are paid in this country."

Fiorina's words came back to haunt her six years later, when she ran as a Republican for a Senate seat in California against the incumbent Democrat, Barbara Boxer. Boxer made prominent use in her television commercials of Fiorina's 2004 declaration and of the job cuts she had made as part of HP's restructuring during her tenure at the company. It is not a good sign when bluntly speaking the truth turns into a negative political advertisement that harms a candidacy.

Home Alone

While the connection between education and economic growth has never been tighter, we don't want our young people to be educated just so that they can be better workers. We want all citizens to be better educated so they can be, well, better citizens. "We want kids to think critically, to read, to create, but not simply because those things will get them jobs and money," said Susan Engel, the Williams College teaching expert, "but because a society made up of such people will be a better society. People will make more informed decisions, invent things that help the world rather than harm it, and at least some of the time, put the interests of others ahead of self-interest."

No question: Education should focus on the whole person—should aim to produce better citizens, not just better test takers. About this, Engel is surely right. If our schools teach American children what it means to be an American citizen, they—and America—will have a much better chance of passing on the American formula for greatness to future generations.

But we simply cannot escape the fact that we as a society have some catching up to do in education generally. When you are trying to catch up, you have to work harder, focus on the fundamentals, and get everyone to pitch in. Give us a country where everyone feels that he or she has a real stake in improving education—where parents are focused on their children's homework, where neighbors care about the quality of their local schools, where politicians demand that their schools be measured against the standards of our peers, where businesses insist that their schools be among the best in the world, and where students understand just how competitive the world is—and we promise you the best teachers will become even be better, the average ones will improve, and the worst ones will truly stick out.

One of the most wrongheaded movies we can imagine came out in late 2010. It was called *Race to Nowhere*, and its theme was that suburban American students are under too much pressure. They have to juggle homework, soccer, Facebook, wrestling practice, the school play, the prom, SAT prep, and Advanced Placement exams. Some would call that stress. We would call it misplaced priorities.

Stress? Stress is what you'll feel when you can't understand the thick Chinese accent of your first boss out of college—in the only job you are offered.

That will be stress.

SEVEN

Average Is Over

W e have a bone to pick with the writers of the movie *The Social Network*. We take exception to the way they depicted Lawrence Summers, who was the president of Harvard at the time in which the movie is set. At one point, two Harvard students, the twin brothers Cameron and Tyler Winklevoss, go to Summers complaining that a fellow student, Mark Zuckerberg, has stolen their idea for something called "the Facebook." Summers hears the twins' tale of woe without a shred of sympathy, then tosses them out with this piece of advice: "Yes, everyone at Harvard is inventing something. Harvard undergraduates believe that inventing a job is better than finding one, so I'll suggest again that the two of you come up with a new, new project."

That line is supposed to make Summers look arrogant, unsympathetic, condescending, and clueless. In fact, his point describes perfectly what "better" education should aspire to achieve: ingenuity, creativity, and the inspiration to bring something "extra" to whatever the student winds up doing in the world.

Woody Allen's dictum that "90 percent of life is just showing up" is no longer true. Just showing up for work will not cut it anymore. Now it is about showing off—not strutting or calling attention to yourself but doing things with an excellence that deserves attention.

America's economic future will depend on how well we are able to get our whole country to resemble Garrison Keillor's fictional Lake Wobegon, "Where all the women are strong, all the men are good-looking, and all the children are above average."

Average is officially over.

In a hyper-connected world where so many talented non-Americans

and smart machines that can do above-average work are now easily available to virtually every employer, what was "average" work ten years ago
is below average today and will be further below average ten years from
now. Think of the world as one big classroom being graded on a curve.
Well, that curve is steadily rising as more brainpower and computing
power and robotic power enters the classroom. As a result, everyone
needs to raise his or her game just to stay in place, let alone get ahead of
other workers. What was an average performance in the past will not earn
an average grade, an average wage, or a middle-class standard of living.

Say you're applying to college next year and you'd like to go to a small
liberal arts college in central Iowa—say, for instance, Grinnell College.
Well, at Grinnell, with 1,600 students in rural Iowa, "nearly one of every
10 applicants being considered for the class of 2015 is from China," *The
New York Times* reported (February 11, 2011). "Dozens of other American colleges and universities are seeing a surge in applications from students in China . . . following a 30 percent increase last year in the
number of Chinese studying in the United States . . . [But this] has created a problem for admissions officers. At Grinnell, for example, how do
they choose perhaps 15 students from the more than 200 applicants
from China? . . . Consider, for example, that half of Grinnell's applicants from China this year have perfect scores of 800 on the math por-
tion of the SAT, making the performance of one largely indistinguishable
from another."

This is just one small reason that whatever your "extra" is—inventing
a new product, reinventing an old product, or reinventing yourself to do
a routine task in a new and better way—you need to fine-tune it, hone
and promote it, to become a creative creator or creative server and keep
your job from being outsourced, automated, digitized, or treated as an
interchangeable commodity.

Everyone's "extra" can and will be different. For some it literally will
be starting a company to make people's lives more comfortable, educated, entertained, productive, healthy, or secure. And the good news is
that in the hyper-connected world, that has never been easier. If you
have just the spark of a new idea today, you can get a company in Taiwan to design it; you can get Alibaba in China to find you a low-cost
Chinese manufacturer to make it; you can get Amazon.com to do your
delivery and fulfillment and provide technology services from its cloud;
you can find a bookkeeper on Craigslist to do your accounting and an

artist on Freelancer.com to do your logo. All you need is that first spark of extra imagination or creativity.

In *Wired* magazine (January 25, 2010), the technology writer Chris Anderson eloquently explained what the hyper-connecting of the world is doing for anyone with an itch to start something:

> Here's the history of two decades in one sentence: If the past 10 years have been about discovering post-institutional social models on the Web, then the next 10 years will be about applying them to the real world. This story is about the next 10 years. Transformative change happens when industries democratize, when they're ripped from the sole domain of companies, governments, and other institutions and handed over to regular folks. The Internet democratized publishing, broadcasting, and communications, and the consequence was a massive increase in the range of both participation and participants in everything digital—the long tail of bits. Now the same is happening to manufacturing . . . The tools of factory production, from electronics assembly to 3-D printing, are now available to individuals, in batches as small as a single unit. Anybody with an idea and a little expertise can set assembly lines in China into motion with nothing more than some keystrokes on their laptop. A few days later, a prototype will be at their door, and once it all checks out, they can push a few more buttons and be in full production, making hundreds, thousands, or more. They can become a virtual micro-factory, able to design and sell goods without any infrastructure or even inventory; products can be assembled and drop-shipped by contractors who serve hundreds of such customers simultaneously. Today, micro-factories make everything from cars to bike components to bespoke furniture in any design you can imagine. The collective potential of a million garage tinkerers is about to be unleashed on the global markets, as ideas go straight into production, no financing or tooling required. "Three guys with laptops" used to describe a Web startup. Now it describes a hardware company, too. "Hardware is becoming much more like software," as MIT professor Eric von Hippel puts it . . . We've seen this picture before: It's what happens just before monolithic industries fragment in the face

of countless small entrants, from the music industry to news-papers. Lower the barriers to entry and the crowd pours in.

But some people are not risk takers—not resilient or entrepreneurial enough to start a new company from scratch. That's okay. In that case, though, they need to re-create themselves within their existing company or line of work by taking a routine creator job or routine server job and turning it into something special for which people will want to pay extra.

For some that will be providing something sophisticated that a cre-ative creator would do—designing a building, writing an innovative legal brief, inventing a new business, composing an ad, redoing a kitchen, or writing an iPad application. But for many others it will mean becoming a creative server and bringing a special passion or human touch to a job in a way that truly enriches the experience for the person paying for it. We all know that when we see it. You see it when you visit a parent in a nursing home and watch as that one health-care worker sits patiently with your father and engages him in a way that so clearly brightens his day that you say to yourself, "I am speaking to the man-ager. I will pay extra just to have her be on duty with Dad every day." You see it when you are waited on by a salesperson in the men's suit depart-ment or the women's shoe department who is so engaging, so up on the latest fashions and able to make you look your best, that you'll come back and ask for that person by name. You see it in that trainer or Pilates instructor who seems to know exactly how to teach each exercise properly—the one everyone is standing in line for, even though he charges more than his colleagues. And you see it on Southwest Airlines, where they manage to take an economy airline seat and give it some-thing extra. Southwest pilots, stewards, and stewardesses try to bring a little humor and a personal touch to everything they do.

The point of this chapter, and the whole education section, is this: For decades there has been a struggle between the American economy's desire to constantly increase productivity and the desire to maintain blue-collar jobs. We watched as more and more machines and cheaper and cheaper foreign workers replaced American manual laborers. We com-pensated for this loss of blue-collar jobs by creating white-collar jobs. But how do we compensate for the loss of white-collar jobs, which are increas-ingly under threat in the hyper-connected world? We do it by inventing new kinds of white-collar jobs. But that requires more start-ups and better education and more investment in research and development to push out the boundaries of science and technology. Today, the Chinese can generate growth just by educating their people enough to do the jobs now done in rich countries. For us to grow, we have to educate people to do jobs that don't yet exist, which means we have to invent them and train people to do them at the same time. That is harder, and it is why we need *everyone* to aspire to be a creative creator or creative server.

There are three mind-sets that are helpful in thinking about how to be a creative creator or creative server: think like an immigrant, think like an artisan, think like a waitress.

Every American worker today should think of himself as a new immigrant. What does it mean to think like an immigrant? It means approaching the world with the view that nothing is owed you, nothing is given, you have to make it on your own. There is no "legacy" slot waiting for you at Harvard or the family firm or anywhere else. You have to go out and earn or create your place in the world. And you have to pay very close attention to the world you are living in. As with immigrants throughout history, Americans now find themselves in new and in many ways unfamiliar circumstances. In important ways, in this hyper-connected world of the twenty-first century we *are* all immigrants.

Everyone should also think like an artisan, argues Lawrence Katz, the Harvard labor economist. "Artisan" was the term used before the advent of mass manufacturing to describe people who made things or provided services with a distinctive touch and flair in which they took personal pride. Prior to the Industrial Revolution, this included just about everyone: the shoemaker, the doctor, the dressmaker, the saddler. Artisans gave a personal touch to whatever they did, and they often carved their initials into their work. It's a good mind-set to have for whatever job you are doing: Would you want to put your initials on it when it's done?

Finally, it would not hurt for all of us at times to think like a waiter or waitress. In late August 2010, Tom was in his hometown of Minneapolis, having breakfast with his friend Ken Greer at the Perkins pancake house. Ken ordered three buttermilk pancakes and fruit. When the waitress came back with the breakfast plates, she put them down in front of each of them, and as she put Ken's plate down she simply said, "I gave you extra fruit." "We gave her a 50 percent tip for that," Tom recalled. That waitress didn't control much in her work environment, but she did control the fruit ladle and her way of trying to do that little extra thing was to give Ken extra fruit. In many ways, we all need to think like that waitress and ask: What is it about how I do my job that is going to differentiate me? More than ever now, we are all waiters and waitresses trying to do that something extra that a machine, a computer, a robot, or a foreign worker.

This kind of "extra" is what "better" education has to achieve and to inspire. For the last 235 years, America expanded and upgraded its educational system again and again in line with advances in technology. When we were an agrarian society, that meant introducing universal primary education; as we became an industrial society, that meant promoting universal high school education; as we became a knowledge economy, that meant at least aspiring to universal postsecondary education. Now the hyper-connected world is demanding another leap. Mark Rosenberg, the president of Florida International University, which has 42,000 students, summed up what it is: "It is imperative that we become much better in educating students not just to *take* good jobs but to *create* good jobs." The countries that educate and enable their workers to do that the best will surely thrive the most.

Indeed, as globalization and the IT revolution continue to merge, expand, and advance, the more they will destroy the old categories of "developed" and "developing" countries. Going forward, we are convinced, the world increasingly will be divided between high-imagination-enabling countries, which encourage and enable the imagination and extras of their people, and low-imagination-enabling countries, which suppress or simply fail to develop their peoples' creative capacities and abilities to spark new ideas, start up new industries, and nurture their own "extra." America has been the world's leading high-imagination-enabling country and now it needs to become a *hyper*-high-imagination-enabling society. That is the only way we can hope to have companies that are increasingly productive *and* many workers with jobs that pay decent salaries.

The big question for American educators, though, is how one actually goes about teaching "extra." The three R's—reading, writing, and arithmetic—we know how to teach and test. Teaching "extra," though, requires both teaching and *inspiring* creativity. There is no one way to do this, and the different attempts to teach creativity and "extra" are among the most exciting experiments in education today. But we know it can be done because people are already doing it.

The Three C's

Tony Wagner, the Innovation Education Fellow at the Technology and Entrepreneurship Center at Harvard and author of *The Global Achievement Gap* and *Learning to Innovate, Innovating to Learn,* has a good definition of a "better" education. It is one that teaches what Wagner calls the "the three C's"—"critical thinking, effective oral and written communication, and collaboration."

Thinking critically, Wagner says, involves asking the right questions—rather than memorizing the right answers. Communication and collaboration involve defining objectives and then working with others to bring them about. A person needs all three C's to become a creative creator or a creative server.

"If you cannot communicate, you cannot collaborate," explains Wagner, "and if you cannot collaborate, you will be less creative." There is a myth, he says, that the most creative and innovative people do their best work alone. "That is simply not true from what I see in the workplace and from talking to highly innovative people. Innovation today is almost always done in teams that are multinational, multilingual, and even virtual." In such teams, he argues, "to work effectively you have to communicate effectively."

But how can we nurture that first C—creative and critical thinking—in a classroom setting? It is not easy to define creativity with any precision, let alone measure it or teach it. Nonetheless, because the merger of globalization and the IT revolution is putting every job under pressure, because well-paying jobs will more and more require a measure of creativity, and because the burden of preparing Americans for the workforce falls so heavily on our schools, the schools must find ways to inspire the three C's while teaching the three R's.

Here we offer a few examples of what strike us as successful efforts to do so. We begin with Steve Jobs and his often cited 2005 commencement speech at Stanford University. Jobs attended Reed College, in Oregon, for one semester, and then dropped out, but that brief experience left its mark.

> I naively chose a college that was almost as expensive as Stanford, and all of my working-class parents' savings were being

spent on my college tuition. After six months, I couldn't see the value in it. I had no idea what I wanted to do with my life and no idea how college was going to help me figure it out. And here I was spending all of the money my parents had saved their entire life. So I decided to drop out and trust that it would all work out OK. It was pretty scary at the time, but looking back it was one of the best decisions I ever made. The minute I dropped out I could stop taking the required classes that didn't interest me, and begin dropping in on the ones that looked interesting.

It wasn't all romantic. I didn't have a dorm room, so I slept on the floor in friends' rooms, I returned Coke bottles for the 5¢ deposits to buy food with, and I would walk the 7 miles across town every Sunday night to get one good meal a week at the Hare Krishna temple. I loved it. And much of what I stumbled into by following my curiosity and intuition turned out to be priceless later on. Let me give you one example:

Reed College at that time offered perhaps the best calligraphy instruction in the country. Throughout the campus every poster, every label on every drawer, was beautifully hand calligraphed. Because I had dropped out and didn't have to take the normal classes, I decided to take a calligraphy class to learn how to do this. I learned about serif and sans serif typefaces, about varying the amount of space between different letter combinations, about what makes great typography great. It was beautiful, historical, artistically subtle in a way that science can't capture, and I found it fascinating.

None of this had even a hope of any practical application in my life. But ten years later, when we were designing the first Macintosh computer, it all came back to me. And we designed it all into the Mac. It was the first computer with beautiful typography. If I had never dropped in on that single course in college, the Mac would have never had multiple typefaces or proportionally spaced fonts. And since Windows just copied the Mac, it's likely that no personal computer would have them. If I had never dropped out, I would have never dropped in on this calligraphy class, and personal computers might not have the wonderful typography that they do.

There are two messages contained in Jobs's speech. The first is the importance of a liberal-arts education. To be sure, no one can be a creative programmer without knowing math or basic computing. And no one can be a creative engineer without knowing basic physics, nor can anyone invent a new drug without a background in biology and chemistry. Being grounded in the three R's and in an intellectual discipline matters. But if, in our rush to get everyone a proper grounding in math and science, we throw out or shrink art, music, journalism, choir, band, film, physical education, dance—and calligraphy—as many public schools are being forced to do, we lose the very things that encourage collaboration and inspire creativity and mash-ups.

The other lesson of Jobs's speech for teaching creativity is the importance of what Wagner calls "play" and "discovery." These two are related in children from an early age. Jobs was indulging himself when he took that calligraphy course, just exploring things he never knew about before or never felt he had time to explore. He was "playing," in the way educators use that word. "Every kid is an artist in kindergarten," explains Wagner. "Play is a form of discovery, and it is how we begin to make sense of the world and discover our passions." The problem with school today, Wagner argues, "is that it doesn't respect play, passion, and purpose—and isolates those who won't conform." Because these attributes cannot be measured, they cannot be tested, so they are not really valued.

Marc Tucker heads the National Center for Education and the Economy. He says that some of the best school systems he has studied, such as Denmark's, promote play with a purpose—but at a very high level. "I observed this in a technical high school in Denmark," said Tucker, "where the class was divided into four or five teams and each was given the assignment to build a dogsled. They competed with one another. First, they had to decide: Do we optimize for speed, for going a long distance, or for carrying heavy loads? You had to announce your criteria in advance and lay out your plan, and then build to it." While teams could decide their own work schedules, it was not just unstructured exploration. "It was supported exploration," said Tucker. "What I mean is that you take a problem that others have worked on before and you work your own way toward solving it. It requires you to draw on but then extend your classroom knowledge, to search for the relevant information you need, to filter out what can and can't be used to solve the problem, to learn how to be skeptical of some information, and ultimately to translate it all into a solution. At each stage you are supported by the faculty, so it is not totally unstructured."

Tucker added, "I have seen lots of project-based curriculum in the U.S. but the substance is often so shallow. To make this work, it has to be built on a solid base of knowledge. You have to know some basic engineering to build a dogsled. If you don't have that solid base of underlying skills, you will get nowhere." The goal, Tucker said, is a classroom situation where students can explore and collaborate, "but it has to be against a set of high standards for the project" so that students cannot just turn in any piece of junk and call it creative.

When it is done seriously, Tucker concluded, "it gives young people confidence, and that is crucial. To be creative, people need to have the confidence that they can do it." They also need the confidence to believe that "they can leave their moorings" and explore somewhere new outside their comfort zone.

The best companies already understand this. The adult version of "play" are programs that companies such as Google and 3M have instituted, in which employees are invited to spend 15 or 20 percent of their week working on projects that they devise, which are loosely connected to the company's main mission but can lead in almost any direction. "It is permission to play on company time," said Wagner. The programs have been a rich source of innovations for both companies. The website eWeek.com ran a piece (October 31, 2008) about Google's "20 percent time rule, which allows programmers and other Google employees to spend one of their five work days per week working on something of their own design. These projects stay in-house for a while, but several have been spun off for use in the outside world . . . Gmail, Google News and Google Talk are among that number."

The Good News

Fortunately, many American educators, at all levels, are aware of this challenge and are exploring unconventional ways to address it.

In 1981, Steve Mariotti had just left his job as an analyst with Ford Motor Company and moved to New York to start a new business when he got mugged jogging along the East River. Five teens jumped him, beat him up, and stole the $10 he was carrying. Afterward, he said, "I felt like if they had only asked for help, I would have given it to them." The son of schoolteachers, Mariotti decided after the incident to quit his job and teach in an inner-city school. The transition was rocky. "On his first day at Brooklyn's Boys and Girls High School," *People* magazine reported (September 13, 2003), "troublemakers called him Mr. Manicotti. One pupil set another kid's coat on fire. 'I was terrified,' he says. 'The principal told me I was the worst teacher in the school . . . I realized the good kids were getting bullied and tormented by the few who were really bad,' says Mariotti, who soon changed his teaching methods."

In a departure from normal practice at that school he decided to teach something that his students wanted to learn—how to make money. Suddenly, said *People*, they were flocking to his new business class, "a mix of basic math, English, commercial skills and trips to places like a wholesale market."

The experience eventually led Mariotti to establish, in 1987, the Network for Teaching Entrepreneurship (NFTE), an organization that helps young people from low-income communities unlock their potential for entrepreneurial creativity by teaching them to start their own businesses, which keeps them in school as they are learning how to do this.

Today more than 330,000 students in junior and senior high schools across America have taken part in a NFTE course or in its national competition for the best new business plan put together by a student age eleven to eighteen. Here is how it works. Once a school has affiliated with NFTE, explained Amy Rosen, the organization's current president, "we hold NFTE University, where the teachers who will be implementing our program are trained to deliver our unique curriculum"—a mix of math, introductory accounting, entrepreneurship, and economics.

NFTE then provides the schools with its own specially designed textbook, now in its eleventh edition, which teaches the basics of entrepreneurship. The students participate either as a stand-alone course or as part of other courses, such as economics, which requires their mastering a certain level of math. Says Rosen, "You cannot figure out return on investment if you cannot multiply fractions." The class starts with each student being given $25 to buy something to resell for a profit at a NFTE-sponsored school bazaar. "That's how you learn the difference between gross and net profits," said Rosen. Then every student has to design a business according to a defined template.

Throughout the year they work on developing a business plan for their own business, which they present and defend in the spring. If they choose, they can then enter local, city, state, and national competitions to become one of the national finalists. In 2010, President Obama met with the finalists, who were chosen from an original pool of 20,000 entrants. The overall winner, Nia Froome, a seventeen-year-old student from Valley Stream, New York, received the $10,000 grand prize for the business she started, Mamma Nia's Vegan Bakery. Bosnian immigrants Zermina Velic and Belma Ahmetovic, from Hartford, took first runner-up for their computer services company, Beta Bytes, which they started to help fellow immigrants deal with their computer problems.

Many students drop out of school today because they can't make a connection with their teachers or their curricula, noted Rosen. "What NFTE does is engage their brains in projects they feel are relevant and bring out that individual thing we all have," she explained. "Remember, free enterprise is all based on individuality and people finding their own path to independence. And when you find a way for kids to engage their brains and combine it with a way for them to discover their individual interest, you have a winning combination."

These students "have a lot of street smarts," Rosen added. "Most of them are surviving in really challenging environments. So if you just give them the minimum amounts of information and show them the world beyond their communities, many of them are natural entrepreneurs. They see all kinds of opportunities. They see a way to make a living in this world in a whole different way."

A documentary about NFTE entitled *Ten9Eight* was released in 2009, which is how we found out about the program. The three finalists that year were an immigrant's son, who took a class from H&R Block and invented a company to do tax returns for high school and college students; a young woman who taught herself how to sew and designed custom-made dresses; and the winner, an African American boy who manufactured "socially meaningful" T-shirts. The young woman who started the clothing business "turned down an Ivy League college to attend Northwestern," said Rosen, "because Northwestern promised her a single room so she could bring her sewing machine to school."

Creative Crimson Tide

Many colleges attempt to teach creativity and critical thinking. One of the more novel programs for this purpose is the Creative Campus, initiated by the University of Alabama. Hank Lazer, the associate provost for academic affairs and the program's executive director, explained to Tom that it all started by accident—by students looking for something extra. In 2005, the university was offering an honors seminar called "Art and Public Purpose," about how public institutions can support the arts. At the end of the term the thirteen students, rather than write individual papers, banded together and "presented a long report and recommendations to the provost on how to broaden and deepen the exposure to the arts by Alabama students on and off campus, so students not majoring in the arts could be more artistically expressive," said Lazer. "They thought it was important." So did the university leadership, which had recently commissioned a study that found that some 70 percent of entering University of Alabama students had participated in a band, a choir, a yearbook staff, a newspaper, or something involving the arts, but only 19 percent did so while in college. "That was a disturbing statistic, coming at a time when 'creativity' was emerging as the new necessity for an educated person—and to get a job," said Lazer.

The university leadership got the message, and in 2006 it initiated a program called Creative Campus, designed to nurture creativity among students by getting them to think about how to promote the arts in their community, on and off campus. The program was given its own prestigious home in Maxwell Hall, the university's old observatory at the highest point of the original UA campus, and, more important, directly across the street from the football stadium! The university was encouraged to fund the program, said Lazer, after visits to the campus by Daniel Pink, author of *A Whole New Mind: Why Right-Brainers Will Rule the Future*, and Sir Ken Robinson, author of *Out of Our Minds: Learning to Be Creative*, "who were touting creativity as the driving force for economic and community development."

Creative Campus works this way: Each year forty to forty-five students are paid between $8 and $10 an hour for ten hours of work a week to come up with ideas that fuse and promote the arts and culture in ways that enrich student life and the artistic life of the surrounding community. They put together their own teams to develop project ideas and to collaborate in executing them. For instance, one project, Lazer explained, "involved Creative Campus interns pulling together a multifaceted partnership with the West Alabama Chamber of Commerce, the City of Tuscaloosa, the City of Northport, and Tuscaloosa County—and Robert McNulty's Partners for Livable Communities—to develop a comprehensive cultural arts and economic development plan for the region." The campaign was called "Culture Builds." Another team put together the Druid City Arts Festival—which is held in downtown Tuscaloosa to highlight a range of local artists and bands, and is now in its second year. Yet another team created a program called Unbound Arts to present the artwork of people with disabilities.

Lazer says that "we are a deliberately unstable and organic group by design." The purpose is to push students into thinking creatively and entrepreneurially about broadening exposure to the arts "in a way that will push every one of our students out of their comfort zone." Interns not only have to learn about the area's art and music scene in depth; they have to propose ideas for engaging it and then work through all the bureaucratic issues involved in staging a major event.

"A lot of the completion of a really creative task is boring," Lazer said, which is why his program aims not only to foster imagination but also to teach execution. "Persistence trumps talent, but it is best to have both," he says. "The students who want to organize an arts festival learn to work with the mayor and the city regulations that they need to negotiate. They learn that that is a big part of doing anything exciting." The whole idea is to let students "play" in a structured way and with a purpose.

Besides thinking creatively and collaboratively, Lazer said, "we are teaching the students two things: self-confidence and resiliency, which is what gives you the ability to get through the failures. It takes you at least ten ideas to come up with the good one," and then persistence squared to get that good one done. "We have one student," Lazer added, "who is graduating in electrical engineering who just decided to take one year off to work on his band. His mom told us she is not upset by this detour, which is probably what it will prove to be, because of the self-confidence she has seen her son develop in the program. I suspect that in two or three years, when he is working for Apple or Google, his band experience will also serve him well."

An Idealab

When you ask Bill Gross what it takes to be creative and a starter-upper, he doesn't say math or liberal arts or collaboration. He says "courage."

Gross knows start-ups and starter-uppers as well as anyone in America's high-tech firmament, for the simple reason that his start-up business manufactures start-ups. Gross founded the Idealab in Pasadena, California, in 1996, describing it as an innovation laboratory that supports "groundbreaking companies whose products and services change the way people think, live, and work." Working out of a big warehouse, Gross hosts and helps to fund half a dozen or more start-ups at a time under one roof. You can walk the halls of his office and find a budding solar company in one corner working next to a budding social-networking game company in another. After his college days at Caltech, Gross says, he was a "serial entrepreneur," starting one company after another, until he realized that he was a "parallel entrepreneur" and became the incubator/partner for many start-ups at once. Gross's Idealab has gotten about a hundred companies up and running since 1996. Among his recent winners was Picasa, a software download sold to Google that helps users organize, edit, and share photos.

"I look at the world and see something I don't like and my immediate instinct is to say, How can I fix that? I don't think I have better skill than other people to do that, but I have less fear than other people to go out and do it." Gross argues that a big part of teaching the creative process at any level involves getting people to overcome their fear of failure and plunge ahead when they have an idea.

Who taught him that? "Failure," says Gross. "We have had one hundred companies over the last twenty years and sixty have succeeded and forty failed, and the failures are where I learned everything. Everybody goes through life and sees things and says, 'I wish that were this way.'" But most people stop there. The successful creators and entrepreneurs are the people who overcome that fear and act. The biggest barrier to creativity, argues Gross, is "lack of self-confidence."

Gross says he gained confidence "from a few failures I had at the beginning—and maybe it came from realizing that a few failures at the beginning didn't feel that bad. Failure that produces learning along the way is not looked on as a scarlet letter. As an employer, I find that when prospects come to me with failures on their résumés that they have taken accountability for and learned from, they are way more exciting to hire than someone who comes with a success that might have been due to luck. Every big company goes through hard times at some point, and having someone who has lived through that is very helpful."

Successful creators, argues Gross, not only have a gift for seeing things before others do. They have another skill that is just as important, if less glamorous. They know how to get things done. "Getting stuff done is really underrated," said Gross. "Bill Gates had a vision but then he just stuck with it and stuck with it and stuck with it. People laughed along the way; he just stuck with it. That you cannot teach . . . You can admire and learn from it."

And as someone who is immersed in this world, Gross has no doubt that everyone needs to aspire to be what we call a creative creator or creative server, but he also believes strongly that there has never been a better time to do so. "This is a great time to be an entrepreneur," he argues. "There is lots of money around. And if you make something happen that catches on, you can reach the whole planet with your idea. You have to make something that gets through the noise, but if you do, you have a global reach that is just unbelievable."

Yes, And

Like Gross, the best educators understand that "extra" and "creativity" are not so much taught as they are unlocked and let out, after which they are usually self-propelled. One school that was designed to foster this is the forty-three-year-old Nueva School, a private school located in Hillsborough, California, between San Francisco and Palo Alto. Nueva is for gifted children. Few public schools can match the resources and teacher-student ratio of Nueva, with more than four hundred pupils and facilities such as a children's workshop with every imaginable tool designed for students to build things. But the principles Nueva applies in teaching young people from a very early age to be creative are things that others can copy, because they don't involve money or class size or even the individual genius of students. They involve intangibles, such as trusting teachers, helping students develop the confidence to take risks, and—most important—learning to say "Yes, and," according to Nueva's head of school, Diane Rosenberg.

Rosenberg says that she and her colleagues approached the issue of how to nurture creativity by starting with a simple question: Who are successful people in life? "As we looked around," she recalled, "the answer was that they were people who pursued their passion with a purpose. And they were all-in in doing so. They did it with their entire being, whatever it was. They were pulled by something inside them, not driven."

That being the case, she said, starting with the four-year-olds in pre-K, the Nueva School encourages all students to find those things that pull them from within, through a combination of classroom fundamentals and project-based learning. Everything starts with a solid grounding in the fundamentals, says Rosenberg, echoing Marc Tucker. "Creativity only comes from a genuine understanding of a discipline," she said. "We try to provide a solid foundation of core concepts and skills and then encourage students to play with ideas which they develop a passion for. But you cannot play with ideas if you don't have the core understanding."

For instance, says Rosenberg, a class might be studying ancient Egypt. They first study all the fundamental information in depth, and then each student is encouraged to explore whatever aspect of that society intrigues him or her—science, the Pyramids, economy, culture—through collaborative project-based research.

"As a teacher, you have to let go a little," said Rosenberg. You don't know exactly what a student might want to explore. Therefore, "you have to know that the kids are going to ask questions that the teacher doesn't have the answers to and that teacher has to be willing to say, 'I don't know, let's find out who does,'" said Rosenberg. "It is about directing them and teaching them how to ask the questions and how to navigate that world . . . Part of that also involves creating a classroom environment where students feel free to pursue any idea without fear of ridicule, so that kids don't feel they have to conform."

Which leads to Nueva's overall teaching philosophy: "Yes, and." Explains Rosenberg: "When a student proposes a project idea, our teachers are encouraged to say, 'Yes, and . . . would you consider taking it this direction?'" The idea is not just to accept any idea but always to begin by building on something coming from inside that student and then trying to guide it in a productive direction. But it has to start with saying "Yes" to student-generated ideas, whenever possible.

Self-motivation is vital now for other reasons as well. In a hyperconnected world where innovation takes place ever more rapidly, what a person knows today will be outdated tomorrow. In such a world one of the most important life skills will be the ability and desire to be a life-long learner. If average is over, then school is never over. Some people are born with the curiosity and drive to keep learning long after they have left school. Others need to have it inspired in them, and that often comes from having had at least one great teacher who got them excited about a subject or embraced their own excitement with "Yes, and." Wherever it comes from, everyone is going to need it because a better education today is one that prepares a student to understand a book that has not yet been written, to master a job that has not yet been created, or to conceive a product that does not yet exist. That is what students in their working lives will have to do, repeatedly.

"Trust," "ownership," and "self-propulsion" are important words when it comes to bringing out people's extras, and Rosenberg uses them a lot. "All great teachers feel like they are working for themselves," she said. And so do all inspired students. The more trust you bring into a classroom—the more administrators can trust principals, principals can trust teachers, and teachers can trust students—the more each one of them, more often than not, becomes self-propelled, doing more than anyone would ever think of demanding from them.

So yes, it is possible to teach creativity, not only with a radical new curriculum but with some very traditional old values: trust, owner-ship, self-confidence, courage, and most of all, two common indis-pensable words in the English language, used together: "Yes, and." Surely every school in America has room for these basic values in its classrooms.

If Carlson's Law is correct and more and better innovation is going to be coming from the bottom up and less from the top down, then a leader or teacher or principal cannot be effective without being able to inspire workers or students.

"You cannot command collaboration and creativity," says Dov Seidman of LRN. "You have to inspire it and create a context and an environment and a culture where it can happen—and where people [who feel] united by a shared vision will then work collectively and col-laboratively to make it happen."

"Extra" also has to be inspired because, as we've said, for many people the extra they have to add will not be a software breakthrough or a rocket design or even the drive to exceed a sales target. It will be something simpler but all too rare these days: the ability to connect with other human beings in a way that no machine ever can—whether you are a doctor, nurse, salesclerk, or teacher. Seidman maintains that "this distinctly human ability to be humane, hopeful, and helpful" cannot simply be taught *to* people; it, too, has to be inspired *in* people.

"I Kill Jobs"

For all these reasons, the merger of globalization and the IT revolution has made average a dangerous place to be on the workplace spectrum, and one way or another everyone needs to find his or her "extra."

No one has more bluntly summed up why average is over, and what it means for education, than John Jazwiec, who has headed a variety of technology start-ups, including RedPrairie and FiveCubits. Blogging on his website, JohnJazwiec.com, he confessed:

> I am in the business of killing jobs. I kill jobs in three ways. I kill jobs when I sell, I kill jobs by killing competitors, and I kill jobs by focusing on internal productivity. All of the companies I have been a CEO of, through best-in-practice services and software, eliminate jobs. They eliminate jobs by automation, outsourcing, and efficiencies of process. The marketing is clear—less workers, more consistent output. I reckon in the last decade I have eliminated over 100,000 jobs in the worldwide economy from the software and services my companies sell. I know the number, because . . . my revenues . . . are based on the number of jobs I kill. I have killed many competitors. Again, I reckon I have eliminated over 100,000 jobs in the last decade. I know the number, because I know I have been in large markets, and have ended up being one of two companies left standing, where there were many more when I took over. Finally, I have killed many internal employees. When I acquire a company, some of the "synergies" [involve] eliminating duplicate jobs. When I buy productivity software or outsource for lower labor costs, I kill internal jobs. Finally, companies that grow demand internal people to grow.

They attract better job candidates. Growing companies kill internal jobs by economic darwinism. So there, I have said it, I am a serial job killer.

He explained: "Any job that can be eliminated though technology or cheaper labor is by definition not coming back. The worker can come back. They most often come back by being underemployed. Others upgrade their skills and return to previous levels of compensation. But as a whole, the productivity gains over the last twenty years have changed the landscape of what is a sustainable job.

What, then, is a sustainable job? Jazwiec asks.

The best way I can articulate what is a sustainable job is to tell you, as a job killer, [sustainable jobs are] jobs I can't kill. I can't kill creative people. There is no productivity solution or outsourcing [strategy] that I can sell to eliminate a creative person. I can't kill unique value creators. A unique value creator is, well, unique. They might be someone with a relationship with a client. They might be someone who is a great salesman. They might be someone who has spent so much time mastering a market that they are subject matter experts . . .

The largest factor in high systemic unemployment is a failure in our schools and workforce to recognize [that] we have entered into a "free agent" era of labor. Everyone is now a free agent. The days [when] people worked for one company have been gone for a long time. But the days where people could assume [that] if they worked hard and the company they worked for was successful, [this] made them "safe," is now over. They are over because job killers like me are lurking everywhere . . . Until our children are taught to be individuals, until our colleges spend more time on creative application, and until we provide training and mentoring for before-gainfully-employed professionals, high systemic unemployment is never going away. In the meantime, the fully employed herd, without creative unique value contribution skills, will continue to be prey to serial job killers like me.

PART III

THE WAR ON MATH AND PHYSICS

EIGHT

"This Is Our Due"

If America had simply underestimated the impact of globalization and the IT revolution and failed to respond to them by improving our system of education, the future would be complicated enough. But we made comparable mistakes with our other two major challenges—the deficit and the intersection of energy and climate. Just when we needed to be husbanding our financial resources and spending every dollar of government revenue in the smartest way possible to advance and upgrade our traditional formula for prosperity, we did the opposite. Between 2000 and 2010 we added more to our national debt in a shorter period of time than during any previous decade in American history. And just when the flattening of the world not only created two billion more competitors but also two billion more consumers, just when some of those new consumers were getting the chance to live in American-size homes, drive American-size cars, and eat American-size Big Macs, just when all the rising energy demand from all these new consumers was affecting the climate and food prices and creating the need for cheap, clean, renewable energy, and just when China recognized all this and began investing heavily in wind, solar, battery, and nuclear power, America dithered, delayed, and underinvested in energy and in the wider foundations of its economic growth.

What makes this all the more troubling is that, unlike the challenges of globalization and IT—which many of us didn't see or fully comprehend—our energy, climate, and deficit challenges were staring us in the face. In the past, we not only understood both problems; we took significant and often politically difficult steps to address them. This time around, however, we did worse than merely ignore these challenges. In the last two decades, a significant segment of Americans denied that they even existed.

To put it bluntly, in the first decade of the twenty-first century, America declared war on both math and physics.

Ron Suskind's book *The Price of Loyalty* recounts the efforts of Paul O'Neill, George W. Bush's first secretary of the Treasury, to block tax cuts he felt the country simply could not afford. According to Suskind, at one point in late 2002 O'Neill tried to warn Vice President Dick Cheney that growing budget deficits—which were expected to exceed $500 billion that fiscal year alone—posed a threat to the economy's long-term health. Cheney cut him off. "You know, Paul, Reagan proved deficits don't matter," he said. Cheney went on: "We won the midterms [the congressional elections]. This is our due." A month later, Cheney told the Treasury secretary, an old friend, to find another job.

Meanwhile, Senator James Inhofe, a Republican from Oklahoma and currently the ranking minority member and former chairman of the Senate Committee on Environment and Public Works, has called global warming the "greatest hoax ever perpetrated on the American people."

In that same vein, Senator Jon Kyl, an Arizona Republican, went on *Fox News Sunday* (July 11, 2010) and declared—with no sense of irony at all—that when Democrats raise spending in one area, the spending needs to be offset by a spending reduction in another area, but when Republicans cut taxes in one area, the cut does not have to be offset by any cut in spending. "You do need to offset the cost of increased spending, and that's what Republicans object to," said Kyl. "But you should never have to offset the cost of a deliberate decision to reduce tax rates on Americans." In other words, raising spending means that one and one make two: the deficit grows. But in the case of lowering taxes without lowering spending, one and one make one: there is no effect on the deficit.

It is as if the law of gravity applies to apples but not to oranges.

To be sure, not all Americans shared this gravity-defying logic, but those who did became a powerful enough force to shape America's overall budget and energy and climate politics and to stymie reform. They prevented the passage of an energy bill in the 111th

Congress and blocked comprehensive deficit reduction. No matter what we Americans say, we are what we do. And this is what we as a country have been doing: waging war on math and physics. We've been simultaneously engaged in deficit denial and climate change denial.

There is no other way to say this: Somewhere in the last twenty years of baby boomer rule, Americans decided to act as if we had a divine right to everything—low energy prices and big cars, higher spending and lower taxes, home ownership and health care, booms without ceilings and busts without massive unemployment—all at a time when the country was waging wars in Afghanistan, Iraq, and then Libya. Our sense of entitlement expanded far beyond Social Security and Medicare to encompass . . . well, everything.

We went to war against math and physics to finance this fantasy. In reality, though, it was actually financed—as the character Blanche DuBois said in the Tennessee Williams play *A Streetcar Named Desire*—by "the kindness of strangers." In our case that was the willingness of China to lend us money, Saudi Arabia to keep us awash in oil and petrodollars, and the market and Mother Nature to show us a certain forbearance. That kindness is surely running out. The choice we face is between reducing deficits and greenhouse gas emissions in a considered and deliberate fashion, and waiting for the market and Mother Nature to force us to do so—rapidly and brutally.

There is plenty of room for debate about the proper response to our energy and climate challenges. And there is plenty of room to debate when and whether to a run a deficit—to stimulate the economy during a recession, for example. And there is plenty of room to debate how large deficits can become without seriously endangering the economy. But it is factually, scientifically, and mathematically untrue that deficits don't matter and that human-driven global warming that could trigger climate change is simply the invention of a global conspiracy of left-wing scientists and Al Gore.

There is something else that our math and physics problems have in common—their solutions. These solutions are not ends in themselves. They are the means to our larger goal—the place we are actually trying to reach. Our goal is to sustain the American dream at home so it can be enjoyed by the next generation and to sustain American power abroad so that the United States can play the stabilizing and example-setting role that the world wants and needs it to play. To achieve both we need sustainable economic growth. And to achieve that we need a systemic response to both our math and physics challenges, not a war on both. In math, such a response involves cutting spending, raising taxes, and investing in our formula for success—all at the same time. In physics, such a response involves increasing energy efficiency dramatically, investing more in research and deployment of cleaner power, and imposing a price on carbon. That, too, requires an integrated approach. We need to do these things not to punish ourselves for our profligacy but to reverse the damage we have done by making war on both math and physics, and most of all to assure economic growth in the future. If we don't, to paraphrase Cheney, we will get what is our due.

In the first decade of the twenty-first century, the attacks on New York and Washington of September 11, Islamic terrorism, Osama bin Laden, Afghanistan, Iraq, and homeland security preoccupied Americans. We believe, however, that if we don't change course, twenty-five years from now the war we undertook with al-Qaeda won't seem nearly as important as the wars we waged against physics and math. We will be paying for these two wars far longer. And that's the optimistic scenario.

If we don't shrink the deficit to a more manageable size while investing in our traditional formula for success, and if we don't address our long-term clean-energy needs while mitigating climate change, we will effectively be outsourcing America's fate to the two most merciless, unemotional, and unrelenting forces on the planet: the market and Mother Nature. These two will determine, each in its own time and its own way, when its limits have been breached, when the laws of nature and of economics will kick in, when the music will stop, and when the adjustment to our lifestyle—which will be nasty, brutish, and long—will start.

The next two chapters explain how we got to this point.

NINE

The War on Math (and the Future)

Arithmetic is not an opinion.

—Italian proverb

In the winter of 2011 *The New Yorker* ran a cartoon showing an elderly man meeting with his banker. The caption underneath had the man saying, "I want to take out one of those mortgages on my grandchildren's future."

That little cartoon summed up not only how we have behaved in the past but how much damage we can still do to our future if we don't change course and bring our national debt, entitlements, and annual deficits under control—in an intelligent way. Given all of our excessive spending since the end of the Cold War, a certain amount of intergenerational conflict over who pays what is now impossible to avoid, as the cartoon suggested. What remains to be determined is whether it is a battle or a full-fledged civil war—the old against the young. The battle lines have already been drawn: Medicare versus Pell Grants for college tuition, nursing homes versus community colleges, the last year of grandma's life in the hospital—which takes up roughly 30 percent of Medicare.—versus the first eighteen years of your child's life in public school.

Even though these battles are being fought today by accountants with calculators, their outcome will be no less important in shaping our nation's course in the decades to come than the battles of Gettysburg and Bull Run were for the nineteenth century. Many Americans now wrongly believe that the issue we face is whether or not we will reduce the annual federal budget and which programs will get dropped or trimmed. Rest assured, the budget will be cut and programs will be trimmed. The markets will eventually make sure of it. We have no choice.

The important question is: On the basis of what priorities and what vision will those cuts be made? Will we reorganize government spending in a way that invests in the future, or in a way that just pours more money into the past? It is a hard choice. Deserving programs and deserving people will be cut because we simply cannot keep all the promises we have made to ourselves. We have made too many, which are too big, for too long. So if we don't take the initiative—if we don't *cut spending, increase revenues, and invest in the future all at the same time,* based on an accurate reading of the world in which we are living and what we will need to thrive in it—we will pay a huge price. It may be possible to grow effectively without a plan, but there is no way to shrink effectively without a plan.

The fix America is in reminds us of a scene in Orson Welles's 1958 film *Touch of Evil*, about murder, kidnapping, conspiracy, and corruption in a town on the Mexican-American border. Welles plays a crooked cop who tries to frame his Mexican counterpart for a murder. At one point, Welles stumbles into a brothel and finds the proprietor, Marlene Dietrich, who is also a fortune-teller, with cards spread out in front of her.

"Read my future for me," Welles says.

"You haven't got any," she replies. "Your future is all used up."

If we don't reshape our budgets properly, reducing our soaring deficits but also reinvesting in our formula for greatness, that will be us: a country with its future all used up.

The rest of this chapter is about how we got into this situation and how we get out of it—with a future.

Paint by Numbers

Beginning in the late 1960s, the United States got out of the habit of paying for what the federal government spends with money the government collected through taxes. Year after year, the government ran a deficit. As the annual deficits accumulated, the total national debt grew, although its proportion of the growing American economy did not increase rapidly. It stood at $5.6 trillion in 2001, but over the next nine years it increased dramatically. By 2011, it had reached $14 trillion—the equivalent of the country's GDP—with the prospect of increasing to $16 trillion by 2012 without countervailing steps.

"Total American general government debt today is at a phenomenal level," said Kenneth Rogoff, a professor of economics and public policy at Harvard University and formerly the chief economist at the International Monetary Fund. Rogoff is also the co-author with Carmen Reinhart of *This Time Is Different: Eight Centuries of Financial Folly*, which surveys the history of debt and financial crises. "By our benchmark," Rogoff added, "when you take local, state, and federal government debt together we are at our all-time high—above 119 percent of GDP. That is even higher than at the end of World War II, which is the only time before now that we have ever been that high . . . We are at the outer edge of the envelope of the last two hundred years of experience. We look at sixty-six countries in our book, going back over two hundred years, and find that debt levels over 120 percent of GDP are quite exceptional.

And soon it will get worse. The retirement of seventy-eight million baby boomers—Americans born between 1946 and 1964—will cause the costs of the two main entitlement programs, Social Security and Medicare, to skyrocket. Between 2010 and 2020 they are scheduled to rise by 70 and 79 percent, respectively. By 2050, paying for both, plus Medicaid, could take a full 18 percent of everything the United States produces in a year. The actual size of the gap between what the country is pledged to pay out to the boomers over the decades of their retirement and the amount of money the government can expect to collect at current tax rates is a matter of debate, but there is no doubt that that gap, if left untended, is very, very large. Estimates of the gap run as high as a staggering $50 trillion to $75 trillion. (Again, the total GDP of the United States in 2010 was about $14 trillion.)

That's a lot of money to borrow. To be sure, borrowing money, for an individual, a firm, or a country, is not always a mistake. Indeed, it is justified, even necessary, when the money borrowed is needed to cope with an emergency, such as the economic crisis of 2008. "In the midst of the global financial crisis," remarked Mohamed El-Erian, the co-CIO of PIMCO, a global investment management firm and one of the world's largest bond investors, "policymakers took the right decision in using public balance sheets to offset the massive disorderly de-leveraging of private balance sheets—those of banks, companies, and households. To use the phrase of my good friend Paul McCulley, the responsible thing was to be irresponsible." Borrowing money also makes sense to enhance a nation's long-term productive capacity because the debt can easily be paid back out of a growing income. A person is well advised to borrow to get an education, a firm to modernize its plant, a country to import cutting-edge technology.

The United States, however, has been borrowing not for investments of this kind and not only to cope with the economic crisis and fight wars but also for consumption. Borrowing money has made it possible for Americans to buy toys, cars, iPods, and vacations, which do nothing to make us better able in the future to pay off the debt the country is piling up. On the contrary, an out-of-control national debt poses serious threats to America's future. In the short term, the country's creditors may lose confidence in its ability, or at least its political will, to repay its debts, and that can lead to a vicious cycle, or feedback loop: a devalued currency spurs inflation, inflation leads to higher interest rates, and then come more devaluations, even higher inflation, and higher interest rates.

We like the way Robert Bennett, the former businessman who served three terms as a Republican senator from Utah before losing the Republican nomination to a Tea Party candidate in 2010, explains it. "If you are asking the wrong questions, the answers don't matter, and increasingly we are asking the wrong questions. There is really only one fundamental question: What is the borrowing power of the United States of America? When I took over the Franklin International Institute, to run it as a business, it had a debt of $75,000. When I stepped down as the CEO, it had a debt of $7.5 million. Well gee, I was a complete failure—except that they could not pay the debt of $75,000, and if the bank had called it, the company would have been shut down. And, when we had a debt of $7.5 million, we had over $8 million in cash in the bank; we had sales approaching $100 million and our pretax margin on those sales was 20 percent. So we were earning close to $20 million a year, and the only reason we didn't pay off the debt is that it had some prepayment penalties. So we clearly had substantially more borrowing power than $7.5 million. So it's the question of: What is the borrowing power of the United States? . . . Nobody can project it because the economy is constantly growing, constantly changing. But there is a feeling certainly in my gut and those of the economists whom I trust that we are approaching that limit. Now, once you go over that limit, wherever it is, you are Greece; you are Ireland; you are Zimbabwe. That's the great issue: How do we make sure that the U.S. government does not approach that unknown number?"

That is indeed the great issue right now, and there is a growing consensus that we are approaching that unknown number. As we do, we should heed Rogoff's advice: "When it comes to the question of how high is too high, nobody really knows. But complex arguments should not defeat common sense that you are taking a risk heading way further down this down road." Or as El-Erian put it: "It is no longer responsible to be irresponsible."

Common sense also says that the right strategy now is neither to slash all discretionary government spending suddenly nor to continue piling up debt to keep the economy stimulated, as if there are no implications for that down the road. The right strategy is to have a strategy—a strategy for long-term American growth and nation-building at home. That will require us to cut spending, to raise taxes, and to invest in the sources of our strength, all in a coordinated way.

But before we discuss that, let's step back for a moment and ask: How in the world did we get into this position?

Present at the Creation

From the end of World War II until Ronald Reagan's presidency, American budget history was pretty boring. The federal government ran manageable annual budget deficits and the economy steadily grew, so our debt-to-GDP ratio fell. Since the big change occurred during the Reagan presidency, we decided to ask someone who was present at the creation: David Stockman, the budget director during Reagan's first term and a sharp critic of recent American fiscal policy. Stockman argues that the ground was prepared for the budget-busting that started in the 1980s by an event that occurred four full decades ago.

On August 15, 1971, the U.S. government put an end to the international monetary system that the United States and Great Britain had devised at Bretton Woods, New Hampshire, in 1944. Under that system, the dollar was tied to the price of gold and international exchange rates were fixed, which imposed fiscal discipline on all participating countries, including the United States. The government couldn't print and spend money as much as its leaders wanted. "When we collapsed Bretton Woods," argues Stockman, "we took discipline out of the global economy. When the dollar was tied to fixed exchange rates, politicians were willing to administer the needed castor oil because the alternative was to make up for any trade shortfall by paying out our reserves, and this would cause immediate economic pain in the form of higher interest rates."

President Richard Nixon scrapped the Bretton Woods system in order to avoid putting the country through a recession to pay for all of the excess government spending going to fund the Vietnam War. As Stockman put it: Nixon, listening to famed University of Chicago economist Milton Friedman, said, Let's just let our currency and everyone else's float and the free market will find the right exchange rates among us all. If we run persistent deficits, our currency will lose value against those of countries that don't and that will quickly wipe out any trade deficits; the hidden hand of the market will ensure that currencies automatically adjust up or down, depending on how we each manage our economic fundamentals. The reality turned out to be more complicated, but it took a while to unfold.

Deficits ballooned during Reagan's first term, when tax cuts, skewed toward the wealthy, reduced the revenue base by a full 5 percent of GDP while the government continued domestic spending virtually unchecked. (It fell by barely 1 percent of GDP and was overwhelmed by the costs of the Reagan defense buildup.) This alarmed Reagan, who was part of the Greatest Generation and who was not at all a fan of deficits. So he enacted five different tax increases over the remainder of his time in office, which, according to Stockman, took back more than 40 percent of the original reductions. Reagan also led a reform of Social Security in 1983 to shore up the system.

Recall the words of former vice president Cheney, whom we quoted earlier: "Reagan proved deficits don't matter." Reagan not only did not prove that deficits don't matter; *he did not believe that deficits don't mat-*

ter. This is a fiction that would be manufactured later by a new generation of conservatives either out of ignorance or for their own selfish or ideological reasons.

"Ronald Reagan never called them taxes," recalled former senator Bennett, the Utah Republican. "They were 'revenue enhancements.' [Senator] Pete Domenici described it to me once: he said, 'We went down to the White House and said, "Mr. President, we can't survive on this level of revenue." And, Reagan said, "Okay, maybe we ought to have some 'revenue enhancements.'"' And so the gas tax went up, which it should have, and should be going up now."

Neither of the presidents who followed Reagan wanted to raise taxes, but to their credit, both decided to do so rather than go to war on math. President George H. W. Bush put his presidency in jeopardy to keep the deficit under control by breaking his famous promise: "Read my lips— no new taxes." Then our first baby boomer president, the Democrat Bill Clinton, made deficit reduction one of his top priorities as well—due, in part, to the strong showing in the 1992 presidential election of H. Ross Perot's third-party candidacy, which was dedicated to slashing the deficit above all else. In 1993 congressional Democrats enacted a deficit-reduction bill without a single Republican vote; Vice President Gore broke a tie on August 6, 1993, to pass the measure in the Senate. Four days later Clinton signed the Budget Reconciliation Act, which included about $240 billion in tax increases for high-income earners and $255 billion in spending cuts.

This is when Reagan's bad imitators began to make themselves felt in the Republican Party. In the wake of Clinton's 1993 budget, Representative Dick Armey, a Texas Republican, predicted that "the impact on job creation is going to be devastating." "The tax increase will lead to a recession and will actually increase the deficit," argued Newt Gingrich, a Republican congressman from Georgia. (In 1995 Armey and Gingrich became majority leader and Speaker, respectively, of the House of Representatives.) No such things happened. Instead, reinforced by the dot-com boom and the peace dividend, the Clinton deficit-reduction measures turned what was then the largest deficit in American history into a budget surplus and laid the foundation for several years of solid economic growth. America was projected to be "debt free" by . . . 2012.

Since the 1970s, actuaries had been issuing reports saying that, given the aging of the baby boomers, a fiscal crunch would occur in America sometime between 2010 and the 2020s. The Clinton administration's economic policies were designed in part to generate budget surpluses that could pay down the deficit before the baby boomers retired and began to draw on Social Security and Medicare. As a result, from 1993 to 2001 America's debt-to-GDP ratio went from 49 percent to 33 percent. Simply put, we cut our debt from half our annual output to a third. That used to be us.

Young Republicans

Then came the administration of George W. Bush. Alan Blinder, a Princeton economist and former vice chairman of the Federal Reserve, summed up what happened in a brief essay in *The Wall Street Journal* (December 17, 2010):

> The nation took leave of its fiscal senses, and simply stopped paying for anything during President Bush 43's eight years. Not for huge tax cuts—once again skewed toward the rich. Not for the Medicare drug benefit—which, in fairness, is skewed toward the poor. Not for two wars. That spree was followed by the financial crisis, the Great Recession, and the policy responses thereto—all of which blew up the deficit massively under President Obama.

This great loosening was brought about, in part, by a generational shift in the Republican Party. The old guard, the members of the World War II generation, which included Richard Nixon, Gerald Ford, George H. W. Bush, Bob Dole, George Shultz, and Ronald Reagan himself, believed in keeping the deficit under control—by raising taxes if necessary. They were succeeded by a new generation of Republicans, led by Newt Gingrich, Tom DeLay, Dick Armey, Dick Cheney, and George W. Bush. The new generation took as its hero an imaginary version of Reagan, one who, unlike the real fortieth president, believed that deficits don't matter and opposed raising any taxes at any time under any circumstances, especially for the wealthiest Americans.

As noted, Bush's first Treasury secretary, Paul O'Neill, was pushed out after resisting the administration's decision to enact a $350 billion tax cut in 2003, having enacted a $1.35 trillion tax cut just weeks after entering office in 2001—at a time when the budget was essentially in balance. "I believed we needed the money to facilitate fundamental tax reform and begin working on unfunded liabilities for Social Security and Medicare," O'Neill said in an interview with *The Washington Post* (May 1, 2011). The White House, he said, was focused on improving economic growth for the fourth quarter of 2004. "They wanted to make sure economic conditions were great going into the president's reelection."

Looking back on the whole period in an essay in *The New York Times* (July 31, 2010), David Stockman wrote:

> In 1981, traditional Republicans supported tax cuts, matched by spending cuts, to offset the way inflation was pushing many taxpayers into higher brackets and to spur investment . . . Through the 1984 election, the old guard earnestly tried to control the deficit, rolling back about 40 percent of the original Reagan tax cuts. But when, in the following years, the Federal Reserve chairman, Paul Volcker, finally crushed inflation, enabling a solid economic rebound, the new tax-cutters not only claimed victory for their supply-side strategy but hooked Republicans for good on the delusion that the economy will outgrow the deficit if plied with enough tax cuts.

As Stockman explained, this "new cadre of ideological tax-cutters" undermined the Republican Party's commitment to fiscal prudence and conservatism.

Republicans gone wild on tax cuts (which they justified by invoking an imaginary version of Reagan), combined with Democrats determined not to cut spending during the first decade of the twenty-first century, along with two wars and the costs of coping with the meltdown of the financial system and the Great Recession: all this created today's huge deficits and massive total debt.

But what happened to the discipline of Milton Friedman's free-currency markets? Why didn't these lead to a sharp devaluation of the dollar and force the White House and Congress to take the castor oil of tax increases and spending cuts? The reason, argued Stockman, was that a totally unanticipated development got in the way and made us think we were flying: We were able, too easily, to finance our growing budget deficits by borrowing from other countries. The biggest pusher for our debt habit turned out to be China, which proved willing to lend us money on a previously unimaginable scale through the purchase of U.S. Treasury bonds. The Chinese government was eager to do this because of its economic strategy of export-led development. To sustain the country's growth, which was necessary for the Communist Party to keep its grip on power in the country, China had to sustain and expand its exports in order to create jobs for more and more Chinese. That required keeping those exports affordable for the chief consumer of Chinese-made products, the United States. By buying American dollars, China kept the dollar strong in relation to the yuan, making it possible for American consumers to continue to buy Chinese products in ever larger quantities.

"What Milton Friedman had failed to anticipate," said Stockman, "was that there would never be a global free market in currencies—that countries such as Japan and China would manipulate their currencies to support their export growth models, and their export growth models turned out to support our consumption growth model." The result was a system that allowed the United States to overborrow from China and others and to overconsume, and this in turn allowed China and its neighbors to develop much more rapidly than they would have in the pre-1970 world by generating growth through massive exports, high savings, and low consumption.

"China and America entered into the perfect symbiotic relationship," said Stockman. "China needed somewhere safe to park its massive currency purchases and it put [those purchases] into our sovereign debt. We suddenly had someone who would buy our paper at a scale we never had before in history . . . We were like two drunks leaning on each other without a lamppost." America got to live beyond its means as a nation for twenty years and build up a combined shortfall in our trade in goods, services, and income of more than $7 trillion. Stockman describes this as "borrowed prosperity on an epic scale."

So when Vice President Cheney declared that "Reagan proved deficits don't matter," he was speaking economic "nonsense," said Stockman, "but he was making an empirically accurate observation. It was morally irresponsible, but empirically accurate. Thanks to China, what everyone feared about deficits was no longer true—you could have 'deficits without tears,' as a famous French economist said."

Of course, that is true only as long as China and others are ready to keep lending, which now seems to be coming into question—and not just for Chinese lenders but also for American ones. If, or rather when, that funding slows or stops, the party will end. And that stop could come very suddenly. At that point the United States will have three unhappy options: raise interest rates sharply to attract capital, thereby triggering an economic downturn; print money to cover the deficit, thereby triggering inflation; or close the gap with a combination of spending cuts and tax increases. Some combination of the three is perhaps the most likely outcome. None is cost-free: all will inflict economic pain on Americans.

The third option, reducing spending while raising taxes and reinvesting in our formula, is, for the sake of the country's long-term well-being, the only sensible option. Although we have passed the point at which we could correct our fiscal errors in a pain-free manner, the sooner we adopt the third option, the less economic pain we will have to suffer.

In the meantime, as one member of the president's deficit commission put it to us: We had better hope that China does not invade Taiwan. "We have a treaty that says we have to defend Taiwan in the event that it is attacked by China," he said. "The only problem is that we would now have to borrow the money from China to do it."

Hey, Big Spender

Unfortunately, the war on math was not confined to the federal government or the Republican Party. The Democrats waged a war on math of their own, particularly at the state and local levels. While Republicans were not innocent of this behavior, Democrats in particular fell into the habit of granting pay and pension increases to public-employee unions—police, firemen, teachers, and civil servants—which were based on wildly optimistic assumptions about future tax revenues and future market returns for pension funds. These estimates were often extrapolations from the fat years of the 1990s and early 2000s, when the peace dividend and dot-com and credit bubbles encouraged a kind of magical thinking about economic matters.

Not simply bad math but also politics were involved. Plenty of governors and mayors, many of them Democrats, entered into mutual back-scratching arrangements with state and local unions. They granted generous pay and pension increases to the unions, and the unions turned around and made generous campaign contributions to local and state politicians, and to the Democratic Party.

Unconstrained by market discipline, public employees' salaries, pensions, and health benefits got out of line with those of the private sector. So, too, did the numbers of employees, as politicians in flush times added political loyalists to the public payrolls. Illinois, New Jersey, New York, and California were the poster children for this phenomenon. The *Chicago Tribune* editorial page has made a practice of railing against such abuses in its state. Here is a tiny sampler:

> During the decade that ended in fiscal 2008, the Civic Federation says, pension pledges at 10 governmental bodies grew by 68.9 percent. In the same years, the funding of all these pension promises grew by only 26.4 percent . . . Did you know that Illinois police and firefighters can receive full pension—75 percent of pay—as early as age 50? (March 9, 2010)

> Citizens in Highland Park have done the right thing since this newspaper exposed what occurred in that northern suburb: Park commissioners awarded their executives fat pre-retirement raises and bonuses. Executive Director Ralph Volpe's salary was $164,204 in 2008, although the district paid him $435,203 that year. That spiked Volpe's pension by more than $50,000, to $166,332 a year. Since that disclosure, infuriated taxpayers have forced their commissioners who were on the Park Board at the time to resign. (September 19, 2010)

> Often when these retirement deals were cut, the public officials and the union leaders were, in effect, seated on the same side of

the negotiating table holding hands. The politicians essentially pledged future tax dollars in return for the cooperation of public sector unions . . . The Republicans and Democrats who cut these deals were playing with other people's money. The pols knew they were creating somebody else's problem. When the devastating costs came due, they would be gone, out of office, retired. (November 28, 2010)

The Wall Street Journal reported (October 15, 2010) that, at a time when other traditional Democratic donors were limiting their campaign contributions,

> public-sector unions have remained a bulwark for Democrats this fall . . . according to a *Wall Street Journal* analysis of Federal Election Commission data. Unions have long bankrolled Democratic campaigns, but some of the biggest public unions are spending more this fall than they did during the prior midterm-campaign cycle in 2006. The National Education Association, the largest U.S. teachers union, has independently spent more than $3.4 million that must be disclosed, including ad buys and direct-mail campaigns, for the key electioneering period from September 1 to October 14. The NEA spent $444,000 during the same stretch in 2006. The American Federation of State, County and Municipal Employees has nearly matched its 2006 midterm outlays. It has spent $2.1 million on electioneering since the beginning of last month, according to FEC filings for two campaign committees associated with the union. That is just shy of the $2.2 million spent for that period in 2006.

This explains why the Republican governors of Wisconsin and Ohio moved to curb collective-bargaining rights by their state public-employee unions early in 2011. They could achieve two goals at once: save money and hurt one of the Democratic Party's key funding sources.

As at the federal level, spending patterns for state and local governments will have to change. John Hood, the president of the John Locke Foundation, a state-policy think tank based in North Carolina, explained it this way in a report he wrote about on this issue, *The States in Crisis*:

"When tax revenues declined precipitously as a result of the 2008 financial crisis, state officials' optimistic budgeting crashed into cold, hard reality." The gaps between promised salaries, pensions, and services and tax revenues are now very large indeed. "State tax revenues," notes Hood, "were 8.4 percent lower in 2009 than in 2008, and a further 3.1 percent lower in 2010." States such as California, Texas, New Jersey, and Illinois face the prospect of huge deficits, amounting to 25 percent and more of their entire budgets, in the immediate future.

At the heart of the states' fiscal problems, explains Hood,

> lies the fact that government pension plans do not function the way most private retirement plans do. Americans with jobs in the private sector are likely most familiar with "defined contribution" retirement programs—like 401(k) accounts—which involve a set contribution (generally some percentage of one's pay). This contribution, made over the course of a person's working years, is channeled into a savings account that accrues interest; upon retirement, that account begins to pay out benefits . . . Such a retirement plan cannot be underfunded, since it pays out in benefits only what one contributes over the course of one's working life. Most government pension plans, by contrast, are "defined benefit" programs. These plans, as the name suggests, guarantee a particular annual benefit to each retiree (generally based on the income he earned while he was working, the number of years he worked, and some cost-of-living adjustment). Instead of disbursing payments based on the amount of money collected over time in a savings account, defined-benefit programs work backwards: They first determine the benefits they will provide, and then try to calculate how to collect enough money to meet those obligations.

The accuracy of the calculation depends on the accuracy of the predictions about how well the stock or bond market will do over time. "If a defined-benefit plan promises excessively generous payouts, or fails to collect enough money to meet its financial pledges to retirees," said Hood, "the result will be a massive accumulation of debt as large numbers of workers begin to retire."

According to a recent report from the Pew Center on the States, which Hood cited, state governments

> face an unfunded liability of $1 trillion for retirement benefits promised to public employees. This figure, which remains the most accurate available assessment of the problem, is based on FY 2008 data—that is, *before* the financial markets and economy really tanked. More recent estimates, calculated by North-western University economist Joshua Rauh and his colleagues, have suggested a figure closer to $3 trillion in unfunded state liabilities (the shortfall in city pensions totaled an additional $574 billion).

To be sure, there are many reasons states and cities find themselves in fiscal crises these days—not just overspending and under-taxing in good times but also runaway health-care costs from federal mandates that the states cannot finance anymore—but there is no question that the overly generous contracts of public-service workers in the last decade belong on that list. Union members in the private sector know that their employers can go broke at any time, which does temper their demands. Public-sector union workers, by contrast, work for city and state monopolies that can never go out of business, and the workers get to play a role in electing the officials who can grant them increases in pay and benefits. To their credit, many public-service employees have been willing to absorb cutbacks as long as the sacrifice has been shared.

In sum, national, state, and local economic and fiscal policies over the last two decades added up to a bipartisan flight from prudence, common sense, and reality that has created an enormous challenge for the United States. If you were a trustee running a private pension fund and you had made the assumptions that state and local Democrats made—about the returns their investments would yield forever—you would have been fired by now. If you were a trustee running a private pension fund and had made the assumptions that national Republicans made—that deficits don't matter if they are the result of tax cuts—you would have been institutionalized by now.

Unfortunately, people holding those views have dominated American political life for at least the last twenty years, one offering an economics based on wishful math, the other an economics based on no math at all. Now the only solution to the problem they jointly created is a prolonged and far from painless period of adjustment to reality.

"When you look at the data on things like spending and deficits and the debt-ceiling limit, you will see that starting in the 1980s we lost our way," said David Walker, the former U.S. comptroller general, a debt expert, and the author of *Comeback America: Turning the Country Around and Restoring Fiscal Responsibility.* "Then we temporarily regained our senses starting in the early 1990s under President Bush 41 and again under President Clinton." These two presidents, one a Republican and one a Democrat, added Walker, did three things in common: "One, they supported the imposition of tough statutory budget controls that kept government from making more promises, when it had already made more promises than it could keep; in addition, they each imposed tough but realistic discretionary spending caps that included defense and security spending. Two, they did not expand entitlement programs, which is arguably the most imprudent thing you can do." And third, Walker added, both Bush 41 and Clinton "broke campaign promises in connection with taxes when they saw the reality of our fiscal situation. So we had one Republican and one Democrat who each batted a thousand. Then Bush 43 came along and totally struck out." President George W. Bush, noted Walker, let the statutory budget controls expire at the end of 2002, he expanded entitlements—with Medicare prescription drugs—"and he never broke his campaign promise to cut taxes. Obama so far is the same thing, but he can still change course."

One way or another, we are all going to have to pay for this. The only questions left are these, framed by the *Washington Post* business columnist Steven Pearlstein (February 22, 2011):

> Will the pain come in the form of prolonged high unemployment? Or wage and salary cuts? Or reduction in the value of homes and financial assets? Or loss of ownership of American companies? Or price inflation? Or higher taxes? Or reductions in government services and benefits? The right answer, of course, is "all of the above." The hole we dug for ourselves was so deep and so wide that we'll need all of them to get us out of it. The central political, economic and social challenge of the

next decade will be to decide how we are going to apportion the adjustment among these various channels, and among the various classes and sectors and regions of the country, without tanking the economy or breaking the bonds that hold our society and our democracy together.

The Return of Gravity

For the sixty years after World War II, to be a mayor, governor, college president, or president of the United States involved, on most days and in most ways, giving things to people. For the next decade at least, to be a mayor, governor, college president, or president of the United States will mean, on more days and in more ways, taking things away from people. As our leaders move from distributing generosity to apportioning sacrifice and deciding how much to take away from whom, we have to be much smarter than we have been recently. We have to cut, tax, and invest in ways that will both get our fiscal house in order and reinvest in the elements of our formula for success. Nations that don't invest in their future tend not to do well there.

That means that every mayor, governor, and member of Congress, not to mention every president we elect, must be guided by this truth: If we keep spending as we have in the past, we are mortgaging—indeed sabotaging—our nation's future. But if we don't spend on the right things, something we have generally done since the nineteenth century, we are just as surely mortgaging, and sabotaging, our future. We can no longer avoid making choices. The future depends not only on keeping markets from crushing us but also on upgrading all the pillars of our formula for success. We not only have to get well as a country; we have to get strong again.

Jack Markell, the governor of Delaware, explained to us that he now confronts this challenge every day. "Governing is twice as hard as it used to be," he said. In the past, "a forward-thinking governor could advance his or her agenda by taking the incremental revenues generated by a growing economy and then have just one fight with the legislature: over where you spend the additional money." That was because, for most states most of the time—save for a few periods of recession over the last sixty years—governors had steadily rising tax revenues at their disposal. That era has ended. "Now you have to have two fights with the legislature," explained Markell. "First you have to fight over where the cuts get made and then, once you have freed up the resources, you have to fight over where you spend the money. So governing is twice as hard as it used to be."

And it is going to get even harder.

In 2010, America was still reeling from the Great Recession and it was unrealistic to expect we would have the budget fight then that we need to have. In early 2011, the struggle got under way in earnest with the bitter wrangle over government funding for the remainder of the fiscal year ending September 30. The government was nearly shut down over whether or not to cut an additional $40 billion from President Obama's budget. That event marked the beginning of what will be a protracted, difficult, and surely bitter political process to correct the country's dangerous fiscal course. For that inevitable process, which will surely involve heated and complicated horse-trading before it is completed, we offer four guidelines for America to follow.

The first guideline is the need for seriousness. We face a huge budgetary problem—the product of three decades of gross irresponsibility. Rhetoric, posturing, marginal changes, future targets—none of these will solve this problem. Anyone who proposes solutions that are not at the scale of the problem and don't require immediate actions is not being serious.

The second guideline involves the purpose of the exercise. It is not simply to reduce the deficit but to ensure prosperity. Solvency is vital, but it is not enough. To uphold American greatness the country will have to do more than get its debt-to-GDP ratio to a reasonable and sustainable level, although it will certainly have to do that. It will also have to equip its people with the skills and the tools that have always been part of our formula for economic growth. Providing them will cost money and require new long-term investments. To assure the nation's economic future we will have to spend more, not less, on some things: certainly infrastructure and research and development, and probably education as well. This will be especially difficult to accomplish at a time when valued programs are shrinking and taxes are rising; but if we do not invest in upgrading our formula, we will forfeit the indispensable condition for sustaining the American dream and maintaining American power in the world: economic growth. Anyone who says we can forgo spending of this kind does not understand either American history or the world in which we are now living.

The third guideline is that the cuts have to take place across the board. One thing we must not do is try to bring the budget back toward balance by making most, let alone all, of the spending cuts in "nonsecurity discretionary spending"—the 12 percent of the budget that does not include Social Security, Medicare, Medicaid, defense, and interest on the national debt. That is the part of the budget where all the education, innovation, and infrastructure programs, essential to our formula for prosperity, reside. To destroy them to save money would be akin to trying to lose weight by cutting off two of your fingers. You won't lose much weight, but you will be forever handicapped in securing and keeping a good job.

That means that reductions in entitlement programs such as Social Security and Medicare are inevitable, as are measures to slow the rate of increase in general health-care costs. Everything has to be on the table, and everything is going to get cut one way or another. Anyone who says that these programs can continue exactly as they are is not being serious. Reform will likely require some form of means-testing Medicare and Social Security benefits; pushing back the retirement ages for Social Security and adjusting the cost of living index; and, most important, finding ways to slow the growth in the costs of Medicare, which covers health insurance for all those over sixty-five, as well as Medicaid and the Children's Health Insurance Program to support the poor. In the 1950s, health-care spending accounted for 4 percent of GDP. Today it is around 17 percent and heading for 30 percent by 2030, but without better outcomes than in countries such as Canada, which spends only 10 percent of its GDP on health care. More than 20 percent of all Medicare spending occurs in the last two months of life, and 30 percent in the last year, using the remarkable new technologies we have invented.

According to CBS's *60 Minutes* (August 8, 2010), in 2009 "Medicare paid $55 billion just for doctor and hospital bills during the last two months of patients' lives. That's more than the budget for the Department of Homeland Security, or the Department of Education. And it has been estimated that 20 to 30 percent of these medical expenses may have had no meaningful impact. Most of the bills are paid for by the federal government with few or no questions asked." Indeed, Medicare is barred by law from rejecting any treatment based on cost. As people live longer and more expensive technology and drugs become available to prolong their lives, the combination becomes a prescription for bankrupting the country—unless we slow down the growth in health spending across the board. This will require some implicit rationing of the end-of-life care for which the government will pay.

"We need a budget for how much we can afford to spend on Medicare," said David Walker. "We cannot keep writing a blank check. Right now Medicare has no budget. We are the only major industrialized nation that does not have a budget for how much public resources are allocated for health care. We are the only country that is dumb enough to write a blank check for health care. Everybody else knows that it can bankrupt you." The United States today, he argues, has first to decide how much it can afford to allocate on government-supported health-care programs—primarily Medicare and Medicaid. Once we have determined the basic health-care budget we can afford, we have to decide how to allocate it. That is, said Walker, "we have to decide what level of universal health care is appropriate, affordable, and sustainable based on society's needs and individual wants." We have promised people a level of health care that we cannot sustain.

As we decide what is affordable and sustainable, particularly care in the last year of people's lives, decisions will have to be evidence based. "If a medical intervention is going to meaningfully improve or extend life, it should be done," argues Walker. "If it is not going to meaningfully improve or extend life, then it should not be done." Today, added Walker, "a lot of it does not pass this test. In fact, some of these high-tech interventions are not even in the patient's interest." Individuals and employers ought to be able to spend as much of their own money as they want for medical care right up to the end of their lives, concluded Walker, "but when you're talking about taxpayer resources, there's a limit to how much resources we have."

As part of controlling health spending, we will have to move to a system whereby hospitals and doctors are reimbursed for proven quality and cost-effective services, rather than for procedures alone. This will require a uniform system of health-care information whereby consumers will be able to access a hospital's or individual doctor's performance records and prices for different procedures. If I am having a kidney re-

moved, I want to go to the doctor with the best record at the best price—
on the basis of criteria established by an independent medical board.
Doctors and hospitals who will not participate will not get reimburse-
ment from government programs or private insurers. Consumers also
must be exposed to the true costs of their health care, and the differences
in quality, so they have incentives to get the best care for the best price.
Currently, the vast majority of health-care bills are paid to the provider
by the government or private insurance companies on the basis of procedures alone ("Here is how much you get for a colonoscopy"), without
reference to outcomes. And most patients never look at a medical bill
showing the costs of care. It is hard to bring prices down when you can't
shop.

Moreover, we are all going to have to take better care of ourselves.
So much of America's health-care spending goes to preventable chronic
illnesses, such as diabetes and complications from obesity—which the
health-care industry then creates all sorts of expensive technologies to
mitigate. We simply can't afford to have so many overweight people, and
we certainly can't afford to have roughly 40 million Americans still
smoking, which, according to the Centers for Disease Control and Prevention, still causes at least 30 percent of cancer deaths and 80 percent
of lung cancer deaths.

In the cuts in spending that America will have to make, foreign
policy cannot be exempt. Defense spending is invariably among the biggest items in the federal budget, and it, too, will have to be reduced. We
favor retaining the American military and political roles in Europe, East
Asia, and the Middle East, which are crucial for the stability and prosperity of those regions. But America will have to find ways to do these
things at a lower cost than in the past.

As Michael argued in his 2010 book, *The Frugal Superpower:
America's Global Leadership in a Cash-Strapped Era*, the country can
no longer afford the kind of military intervention that became common
in the post–Cold War era. In that period the United States has conducted military operations in Somalia, Haiti, Bosnia, Kosovo, Afghanistan, Iraq, and Libya—and sent troops to all except the last country. The
dispatch of troops involved America in the unexpected, unwanted, protracted, difficult, frustrating, expensive, and seldom entirely successful
task of nation-building: that is, building the institutions of government

where they have collapsed, or never existed at all. Whatever the intrinsic value of these interventions, they have become too expensive. We need the resources they consume to reduce our deficits and to upgrade our formula for prosperity. We need these resources, in other words, for nation-building in America.

The fourth guideline is that we cannot simply cut our way to fiscal sanity. We also will have to raise revenue through taxation—and as many Americans as possible have to contribute something. While the best-off among us ought to contribute proportionally more than the least afflu-ent, no one can be entirely exempt. No segment of the Greatest Gener-ation opted out of World War II or the Cold War, and no part of the baby boom generation—ultrarich, upper class, middle class, lower class, retir-ees—can be excused from the task the nation confronts. As a society, we need to pick some functional level of poverty, and every American above that level should contribute something by way of income taxes. Some combination of tax reform that includes the closing of loopholes, taxing energy, eliminating farm subsidies, and raising marginal rates for the wealthy—and for the middle class as well—will be needed. Anyone who says that we can restore order to our nation's finances today without rais-ing taxes is not being serious.

In the end, both parties are going to have to give up on their ideolo-gies and accept a blended arrangement of across-the-board cuts in entitle-ments, defense, and discretionary programs, along with across-the-society tax increases and the closing of tax loopholes, plus some targeted invest-ments. The proposal by the 2010 bipartisan National Commission on Fiscal Responsibility and Reform, chaired by Alan Simpson and Erskine Bowles, is the kind of framework that is required. Unfortunately Ameri-can politics in the second decade of the twenty-first century do not lend themselves to such a national effort.

"It has been so long since the two parties have worked together to take things away from people," David Stockman observed, that "they are out of shape."

We had better get into shape. Reducing the deficit is not just an ac-counting issue or a food fight among policy wonks. It is the baby boomers' Greatest Generation moment. The future of the country is in our hands, as it was for the GIs on the beaches of Normandy. We have to do something hard, we have to do it now, and we can only do it together.

Atlanta's mayor, Kasim Reed, understands what we have to do because he starred in the off-Broadway mini-version of this play in his own city. A former Georgia state senator, Reed won Atlanta's mayoral race in December 2009 by 714 votes. The day he took office, Atlanta had only $7.4 million in reserves and an out-of-control budget, and was laying off so many firefighters there were often only three firemen on a truck, which is below national standards. Reed started his reforms by enlisting two professionals, not cronies, to help run the city: Peter Aman, a partner at the consulting firm Bain & Company, to be his chief operating officer; and John Mellott, the former publisher of *The Atlanta Journal-Constitution*, to lead a pension-review panel. To end the war on math in Atlanta politics, Reed had to bring in outsiders whose assessment of exactly where the city stood financially was unimpeachable. When he took over the mayor's chair in early 2010, runaway city pensions—which had increased by 30 percent in the early 2000s and been made retroactive for all city police, fire, and municipal union workers—were eating up 20 percent of tax revenues, and rising. So between 2001 and 2009, Atlanta's unfunded defined-pension obligation grew from $321 million to $1.484 billion. Reed couldn't cut existing pensions without lawsuits, but he reduced pensions for all new employees to pre-2000 levels and raised the vesting period from ten to fifteen years. When union members picketed city hall, Reed invited them all into his office—in shifts—and patiently explained, with charts and spreadsheets, that without pension reform everyone's pensions would eventually go bust. By getting the city's budget under control, Reed then had some money to invest in more police and, what he wanted most, to reopen the sixteen recreation centers and swimming pools in the city's most disadvantaged neighborhoods, which had been shuttered for lack of funds. "People were shooting dice in the empty pools," he said. Local businesses have since funded some after-school job-skills programs in the reopened centers.

Cutting some programs, raising some taxes, and increasing some necessary investments—that will be the essence of American politics as we try to overcome our dalliance with the notion that math doesn't matter. Here we are in total agreement with Erskine Bowles, who said that the biggest lesson he drew from co-chairing the president's commission with Alan Simpson was this: "When we started out on this project, we said, 'We're doing this for our grandchildren.' Then we said, 'We're doing this for our children.' Now we realize that this is for us."

He is absolutely right. This is our job. This is our mess. It cannot wait. We made it. We need to fix it in our time, at our expense—but with an eye on the future, not just the present. What is at stake here is nothing less than whether or not we're going to give the next generation a chance at the American dream.

TEN

The War on Physics and Other Good Things

Virtually all of America's energy and climate challenges today can be traced back to one pivotal year and the way life imitated one dramatic film.

The year was 1979, and the film was *The China Syndrome*.

Set in California's fictional Ventana nuclear plant, *The China Syndrome* stars Jane Fonda as a television reporter, Michael Douglas as her cameraman, and Daniel Valdez as her soundman. The movie opens with the three of them being escorted to the observation room at the nuclear reactor to do a feature story on its operations for a local TV station. The room has large soundproof windows that overlook the control room below. Douglas is told not to film but surreptitiously does so anyway. Suddenly there is a panic in the control room. A close-up of a watercooler shows bubbles floating to the top. There is a vibration. "What the hell is that?" asks the shift supervisor, played by Jack Lemmon. An alarm sounds. He taps a gauge, which quickly changes to show the level of coolant to be low. "We have a serious condition!" he says. The panicked staff watches the gauge, as it appears that the reactor core could be exposed. Eventually the coolant levels return to normal and everyone breathes a sigh of relief. In an editing room back at the TV station, Douglas shows his footage to his colleagues. His producer refuses to air it for fear of a lawsuit.

Leaving the station after the evening news, Fonda is told that Douglas has absconded with the film and that she has to get it back. She finds Douglas in a screening room showing the film to a physics professor and a nuclear engineer. The engineer says that it looks as if the reactor's core indeed may have come close to exposure. The professor says that that could have led to the "China Syndrome." "If the nuclear core is exposed," he says, "the fuel heats up and nothing can stop it. It will melt through the bottom of the plant, theoretically to China. As soon as it hits groundwater, it blasts into the atmosphere and sends out clouds of radioactivity. The number of people killed would depend on which way the wind is blowing."

The professor then adds ominously, "This would render an area the size of Pennsylvania uninhabitable."

In the film's final scenes, Fonda, Douglas, and Lemmon commandeer the control room, locking it from the inside, and begin to broadcast an exposé of the plant's dangers. Security guards break in and gun down Lemmon. Suddenly the room begins to shake violently. Part of the cooling system begins to crack apart, but the reactor holds. The movie ends with Fonda on live television saying, "I'm convinced that what happened tonight was not the actions of a drunk or a crazy man. Jack Godell [Lemmon] was about to present evidence that he believed would show this plant should be shut down."

Films often express our unspoken fears. *The China Syndrome* first appeared in U.S. movie theaters on March 16, 1979. Just twelve days later, on March 28, 1979, the worst nuclear accident in American history took place at Metropolitan Edison's nuclear power plant—Three Mile Island Unit 2—outside Harrisburg, Pennsylvania.

An incorrect reading of equipment at Three Mile Island made the control operators overestimate the amount of coolant covering the plant's nuclear core. In fact, the coolant was low, leaving half of the reactor's core exposed. One report estimated that roughly one-third of the core may have reached temperatures as high as 5200 degrees Fahrenheit. Had the situation not been brought under control, the melting fuel core could have cracked open the reactor vessel and containment walls, leading to the China Syndrome. Radiation would have spewed out into the air, and would have done exactly what that professor in the movie warned of—"render an area the size of the state of Pennsylvania permanently uninhabitable."

As in the movie, Three Mile Island ended without a single person being killed or seriously injured. The releases of radioactive gas and water were inconsequential, and there has been no unusual incidence of cancer or other diseases for neighborhood residents since then. Three Mile Island's long-term impact on America's economic, geopolitical, and environmental health, however, was radioactive in the extreme.

The coincidence of the movie *The China Syndrome* and the real-life Three Mile Island—and, most important, the steadily soaring costs and legal liabilities of building nuclear power plants that hit in the 1980s—gradually combined to bring a halt to the construction of any new commercial nuclear facilities in America. Unlike solar or wind power or batteries, which get cheaper with each new generation of technology, nuclear power plants have gotten more and more expensive to build. A one-gigawatt nuclear power plant today costs roughly $10 billion to construct and could take six to eight years from start to finish. So what began with fears of runaway reactors and morphed into fears of runaway construction budgets has resulted in this stark fact: It has been more than thirty years since the Nuclear Regulatory Commission has approved construction of a new commercial nuclear power plant in America. The last new nuclear power plant to be completed in America was in 1996—the Watts Bar Nuclear Plant in Tennessee. That plant was approved in 1977.

At the time America abandoned nuclear energy, though, we actually led the world in generating electricity from carbon-free power. Our existing nuclear fleet of 104 reactors now has an average age of thirty years. Just to maintain the current contribution that nuclear power makes to America's total output of electricity—about 20 percent of national usage—we will need to rebuild or modernize virtually our entire fleet over the next decade. The earthquake and tsunami-triggered Japanese nuclear disaster at the Fukushima Daiichi Nuclear Power Plant in March 2011—which led to a release of radiation in both the air and water—makes a renewed emphasis on nuclear power in America politically difficult at best and impossible at worst. Because we have not increased the nuclear component of our energy mix for more than thirty years, as our total energy demand grew we came to rely all the more heavily on fossil fuels—coal, crude oil, and natural gas.

The year 1979 proved crucial for energy and the environment for other reasons as well. The cost of oil skyrocketed that year as did oil's toxic geopolitical consequences. The sequence of events began in January 1979, with the overthrow of the shah of Iran and the subsequent takeover in Tehran by Ayatollah Khomeini and his followers. Months later, on November 20, 1979, the Grand Mosque in Mecca, Saudi Arabia, was seized by violent Sunni Muslim extremists, who challenged the religious credentials of the Saudi ruling family. After retaking the mosque, the panicked Saudi rulers responded by forging a new bargain with their own Muslim fundamentalists, which went like this: "Let us stay in power and we will give you a free hand in setting social norms, veiling women, curtailing music, restricting relations between the sexes, and imposing religious education. We will go even further and lavish abundant resources on you to spread the austere Sunni Salafi/Wahhabi form of fundamentalism abroad." This set up a competition between Shiite Iran and Sunni Saudi Arabia to be the leader of the Muslim world, each exporting its puritanical version of Islam. In 1979, "Islam lost its brakes," said Mamoun Fandy, an Egyptian expert on the Middle East. Mosques and schools all over the Muslim world tilted toward more fundamentalist interpretations of the faith. There was no moderate counter-trend, or at least none backed by resources remotely comparable to those of Iran and Saudi Arabia.

As if that weren't enough for one year, the Soviet Union invaded Afghanistan on December 24, 1979. In response, Arab and Muslim mujahideen fighters flocked there to drive the Russians out, a jihad financed by Saudi Arabia at America's behest. In the process, both Pakistan and Afghanistan moved toward a more austere Islamist political orientation. Eventually, the hard-core Muslim fighters in Afghanistan, led by the likes of Osama bin Laden, turned their guns on America and its Arab allies, culminating on September 11, 2001.

Gone were the harmless good old days when our foreign gasoline purchases merely bought villas and yachts on the Riviera for Saudi princes, not to mention gambling sprees in London and Monte Carlo. After the assault on Mecca and the Iranian revolution, our oil addiction started funding madrassas in Pakistan, fundamentalist mosques in Afghanistan and Europe, and Stinger missiles for the Taliban, all of which came back to haunt America in subsequent years. In other words, before 1979 our oil addiction was esthetically distasteful; after 1979 it became geopolitically lethal. We were funding both sides of the war with radical Islam—simultaneously paying for our own military with our tax dollars and indirectly supporting our enemies and their jihadist ideology with our oil dollars.

Hard to believe, but 1979 was just getting started. The energy world would be substantially affected by two other political events of that year. Margaret Thatcher was elected prime minister of Great Britain on May 4, 1979. She and Ronald Reagan, who took office as president of the United States in 1981, implemented free-market-friendly economic policies that helped to pave the way for the expansion of globalization after the fall of the Berlin Wall. This increased economic activity the world over, massively increasing the number of people who could afford cars, motor scooters, electric appliances, and international travel.

Less noticed but just as important, in 1979, three years after Mao Tse-tung's death, China's communist government permitted small farmers to raise their own crops on individual plots and to sell the surplus for their own profit. The agricultural reforms had started in the countryside in 1978, but in 1979 capitalism broke out from China's rural farms into the broader Chinese economy.

In 1979, "the first business license in China was given to Zhang Huamei, a nineteen-year-old daughter of workers in a state umbrella factory who illegally sold trinkets from a table [but] who wanted to conduct her business legally," according to a historical reconstruction of this era published in *The Times* of London (December 5, 2009). *The Times* noted that Zhang is now a dollar millionaire and head of the Huamei Garment Accessory Company, a supplier of many of the world's buttons. Of her initial sale she said, "The first thing I sold was a toy watch. It was a sunny morning in May 1978. I bought it for 0.15 yuan and sold it for .20. I was very, very excited to make a profit. But I was also very nervous and very afraid the local government staff would come to stop it." When the government granted her a business license in 1979, the shift of 1.3 billion people from communism to capitalism was on its way. That shift, which produced, among many other things, the conference center in Tianjin with which we began this book, has dramatically increased both global energy demand and the amount of greenhouse gases being pumped into the atmosphere. On January 7, 2010, China's *People's Daily* reported that "a total 16.7 million vehicles were sold in China last year, bringing the country's total vehicles to more than 186 million," about half of which are motorcycles. In 1979 virtually no Chinese owned a private car.

One final notable event occurred in 1979. It drew almost no attention. America's National Academy of Sciences raised its first warning about something called "global warming." In a 1979 study, called *The Charney Report*, the academy stated that "if carbon dioxide continues to increase, [we find] no reason to doubt that climate changes will result and no reason to believe that these changes will be negligible."

Put all these events together and it becomes clear why 1979 was pivotal in creating today's energy and climate challenge. The details of that challenge are complicated, and we will discuss some of them in the rest of this chapter. But the key to meeting it is straightforward. The United States must reduce its use of fossil fuels as fast and as far as is prudently possible. We have not begun to do this. All of us are ducking the challenge and some of us are denying that it even exists. This failure could not be more dangerous to our country and our planet, because matters of energy and climate touch on every big issue in American life. That is why we include them as one of the four great challenges the country faces. How we address, or do not address, our energy and climate challenge will affect our economic vitality, our national security, our food supply, and our capacity to benefit from what will be among the biggest industries of the future. Energy policy affects our balance of payments and the value of our currency. It affects the quality of the air we breathe and the level of the oceans on our shores. America will not thrive in the twenty-first century without a different energy policy, one better adapted than the policy we have now to the realities of the flatter world in which we live.

Unfortunately, instead of debating *how* to generate more clean energy and to slow climate change, we are debating *whether* to do so. Instead of debating the implications of what is settled science, we are debating the integrity of some scientists. Instead of ending an oil addiction we know is unhealthy for our economy, our air, and our national security, we are begging our pushers for just one more hit from the crude-oil pipe.

While there is much that we don't know about when and how global warming will affect the climate, and what that will do to weather patterns, to call the whole phenomenon a hoax, to imply that we face no problem at all—that all the scientific evidence for its existence is bogus—is to deny the laws of physics. And while there is also much we do not know about when the earth's supplies of oil, natural gas, and coal will be exhausted, to behave as if we can consume all we want forever without staggering financial, environmental, and geopolitical consequences is to deny not only the laws of physics but those of math and economics and geopolitics as well.

Finally, to do all this at once is to mock the market and Mother Nature at the same time. It is to invite each of them to respond violently, suddenly, and at a time of its own choosing.

Honk If You Believe in Climate Change

In February 2010, after a particularly heavy snowfall in Washington, D.C., Oklahoma Republican senator James Inhofe's daughter, Molly Rapert, her husband, and their four children built an igloo on the Mall near the Capitol in Washington. On one side they stuck a sign that said AL GORE'S NEW HOME. On the other they put one that read HONK IF YOU ♥ GLOBAL WARMING.

We would not have honked.

And neither would 99 percent of the scientists who have studied the problem. This is actually not complicated. We know that global warming is real because it's what makes life on Earth possible. About this there is no dispute. We have our little planet Earth. It is enveloped in a blanket of naturally occurring greenhouse gases that trap heat and warm the Earth's surface. Without those gases, our planet's average temperature would be roughly zero degrees Fahrenheit. About that there is no dispute.

We also know that this concentration of greenhouse gases in the Earth's atmosphere has been increasing since the Industrial Revolution, because we can actually measure levels of carbon dioxide in the atmosphere. There is no other scientifically plausible explanation for the increase in greenhouse gases than the increased burning of fossil fuels— coal, oil, and natural gas—that began with the Industrial Revolution and surged in the last three decades with the latest stage of globalization. When the Industrial Revolution began, the concentration of carbon dioxide (CO_2) in the Earth's atmosphere was roughly 280 parts per million by volume. By 2011 it was 390 parts per million. About that there is also no dispute.

This naturally had an effect on global average temperatures, which, again, we can measure. As we thickened the blanket of greenhouse gases around the Earth, it trapped more of the sun's rays and the heat that they generated. As the Earth Policy Institute, a nonpartisan research center dedicated to tracking climate change, notes in its report for 2010:

> The earth's temperature is not only rising, it is rising at an increasing rate. From 1880 through 1970, the global average temperature increased roughly 0.03 degrees Celsius each decade. Since 1970, that pace has increased dramatically, to 0.13 degrees Celsius per decade. Two thirds of the increase of nearly 0.8 degrees Celsius (1.4 degrees Fahrenheit) in the global temperature since the 1880s has occurred in the last forty years. And nine of the ten warmest years happened in the last decade.

The EPI report explains that global average temperature is influenced—up and down—by a number of factors besides carbon emissions, including various naturally occurring cycles involving the sun and atmospheric winds. But the current natural cycles should be causing global average temperatures *to go down, not up.* The recorded rise in global temperatures is therefore doubly worrying.

The EPI report concludes as follows: "Topping off the warmest decade in history, 2010 experienced a global average temperature of 14.63 degrees Celsius (58.3 degrees Fahrenheit), tying 2005 as the hottest year in 131 years of recordkeeping." In addition, "while 19 countries recorded record highs in 2010, not one witnessed a record low temperature . . . Over the last decade, record highs in the United States were more than twice as common as record lows, whereas half a century ago there was a roughly equal probability of experiencing either of these."

As the Earth's greenhouse blanket traps more heat and raises global average temperatures, it melts more ice. According to the EPI, 87 percent of marine glaciers on the Antarctic Peninsula have retreated since the 1940s. There is enough water frozen in Greenland and Antarctica to raise global sea levels by more than 230 feet if they were to melt entirely.

These are facts about which there can be no dispute. They all can be measured.

While no single weather event can be attributed directly to climate change, the large number of extreme weather events of 2010 are all characteristic of what scientists expect from a steadily warming climate. Climate change, they argue, will make the wets wetter, the snows heavier, and the dries drier, because warmer air holds more water vapor and that extra moisture leads to heavier storms in some areas and even less rainfall in others. The record events in 2010 included floods in Australia and Pakistan, a heat wave in Russia that claimed thousands of lives, unprecedented forest fires in Israel, landslides in China, record snowfall across the mid-Atlantic region of the United States, and twelve Atlantic Ocean hurricanes. That is why we believe the term "global weirding," coined by L. Hunter Lovins, a co-founder of the Rocky Mountain Institute, is a more accurate way to describe the climate system into which the world is moving than is "global warming." Global warming . . . It sounds so cuddly. It will be anything but that.

Beyond these well-established core facts lie many uncertainties. We do not know how hot the world will become or how rapidly it will warm. This is so not only because we cannot forecast precisely how much greenhouse gas the planet's 6.8 billion humans will produce but also because, as many climate scientists believe, the Earth's temperature may well rise at a rate even higher than greenhouse gas emission alone would cause, through what are called "feedback effects." Higher temperatures, for example, could melt the tundra found in the world's northern latitudes (this has already begun), releasing the potent greenhouse gas methane, which lies beneath it, and thereby thickening the heat-trapping blanket that surrounds the Earth. Nor can we be sure what the consequences of higher temperatures will be for the planet. The Earth's atmosphere and its surface are complicated interrelated systems, too complicated to lend themselves to precise prediction even by the best scientists using the most sophisticated mathematical models. The social and political effects of the geophysical consequences of higher global temperatures involve even greater uncertainties. They could include famines, mass migrations, the collapse of governmental structures, and wars in the places most severely affected. Unfortunately, it is not possible to know in advance how, whether, and when global warming will trigger any or all of these things.

So, yes, there are uncertainties surrounding the *effects* of climate change, but none about whether it is real. The uncertainties concern how and when its effects will unfold. Moreover, one thing that usually gets lost in the debate about these uncertainties is the fact that uncertainty cuts both ways. True, the consequences of the ongoing increase in the global temperature could turn out to be more benign than the forecasts of most climate scientists. Let's hope that they do. But they could also turn out to be worse—much worse.

You would not know that, though, from reading the newspapers in 2010. Climate skeptics, many funded by the fossil-fuel industries, seized on a few leaked e-mails among climate scientists working with Great Britain's University of East Anglia's Climatic Research Unit to gin up a controversy about the conduct of some of its scientific investigators. Whatever one thinks of this specific case, it hardly invalidates the scientific consensus on global warming based on independent research conducted all over the world, nor do a few minor mistakes in the UN's massive Intergovernmental Panel on Climate Change report. But for a public too busy to take the time to study these issues, without the background to appreciate fully how little these errors touched on the larger scientific certainties and disinclined to ask why and how climate scientists all over the world could organize a vast conspiracy to get people to believe this problem was more serious than it is, these news stories created doubt and confusion about the issue and helped to stall any U.S. climate legislation.

The climate skeptics took a page right out of the tobacco industry's book, said Joseph Romm, the physicist and popular Climateprogress.org blogger. "When the whole smoking-causes-cancer issue came up, the tobacco industry figured out that it did not have to win the debate, it just had to sow enough doubt to pollute what people thought. It was: 'I don't have to convince you that I am right. I just have to convince you that the other guy may be wrong.' The tobacco people wrote a famous memo that said 'Doubt is our product.' It is a much easier threshold to meet." The other thing the skeptics have on their side is that their goal is to persuade you that the way you are living your life is just fine. It is human nature to "remember and latch on to things that confirm your worldview and ignore and discount those things that don't. It is called 'confirmation bias,'" said Romm.

At the same time, scientists, who tend to focus on what they don't know more than on what they do, also tend to be poor communicators and defenders of their positions. As Romm put it: "Scientists do live in ivory towers. They believe that facts win debates and speak for themselves and that you don't need to market your ideas or repeat them over and over again. And they are even distrustful of people who repeat themselves or cultivate too high a public profile."

Eventually, though, the irresponsible campaign against the science of climate change reached the point that it triggered an open letter signed by 255 members of America's National Academy of Sciences, the nation's top scientific society, which was published in *Science* magazine on May 7, 2010. Here is what the scientists said:

> All citizens should understand some basic scientific facts. There is always some uncertainty associated with scientific conclusions; science never absolutely proves anything. When someone says that society should wait until scientists are absolutely certain before taking any action, it is the same as saying society should never take action. For a problem as potentially catastrophic as climate change, taking no action poses a dangerous risk for our planet.
>
> Scientific conclusions derive from an understanding of basic laws supported by laboratory experiments, observations of nature and mathematical and computer modeling. Like all human beings, scientists make mistakes, but the scientific process is designed to find and correct them. This process is inherently adversarial—scientists build reputations and gain recognition not only for supporting conventional wisdom, but even more so for demonstrating that the scientific consensus is wrong and that there is a better explanation. That's what Galileo, Pasteur, Darwin, and Einstein did. But when some conclusions have been thoroughly and deeply tested, questioned, and examined, they gain the status of "well-established theories" and are often spoken of as "facts."

The letter went on to list the fundamental, well-established scientific conclusions about climate change:

> (i) The planet is warming due to increased concentrations of heat-trapping gases in our atmosphere. A snowy winter in Washington does not alter this fact. (ii) Most of the increase in the concentration of these gases over the last century is due to

human activities, especially the burning of fossil fuels and de-forestation. (iii) Natural causes always play a role in changing Earth's climate, but are now being overwhelmed by human-induced changes. (iv) Warming the planet will cause many other climatic patterns to change at speeds unprecedented in modern times, including increasing rates of sea-level rise and alterations in the hydrologic cycle. Rising concentrations of carbon dioxide are making the oceans more acidic. (v) The combination of these complex climate changes threatens coastal communities and cities, our food and water supplies, marine and freshwater ecosystems, forests, high mountain environ-ments, and far more.

Honk If You Think Like Dick Cheney

The conclusion that emerges from the summary is that while climate change does involve substantial uncertainties, they concern when and how, not whether, it will affect the planet. Sigma Xi, the Scientific Re-search Society, concluded in its February 2007 report for the United Nations that the only sensible response now to the reality of global warming is a two-pronged action strategy to "avoid the unmanageable (mitigation) and manage the unavoidable (adaptation)"—because some significant climate change is coming, even if we don't know when or how much damage it will do.

In other words, uncertainty is a reason to act and not a reason not to act. After all, people in Kansas buy insurance on their homes not be-cause they are certain that a tornado will smash it one day but because they cannot be sure one will not. When faced with a credible threat with potentially catastrophic consequences, uncertainty is why you act—especially with this climate problem, because buying energy and cli-mate insurance will not only pay for itself, it will eventually make a profit. For both these reasons, we favor the "Dick Cheney Strategy" when dealing with the climate issue.

Why do we call it that? In 2006, Ron Suskind published *The One Percent Doctrine*, a book about the U.S. war on terrorists after 9/11. The title came from an assessment by then vice president Dick Cheney, who, in the face of concerns that a Pakistani scientist was offering nuclear-weapons expertise to al-Qaeda, reportedly declared: "If there's a 1% chance that Pakistani scientists are helping Al Qaeda build or develop a nuclear weapon, we have to treat it as a certainty in terms of our response." Cheney contended that the United States had to confront a very new type of threat: a "low-probability, high-impact event."

Soon after Suskind's book was published, the legal scholar Cass Sunstein, then at the University of Chicago, pointed out that Cheney seemed to be endorsing the same "precautionary principle" that animated environmentalists. Sunstein wrote in his blog: "According to the Precautionary Principle, it is appropriate to respond aggressively to low-probability, high-impact events—such as climate change. Indeed, another vice president—Al Gore—can be understood to be arguing for a precautionary principle for climate change (though he believes that the chance of disaster is well over 1 percent)."

Cheney's instinct on nuclear weapons in the hands of rogue states is the right framework for thinking about the climate issue. It's all a game of odds. We've never been here before, but we do know two things. First, the CO_2 we put into the atmosphere stays there for several thousand years, so it is "irreversible" in real time (barring some not-yet-invented technique of geo-engineering to extract greenhouses gases from the atmosphere). And second, the CO_2 buildup, if it reaches a certain point, has the potential to unleash "catastrophic" global warming—warming at a level that no humans have ever experienced. We do not know for sure (and cannot know until it is too late) that this *will* happen, but we do know that it *could* happen. Since the buildup of greenhouse gases is irreversible and the impact of that buildup could be "catastrophic"—that is, it could create such severe and irreparable damage to the Earth's ecosystem that it would overturn the normal patterns of human life on the planet—the sensible, prudent, *conservative* thing to do is to buy insurance.

This is especially advisable when there is every chance our response will eventually turn a profit and serve as an antidote to almost every energy/climate problem set in motion in 1979. If we prepare for climate change by gradually building an economy based on clean-power systems but climate change turns out not to be as damaging as we expect, what would be the result? During a transition period, we would have higher energy prices, while new technologies providing both clean power and greater efficiency achieved scale from mass production. Very quickly, though, we would have higher energy *prices* but lower energy *bills*, as well as lower greenhouse gas emissions, as the new technologies dramatically improved efficiency to give us more power from less energy for less money. In its 2009 report *Unlocking Energy Efficiency in the U.S. Economy*, the McKinsey consultancy found that if serious but affordable energy-efficiency measures were implemented throughout the U.S. economy through 2020, this would yield gross energy savings worth more than $1.2 trillion—more than twice the $520 billion investment in such measures needed in that time frame. Energy efficiency, that is, would save more than twice as much as it would cost.

At the same time, as a result of buying insurance by starting the transition to clean energy, we would become competitive in what is sure to become the next great global industry. Even if global warming did not exist at all, the fact that the planet is on track to move from 6.8 billion people today to 9.2 billion by 2050, and more and more of these people will indeed live in American-size homes, drive American-size cars, and eat American-size Big Macs, means that global energy demand for oil, coal, and gas will surge. Fossil fuels will therefore become more expensive, and the pollution they cause will increase. This will raise the demand for clean, renewable energy, and rising demand will stimulate an increasing supply. There is every reason to believe, in other words, that clean energy will become the successor to information technology as the next major cutting-edge industry on which the economic fortunes of the richest countries in the world will depend. That is the bet that China has made in its twelfth five-year plan, authorized in March 2011, which stresses that development of renewable energy will be the key to China's energy security for the next decade. That plan places special emphasis on developing solar and nuclear energy.

Moreover, renewable energy depends on new technology, which the United States has historically led the world in developing. China is now seeking to seize that position. "Chinese solar panel manufacturers accounted for slightly over half the world's production last year," Keith Bradsher, the *New York Times* Hong Kong business reporter, wrote (January 14, 2011). "Their share of the American market has grown nearly sixfold in the last two years, to 23 percent in 2010, and is still rising fast . . . In addition to solar energy, China just passed the United States as the world's largest builder and installer of wind turbines." Bradsher also noted that since 2007, China has become the world's leading builder of more efficient, less polluting coal power plants, mastering the technology and driving down the cost. "While the United States is still debating whether to build a more efficient kind of coal-fired power plant that uses extremely hot steam, China has begun building such plants at a rate of one a month," Bradsher wrote (May 10, 2009). China is also building far more nuclear power plants than the rest of the world combined.

America does not have in place the rules, standards, regulations, and price signals—the market ecosystem—to stimulate thousands of green innovators in thousands of green garages to devise the breakthrough technologies that will give us multiple sources of abundant, cheap, reliable, carbon-free energy. Solar "is an industry we pioneered and invented," explained Phyllis Cuttino, the director of the Pew Charitable Trusts' Clean Energy Program. "We used to be the leading manufacturer of solar in the world, and now the largest manufacturers of solar and wind are China and Germany. In 2008, we led the world in private investment and financing of clean energy. In 2009 China took the lead at $54 billion, Germany is attracting $41 billion, and we are at $34 billion."

A key reason for the rise of Germany and China in clean power, Cuttino noted, is that they both used "domestic policy tools to create huge internal demand." If we set high energy-efficiency standards for our own buildings, trucks, cars, and power plants, we would trigger innovation by American companies, which would then be better positioned to compete globally. If, on the other hand, we lower those standards, we invite competition from low-cost, low-standards competitors.

Beyond the potential for spawning new industries, taking climate change and our oil addiction seriously would surely bring strategic advantages. Led by Ray Mabus, President Obama's secretary of the navy and the former U.S. ambassador to Saudi Arabia, the navy and marines are not waiting. Using their own resources, they have been building a strategy for "out-greening" al-Qaeda, the Taliban, and the world's petro-dictators. Their efforts derive from a Pentagon study from 2007 data that found that the U.S. military suffers one person killed or wounded for every twenty-four fuel and water convoys it runs in Afghanistan. Today, many hundreds of these convoys are needed each month to transport the fuel to run air conditioners and to power diesel generators—to remote bases all over Afghanistan.

On April 22, 2010, Earth Day, the navy flew an F/A-18 Super Hornet fighter jet powered by a fifty-fifty blend of conventional jet fuel and camelina aviation biofuel made from pressed mustard seeds. That fighter jet flew at Mach 1.2 (850 miles per hour) and has since been tested on biofuels at Mach 1.7 (nearly 1,300 miles per hour)—without a hiccup. As Scott Johnson, general manager of Sustainable Oils, which produced the camelina, put it in *Biofuels Digest*: "It was awesome to watch camelina biofuel break the sound barrier."

Mabus believes that if the navy and marines could deploy generators in Iraq and Afghanistan with renewable power, as well as more energy-efficient tents; could run more ships on nuclear energy, biofuels, and hybrid engines; and could fly some of its jets with biofuels, it would gain a major advantage over the Taliban and America's other adversaries. This is still a long, long way off, but it is heartening to see the Pentagon taking some leadership on this issue—which is no surprise, since for the marines it is a life-and-death issue. The best way to avoid a roadside bomb is not to have vehicles on the roads trucking fuel in the first place. Similarly, the best way not to have to kowtow to petro-dictators is to take away, or reduce the value of, the only source of income they have. And the best way to make it possible for the United States to cut its military budget without harming the nation's security is to reduce our and the world's addiction to oil. Making oil less important would reduce the military forces we have to keep on station to protect its flow from the Persian Gulf to the rest of the world. And, of course, importing less oil would strengthen the dollar. Americans currently send more than $1 billion a day abroad to purchase both crude oil and refined petroleum products from around the world. Bring that number down with energy efficiency and clean power, and America's trade deficit would improve. As a bonus, the air we breathe would be cleaner, so our health-care bills would be lower.

Any of these points individually would argue for adopting a different policy on energy and climate. All of them together add up to a case that is overwhelming. No single measure would do more to make America stronger, wealthier, more innovative, more secure, and more respected than implementing a sound energy strategy—putting a price on carbon, or increasing the gasoline tax, or establishing national energy-efficiency standards for every building and home. To dismiss global warming as a hoax and refuse to take any of these steps to reduce our addiction to oil, therefore, is to wage war not just against physics but against the American national interest and against elementary prudence.

China has a different approach. "There is really no debate about climate change in China," said Peggy Liu, chairwoman of the Joint U.S.-China Collaboration on Clean Energy, a nonprofit group working to accelerate the greening of China. "China's leaders are mostly engineers and scientists, so they don't waste time questioning scientific data." Air pollution is much worse in China than in the United States because the country burns huge quantities of cheap coal. That creates serious health problems of a kind that, fortunately, we in the United States do not face. For this reason, Liu added, the push to be green in China "is a practical discussion on health and wealth. There is no need to emphasize future consequences when people already see, eat, and breathe pollution every day." And because runaway pollution in China means wasted lives, air, water, ecosystems, and money—and wasted money means fewer jobs and more political instability—the regime takes it seriously. Energy efficiency achieves three goals at once for China. The country saves money, takes the lead in the next great global industry, and earns some credit with the world for mitigating climate change.

Why is that attitude so hard for America to duplicate? Why has the United States failed so abjectly to meet the related challenges of climate change and energy?

Of Science and Political Science

For starters, climate change occurs gradually and may not produce an equivalent of Pearl Harbor—until it is too late. That is, it's another one of those slowly unfolding problems—like the deficit—in which there is a fundamental mismatch between the cause and the people who cause it, on the one hand, and the effect and the people who will be most affected, on the other. The effects lag far behind the causes.

So, for example, whatever global warming effects we're experiencing today, which are relatively mild, are the product of CO_2 emissions from

decades ago, before China and India and Brazil became economic pow-
erhouses. And the emissions that we are pouring into the atmosphere
today will be felt by our grandchildren in 2050. When people cannot see
any immediate effect of what scientists tell them is harmful behavior,
generating collective action to stop that behavior is extremely difficult.
But this also means that if and when the environmental equivalent of
Pearl Harbor does come, the response will have to be sweeping and
disruptive.

"Time here is indeed the enemy," said Hal Harvey, the CEO of the
ClimateWorks Foundation, which promotes the best practices for energy management and climate-change mitigation around the world.
"Things that happen suddenly, like a pinprick or a tornado, capture our
attention. But we don't even notice things that unfold over years or
decades."

Another reason we keep putting off action on global warming is that
the solution requires putting a price on carbon and setting stronger
energy-efficiency standards. Since politicians don't want to propose either of those, they prefer not to talk about the problem. This did not
use to be us. Under the leadership of presidents Gerald Ford and Jimmy
Carter, the United States reacted to the 1973–1974 Arab oil embargo by
putting in place higher fuel-economy standards for cars and trucks. In
1975, Congress, with broad bipartisan support, passed the Energy Policy
and Conservation Act, which established corporate average fuel economy
standards that required the gradual doubling of efficiency for new pas-
senger vehicles—to 27.5 miles per gallon—within ten years. As a result
of that, said Amory Lovins of the Rocky Mountain Institute, "we raised
our oil productivity 5.2 percent a year for eight years from 1977 through
1985; oil imports fell 50 percent and oil imports from the Persian Gulf
fell 87 percent. We broke OPEC's pricing power for a decade by cutting
their sales in half." Oil tumbled in price to below $15 a barrel. "Just
think," added Lovins, "with today's innovations, we could rerun that old
play so much better, and imagine what the impact would be."

It was a Republican president, Richard Nixon, who signed into law
the first pieces of major environmental legislation in the United States,
which addressed our first generation of environmental problems—air
pollution, water pollution, and toxic waste. In particular, Nixon pushed
Congress to pass the landmark Clean Air Act of 1970, and to oversee

environmental protection, he also created both the Department of Natural Resources and the Environmental Protection Agency.

It was Ronald Reagan's secretary of state, George Shultz, who oversaw the negotiation of the Montreal Protocol on Substances That Deplete the Ozone Layer—a landmark international agreement designed to protect the stratospheric ozone layer that shields the planet from damaging UVB radiation. And it was President George H. W. Bush who introduced the idea of "cap and trade" to address an environmental problem. Yes, you read that correctly.

In an article entitled "The Political History of Cap and Trade," published in *Smithsonian* magazine (August 2009), Richard Conniff details the story of how "an unlikely mix of environmentalists and free-market conservatives hammered out the strategy known as cap-and-trade." As Conniff explained it,

> The basic premise of cap-and-trade is that government doesn't tell polluters how to clean up their act. Instead, it simply imposes a cap on emissions. Each company starts the year with a certain number of tons allowed—a so-called right to pollute. The company decides how to use its allowance; it might restrict output, or switch to a cleaner fuel, or buy a scrubber to cut emissions. If it doesn't use up its allowance, it might then sell what it no longer needs. Then again, it might have to buy extra allowances on the open market. Each year, the cap ratchets down, and the shrinking pool of allowances gets costlier . . .
>
> Getting all this to work in the real world required a leap of faith. The opportunity came with the 1988 election of George H. W. Bush. [Environmental Defense Fund president] Fred Krupp phoned Bush's new White House counsel [C. Boyden Gray] and suggested that the best way for Bush to make good on his pledge to become the "environmental president" was to fix the acid rain problem, and the best way to do that was by using the new tool of emissions trading. Gray liked the marketplace approach, and even before the Reagan administration expired, he put EDF staffers to work drafting legislation to make it happen . . .
>
> John Sununu, the White House chief of staff, was furious.

He said the cap "was going to shut the economy down," Boyden Gray recalls. But the in-house debate "went very, very fast. We didn't have time to fool around with it." President Bush not only accepted the cap, he overruled his advisers' recommendation of an eight million-ton cut in annual acid rain emissions in favor of the ten million-ton cut advocated by environmentalists . . .

Almost 20 years since the signing of the Clean Air Act of 1990, the cap-and-trade system continues to let polluters figure out the least expensive way to reduce their acid rain emissions.

Alas, today's Republican Party is different. An October 2010 poll by the Pew Research Center for the People & the Press found that a "53%-majority of Republicans say there is no solid evidence the earth is warming. Among Tea Party Republicans, fully 70% say there is no evidence. Disbelief in global warming in the GOP is a recent occurrence. Just a few years ago, in 2007, a 62%-majority of Republicans said there is solid evidence of global warming, while less than a third (31%) said there is no solid evidence."

Not all Republicans are happy about this. As Sherwood Boehlert, a Republican who represented New York's Twenty-fourth District in Congress from 1983 to 2007, put it in *The Washington Post* (November 19, 2010),

I call on my fellow Republicans to open their minds to re-thinking what has largely become our party's line: denying that climate change and global warming are occurring and that they are largely due to human activities. The *National Journal* reported last month that 19 of the 20 serious GOP Senate challengers declared that the science of climate change is either inconclusive or flat-out wrong. Many newly elected Republican House members take that position. It is a stance that defies the findings of our country's National Academy of Sciences, national scientific academies from around the world and 97 percent of the world's climate scientists . . . There is a natural aversion to more government regulation. But that should be included in the debate about how to respond to climate change, not as an excuse to deny the problem's existence . . . My fellow

Republicans should understand that wholesale, ideologically based or special-interest-driven rejection of science is bad policy. And that in the long run, it's also bad politics. What is happening to the party of Ronald Reagan? He embraced scientific understanding of the environment and pollution and was proud of his role in helping to phase out ozone-depleting chemicals. That was smart policy and smart politics.

There is another new factor blocking legislative action against climate change: the shift in Senate rules whereby it now requires sixty votes to shut off a filibuster and thereby pass any significant legislation such as an overhaul of our energy system. A significant majority of Democratic senators were ready to pass such legislation, the Waxman-Markey cap-and-trade bill, in President Obama's first two years, but even though the Democrats had a sixty-vote majority, they could only muster from fifty to fifty-two votes, because oil-state and coal-state Democrats could not be brought on board. Surely, however, they could have found ten Republicans who would support such legislation or offer their own simpler alternative to cap and trade, such as a carbon tax, could they not?

After all, as Senator Lindsey Graham of South Carolina told Tom in an interview in February 2007, when this legislation was being debated, it was vital for the country and his party to help produce some clean-energy legislation. "I have been to enough college campuses to know if you are thirty or younger this climate issue is not a debate," said Graham. "It's a value. These young people grew up with recycling and a sensitivity to the environment—and the world will be better off for it. They are not brainwashed . . . From a Republican point of view, we should buy into it and embrace it and not belittle them. You can have a genuine debate about the science of climate change, but when you say that those who believe it are buying a hoax and are wacky people, you are putting at risk your party's future with younger people."

Graham's approach to bringing around the conservative state he represents was to avoid talking about "climate change." Instead, he framed America's energy challenge as a need to "clean up carbon pollution," to "become energy independent," and to "create more good jobs and new industries for South Carolinians." He proposed "putting a price on carbon," starting with a focused carbon tax rather than an economy-wide cap-and-trade system, so as to spur both consumers and industries to invest in and buy new clean-energy products. He included nuclear energy, and insisted on permitting more offshore drilling for oil and gas to provide more domestic sources as we make the long transition to a new clean-energy economy.

"You will never have energy independence without pricing carbon," Graham argued. "The technology doesn't make sense until you price carbon. Nuclear power is a bet on cleaner air. Wind and solar is a bet on cleaner air. You make those bets assuming that cleaning the air will become more profitable than leaving the air dirty, and the only way it will be so is if the government puts some sticks on the table, not just carrots. The future economy of America and the jobs of the future are going to be tied to cleaning up the air, and in the process of cleaning up the air this country becomes energy independent and our national security is greatly enhanced." Remember, he added, "we are more dependent on foreign oil today than after 9/11. That is political malpractice, and every member of Congress is responsible."

We have no problem with this more conservative approach. Unfortunately, Graham could not get a single Republican senator to join him when he worked out a draft bill—with senators Joseph Lieberman and John Kerry—that included a complex mechanism for pricing carbon, which was never called a tax but was tantamount to it. As *The New Yorker*'s Ryan Lizza noted in a reconstruction of the failure by the Senate to produce an energy bill (October 11, 2010), Republican senators looking to follow Graham's lead were bombarded with allegations that they were raising taxes and killing jobs. As a result, each and every one of them backed off, including Graham. A lot of this had to do with intra-Republican politics. Lizza reported, "Graham warned Lieberman and Kerry that they needed to get as far as they could in negotiating the bill 'before Fox News got wind of the fact that this was a serious process,' one of the people involved in the negotiations said. 'He would say: The second [the Fox newscasters] focus on us, it's gonna be all cap-and-tax all the time, and it's gonna become just a disaster for me on the airwaves. We have to move this along as quickly as possible.'" Unfortunately, they couldn't. Fox found out, Graham backed off, and the bill died.

In addition, the vested interests in the oil, coal, and gas industries, and the U.S. Chamber of Commerce, spread their political donations around to make sure that nothing happened. As Lizza noted, "Newt Gingrich's group, American Solutions, whose largest donors include coal and electric-utility interests, began targeting Graham with a flurry of online articles about the 'Kerry-Graham-Lieberman gas tax bill.'"

In the middle of all this, President Obama decided that he would not spend any significant political capital to press for the clean-energy legislation, to set a price on carbon, or to refute aggressively the climate-change deniers. His political advisers told him it would not be good politics heading into the 2012 election. Rather than change the polls, the president chose to read the polls.

So 2010 turned out to be a microcosm of all the forces undermining our ability to get something big, or even something small, done to deal with our energy and climate challenges. The Democrats were cowardly, and the Republicans were crazy. The Democrats understood the world they were living in but did not want to pay the political price—alone—for adapting to it. The Republicans simply denied the reality of this world. Democrats didn't have the courage of their convictions. Republicans had the wrong convictions. In the end, both parties acted as if a serious energy and climate policy is a luxury that can be put off indefinitely or achieved simply with investments and incentives but without a price signal.

By the end of 2010, the energy debate shifted to the prospect of abundant domestic natural gas, which emits only half as much carbon dioxide as coal. Recently, new exploration and drilling technologies have made vast new gas reserves economically attractive. Because of this, America's recoverable gas reserves have grown ten- to twentyfold in just the last few years. This sounds great—and it might be—but it could equally portend real trouble if not put in the proper context. If we just opt for one more fix of cheap hydrocarbons, consuming it as fast as we can, this bonanza will simply extend our energy and climate denial, make things far worse, and miss the next great global industry. If we choose to use gas as an intelligent bridge to a clean-energy future, it can make the transition easier. Where possible, we should use gas to shut down our oldest, dirtiest coal power plants as rapidly as we can. But to exploit these new reserves of natural gas, which are embedded in deep formations, special drilling techniques known as "fracking" are required, and these can be environmentally destructive. The natural gas industry and the environmental community need to work together to develop guidelines that determine where drilling for natural gas can safely take place and how to avoid contaminating aquifers.

Hot, Flat, and Crowded; Hungry, Thirsty, and Unstable

We began this chapter by recounting the events of 1979 that fed off one another to create a giant feedback loop that has fueled the energy and climate challenge faced by America and the world ever since. A similarly toxic feedback loop, or vicious cycle, appeared in 2010. Unless we create a virtuous cycle to counter it, it will wreak even greater havoc.

Here is what we mean: The UN Food and Agriculture Organization tracks the global prices of fifty-five food commodities. In December 2010, the FAO Food Price Index hit its highest level since records began being kept in 1990, climbing above the peak reached during the 2008 food crisis. Those rising food prices were one factor, perhaps the last straw, that sparked the political uprising in Tunisia, which quickly spread to Egypt, Libya, Bahrain, Syria, Yemen, and across the Arab world. Those uprisings then triggered disruptions in oil production and speculations in oil futures, sending global oil prices soaring toward their historic peaks. Higher oil prices, in turn, raised food costs, because of oil's prominence in fertilizers, food production, and transportation. So the prices for rice, corn, potatoes, and other staples that sustain the world's poor all spiked. Rice alone is a basic food for three billion of the world's people. The continually rising food prices heightened discontent in the Arab world (and elsewhere), which kept pressure on oil prices, which kept pressure on food prices, and so on . . .

This inner loop is being reinforced by another loop of steadily rising world population, plus steadily rising standards of living, plus steadily rising climate change. Egypt alone has grown from twenty-two million people in 1950 to eighty-two million today. That is one reason that FAO experts estimate that global food production will have to increase by some 70 percent by 2050 to keep up with the world's population growth from 6.8 billion to 9.2 billion. Meanwhile, thanks to the hyper-connecting of the world, more and more people will be living, driving, and eating like Americans, increasing the demand for fossil fuels, which will put even more stress on global natural resources and oil prices. China faces major water shortages already, with industrial demand for water roughly doubling every seven to eight years. Yemen may be the first country in the world actually to run out of water.

Some of the world's leading investors believe this is the start of a major global shift in resource supply and demand. "Accelerated demand from developing countries, especially China, has caused an unprecedented shift in the price structure of resources: after 100 years or more of price declines, they are now rising, and in the last 8 years have undone, remarkably, the effects of the last 100-year decline," the noted money manager Jeremy Grantham wrote in his April 2011 report to investors. "Statistically, also, the level of price rises makes it extremely unlikely that the old trend is still in place . . . From now on, price pressure and shortages of resources will be a permanent feature of our lives. This will increasingly slow down the growth rate of the developed and developing world and put a severe burden on poor countries. We all need to develop serious resource plans, particularly energy policies. There is little time to waste."

All these trends are being exacerbated by the fact that the more people there are on the planet, the more urbanized the world becomes. Urbanization increases global warming, which, as we have noted, many scientists predict will set off even more severe storms, droughts, deforestation, and floods of the kind that ruined harvests all over the world in 2010. The more that harvests are disrupted, the higher food prices will rise. The higher food prices rise, the more political uprisings there will be. The more uprisings, the higher fuel prices will rise. Welcome to our own 1979-like feedback loop in 2011. The only way to stop it is for America, and other big industrialized countries, to launch a virtuous cycle to counter this emerging vicious one.

"We need to bring our own cause-and-effect logic" to this dangerous feedback loop gathering momentum today, argues Hal Harvey, the ClimateWorks CEO. He proposes an approach with three parts: performance standards, a price on carbon, and research and innovation. Melded together, they can create a powerful virtuous cycle.

Twenty years' experience in California demonstrates the gains in efficiency and innovation that can come from steadily rising performance standards. California's strategy reduced electricity consumption in refrigerators by a full 80 percent. New houses, built with ever higher performance standards, known as building codes, have cut energy use in new homes there by 75 percent compared to precode versions. Together, these policies now save the average California family some $1,000 per year. The state is going further: It has led the nation in raising mileage standards for cars and trucks, and in raising requirements for utilities to provide energy produced from solar, wind, hydro, or nuclear sources. These performance standards are transforming the California energy economy.

As technology improves, performance standards need to advance as well. As noted earlier, in 1974, in the wake of the Arab oil embargo, Congress doubled the average efficiency standard for new automobiles sold in the United States, from about thirteen miles per gallon to more than twenty-five, over the next decade. Unfortunately, "this improvement, designed as a floor, turned into a de facto cap on fuel economy for most manufacturers, and fuel economy remained stuck for two decades," said Harvey. One reason was that Detroit fiercely—and, as it turns out, suicidally—fought any change in the standards the whole time. "Imagine if, instead, the fuel economy level had grown just 2 percent per year after 1985," said Harvey. "U.S. cars would have reached an average of forty-four miles per gallon this year, Detroit would be a technology leader, U.S. oil consumption would be three million barrels per day less." We would have saved hundreds of millions of dollars, and the recent oil shocks would have been avoided or been far less severe.

It is never too late to get this right, because the gains are so huge and the costs so low. In 2011, the Obama administration is expected to issue a proposal for new mileage standards to take us from 2017 to 2025. It is considering mandating annual improvements ranging from 3 percent to 6 percent. The current rules, which run from 2012 through 2016, compel automakers to decrease emissions—the proxy for fuel efficiency—by 5 percent each year. Automakers are pushing for 3 percent or less. We must go for 6 percent—and Dan Becker, a longtime environmental lobbyist and expert on this subject, explains why: "The technology to achieve 6 percent is on the shelves today. Most cars would get the mileage of today's Prius. SUVs and other light trucks would average what today's Ford Escape hybrid averages. This is auto mechanics, not rocket science. Most changes would be under the hood—better engines and transmissions, for example—and improved aerodynamics. The differences between strong and weak standards are huge: At 6 percent, we'll save 2.5 million barrels of oil a day in 2030. That is more than our daily imports from the Persian Gulf. But if the standard calls for only a 3 percent decrease in emissions, we'll save just over 1 million barrels a day. With the weaker standard, we'll use an extra 1.5 million barrels of oil each day. That's no way to curb our oil appetite." By using less gas, the country would spend $645 billion less at the pump from 2017 to 2030, assuming gas costs $3.50 a gallon, according to the Union of Concerned Scientists.

Once we put in place steadily rising efficiency standards across the nation, a price signal—a tax on carbon and/or an increase in the federal gasoline tax—would reinforce them. People would have even greater incentives to look for more efficient homes, cars, and appliances, which the market would have made available thanks to the performance standards. "Then you have this huge market signal pulling you where the government is pushing you," said Harvey.

Finally, when the market and the efficiency standards are both driving behavior in one direction, this creates a major incentive for private-sector investment and innovation. "California building codes get tighter every three years," said Harvey. This has spawned ever more sophisticated window manufacturers, heating-and-cooling equipment producers, and insulation makers. These companies, in turn, have become a lobby for higher standards because with higher standards they have more customers for their higher-performing products and fewer competitors, especially cheap foreign competitors. "When Washington tried to pass a carbon cap, it got pecked to death by the vested interests," said Harvey. "California passed a far more aggressive policy because the old vested interests from the fossil-fuel industries and the [U.S.] Chamber of Commerce have been supplanted by new vested interests that are part of this virtuous cycle."

These new interests know that if they can meet California's standards, they can compete against anyone globally. This, in turn, gives both government and business the incentives to invest more in research and development. The pipeline of new products steadily drives more efficiency, making it easier and cheaper for consumers to adjust to a price signal. "The price signal becomes a transformation device, not a punishment device," said Harvey. "If I make gasoline more expensive but I have access to great electric car batteries at falling prices, it doesn't matter." The consumer ends up saving money.

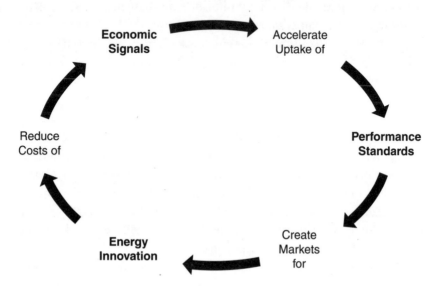

Putting all three together—efficiency standards, carbon prices, and innovation—creates a powerful engine for driving down the price for clean power and driving up demand for their production. (See Harvey's graphic above.) "And then your innovation radically increases," said Harvey, "because the venture capital guys see a market and the finance guys see an income stream and that really starts to change the world." Harvey added that this is precisely the ecosystem that China is trying to put in place. "They want to have the highest-performing globally competitive businesses in the clean-energy space, and that is exactly where they are going."

We wish we could say the same for America. But we can't. America's choices are clear: We can opt for living with the vicious energy-climate cycles set off in 1979 and 2010 that are making us less secure, less healthy, less wealthy, and more exposed than ever to the whims of the two most brutal forces on the planet—the market and Mother Nature. Or we can set in motion our own virtuous cycle that makes us healthier, more pros-perous, more secure, and more resilient in today's hyper-connected world.

Given the dangers and disruptions posed by the first choice and the economic and strategic benefits offered by the second, we consider the proper alternative to be obvious. We hope that a majority of Americans will soon see it that way as well. It is not at all an exaggeration to say that our future and the planet's future are riding on it.

PART IV
POLITICAL FAILURE

ELEVEN

The Terrible Twos

MAN LEAPS FROM WINDOW, SAVED BY UNCOLLECTED
TRASH, January 3, 2011, 12:07 PM ET NEW YORK (Reuters)—A man
who jumped out of a ninth-floor window in New York was alive on Mon-
day after he landed in a giant heap of trash uncollected since the city's
huge snowstorm a week ago.

Two scenes from Capitol Hill—five years apart—pretty well sum up
America's reckless behavior in the last decade. The first took place on
March 18, 2005, when a group of America's greatest baseball players tes-
tified before Congress. It wasn't pretty. Curt Schilling, Rafael Palmeiro,
Mark McGwire, Sammy Sosa, and José Canseco appeared together at
one table—sitting "biceps-to-biceps"—before the House Committee on
Oversight Government Reform for a hearing on steroids in baseball.
They had come in response to repeated threats by Congress to pass leg-
islation that would govern drug testing in baseball and other sports.
ESPN.com described McGwire's testimony:

> In a room filled with humbled heroes, Mark McGwire hemmed
> and hawed the most. His voice choked with emotion, his eyes
> nearly filled with tears, time after time he refused to answer the
> question everyone wanted to know: Did he take illegal steroids
> when he hit a then-record 70 home runs in 1998—or at any
> other time? Asked by Rep. Elijah Cummings, D-Md., whether
> he was asserting his Fifth Amendment right not to incriminate

himself, McGwire said: "I'm not here to talk about the past. I'm here to be positive about this subject." Asked whether use of steroids was cheating, McGwire said: "That's not for me to determine."

José Canseco, whose best-selling book, *Juiced*, drew lawmakers' attention, said anew that he used performance-enhancing drugs as a player. Baltimore Orioles teammates Sammy Sosa and Rafael Palmeiro said they haven't . . . "Steroids were part of the game, and I don't think anybody really wanted to take a stance on it," Canseco said. "If Congress does nothing about this issue, it will go on forever."

It was painful to watch these heroes of our national pastime confess by their evasions that their record-setting performances not only were the product of hard work on the field and in the gym but were boosted by steroid injections in a dark corner of the locker room (and one of them, Palmeiro, later actually failed a drug test).

Almost five years later, on January 13, 2010, in another committee hearing room just down the hall, Congress was at it again, with another panel investigating steroid use—this time financial steroids. The scene was eerily similar, but instead of baseball stars sitting biceps-to-biceps, it was investment bankers sitting briefcase-to-briefcase. Their huge bonuses and paydays were the Wall Street equivalent of grand-slam home runs—home runs also hit, it was suspected, with artificial stimulants. Some of America's biggest financial sluggers jammed together at one long witness table: Goldman Sachs CEO Lloyd Blankfein, JPMorgan Chase CEO Jamie Dimon, Bank of America CEO Brian Moynihan, and Morgan Stanley chairman John Mack. This was the first public hearing of the Financial Crisis Inquiry Commission.

Here is how Reuters described what happened:

Wall Street's chiefs acknowledged taking on "too much risk" . . . but stopped short of an apology as they sparred with a commission looking into the origins of the financial crisis . . .

With U.S. unemployment near a 26-year high after the worst recession in decades, public fury is growing over the cost of U.S. taxpayer bailouts and huge bonuses for bankers, now that the banking industry has stabilized from the 2008 meltdown.

Phil Angelides, chairman of the commission and a former state treasurer of California, confronted the pugnacious, arm-waving Lloyd Blankfein, chief executive of Goldman Sachs, over his firm's pre-meltdown practices.

Angelides compared Goldman's practice of creating, then betting against, certain subprime mortgage-backed securities to "selling a car with faulty brakes and then buying an insurance policy on the buyer."

Just as baseball players in the 1990s injected themselves with steroids to build muscle artificially for the purpose of hitting more home runs, our government injected steroids into the economy in the form of cheap credit so that Wall Street could do more gambling and Main Street could do more home buying and unskilled workers could do more home-building. The fastest-growing job sectors during the steroid-injected bubble years of the early 2000s were construction, housing, real estate, homeland security, financial services, health care, and public employment—all of them fueled by low interest rates and deficit spending. New value-creating industries grew very little.

Warren Buffett likes to say that when the tide goes out, you see who isn't wearing a bathing suit. The economic tide went out with the financial meltdown and deep recession at the end of the first decade of the twenty-first century, and it showed with brutal clarity who was swimming naked.

It was us.

Thanks to the peace dividend, the creation of the dot-com industry, the portable-computing and cell-phone industries, and the tax increase pushed through by President Bill Clinton, the first decade after the end of the Cold War was, on balance, positive for America. We almost erased the deficit, and employment grew steadily. The Clinton administration tried to pass an energy tax and nearly succeeded in doing so. Welfare was reformed, and corporate America seemed to be adjusting and adapting to the flat world, because it had no choice. Alas, the second decade after the Cold War ended—the first decade of the twenty-first century—was not so benign. There is really no other way to say it: By the standards of elementary prudence and our own history, we went nuts.

When America failed to see what a profound challenge the end of the Cold War posed, this could be chalked up to ignorance or inattention. We simply didn't understand the world in which we were living. But when we decided to go to war on math and physics, we did so with eyes wide open. And *when we did all of these things at once*, we made a radical departure from the norms of American history. That is why we call this initial decade of the twenty-first century the "Terrible Twos."

This term comes originally from child psychology. It refers to the developmental stage, beginning sometime after a child turns two, when the child becomes cranky, moody, and willful about almost everything. Pediatricians reassure anxious parents of such cantankerous toddlers that the behavior pattern is normal. They'll grow out of it. American behavior in the Terrible Twos, by contrast, was anything but normal, and we have not yet grown out of it.

As a country, we lost the plot. We forgot who we were, how we had become the richest and most powerful country in the history of the world, where we wanted to go, and what we needed to do to get there. We failed to update our five-part formula for greatness—education, infrastructure, immigration, research and development, and appropriate regulation—just at a time when changes in the world, especially the expansion of globalization and the IT revolution, made adapting that formula to new circumstances as important as it had ever been. Then we fell into the pit of the Great Recession, while fighting two wars in the Middle East and being the first generation of Americans not only to fail to raise taxes to pay for a war but actually to cut them.

In short, we were the generation of Americans that threw out its umbrella just before the storm. In so doing, we broke with one of the main patterns of American history. "In the past we not only met challenges, we did it in ways that left people in our dust—so as to emphatically assert or reassert our leadership," said Dov Seidman, the author of *How*. We did nothing of the sort in the Terrible Twos, and that has left us in very difficult circumstances. "Instead of being twenty years behind, we should be twenty years ahead right now—so we are actually forty years behind where we should be," Seidman added.

And while the steroid-enhanced sluggers' achievements remain, at least for now, part of baseball's record books, the artificially created wealth of the Terrible Twos has evaporated. The numbers don't lie. On January 2, 2010, as that radical decade was coming to an end, *The Washington Post* did the math—the real math. It ran an article by Neil Irwin entitled "Aughts Were a Lost Decade for U.S. Economy, Workers," which is worth quoting at length:

> For most of the past 70 years, the U.S. economy has grown at a steady clip, generating perpetually higher incomes and wealth for American households. But since 2000, the story is starkly different. The past decade was the worst for the U.S. economy in modern times, a sharp reversal from a long period of prosperity that is leading economists and policymakers to fundamentally rethink the underpinnings of the nation's growth. It was, according to a wide range of data, a lost decade for American workers. The decade began in a moment of triumphalism— there was a current of thought among economists in 1999 that recessions were a thing of the past. By the end, there were two, bookends to a debt-driven expansion that was neither robust nor sustainable. There has been zero net job creation since December, 1999.
>
> No previous decade going back to the 1940s had job growth of less than 20 percent. Economic output rose at its slowest rate of any decade since the 1930s as well. Middle-income households made less in 2008, when adjusted for inflation, than they did in 1999—and the number is sure to have declined further during a difficult 2009. The Aughts were the first decade of falling median incomes since figures were first compiled in the 1960s. And the net worth of American households—the value of their houses, retirement funds and other assets minus debts— has also declined when adjusted for inflation, compared with sharp gains in every previous decade since data were initially collected in the 1950s.

The financial shenanigans that produced the meltdown triggered by the collapse of the investment bank Lehman Brothers on September 15, 2008, made a huge contribution to these dismal, shocking, and unprecedented figures. The titans of banking have a lot to answer for. But financial misdeeds were not the only cause. Just as responsible for the nation's abysmal economic performance during the Terrible Twos, if not more responsible for it, was the nation's collective failure to maintain and upgrade the American formula that had served us so well for so long. We let each one of the pillars of our formula erode significantly during the last decade, and that, in our view, is what made the Terrible Twos so terrible. Here is a scorecard.

If 2 Plus X Equals 4, What Is the Value of X?

On October 24, 2010, *The Hartford Courant* ran a cartoon by the paper's resident cartoonist, Bob Englehart, featuring four versions of the famed recruiting poster—the one with Uncle Sam pointing outward. In the first poster Uncle Sam is saying, "I WANT YOU." In the second poster, he has both hands up, flashing stop, under the caption "NO, WAIT. NOT YOU." In the third poster he is pointing out again, under the caption "WELL, OK, YOU." In the final poster he has both hands up again, warning stop, under the caption "NO, WAIT . . ."

We wonder if he drew that cartoon in anticipation of a study that made headlines on December 21, 2010, which found, according to an Associated Press report that day, that "nearly one-fourth of the students who try to join the U.S. Army fail its entrance exam, painting a grim picture of an education system that produces graduates who can't answer basic math, science and reading questions." The study, conducted by the Education Trust, a Washington, D.C.–based children's advocacy group, "found that 23 percent of recent high school graduates don't get the minimum score needed on the enlistment test to join any branch of the military. Questions are often basic, such as: 'If 2 plus x equals 4, what is the value of x?'"

The AP story noted that this was the first time the U.S. Army had released such test data publicly. Tom Loveless, an education expert at the Brookings Institution think tank, was quoted saying the results echo those on other tests. In 2009, 26 percent of seniors performed below the basic reading level on the National Assessment of Educational Progress. Other tests, like the SAT, look at students who are going to college. "A lot of people make the charge that in this era of accountability and standardized testing, we've put too much emphasis on basic skills," Loveless said. "This study really refutes that. We have a lot of kids that graduate from high school who have not mastered basic skills."

In chapter 6, we cited the unimpressive showing of American fifteen-year-olds in the international PISA test, which measures student skills in reading, math, science, and critical thinking. But many other warning signs that America's education system was underperforming at all levels showed up in the Terrible Twos.

In a speech to the Council on Foreign Relations (October 19, 2010), Arne Duncan, the secretary of education, issued his own report card on the status of American education. On a broad set of metrics of educational attainment, we didn't do well.

> Just one generation ago, the United States had the highest proportion of college graduates in the world. Today, in eight other nations, including South Korea, young adults are more likely to have college degrees than in the U.S. In South Korea, 58 percent of young adults have earned at least an associate's degree. In America, just 42 percent of young adults have achieved the same milestone. In many other developed countries, the proportion of young adults with associate's or bachelor's degrees soared in the last 15 years. Here in the United States, we simply flat-lined. We stagnated, we lost our way—and others literally passed us by . . . Just as troubling, about one in four high school students—25 percent—in the U.S. drops out or fails to graduate on time. That's almost one million students leaving our schools for the streets each year. That is economically unsustainable and morally unacceptable. High school dropouts today are basically condemned to poverty and social failure. One of the more unusual and sobering press conferences I participated in last year was the release of a report by a group of top retired generals and admirals that included General Wesley Clark and Major General James Kelley. They were deeply troubled, as I am, by the national security burden created by America's underperforming education system. Here was the stunning figure cited in the generals' report: 75 percent of young Americans, between the ages of 17 to 24, are unable to enlist in the military today because they have failed to graduate from high school, have a criminal record, or are physically unfit. So, to borrow a phrase from the space race era—yes, Houston, we have a problem.

In a follow-up essay in *Foreign Affairs* (November–December 2010), Duncan added that young Americans today have almost identical college completion rates as their parents. In other words, we've made no improvement. The numbers tell the story.

"Currently," Duncan wrote, "about one-fourth of ninth graders fail to graduate high school within four years. Among the OECD countries, only Mexico, Spain, Turkey, and New Zealand have higher dropout rates than the United States." The numbers do not improve as American students move through the educational system.

> College entrance exams suggest that merely one quarter of graduating high school seniors are ready for college, and 40 percent of incoming freshmen at community colleges have to take at least one remedial class during their first semester. In June, the Center on Education and the Workforce projected that by 2018, the U.S. economy will need about 22 million more college-educated workers, but that, at current graduation rates, it will be short by at least three million. With not enough Americans completing college, the center warned, the United States is "on a collision course with the future."

American colleges and universities, Duncan added, still have one of the highest enrollment rates in the world—"nearly 70 percent of U.S. high school graduates enroll in college within one year of earning their diplomas. But only about 60 percent of students who enroll in four-year bachelor's programs graduate within six years, and only about 20 percent of students who enroll in two-year community colleges graduate within three years."

Much of what Duncan described is taking place in middle-class communities, but the picture that emerges from more challenged areas is breathtakingly bleak. A May 2011 study by the Detroit Regional Workforce Fund found that 47 percent of adult Detroit residents, or about 200,000 people, are functionally illiterate—which means that nearly half the adults in the city can't perform simple tasks such as reading an instruction book, reading labels on packages or machinery, or filling out a job application. Depressingly, about 100,000 of those functionally illiterate adults have either a high school diploma or the GED equivalent. You can stimulate the Detroit economy all you want, but even if jobs come back, people who can't read won't be able to do them.

We as a country already pay staggering sums to fund remedial education for students who enter the workplace with high school and college degrees—degrees that were supposed to prepare them for jobs but did not. A 2004 study of 120 American corporations by the National Commission on Writing (a panel established by the College Board) concluded that a third of the employees in the nation's blue-chip companies wrote poorly and that businesses were spending as much as $3.1 billion annually on remedial training. *The New York Times*'s education writer, Sam Dillon, reported (December 7, 2004) that

> R. Craig Hogan, a former university professor who heads an online school for business writing [in Illinois], received an anguished e-mail message recently from a prospective student: "i need help," said the message, which was devoid of punctuation. "i am writing a essay on writing i work for this company and my boss want me to help improve the workers writing skills can yall help me with some information thank you." . . . "E-mail is a party to which English teachers have not been invited," Dr. Hogan said.

On education, in short, we have not updated our formula for greatness the way we did when we made sure that every American had access to a tuition-free high school education. "We have not made an equivalent commitment to the twenty-first century—to say everyone should be able to get postsecondary schooling free of tuition," said Lawrence Katz, the Harvard labor economist. Just when we needed to speed up, we stayed where we were. Katz quoted a telling, discouraging statistic: "American fifty-five-year-olds are still the most educated people in their cohort in the world. But American twenty-five-year-olds are in the middle of the pack. That," he added, "is a new phenomenon."

Bridges

If all Americans could compare Berlin's luxurious central train station today with the grimy, decrepit Penn Station in New York City, they would swear we were the ones who had lost World War II. When you ride from New York to Washington on the Amtrak Acela, America's bad imitation of a Japanese bullet train, trying to have any kind of sustained cell-phone conversation is an adventure, to say the least. Your conversation can easily be aborted three or four times in a fifteen-minute span. Whenever, we, the authors, have a cell-phone conversation from the Acela, one of us typically begins by saying, "Speak fast, I'm not calling from China. I'm on the Acela." Our airports? Some of them would probably qualify as historic monuments. We would nominate both Los Angeles International and several terminals at John F. Kennedy in New York for this distinction. LAX's dingy, cramped United Airlines domestic terminal feels like a faded 1970s movie star who once was considered hip but has had one too many face-lifts and simply can't hide the wrinkles anymore. But in many ways, LAX, JFK, and Penn Station are us. We are the United States of Deferred Maintenance. (China, by contrast, is the People's Republic of Deferred Gratification.)

In the Terrible Twos, our roads got more crowded, our bridges got creakier, our water systems got leakier, and the lines in our airports got longer. In 2009, the American Society of Civil Engineers (ASCE) issued a *Report Card for America's Infrastructure*, and gave America an overall grade of D. The report also gave individual grades to fifteen infrastructure categories. None got higher than C+. "Decades of underfunding and inattention have endangered the nation's infrastructure," the engineers said, adding that since the ASCE's last report card in 2005, there has been little change in the condition of America's roads, bridges, drinking-water systems, and other public works, but the cost of repairing them (when they do get repaired) has risen. ASCE estimated in 2009 that America's infrastructure needed $2.2 trillion in repairs—up from the $1.6 trillion price tag in 2005.

"In 2009, all signs point to an infrastructure that is poorly maintained, unable to meet current and future demands, and in some cases, unsafe," the engineers said. A story on the Environment News Service (January 28, 2009) about the infrastructure study noted that the engineers gave "solid waste management the highest grade, a C+. The condition of the nation's bridges receives the next highest grade, a C, while two categories, rail as well as public parks and recreation scored a C−. All other infrastructure categories were graded D or D−, including: aviation, dams, hazardous waste, inland waterways, levees, roads, schools, transit and wastewater."

The condition of American infrastructure is even worse than the report suggests. "The U.S. government defines 18 of America's infrastructures as 'critical' to the nation," wrote Mark Gerencser in an article entitled "Re-imagining Infrastructure" in *The American Interest* (March–April 2011). "Of the 18 categories, three are basic, underlying 'lifeline' infrastructures: energy, transportation and water. As it happens, all three are beyond mature; they are nearing the end of their useful operating lives and are in desperate need of recapitalization and modernization to accommodate both new needs and the increased demands of our population growth." The ASCE report quoted Pennsylvania governor Ed Rendell as saying, "The longer we wait the more expensive it will be . . . This is as urgent an imperative as health care." We have already waited too long—we've let things slide for two full decades. The price for making a comeback, for becoming again the people and the country we used to be, is only mounting.

Brain Drain

In March 2010, a large gala dinner was held at the National Building Museum in Washington, D.C.—black ties, long dresses. But this was no ordinary dinner. There were forty guests of honor. So here's our brainteaser for readers: We will give you the names of most of the honorees, and you tell us what dinner they were attending. Ready?

Linda Zhou, Alice Wei Zhao, Lori Ying, Angela Yu-Yun Yeung, Lynnelle Lin Ye, Kevin Young Xu, Benjamen Chang Sun, Jane Yoonhae Suh, Katheryn Cheng Shi, Sunanda Sharma, Sarine Gayaneh Shahmirian, Arjun Ranganath Puranik, Raman Venkat Nelakanti, Akhil Mathew, Paul Masih Das, David Chienyun Liu, Elisa Bisi Lin, Yifan Li, Lanair Amaad Lett, Ruoyi Jiang, Otana Agape Jakpor, Peter Danming Hu, Yale Wang Fan, Yuval Yaacov Calev, Levent Alpoge, John Vincenzo Capodilupo, and Namrata Anand.

Sorry, wrong, it was not a dinner of the China-India Friendship Association. Give up? All these honorees were American high school students. They were the vast majority of the forty finalists in the 2010 Intel Science Talent Search, which, through a national contest, identifies and honors the top math and science high school students in America, based on their solutions to scientific problems. As the list of names makes clear, most finalists hailed from immigrant families, largely from Asia.

If you need any convincing about the virtues of immigration, attend the Intel science finals. We need to keep a constant flow of legal immigrants into our country, whether they wear blue collars or lab coats. It is a part of our formula that very few countries can copy. When all of these energetic, high-aspiring people are mixed together with a democratic system and free markets, magic happens. If we want to keep that magic, we need immigration reform that guarantees that we will always attract and retain, in a legal, orderly fashion, the world's first-round aspirational and intellectual draft choices.

The overall winner of the 2010 Intel contest—a $100,000 award for the best project out of the forty—was Erika Alden DeBenedictis of New Mexico, who developed a software navigation system that would enable spacecraft to "travel through the solar system" more efficiently. To close the evening, Alice Wei Zhao of North High School in Sheboygan, Wisconsin, was chosen by her fellow finalists to speak for them. She told the audience: "Don't sweat about the problems our generation will have to deal with. Believe me, our future is in good hands."

We are sure she is right, as long as America doesn't shut its doors—but that is exactly what it is doing. In the past, the country overcame its shortages in science and engineering talent by importing it. That practice is unfortunately becoming more difficult and less common.

A comment by Vivek Wadhwa, an Indian-born scholar of this subject, makes the point pithily: "America is suffering the first brain drain in its history and doesn't know it." Wadhwa, an entrepreneur himself, and a senior research associate at the Labor & Worklife Program at the Harvard Law School and an executive in residence at Duke University, has overseen a number of studies on the connection between immigration and innovation. They all show that it is vital to America's future to nurture that connection and to strengthen our attraction for talent because so many other countries are now strengthening theirs.

"As the debate over the role of highly skilled immigrants intensifies in the U.S., we're losing sight of an important fact: America is no longer the only land of opportunity for these foreign-born workers," Wadhwa noted in *Bloomberg BusinessWeek* (March 5, 2009).

There's another, increasingly promising, destination: home. New research shows that many immigrants have returned to their native countries—especially India and China—to enjoy what they see as a better quality of life, better career prospects, and the comfort of nearby family and friends. The trend has accelerated in the past few years, in part because these workers have also lost patience with the U.S. visa backlog. At the end of 2006, more than a million professionals and their families were in line for the yearly allotment of just 120,000 permanent-resident visas. The wait time for some has been longer than 10 years.

All this matters, Wadhwa writes, "because immigrants are critical to our long-term economic health. Although they represent just 12% of the U.S. population, they have started 52% of Silicon Valley's tech companies and contributed to more than 25% of U.S. global patents. They make up 24% of science and engineering workers with bachelor's degrees and 47% of those with Ph.D.s." He and two colleagues conducted a survey of 1,203 Indian and Chinese immigrants to the United States who had returned to their home countries. The vast majority were young and highly skilled, and had earned advanced degrees. Asked why they had left, 84 percent of the Chinese and 69 percent of the Indians cited professional opportunities. For the vast majority, a longing for family and friends was also a crucial element. Asked if U.S. visa issues played a role in their decisions, a third of the Indians and a fifth of the Chinese answered in the affirmative. Most of the returnees, Wadhwa said, "seem to be thriving. With demand for their skills growing in their home countries, they're finding corporate success. About 10% of the Indians polled had held senior management jobs in the U.S. That number rose to 44% after they returned home. Among the Chinese, the number rose from 9% in the U.S. to 36% in China."

Some opponents of reforming the visa system to attract and keep more highly skilled non-Americans have charged that giving a job to a foreigner takes a job away from a U.S. citizen. In some cases, Wadhwa noted in a *Bloomberg BusinessWeek* article (May 4, 2009), that is true. Some companies have used H-1B visas to hire foreign labor to lower their labor costs. "But in the aggregate, the preponderance of evidence shows that the more foreigners are working in science and technology jobs in the U.S., the better off the U.S. economy is. Increasingly, the number of H-1B holders in a region correlates to increased filings of patents in that region. And for every 1% increase in immigrants with university degrees, the number of patents filed per capita goes up 6%."

American immigration policy today is just "plain stupid," concluded Peter Schuck of the Yale Law School and John Tyler, general counsel of the Ewing Marion Kauffman Foundation, which studies innovation. They noted in an essay in *The Wall Street Journal* (May 11, 2011) that of "more than one million permanent admissions to the U.S. in 2010, fewer than 15% were admitted specifically for their employment skills. And most of those spots weren't going to the high-skilled immigrants themselves, but to their dependents." The H-1B program that gives a pass for high-skilled immigrants to work in America on renewable three-year visas, which can lead to permanent status, is tiny. "The current number of available visas," they added, "is only one-third what it was in 2003."

It cannot be said often enough: Well-paying jobs don't come from bailouts. They come from start-ups, which come from smart, creative, inspired risk takers. There are only two ways to get more of these people: growing more at home by improving our schools, and importing more by recruiting talented immigrants. Surely we need to do both. "When you get this happy coincidence of high-IQ risk takers in government and a society that is biased toward high-IQ risk takers, you get above-average returns as a country," argued Craig Mundie, the chief research and strategy officer of Microsoft. "What is common to Singapore, Israel, and America? They were all built by high-IQ risk takers and all thrived—but only in the U.S. did it happen on a large scale and with global diversity, so you had a really rich cross-section."

In the Terrible Twos we combined cutbacks in higher education with limits on admitting talented immigrants to our shores. The combination is eating away at our capacity to produce and attract creative risk takers at a time when other countries are better and better able to keep their own at home.

If we don't reverse this trend, over time "we could lose our most important competitive edge—the only edge from which sustainable advantage accrues—having the world's biggest and most diverse pool" of high-IQ risk takers, said Mundie. "If we don't have that competitive edge, our standard of living will eventually revert to the global mean."

Unfortunately, in the Terrible Twos the American political system failed to enact legislation to reform the nation's immigration system. President George W. Bush made a mighty effort but was blocked largely by members of his own party, who were so outraged by illegal immigration that they could not think straight about the vital importance of legal immigration. "The H-1B visa program—that is the key to making us the innovators of energy and computers," said Senator Lindsey Graham, the South Carolina Republican, who has been critical of his own party's obstinacy on this issue. "It has been for most of our life. If you wanted to get really smart and have a degree that would allow you to be a leader in the world, you came to America. Well, it's hard as hell to get to America now. And once you get here, it's hard to stay."

Immigration reform that better secures the borders, establishes a legal pathway toward citizenship for the roughly twelve million illegal immigrants who are here, and enables, even recruits, high-skilled immigrants to become citizens is much more urgent than most of us realize. We need both the brainy risk takers and the brawny ones. Low-skilled immigrants may not be able to write software, but such people also contribute to the vibrancy of the American economy. As the Indian American entrepreneur Vivek Paul once remarked to Tom: "The very act of leaving behind your own society is an intense motivator. Whether you are a doctor or a gardener, you are intensely motivated to succeed."

Million? You Must Mean Billion? No. Million!

In the fall of 2010, Tom had a visit from Kishore Mahbubani, a Singaporean academic and retired diplomat. In the course of their conversation, Tom told him of the Obama administration's plan to set up eight innovation hubs to work on the world's eight biggest energy problems. It was precisely the kind of project that could expand the boundaries of basic science across the entire energy field and launch new industries. Tom explained that the program had not yet been fully funded because Congress, concerned about every dime America spends these days, was reluctant to appropriate the full request of $25 million for each energy breakthrough project, let alone for all eight at once. Only three projects were therefore moving ahead, Tom told him, and none of the three would get the full $25 million. Mahbubani interrupted him in mid-sentence.

"You mean billion," he said.

"No," Tom replied, "we're talking about $25 million."

"Billion," Mahbubani repeated.

"No. Million," Tom insisted.

Mahbubani was stunned. He could not believe that while his little city-state was investing more than $1 billion to make itself a biomedical science hub and attract the world's best talent, America was debating about spending mere millions on game-changing energy research. That, alas, is us today: Think small and carry a big ego. This may seem to be a minor issue, but it is not.

Nations usually thrive or languish not because of one bad big decision but because of thousands of bad small ones—decisions in which priorities get lost and resources misallocated so that the country does not achieve its full potential. That is what happened to America in the Terrible Twos. A graph from *The Washington Post* (April 30, 2011) makes the point: At a time when the pace of change in the global economy and the rising economic importance of knowledge make increasing investment in research and development an urgent priority, our spending in this vital area is actually declining.

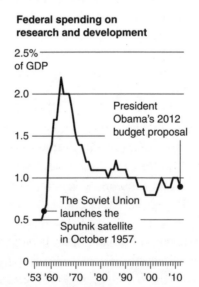

Federal spending on research and development

NOTE: 2011 and 2012 data are projections.

Source: From the Washington Post, © April 30, 2011 The Washington Post. All rights reserved. Used by permission and protected by the Copyright Laws of the United States. The printing, copying, redistribution, or retransmission of the Material without express written permission is prohibited.

In 2005, both the Senate and the House encouraged the National Academies (of sciences, engineering, and medicine) and the National Research Council to conduct a study of America's competitiveness in the global marketplace. They produced a report entitled *Rising Above the Gathering Storm*, which assessed America's standing in each of the principal areas of innovation and competitiveness—knowledge capital, human capital, and the existence of a creative "ecosystem." According to the National Academies website, "Numerous significant findings resulted . . . It was noted that federal government funding of R&D as a fraction of GDP has *declined* by 60 percent in 40 years. With regard to human capital, it was observed that over two-thirds of the engineers who receive PhD's from United States universities are not United States citizens. And with regard to the Creative Ecosystem it was found that United States firms spend over twice as much on litigation as on research."

The *Gathering Storm* report eventually led to a bill called the America COMPETES Act, which authorized investments in a broad range of basic research. It did so on the grounds that

> a primary driver of the future economy and concomitant creation of jobs will be innovation, largely derived from advances in science and engineering . . . When scientists discovered how to decipher the human genome, it opened entire new opportunities in many fields including medicine. Similarly, when scientists and engineers discovered how to increase the capacity of integrated circuits by a factor of one million, as they have in the past forty years, it enabled entrepreneurs to replace tape recorders with iPods, maps with GPS, pay phones with cell phones, two-dimensional X-rays with three-dimensional CT scans, paperbacks with electronic books, slide rules with computers, and much, much more.

Most of the original funding for the expanded research recommended by the *Gathering Storm* report got passed only due to the stimulus legislation enacted after the financial meltdown in 2008—and most of that was for only a limited duration. So in 2010, the same group gathered and issued an update, entitled *Rising Above the Gathering Storm, Revisited: Rapidly Approaching Category 5.*

"So where *does* America stand relative to its position of five years ago when the Gathering Storm report was prepared?" the new report asked. "The unanimous view of the committee members participating in the preparation of this report is that our nation's outlook has worsened. While progress has been made in certain areas . . . the latitude to fix the problems being confronted has been severely diminished by the growth of the national debt over this period from $8 trillion to $13 trillion."

To drive home the point, the updated report began with a series of statistics, which included the following:

In 2009 United States consumers spent significantly more on potato chips than the government devoted to energy research and development—$7.1 billion versus $5.1 billion.

China is now second in the world in its publication of biomedical research articles, having recently surpassed Japan, the United Kingdom, Germany, Italy, France, Canada, and Spain.

In 2009, 51 percent of U.S. patents were awarded to non-U.S. companies. Only four of the top ten companies receiving U.S. patents last year were U.S. companies.

Federal funding of research in the physical sciences as a fraction of GDP fell by 54 percent in the twenty-five years after 1970. The decline in engineering funding was 51 percent.

Sixty-nine percent of U.S. public school students in the fifth through eighth grade are taught mathematics by a teacher without a degree or certificate in mathematics.

Ninety-three percent of U.S. public school students in the fifth through eighth grade are taught the physical sciences by a teacher without a degree or certificate in the physical sciences.

Thirty years ago, 10 percent of California's general revenue fund went to higher education and 3 percent to prisons. Today nearly 11 percent goes to prisons and 8 percent to higher education.

The total *annual* federal investment in research in mathematics, the physical sciences, and engineering is now equal to the *increase* in U.S. health-care costs every nine weeks.

China's Tsinghua and Peking Universities are the two largest suppliers of students who receive Ph.D.'s—in the United States.

And finally, our embarrassing favorite: 49 percent of U.S. adults do not know how long it takes for the Earth to revolve around the Sun.

Rules

An essential part of America's traditional formula for prosperity is the appropriate regulation of American business. When conceived and administered properly, regulation has occupied a middle ground: neither so strong as to stifle innovation, entrepreneurship, and economic growth, nor too light to prevent the excesses and failures to which the free market is susceptible. In the Terrible Twos we managed the trick of going too far in both directions.

The thicket of federal regulations under which the private sector must operate continued to grow during the last decade. In 2007, the Code of Federal Regulations, which includes the text of existing regulations, totaled 145,816 pages, and has since expanded. It is difficult to believe that every one of the listed regulations enhances the well-being of American citizens. Moreover, regulation can have unintended adverse consequences. In 2005 Congress, under pressure from the credit card and financial services industries, passed the Bankruptcy Abuse Prevention and Consumer Protection Act, a law making it much more onerous for a person or an estate to file for Chapter 7 bankruptcy and then start over with a clean slate. Under the new law, explained the website eFinanceDirectory.com, "you can no longer claim Chapter 7, and therefore dismiss all of your debts, unless you make less than your state's median wage. Chapter 7 now stipulates that you must take a debt management class affiliated with the National Foundation for Consumer Credit at least 6 months BEFORE you're eligible to apply for bankruptcy." We are not in favor of encouraging recklessness, but we are in favor of encouraging risk-taking. And some experts speculate that one reason for the sharp drop-off in entrepreneurial start-ups during the Great Recession—a drop of 23 percent as opposed to the usual 5 percent in previous recessions, according to McKinsey's research—is that fewer people are willing to take calculated risks and start new companies owing to this change in the bankruptcy laws. Ever since the dot-com boom, many small entrepreneurs have used their credit cards as their original source of venture capital. Now it is much riskier to do so.

In the Terrible Twos, however, other areas of the financial and energy sectors in the United States suffered from too little regulation. The catastrophic financial meltdown of 2008 occurred in the wake of considerable deregulation of the nation's financial system, which was spurred by, among other things, the belief that the financial industry could largely regulate itself, and that the separations between traditional commercial banking, on the one hand, and investment banking and proprietary trading on a bank's own behalf, on the other—separations put in place to prevent a recurrence of the Great Depression—were no longer necessary. This belief turned out to be wrong, and devastatingly so.

To be sure, the 2008 subprime meltdown was the product of many causes. A mountain of excess savings built up in Asia was looking for a higher return and flowed to subprime bonds—which paid significantly higher interest rates because they were made up of mortgages granted to people who were higher lending risks. The government directly relaxed mortgage standards to help more Americans buy homes. Banks and rating agencies relaxed their standards to get their share of the subprime housing bubble. Government failed to regulate exotic new financial instruments such as derivatives, under pressure from a financial industry that wanted free rein in this lucrative new area.

The University of California Berkeley economist Barry Eichengreen argues that the subprime crisis was partly a case of regulation and regulators not having kept up with the consolidation and internationalization of the commercial banking, investment banking, and brokerage industries. In other words, we did not update our formula in this area. Over the previous two decades, some of the key firewalls erected after the 1929 crash came down, along with regulations stipulating the amount of reserves banks had to keep on hand. The merging of the different financial industries was actually "sensible and well-motivated," argues Eichengreen. It lowered the costs of stock trading for consumers, reduced borrowing costs, and created new financial products that, in theory, could promote growth in different markets. The problem was that this kind of global financial integration was a total misfit with the fragmented, outdated American financial regulatory system, so it was very hard for regulators to get the full picture of the level of risk and leverage different players in the market were taking on. "At the most basic level," Eichengreen argued in an October 2008 paper entitled *Origins and Responses to the Crisis*, "the subprime crisis resulted from the tendency for financial normalization and innovation to run ahead of financial regulation." It ran so far ahead that not only did the regulators not fully understand the level of risks being piled up by different financial houses, but even the CEOs of these firms did not understand what the rocket scientists turned bankers were concocting under them.

One of those new financial instruments—a derivative known as the credit-default swap, a form of private insurance that paid off if a sub-prime package of loans defaulted—was specifically kept out of the juris-diction of government regulators through aggressive lobbying by the financial industry. We wound up with a trillion-dollar market in these swaps without either meaningful government oversight or transparency. Its implosion helped to create the worst financial crash since 1929.

That lack of oversight was a bipartisan effort. In 1999, Republicans passed legislation specifically exempting credit-default swaps from regu-lation—and President Bill Clinton signed it. There is a fine line between a regulatory environment that promotes the risk-taking that is neces-sary in a market economy and an environment that fosters destructive recklessness. In the Terrible Twos, we crossed that line, in part because some important people, chief among them Federal Reserve chairman Alan Greenspan, came to believe that the markets could be "self-regulating"—and that big financial institutions would police themselves because it would be in their self-interest to do so—and in part because the financial industry used its ever greater clout on Capitol Hill to en-sure lax regulation in the new markets it had pioneered and to "capture" regulators. It did so in order to maximize risk-taking so as to create astro-nomical sums of personal wealth for its executives.

Better regulation and regulators might not have prevented the eco-nomic crisis in the last part of the Terrible Twos, but it surely would have made the crisis less severe. In the wake of the crisis, Congress passed and the president signed the Dodd-Frank Wall Street Reform and Con-sumer Protection Act, which imposed new regulations on the financial industry with the goal of making its operations safer. The banking in-dustry, however, did everything it could to weaken that legislation, and the ultimate impact of the reforms remains to be seen.

The result, as the Columbia University economist Jagdish Bhagwati observed, was that a financial industry built to finance "creative destruc-tion" (the formation of new companies and industries to replace old ones) ended up promoting "destructive creation" (the buying and selling of financial instruments with little intrinsic value), the collective implo-sion of which threatened the whole economy.

The fact that virtually none of the main culprits in bringing about this huge destruction of wealth has suffered any legal penalties suggests that our regulations need some updating. At the very least, we should heed what Warren Buffett told the Berkshire Hathaway annual shareholders meeting (April 30, 2010): "Any institution that requires society to come in and bail it out for society's sake should have a system in place that leaves its CEO and his spouse dead broke."

Striking the proper balance between the under- and overregulation of financial markets will be difficult. There is no magic formula for this, and we surely do not wish to stifle all innovation in this area. But finding that balance is crucial because, as we saw in 2008 and thereafter, a major failure in this sector of the economy can inflict massive and long-lasting damage on the economy as a whole.

Income Inequality

A critical reason that America has failed to update its formula by reinvesting in education, infrastructure, and research and development, and hasn't adjusted our immigration policy to promote economic growth or implemented appropriate economic regulations, is that all these require collective action—America as a whole has to act—and lately we have lost our capacity for collective action. One reason for this damaging form of paralysis is the growth of inequality in America, itself the product, among other things, of the further flattening of the world. That flattening has created a global market for the goods and services of people skilled enough to take advantage of it. The earnings in this huge global market can be staggering for the "winners." Consider what a basketball player such as LeBron James can earn in this era when the National Basketball Association sells its branded products from Stockholm to Shanghai—we are talking tens of millions of dollars—compared to the biggest star of the early 1950s, George Mikan of the then Minneapolis Lakers, whose earnings were limited to the United States and were measured in the tens of thousands of dollars.

It is harder to generate collective action when people are living in different worlds within the same country, argues the Nobel Prize–winning economist and Columbia University professor Joseph E. Stiglitz. Historically, Americans have tended to be less troubled by inequality than citizens of other countries. Both the myth and the reality of individual opportunity and upward mobility in America have been so powerful and so deeply ingrained that the socialist narrative of government-sponsored redistribution has never taken root. But the income gaps during the Terrible Twos grew so large, and could well grow larger still, that inequality now threatens to fracture the body politic in ways that could undermine our ability to do big hard things together.

According to Stiglitz, the top 1 percent of Americans now takes in roughly one-fourth of America's total income every year. In terms of wealth rather than income, says Stiglitz, the top 1 percent now controls 40 percent of the total. This is new. Twenty-five years ago, the corresponding figures were 12 percent and 33 percent, he noted. Meanwhile, people in the top 1 percent have seen their incomes rise 18 percent over the past decade, while the incomes of those in the middle have actually fallen. For men with only high school degrees, the decline has been especially pronounced: 12 percent in the last twenty-five years alone, said Stiglitz.

The more divided a society becomes in economic terms, the more likely it is that the wealthy will opt out of paying for public goods and common needs. "You did not need that much collective action in America two hundred years ago," said Stiglitz. "Our defense needs were small. We had no natural enemies. We needed a post office and basic government infrastructure." Today, though, he added, "we need collective action to deliver education, research, modern infrastructure, and all the other public goods that are at the core of a successful society. And that is where inequality fits in, because it impedes our ability to act collectively . . . I would trace it back to Reagan and the unraveling of the social contract."

Today the rich don't need the benefits of collective action, said Stiglitz, because they can create their own "subsociety" with its own collective goods. "They have their country clubs, which are their own parks. They have their own private schools. They don't have to go to public schools and they would not want to have their kids educated there. They have their own transportation system with private jets and chauffeured cars, so they don't really care about the deterioration in public transport. They don't care if there are long lines at the airport, because they are not in them."

Chasing the Losers

If during the Cold War we had let the key features of our formula for greatness—which are the major determinants of economic growth and therefore of power and influence in the world we are living in— deteriorate the way we did during the Terrible Twos, it would have been considered the equivalent of unilateral disarmament. Politicians would have accused one another of creating or tolerating an "education gap" or an "infrastructure gap," like the "missile gap" of the 1950s. The charges and countercharges would have dominated national elections. In the Terrible Twos, something far worse happened.

We didn't notice. Declining numbers in the important categories of national life became normal.

Then we made things even worse. Having underestimated the challenge posed to America by 11/9—November 9, 1989, the day the Berlin Wall fell—we compounded the error by overestimating the challenge of 9/11. We spent the rest of the decade focusing our national attention and resources on the losers from globalization—al-Qaeda, Iraq, Pakistan, and Afghanistan—when our major long-term challenge comes from the winners, most of them in Asia. We devoted ourselves to nation-building in Mesopotamia and the Hindu Kush when we should have been concentrating on nation-building at home.

Since the authors of this book both supported the war in Iraq, to date the more controversial and expensive of the two projects, we need to say what we got wrong and what we still believe. Both of us believed then and believe now that finding a way to bring democracy into the heart of the Arab world was a strategic and moral imperative. We knew it would be difficult and costly, and said so at the time, but even so, we underestimated just how difficult and how costly. We have nothing but regret for the excessive price that America and Iraq have had to pay in lives and treasure.

The losers from globalization—specifically al-Qaeda and Saddam Hussein—did pose significant security problems. We had to strike back against the al-Qaeda perpetrators of 9/11, not simply to deter another attack but also to disrupt what they might have been planning next. But Saddam Hussein was not part of 9/11. The Bush administration asserted that his regime had to be toppled because it had weapons of mass destruction. Neither of us shared that view. Michael believed that the weapons of mass destruction that Saddam Hussein was thought to possess—chemical weapons—did not pose a severe enough threat to justify an attack. What did justify removing him from power was the prospect that at some point in the future he would acquire the far more dangerous nuclear weapons.

Tom's view was that the long-term threat to the United States from the Middle East came less from weapons of mass destruction than from *people* of mass destruction, produced in a region where autocratic regimes were stifling and enraging the people they governed. That was his view in 2001, not just in 2011, when uprisings around the Arab world occurred, triggered by deep frustration and anger at the long-ruling dictatorships and motivated as well, in many cases, by democratic yearnings. His hope was that America could collaborate with a free Iraq to create a decent, democratic model of development in a region that had none.

It was neither foolish nor irresponsible for President George W. Bush to want to use Iraq as a lever to pry open the closed and autocratic world of Arab politics. It was, however, both foolish and irresponsible to try to do so without a well-thought-out plan, without enough troops, and without an adequate understanding of the scale and complexity of what was required. Execution matters.

America's initial policy in Iraq offers, alas, a metaphor for much of American public policy in the Terrible Twos: Our reach exceeded our grasp and ability to execute. We simply, casually, and wrongly assumed that things would work out. We willed the ends but not the means.

We cannot say what would have happened had we done things well in Iraq. We can say, though, that if a decent, democratizing Iraq does finally emerge one day it will be something well worth having, and the lives and treasure expended there will not have been in vain. To the contrary, in that case we will have supported something transformational, of great value to both Iraqis and the world. But even in that case, we will have overpaid for the benefits we get, although by how much will depend on how Iraq evolves. Especially given America's other needs, the American intervention there has cost far too much in lives, money, and the government's attention. The same is true for the wars in Afghanistan and Libya, enterprises with far less potential strategic benefit. In sum, America—and we very much include ourselves in this mistake—acted as if the world that was created on 9/11 was a whole new world. The events of 9/11 did reveal a serious security threat. They posed a real problem. But it was not, in retrospect, the equivalent of a life-threatening disease that required dropping everything and changing everything; it was a chronic disease that we had to keep under control but in a way that allowed us to get on with the rest of our lives. September 11 was diabetes; it wasn't cancer. And the rest of our lives that we had to get on with involves addressing the four major challenges of the post–Cold War era by updating and upgrading our formula for greatness.

We overpaid not only for Iraq but for homeland security as well, because no politician wanted to be accused of negligence by some future investigatory commission. Moreover, we paid for all of this—Iraq, homeland security, Afghanistan, Libya—with borrowed money. We gave ourselves a tax cut rather than a tax hike, added a new entitlement—Medicare prescription drugs—and did it all on the eve of the biggest entitlement payout in American history, which will come with the retirement of the baby boomers.

The contrast with a previous era and a previous Republican presidency is striking. In the 1950s, the Eisenhower era, we used a major conflict—the Cold War—as a lever to upgrade our formula for success to ensure a prosperous future for the nation as a whole. In the Terrible Twos, the George W. Bush era, we used another conflict—the war with al-Qaeda, Saddam Hussein, and radical Islam—to avoid doing the things we had to do to assure a prosperous future. In the first period we sacrificed for and invested in the future. In the second we indulged and splurged in the present at the expense of the future.

Crazy Heart

Looking back on the last decade, we could not help but be struck by some of the lyrics to one of the songs in the 2009 movie *Crazy Heart*. Jeff Bridges won the Oscar for best actor for his portrayal of an alcoholic country singer trying to make a comeback. The song, entitled "Fallin' & Flyin'," makes an all too fitting anthem for the Terrible Twos.

> I was goin' where I shouldn't go
> Seein' who I shouldn't see

Doin' what I shouldn't do
And bein' who I shouldn't be
A little voice told me it's all wrong
Another voice told me it's all right
I used to think that I was strong
But lately I just lost the fight

Funny how fallin' feels like flyin'
For a little while
Funny how fallin' feels like flyin'
For a little while

I got tired of bein' good
Started missin' that ol' feelin' free
Stop actin' like I thought I should
And went on back to bein' me
I never meant to hurt no one
I just had to have my way
If there's such a thing as too much fun
This must be the price you pay

That was America in the Terrible Twos, and we have only begun to pay the price. How did it all happen? The short answer: Our political system got paralyzed and our values system got eroded.

TWELVE

"Whatever It Is, I'm Against It"

In the spring of 2011, the co-chairs of the presidential deficit re-duction commission—Alan Simpson, the former Republican senator from Wyoming, who served from 1979 to 1997, and Erskine Bowles—held a dinner briefing at the Jefferson Hotel in Washington. After the dinner broke up, Simpson, a great raconteur, shared with Tom some thoughts about the state of American politics today, including this story: "A few years ago I went back to the Senate just to check in, and I saw my old and dear friend Dale Bumpers [a Democratic senator from Arkansas]. So I went over across the chamber and gave him this big hug. He's a great guy. When I came back over to the Republican side, [a Republican senator whom Simpson didn't want to name] pulled me aside and said, 'What were you doing over there with Bumpers?' I said, 'He's my friend.' [The Republican senator] said to me, 'He's no good. He's a Democrat. He's a rabid liberal. You shouldn't be hugging him.'"

Simpson was appalled. Things didn't use to be that way. To be sure, political polarization—even hostility—between the country's two major political parties is not new. But the American political system today is not only more polarized than when Simpson served. *It is paralyzed*—by a combination of factors. The two parties, which used to be coalitions of liberals and conservatives, are both now ideologically nearly homogenous, and so stand further apart from each other politically than ever before. Their core agendas were formed in the last century and have not been updated to meet the challenges of this one. The gerrymandering of legislative districts now favors the election of hyper-partisan ideologues rather than moderate problem-solvers. Super-empowered and super-funded interest groups now clog the system's arteries; the new media highlight the loudest and most partisan voices, and more and more depict politics as sports, where all that matters is who won today's game. And, finally, unlike in the past, there is now no big external enemy to enforce a sense of purpose, seriousness, and national unity.

To be sure, there has never been a golden age when partisan divisions in America were trivial and the two parties calmly worked out all the differences they had, but the costs of today's partisanship is far higher than before. When we were more polarized, as in the first half of the nineteenth century, we did not need the federal government to do as much as it must do today; and when we did need it to do as much, as we did for much of the twentieth century, our politics were far less polarized. Today, we have the worst of both worlds: a huge, complicated, and difficult agenda, and a political system incapable of addressing it at the speed and scale we need.

We cannot possibly meet our four major challenges, let alone update America's traditional formula for greatness, without a vibrant federal government able to accomplish big, hard things. But the pathologies of the political system, especially its extreme polarization, block precisely the kind of initiatives we need. The title of Ronald Brownstein's book on the subject—*The Second Civil War*—from which we draw here, is a deliberate exaggeration: Republicans and Democrats are not about to take up arms against each other. The book's subtitle, however—*How Extreme Partisanship Has Paralyzed Washington and Polarized America*—accurately describes one of the chief obstacles to the public policies America needs to thrive in the decades ahead.

We forget that it was not always so. Most Americans today would probably be shocked to learn that Congress established the cornerstone of its social safety net, Social Security, in 1935, established the interstate highway system in 1954, passed civil rights legislation in 1964, and authorized Medicare in 1965, all with a solid majority *of each party* in both the House of Representatives and the Senate voting in favor of the measures.

In recent years, by contrast, the pattern of one party supporting a measure and the other emphatically and overwhelmingly opposing it has become the norm. Each of the last three presidents failed to persuade members of the other party to support his most important programs. Not a single Republican voted for Bill Clinton's initial economic package, which included tax increases, or endorsed his health-care initiative. Only twenty-eight Democrats in the House and twelve in the Senate supported George W. Bush's tax cuts in the spring of 2001, and none endorsed his proposed reform of Social Security, which included private accounts, in 2005. No Republican voted for Barack Obama's 2009 economic stimulus package or his 2010 health-care plan. Both parties go to ever greater lengths to block the other's initiatives, such as through the filibuster—a delaying tactic that one party uses when the other has enough votes to pass a bill. From 1955 to 1961 a vote had to be called to end a filibuster only once. In 2009 and 2010, this happened eighty-four times.

Over the past couple of decades, in fact, Democrats and Republicans have become more like hostile tribes than colleagues with different political views but common goals. Demonization has now become a staple of political rhetoric. In 1994 the Republican Speaker of the House, Newt Gingrich, called the Clinton administration "the enemy of normal Americans." In the next administration, in 2004, the Democratic Senate majority leader, Harry Reid, called President George W. Bush a "liar" who "betrayed his country." When control of the White House passed back to a Democratic president, Republicans called into question Barack Obama's patriotism, his truthfulness, and even the circumstances of his birth—suggesting that he had not been born in the United States and was therefore ineligible for the presidency.

The two parties have become polarized on foreign policy as well as domestic issues. The country was divided over the wars in Korea and Vietnam, but in neither case did the division run mainly along partisan lines. Democrats and Republicans alike both opposed and supported both wars. Aggregated Gallup poll data collected between August 7, 1968, and September 22, 1969, revealed that 51 percent of Democrats and 56 percent of Republicans believed the war to have been a mistake, while 37 percent of Democrats and 34 percent of Republicans believed it had not been a mistake. For the Iraq war that began in 2003, by contrast, the supporters were mainly Republicans and the opponents mainly Democrats—in no small part because a Republican president had chosen to wage the war. A 2005 Gallup poll that asked whether the war had been a mistake found that Democrats said that it *had* been a mistake by 81 percent to 18 percent, while Republicans said it had *not* been a mistake by 78 percent to 20 percent. For much of the twentieth century, partisanship stopped at the water's edge. In the twenty-first century, it sails the high seas and plants its flag from the halls of Montezuma to the shores of Tripoli.

This sharp partisan split has given rise to the frequently cited image of a political map in which the country is divided between Republican "red" states and Democratic "blue" ones, with little in common between the two. In red and blue America, partisan polarization extends to social issues and social life, a feature expressed by a billboard on the West Side of deep-blue Manhattan that reads NYC: WHERE PEOPLE ARE OPENLY GAY & SECRETLY REPUBLICAN. Russ Feingold, a Democrat who represented Wisconsin in the Senate from 1993 to 2011, told us that at the rate polarization is proceeding, partisans will soon demand that consumer products reflect their politics: "We're going to have Republican and Democrat toothpaste."

The movies of the Marx Brothers, the funniest comedy team America has ever produced, satirize respectable but stuffy institutions such as grand opera and the medical and legal professions. In *Horse Feathers* their target is academia, but a song that Groucho Marx sings applies all too well to today's Republicans and Democrats:

> Your proposition may be good,
> But let's have one thing understood,
> Whatever it is, I'm against it.
> And even when you've changed it or condensed it,
> I'm against it.

The Great Disjunction

It would be logical to assume that America's two main political parties, and the public officials who belong to them, have become polarized because the country itself has become polarized. It would be logical to assume that a polarized political system rests on an equally polarized society, in which, as in the Gilbert and Sullivan song,

> Every boy and every gal
> Who's born into this world alive

Is either a little liberal
Or else a little conservative.

In fact, that is *not* the case. *Culture War? The Myth of a Polarized America*, a careful 2004 study of the subject by the political scientist Morris Fiorina (with the assistance of Samuel J. Abrams and Jeremy C. Pope), demonstrates that while the political views of Republican and Democratic activists have pulled apart, those of Americans in general have not changed much, and that the public's views skew closer to the center of the political spectrum than the beliefs and preferences of the officials they elect. Americans are closely divided, Fiorina explains, but they are not deeply divided. "We are closely divided because many of us are ambivalent and uncertain, and consequently reluctant to make firm commitments to parties, politicians or policies," he writes. "We divide evenly in elections or sit them out entirely because we instinctively seek the center, while the parties and candidates hang out on the extremes."

More support for this finding comes from the way the successful presidential candidates of the last two decades presented themselves to the electorate. Each signaled during the campaign that he would govern in moderate fashion and lower the level of partisan rancor in the country, although none has had any discernible success in actually reducing partisanship. George H. W. Bush promised to preside over a "kinder, gentler" America, suggesting that his policies would be less harsh than those of his Republican predecessor, Ronald Reagan. Bill Clinton styled himself a "different kind of Democrat"—that is, a less liberal figure than most other members of his party. Acknowledging the country's distaste for the partisan warfare of the Clinton years, George W. Bush described himself as "a uniter, not a divider." He promised to govern as a "compassionate conservative." When the Bush years proved to be, if anything, even more divisive than the Clinton ones, the American people turned to a first-term senator who had introduced himself to them in 2004 with a speech to the Democratic convention featuring the memorable line "There isn't a liberal America and a conservative America—there's the United States of America."

The difference between the opinions of politically active Americans and those of the electorate as a whole, between what the wider public apparently wants from its government and the kind of polarized governance that it gets, means that a serious disjunction exists between the American people and the government they elect. It means that representative government in America today does not accurately represent Americans.

Writing in the journal *Hoover Digest* (October 30, 2004), Fiorina, who is a political scientist at Stanford, elaborated on this critical point, which is at the center of his research:

> Observers of contemporary American politics have apparently reached a new consensus around the proposition that old disagreements about economics now pale in comparison to new divisions based on sexuality, morality, and religion, divisions so deep and bitter as to justify talk of war in describing them. Yet research indicates otherwise. Publicly available databases show that the culture war script embraced by journalists and politicos lies somewhere between simple exaggeration and sheer nonsense. There is no culture war in the United States; no battle for the soul of America rages, at least none that most Americans are aware of.

To be sure, said Fiorina, there are noisy warriors on both sides who like to skirmish and joust, and, no doubt, "many of the activists in the political parties and the various cause groups do hate each other and regard themselves as combatants in a war. But their hatreds and battles are not shared by the great mass of Americans—certainly nowhere near '80–90 percent of the country'—who are for the most part moderate in their views and tolerant in their manner. A case in point: To their embarrassment, some GOP senators recently learned that ordinary Americans view gay marriage in somewhat less apocalyptic terms than do the activists in the Republican base."

If centrist swing voters have vanished from American politics, said Fiorina,

> how did the six blue states in which George Bush ran most poorly in 2000 all elect Republican governors in 2002 and how did Arnold Schwarzenegger run away with the 2003 recall in blue California? If almost all voters have already made up their

minds about their 2004 votes, then why did John Kerry surge to a 14-point trial-heat lead when polls offered voters the prospect of a Kerry-McCain ticket? If voter partisanship has hardened into concrete, why do virtually identical majorities in both red and blue states favor divided control of the presidency and Congress, rather than unified control by their party? Finally, and ironically, if voter positions have become so uncompromising, why did a recent CBS story titled "Polarization in America" report that 76 percent of Republicans, 87 percent of Democrats, and 86 percent of Independents would like to see elected officials compromise more rather than stick to their principles?

No question, Republican and Democratic elites are polarized, Fiorina concluded, "but it is a mistake to assume that such elite polarization is equally present in the broader public. It is not. However much they may claim that they are responding to the public, political elites do not take extreme positions because *voters* make them. Rather, by presenting them with polarizing alternatives, elites make voters appear polarized, but the reality shows through clearly when voters have a choice of more moderate alternatives—as with the aforementioned Republican governors."

Voters have recognized this. A Rasmussen poll taken in October 2010 (just before the midterm elections) found that a plurality—43 percent—of likely voters believed that neither the Democrats nor the Republicans in Congress were "the party of the American people."

This disjunction is a major fact of the nation's political life. It is a major reason that the United States has failed to address the four major challenges that it faces. It also bears on the question of what can and should be done to shock the political system into addressing those challenges, a question that we take up in chapter 15. How could this gap between American politics and American society have become so large?

The Way We Were

In the 1950s and 1960s, when the baby boom generation was growing up, both the Democratic and the Republican Parties were coalitions of liberals and conservatives. (Some political scientists at the time even called it a "four-party system.") The Democrats included conservative Southerners, whose opposition to the Republican Party dated from the Civil War. They became known as "Dixiecrats" when they temporarily bolted the party in 1948 over the issue of segregation to support the independent pro-segregationist candidacy of the then South Carolina governor Strom Thurmond.

The Republican Party included people with fairly liberal social views who tended to be more conservative in economic terms than most Democrats. Most lived in the Northeast, and in the 1960s, as their ranks began to thin, they came to be known as "Rockefeller Republicans," after New York governor Nelson Rockefeller. One of their number at the beginning of his political career was George H. W. Bush, who grew up in Connecticut, a son of Prescott Bush, a businessman who later served as a senator from Connecticut and belonged to the moderate wing of the Republican Party. (The other, more conservative wing had its center of gravity not in the South, as is the case today, but in the Midwest.) In George H. W. Bush's two terms as a Republican congressman from Texas, he was such an enthusiastic proponent of Planned Parenthood, an organization in disfavor among most Republicans today, that he earned the nickname "Rubbers."

In the days when both parties included both conservatives and liberals in large numbers, compromise was easier than it is today because each party contained factions sympathetic to the views of elements in the other one. Moreover, because these ideologically more diverse parties had to compromise within their own ranks just to arrive at positions on various issues that all party members could support, their positions were often not all that far apart, and they were accustomed to resolving differences.

What happened to change the situation, to create the ideologically pure parties we have today? Broad social changes over the last four decades played a big part. Ron Brownstein calls this "the great sorting out"—the migration of politicians into much more internally uniform camps of conservatives and liberals. Beginning in the 1960s, opposition to the civil rights movement, a movement that was embraced by the Democratic presidents Kennedy and Johnson, led Southern conservatives to defect to the Republican Party. A decade later the rise of social conservatism within that party, in connection with issues such as abortion, school prayer, feminism, and gay marriage, pushed Northern Republicans of moderate social views into the Democratic camp. The number and the proportion of liberals in the Democratic Party increased, as did the number and weight of conservatives among Republicans. Over time, centrist groups within the respective parties (such as the Democrats' Democratic Leadership Council and the Republicans' Ripon Society) all but disappeared. Liberals and conservatives tended to be the people most active in political affairs, and so exercised more influence in each party than in previous eras. The other party was increasingly viewed as the enemy and the rules of engagement were "take no prisoners."

At the same time, at the politicians' behest, the boundaries of congressional districts at the national level, and legislative districts at the state level, were redrawn so as to concentrate members of one party or the other and thereby make that district "safe" for either a Republican or a Democratic candidate. This practice, known as "gerrymandering," is an old one. As Jeff Reichert, the director of the documentary film *Gerrymandering*, explained on NPR (November 11, 2010):

> Redistricting is supposed to be just a benign kind of administrative practice that takes place every 10 years. We have to adjust the lines to account for population. The problems come in when you have political manipulation of the process. And the term comes from 1812. There was a governor of Massachusetts by the name of Elbridge Gerry who was in office, and his party decided to disadvantage the other party, and they drew a district that packed the members of the other party into that one place. And it looked to a political cartoonist of the day like a salamander. And so he said, it's not a salamander, it's actually a gerrymander.

With computerized databases and Google maps, gerrymandering has become much more sophisticated. So effectively can the state legislatures, which draw electoral boundaries, carve out districts so that one party or the other is virtually certain to win that these days, it is said that elected officials are the ones who choose their voters as much as it is the voters, exerting their democratic right, who choose their officials. The state of California provides a vivid example. The state has fifty-three congressional districts. In the four elections between 2004 and 2010—a total of 212 electoral contests—only one district shifted from one party to the other.

Illinois (*Congressional District 4*)

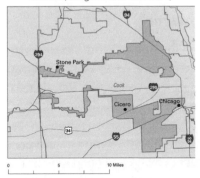

North Carolina (*Congressional District 12*)

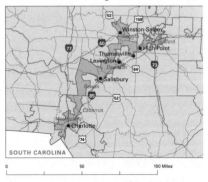

Source: National Atlas of the United States®

What this means is that in "safe" districts the crucial election is the primary, in which registered Democrats or Republicans select the party's candidate. Once you win the primary in a district gerrymandered to your party's advantage, whether you are a Democrat or a Republican, you are virtually guaranteed to win the general election. Because the voters in primaries generally must be registered members of the party, and because the ones who vote in primaries tend to be the most ideologically committed members of the party, candidates nearer the extremes of the political spectrum tend to do better in primaries than those positioned closer to the center. After winning the primary, the extreme candidate is then in a position to get the votes of more moderate voters in the general election—because in effect the only other choice is the extreme candidate from the other party. Moreover, once elected, the official knows that the only politician who can knock him or her out of office is not a candidate from the other party, whose chances have been reduced almost to zero by gerrymandering, but a more extreme candidate within his or her own party, who can pose a challenge in the next primary. The desire avoid a primary challenge discourages moderation and compromise with the other party while the representative is in office.

In this way, moderate voters elect extreme candidates: The political system does not offer them moderate choices. It works so that, as former senator Evan Bayh, a centrist Democrat who represented a relatively conservative state, Indiana, told us, "It's the people in the middle—the moderates, the independents—who get turned off and drop out, which only accentuates the power of the two extremes."

A Broken System

The geographically grotesque, politically uncompetitive electoral districts that gerrymandering can produce are the result of the political machinations of Democrats and Republicans working in state legislatures around the country. But the polarization of the American political system—seen, above all, in the great sorting out of the two parties so that liberals are concentrated in the Democratic Party and conservatives in the Republican Party—is also the product of broad and deep social, economic, and technological forces that have shaped American society for half a century and more.

Nor is a deep division between the two major parties an altogether novel development in American history. American politics have been polarized in several eras prior to this one, but the previous occasions do not offer useful precedents for dealing effectively with the nation's major challenges.

In the early years of the republic, the Federalists and anti-Federalists stood at least as far apart from each other politically as Democrats and Republicans do today, and harbored, if anything, even greater distrust and distaste for each other. In the presidential election of 1800, the allies of Thomas Jefferson hinted that his opponent, John Adams, was a secret monarchist bent on restoring the kind of regime against which the colonies had successfully rebelled. The Adams camp claimed that Jefferson was a North American version of the Jacobins, who had shed so much blood in the French Revolution.

This animosity did not cripple the American government, because that government, presiding as it did over a small agrarian country far removed from the European center of international affairs, had little to do. The duties of the continent-sized, twenty-first-century, postindustrial superpower of more than 300 million people, with the world's largest and most complex economy, are considerably more extensive, and the costs of governmental dysfunction therefore are far greater.

In the middle of the nineteenth century, political polarization over slavery went so far that it led to violence on the floor of the Senate. On May 19, 1856, Senator Charles Sumner of Massachusetts, a Republican, was delivering an antislavery speech when Preston Brooks, a Democratic congressman from South Carolina, set upon him with a walking stick and beat him nearly to death. A few years later, of course, the entire country was convulsed in violence over the same issue—hardly a good model for our own times.

Even short of such terrible violence, a polarized political system cannot furnish the responses to America's principal challenges that the country needs. It cannot do so because, in contrast with the broad voting public, the activists in America's two major parties are both *deeply divided and closely divided.* "Great innovations should not be forced upon a slender majority," Thomas Jefferson once said, and in the twenty-first-century United States they cannot be. Power in America is constitutionally dispersed between the executive and the legislative branches and between the House and the Senate. For that reason, a political party would have to be very powerful over an extended period of time to be able to enact a comprehensive program. Because the two are relatively evenly matched, neither the twenty-first-century Republicans nor their Democratic counterparts have any real prospect of achieving such political dominance. But even if they could, that would not necessarily be a good thing, because neither party alone has all the answers for dealing with globalization, the IT revolution, the nation's deficits, and its pattern of energy usage. As we have tried to demonstrate, we need a hybrid of the best of both right and left now—better public schools *and* more charter schools, more domestic drilling for oil and gas *and* a carbon tax to drive energy efficiency and clean power innovation, more tax revenue *and* more spending cuts. Just bouncing back and forth between the two extreme party positions is not going to solve our problems.

There is another way in which hyper-partisanship blocks needed action on the nation's major challenges. The partisan rancor, the name-calling, the mutual distrust, and the resulting paralysis on the issues of greatest importance for the nation's future have made a predictably bad impression on the American public, resulting in a loss of credibility for all political leaders. Michael's maternal grandfather, who immigrated to the United States from Eastern Europe in the early part of the last century, once told Michael about a three-way debate among candidates for mayor of New York City. After the Republican and the Democrat had spoken, the Socialist began his speech with these words: "I want to tell you that you can believe what my opponents say. That's right! I am here to vouch for their truthfulness. When the Democrat tells you that the Republican is no good, you can believe him. And when the Republican tells you that the Democrat is no good, you can believe him, too."

The American people have evidently been persuaded by what Republicans and Democrats have said about each other, and as a result public esteem for government has fallen to all-time lows. This has a huge cost. As the *Wall Street Journal* columnist Gerald Seib once noted: "America and its political leaders, after two decades of failing to come together to solve big problems, seem to have lost faith in their ability to do so. A political system that expects failure doesn't try very hard to produce anything else."

Mike Murphy, the veteran Republican campaign director who for a time headed Senator John McCain's 2000 presidential bid, has been to the puppet show and seen all the strings close-up. "When I did my first campaigns as a student at Georgetown [University], there were rules in terms of what you could get away with in an ad," he explained. "Not anymore. Everyone wants to blame political consultants, but we chase the voters. We give them what they want. They chase this stuff. Here is a question: How can you tell the difference between a negative ad and a positive ad? The negative ad has at least a partial fact in it."

The toll we're taking on ourselves is just getting bigger and bigger, said Murphy, who is not running political campaigns anymore. "Our politics [today] is almost like a parasite eating at the national interest for short-term gratification—so that your team can cheer and feel good for a few minutes," he told us. "If we don't save the store, the questions between the center right and center left, between apples and oranges, will be irrelevant. We will all be working at TGI Friday's in Beijing."

Murphy then paused for a moment to recall one of the best pieces of advice he ever got from a wise old hand in the ad business. "Negative ads work," the old hand told Murphy, but then added a word of caution: "Do you know why McDonald's never ran a negative ad against Burger King, saying their burgers were all full of maggots? It might have worked for a year or two but then no one would have ever eaten another hamburger." The old hand concluded with this piece of advice for Murphy: "Never destroy the category."

Reflecting on that insight, Murphy note that just at a time when we need politics in America to be at its most credible and constructive in order to define and pursue the national interest, "we've destroyed the category."

Mount Rushmore

These problems are compounded by the fact that the two parties' programs are rooted in narrow readings of their histories that are much less useful for the future than they were in the past. The parties trace these programs to the two most celebrated presidents not on Mount Rushmore: in the case of the Democrats, Franklin D. Roosevelt, who has had to settle for his profile on the dime; and for the Republicans, Ronald Reagan, whose name adorns a Washington-area airport. Each is regarded as the founder—even the prophet—of the modern version of his party, the man who established the core agenda that defines what it is to be a Democrat and a Republican today. In the case of Democrats, their central priority is the preservation and expansion of federal social welfare programs—which means resisting any modification to Social Security and Medicare and promoting universal health-care coverage. In the case of Republicans it is the reduction of taxes—which means resisting any new tax for any reason at all. At different moments in our history, both agendas made significant contributions to American growth and power. And, to be sure, all other things being equal, continuing to do both would be highly desirable.

But all things are not equal in the wake of the Terrible Twos, and behaving as if they are is getting in the way of our responding—vigorously, sensibly, and expeditiously—to our four big challenges. You wouldn't know that to listen to the debates today. As Senator Robert Bennett remarked to us, "We have great issues in politics, and then we have great diversions, and we spend most of our political time arguing over the great diversions and never facing the great issues."

It is not that every issue that each party favors is trivial or unworthy, but if our political system cannot put the nation's priorities in order— increase revenues, reduce benefits, and reinvest in the sources of our strength—this too will have a huge cost. Ironically, neither party's iconic president believed precisely what his contemporary disciples think he believed. Roosevelt, although the founder of the modern American welfare state, announced, when campaigning for the presidency in 1932, his intention to engage in "bold, persistent experimentation." In office, he practiced what he preached. He would surely not have regarded any federal program as untouchable for all time. Reagan, although a champion of low taxes, also embraced fiscal responsibility, and raised taxes when the economics dictated this. But being misunderstood is a characteristic fate of prophets.

To make matters worse, not only do the core agendas of the Democratic and Republican Parties not address the country's major challenges in ways that promise viable solutions to them, the parties' almost religious adherence to those agendas is making one of those challenges—the deficit—even more difficult to fix than it otherwise would be. When Democrats advocate increasing government spending while raising taxes only on the wealthy and Republicans call for lowering taxes without reducing spending sufficiently, it becomes impossible for us to address the country's deficit problem at the scale required. Our fiscal diet of all dessert and no vegetables, the result of uncompromising partisan allegiance to core Democratic and core Republican agendas, has given the country what the columnist Christopher Caldwell has aptly described as "a social-democratic government on an anarchist budget."

Meet Me in the Lobby

"Lobbyists" are so named, legend has it, because in the 1870s men who wanted things from the government would wait for President Ulysses S. Grant in the lobby of the Willard Hotel next to the White House, hoping to press their cases on him when he stopped by for a nightcap.

It was their right. The first amendment to the Constitution reads: "Congress shall make no law respecting an establishment of religion, or prohibiting the free exercise thereof; or abridging the freedom of speech, or of the press; or the right of the people peaceably to assemble, and to petition the Government for a redress of grievances."

That, strictly speaking, is what lobbyists do: "petition the Government for a redress of grievances." In our day, more than ever, the act of petitioning the government is dominated by special interests and their lobbyists. The term "special interests" connotes a selfish disregard for the interests of all Americans. Politicians like to boast of serving the national interest or the public interest, but they serve special interests as well, sometimes above all. As government has grown, so have the special interests and their lobbies in Washington—to the point where they often stand in the way of the policies the country needs. No less than hyperpartisan politics, super-funded and super-empowered special interests are crippling our capacity to define and act in the national interest—which involves meeting our big challenges and reviving our formula for prosperity. The attention paid to special interests also diverts our politicians—and our citizenry—from seeing our big problems, and it keeps us from tackling them with the speed, scope, and scale we need.

While it is no longer possible to buttonhole the president of the United States in a hotel bar, ever since Grant's time lobbyists have plied their trade by influencing politicians and shaping legislation. To do this, they need access to those politicians and the hope of getting a sympathetic hearing for their concerns. They get this access, in no small part, by doing favors for those politicians, including making campaign contributions—which often come close to crossing the line that separates legal from illegal acts. As Russell Long, a former chairman of the Senate Finance Committee, once put it: "The distinction between a campaign contribution and a bribe is almost a hairline's difference. You can hardly tell one from the other."

Lobbyists not only donate to campaigns. They also organize fund-raising events for candidates at which others donate. They help to create and operate political action committees that donate to candidates, and sometimes they even serve as finance chairs and treasurers of campaigns. These services naturally earn them the gratitude and goodwill of the politicians they help. As the longtime Senate Republican leader Bob Dole said of political action committees, when they give money "they expect something in return other than good government."

In our day, the most notorious lobbyist is Jack Abramoff, who was jailed in 2006 after pleading guilty to three criminal felony counts relating to the corruption of public officials and the defrauding of American Indian tribes whose legalized gambling interests he lobbied for in

Washington. The exploits of "Casino Jack" got enough attention to serve as the basis for not one but two feature-length movies. But lobbying actually isn't notably more corrupt today than it was in the past. In the post–Civil War period, bribery of public officials by railroad interests was standard operating procedure. In the 1920s, the Harding administration presided over the Teapot Dome scandal, in which the secretary of the interior received loans from businesses in exchange for the granting of leases on government-owned oil fields. The best novel about lobbying (and about Washington politics in general), *Democracy*, by Henry Adams, in which a woman declines to marry a senator after she learns that he has accepted a bribe, was first published in 1880.

Senator Evan Bayh, a Democrat from Indiana, told us a story in which someone asked then senator Bob Dole whether Congress had gotten more corrupt. "And he said, 'Oh, not even close!' When he got started in Congress back in the early 1960s, people literally had bags of cash that would be distributed and so forth," Bayh said. "That doesn't happen today." (Now the money comes via campaign contributions, airplane rides, golf outings—and more campaign contributions.)

What is new is the sheer number and power of lobbyists and the interests they represent. In 2010 there were 1,900 firms, employing more than 11,000 lobbyists (more than twenty for every member of Congress), registered to operate in Washington. The lobbyists were paid about $3.5 billion, which was twice as much as they had collectively earned only a decade earlier. Why the growth in their numbers, their salaries, and, most important, their power? The answer is contained in the title of Robert G. Kaiser's valuable 2009 book about lobbyists, *So Damn Much Money: The Triumph of Lobbying and the Corrosion of American Government*, which we draw on here.

The rising influence of lobbyists on our political life is the consequence of a broad, long-term trend: the steady growth in the size of the American government. Over the decades, the American people, through their elected representatives, have decided that they want their government to do more and more things and to spend more and more money doing them. The federal budget for fiscal year 2010 involved the expenditure of $3.55 trillion, so it is not surprising that special interests hire lobbyists to get it spent on their behalf and not somebody else's.

Lobbying has its constructive side. Lobbyists can represent small but worthy interests whose voices would otherwise not be heard (such as the group that wants to save the old covered bridge in your hometown), or broad public interests such as environmental protection that have no natural, moneyed, private-sector champions. Lobbyists can also help government officials understand complicated issues involving the companies and interests they work for—and can walk them through the thickets of corresponding legislation. In 2006, the federal tax code was 44,000 pages long, with 5.5 million words. The stimulus bill that Congress passed in early 2009 covered 407 pages. The health-care legislation it enacted the next year was 906 pages long. The financial-reform act of that year took up 2,319 pages. Even the sharpest elected officials cannot hope to understand such bills by themselves. That is where—for good and for ill—lobbyists come in. The diverse and complex nature of so much legislation today opens the way for lobbyists to shape and even write portions of bills, ostensibly for the national interest, certainly for the benefit of the special interests they are paid to represent.

Former senator Simpson has referred to lobbyists as "practitioners of the dark arts" who would, he predicted, resist any serious effort to implement the budget cuts he favored. Behind closed doors, lobbyists work to enact subsidies and to open loopholes that favor already wealthy and not particularly deserving interests, measures that would outrage the public if they received any publicity. As Robert Kaiser, the *So Damn Much Money* author, noted in an essay on Amazon.com in the fall of 2008:

> The House of Representatives set off a sudden collapse of the stock market by voting against the first version of the "bailout" legislation that had been hurriedly written to try to stabilize American banks and other financial institutions. Supporters of the bailout scrambled to change the legislation in ways that would win support for it from a majority of Congressmen. In a matter of days new provisions were added: extension of an excise-tax rebate for makers of Puerto Rican rum (cost to the Treasury, $192 million); extension of a special tax break for the owners of stock car racing tracks (cost, $100 million); a tax break for makers of movies within the borders of the United States (cost over ten years, $478 million) and more. These

"sweeteners"—a revealing bit of Washington jargon—did the trick. Days after rejecting the $750 billion bailout, the House approved it.

While there is so much work and money for lobbyists today because of the big, complex, and steadily growing government we have chosen to have, the proliferation of lobbyists can take a toll on a country's rate of growth—and is already taking a toll on ours. In 1982, the economist Mancur Olson published a book entitled *The Rise and Decline of Nations,* in which he noted the universal tendency of interest groups to form and to lobby on their own behalf, especially in democracies, where they are free to do so. Olson called these groups "distributional coalitions" because they are "overwhelmingly oriented to struggle over the distribution of income and wealth rather than to the production of additional output." They concentrate, that is, on gaining larger shares of the economic pie for themselves, not on making the pie bigger.

Over time such groups, in Olson's words, "slow down a society's capacity to adopt new technologies and to reallocate resources in response to changing conditions." That is why special interests pose such a threat to America's future. Adopting new technologies and reallocating resources in response to changing conditions is precisely what America needs to do.

The fossil fuel lobby (aka Big Oil and Big Coal) has consistently opposed the clean-energy policies needed to respond to the challenges of climate change and America's oil addiction. The most important such policy is the imposition of a higher price on carbon-based fuels—through a tax on carbon—so that non-carbon sources of energy can become commercially competitive with them. This would hasten the transition from fossil fuels to clean-power technologies and, by weakening our oil-exporting adversaries, would make America stronger and more secure internationally. But the oil, coal, and natural gas industries, as well as the U.S. Chamber of Commerce and the National Association of Manufacturers, employ platoons of lobbyists to fight any increase in taxes or clean-air regulations on their fuels, which they say would harm their businesses.

The website ClimateProgress.Org reported (October 3, 2010) that "the oil, gas, and coal industries have spent over $2 billion lobbying

Congress since 1999. These three industries combined spent a whopping $543 million on lobbying in 2009 and the first two quarters of 2010. Meanwhile, alternative energy companies spent less than $32 million on lobbying efforts in 2009, and have only spent $14.8 million this year."

The lobbyists are so effective that their backers can essentially order up a particular policy or change in regulations and the lobbyists will deliver it. An analysis by ProPublica, the nonpartisan investigative news service, about the oil and gas money received by members of the Natural Gas Caucus (January 4, 2011) found that they received "19 times more money from the oil and gas industry between 2009 and 2010" on average than members of Congress who signed a letter in support of a pro-environment proposal to require companies that engage in fracking—a technique to crack open underground formations to unlock natural gas—to disclose the chemicals they use when drilling on public lands.

The most powerful special interest of all is not a labor union or an industry. Most of its members are not wealthy and do not think of themselves as having lobbyists who do their bidding in Washington. Yet it shapes the federal government's response to one of the country's most serious problems—our fiscal deficits—and does more to divert resources from the kinds of programs needed to master the challenges America faces than any other group.

This special interest group is older Americans, and its lobby is the American Association of Retired Persons (AARP). We know this is a controversial position, but it seems to us that older Americans' interests qualify as "special" because, while a secure and dignified retirement for America's seniors is vital, that interest has to be better balanced with other vital interests than it is now. If the budgets for Social Security and Medicare cannot be cut at all, then the budgets for education, infrastructure, and research and development will surely be cut too much.

The federal budget deficit exploded during the Terrible Twos, even before the Great Recession of 2008. Even if we see a full recovery from the recession, though, the country's deficits and debt are on course to explode again because of the rapid rise in the number of older Americans. The retirement of seventy-eight million baby boomers—Americans born between 1946 and 1964—will cause the costs of Social Security and Medicare to skyrocket. Between 2010 and 2020 those costs are expected to rise by 70 and 79 percent, respectively. By 2050, according to Michael Tanner of the Cato Institute, a libertarian think tank, these two programs plus Medicaid will take 18.4 percent of everything the United States produces.

The country has not put aside the money needed to pay the boomers the benefits to which they are entitled by law. The two main programs are funded on a pay-as-you-go basis, with the taxes of people presently in the workforce supporting, through their payroll contributions, those who have retired. The shortfall in revenue at current tax rates as the boomers retire will be immense: into the trillions of dollars. Without serious adjustments—that is, reductions—in Social Security and Medicare benefits, the prospect is for bigger and bigger deficits, requiring more and more borrowing, leading to a larger and larger national debt.

Members of Congress certainly understand this, but they—especially Democrats—have shied away from supporting serious measures to reduce Social Security and Medicare benefits because of the political power of America's senior citizens. That power stems from two hard realities: there are many people sixty-five and older—more than forty million, comprising 13 percent of the population, in 2009, with the percentage expected to rise to 20 percent by 2050—and proportionally more of them vote than do people in other age groups. The AARP is a potent lobby, but what gives it its power is something bigger than money or expertise in the labyrinthine statutes and regulations of the federal government. It is numbers, numbers that can be mobilized for the battles that matter most to politicians—elections.

In the 1930s, when Social Security was established, old-age pensions of any kind were rare, and senior citizens were the poorest age cohort in America. Now, by some measures, seniors are overall the richest, while the poorest rung on the American ladder of wealth is occupied by children. But our entitlement programs transfer resources from the working population to the old at the expense of the young. Children are, as the cliché has it, our future, which means that our entitlement programs represent an investment in the past at the expense of the future. The national interest depends on everyone, including seniors, making some sacrifice so that the country can make the investments it needs in America's future.

Persuading seniors to do so will be hard; not all of them are well-to-do "greedy geezers." The baby boom generation as a whole has a dismally low savings rate, which means that its members are counting on Social Security payments as a much-needed source of income for their retirement years. Serious cuts to Medicare spending would likely affect the quality of care, probably shortening the lives of some of the older Americans who will depend on it. Yet some restraints on the otherwise soaring costs of these two programs are necessary, as the AARP itself has recognized in the case of Social Security, if America is to renew its formula for greatness and tackle its major challenges.

While reducing Social Security and Medicare may be unfair to older Americans, under-investing in education is harmful to everyone. In this sense, entitlements serve a special interest, while education serves the national interest. Virtually all studies of the subject show that the earlier in an individual's life an investment in his or her education is made, the greater will be the payoff in productivity and income earned in the course of that person's life. A dollar wisely invested in early education can do far more to meet the challenges of the world we are living in than a dollar spent on a senior citizen, no matter how deserving he or she may be.

Show Me the Money

The novelist William Faulkner, the recipient of the 1949 Nobel Prize in Literature, once said that "to live anywhere in the world of AD 1955 and be against equality because of race or color is like living in Alaska and being against snow." So is being against money in politics. Money has always been a part of politics—at least of democratic politics—and always will be. Like partisanship and special interests, however, money has taken on a markedly more pronounced political role in recent years, to the detriment of the policies America desperately needs to enact.

Much of the money goes to pay for the ever more elaborate technology of contemporary political campaigns: polling, direct-mail solicitation, robo-calling, and television advertising. In 1974, the money spent on the congressional election—the combined spending by all the candidates for the House of Representatives and the Senate—was $75 million. During the next several election cycles this sum escalated sharply, reaching $343 million in 1982. The amount of money spent on campaigns has continued to climb upward ever since. Altogether, the candidates for the 2010 congressional election spent $879 million.

Where do candidates get all that money? Some of it comes from organizations dedicated to promoting particular causes or issues that tend to fall at either end of the ideological spectrum: gay rights and the environment for Democrats, abortion and gun rights for conservatives. Committed partisans give more money than people in the middle, which aggravates the polarization of American politics.

But candidates' money also comes in large quantities from special interests. Politicians spend an enormous amount of time raising the money they get and spend. The constant need to raise money not only empowers the special interests, which have the money to give; it also disempowers the politicians, by forcing them to spend almost as much time raising money as they do governing. The politicians we spoke to estimated that it routinely takes up a quarter of their working days, and sometimes more. Senator Evan Bayh, the Indiana Democrat who retired in 2011 after two terms, told us that when his father served in the Senate, from 1963 to 1981, "the saying was that you legislate for four years and campaign for two." Now, by contrast, campaigning—especially in the form of fund-raising—goes on all the time. "There are people," Bayh said, referring to his Senate colleagues, "who go from their swearing-in to a fund-raiser that night for their reelection that's six years away. That has happened and is happening! So it never stops.

"If fund-raising and all things political are constantly in the forefront of your mind, it makes it harder to legislate absent those kinds of considerations," added Bayh. "Yeah, it's all politics all the time . . . Political calculus is more prominent in people's thinking when they're forced to think about campaigning and politics 24/7 for six years. Money is a big part of it. And why? Because there are going to be sleazy ads running against you, attacking your character—you've got to be able to set the record straight. And this comes back to the media again, just the cost of television. The atomization—again, even ten years ago, twelve years ago, the number of commercials you had to run to communicate effectively with the electorate was much less than today because they didn't have all these cable channels. The audience is so fragmented. You have to run three or four more times the number of commercials to get the same exposure. And obviously, that's big money. And the cost keeps going up per commercial. So when you combine those two factors, it's just exploded."

Bayh explained that "75 percent of the time a senator is 'in cycle' [meaning that the senator faces an election within two years] is spent raising money—not meeting with constituents, not talking to policy experts, not sitting down with colleagues trying to hammer out a principled compromise. It's getting on the phone and asking for campaign cash or traveling to fund-raisers. You know, that's the reality of it, unless you are überwealthy or are an Internet star or something. The final thing I'd say is . . . remember when Justice [Samuel] Alito had that moment when the president was saying the Citizens United case [striking down the law restricting corporate campaign contributions] was going to lead to a flood of secret cash into our campaigns, and Alito seemed to be mouthing the words 'not true'? Come on! This is exactly what happened. You can say it's good constitutional law, but you cannot [deny] what the obvious consequences of this are going to be. And it's exactly what happened. And we ain't seen nothing yet. There are going to be hundreds of millions of dollars in large increments of secret money influencing the elections of the highest offices in the land. I mean, it's astonishing! . . . What's going to happen [is this]: Senator A is running and is now aware that one of these secret groups will be attacking him with millions of dollars. [So you need] a secret group who's going to be fighting on your behalf in $5, $10, $15 million increments. And that is the only way to level the playing field.

"So both sides will have their secret groups. They'll be taking megamillion-dollar [corporate] contributions. So what will happen is, [a senator] will say, 'Who is going to defend me?' And then [the senator] will go to [one of these deep-pocketed corporate groups] and say, 'I need your help.' And they'll say, 'We love you. You've been a good friend. We will definitely help you out. But you know, the bylaws of our organization will only permit us to do that for people who are with us 90 percent of the time. So here's a list of our top ten issues. Why don't you go study that, fill it out, and give it back to us, because we'd love to help you out.' And these are going to be real votes on specific pieces of legislation! And this [senator] is going to be looking at that, knowing that millions of dollars hang on how he fills out that questionnaire and the commitments he makes on real votes. It's about as close to corruption as you can come without actually crossing the line. And to the average citizen, that would absolutely look corrupt. And you know what's going to change that? It's going to take another Jack Abramoff thing on steroids or another Watergate—it's going to take a huge scandal that will be so shocking that not to change the system would be self-destructive."

Together, the power of special interests and the financial demands of campaigns place Congress—as its own members admit—in danger of becoming a fund-raising organization that dabbles in legislation on the side. It is increasingly beholden to the wealthiest and most politically extreme interests in America at a time when the country urgently needs it to be attentive to the national interest.

Media Madness

Senator Lindsey Graham leaned back in his chair in his Senate office, trying to imagine for us what would have happened if America's current media had been around to cover the Constitutional Convention in Philadelphia. We'd probably still be living as separate colonies, he said.

"Let's go back in time," mused Graham. It is 1787 "and we're in Philadelphia, we're trying to hammer out the Constitution. Tell me how the twenty-four-hour news cycle would have affected writing the Constitution. Cable networks are outside Independence Hall. Ben Franklin walks out. He gets ambushed by Fox News. 'Is it true you're caving on a small [state] representation? What power do you give small states?' I've always thought *Saturday Night Live* should do this. Think of a skit in which Ben Franklin is walking down the streets and people are just eating him alive. And you have Glenn Beck right outside saying, 'They're selling us out.' You've got Rachel Maddow throwing herself in front of the door. Okay, so now, fast-forward. The twenty-four-hour news cycle makes compromise difficult because things get leaked and the momentum to find consensus is deterred. It's hard to maintain momentum for controversial topics in the twenty-four-hour news cycle. You saw it on the energy bill—when somebody from the White House told Fox News that Lindsey Graham is pushing the carbon tax, remember that?" That report generated so much conservative opposition in South Carolina before Graham got a chance to put it in context that he was unable to continue his support for the bill.

All of the forces of polarization that have weakened our political system's ability to address our biggest problems are reinforced by a hyper-fragmented, hyper-energized media environment, which has turned the war between the parties into a much more intense form of entertainment and blood sport than ever before.

"The twenty-four-hour news cycle is about defining things," Graham continued. "You're always in a constant cycle to make sure that your proposal is not defined in a way that would destroy your ability to get the necessary votes . . . What does this mean? It means that Social Security reform, Medicare reform, tax-code reform, are going to be incredibly difficult—because all it takes is one or two liberal or conservative special interest groups to be able to get traction [by the way they define the issue in the media and] then you start losing people."

Technology makes these problems more acute. Where once working politicians had to follow, and contend with, only newspapers and the three major television networks, now talk radio, cable television news, the Internet, and the blogosphere are inescapable aspects of their working lives. From our interviews, it appears that the time politicians spend obsessing on what is written about them in the blogosphere rivals the time they spend dialing for dollars.

The new media have turned news into something that is distributed through many channels, that is updated constantly, and that is available everywhere. Because of blogs and Twitter, anyone can be a reporter or a columnist. Because of websites, the news is reported twenty-four hours a day, seven days a week—in the back of a taxi to the airport, in the waiting room at the airport, and on the plane itself. Because of satellites, digital cameras, and cell phones, anything that happens anywhere that is of interest to anyone can and will be broadcast, instantaneously, around the world. These developments have broadened the range of news sources and opinions, which we believe is healthy for our democracy. But they have also created an appetite, and platforms, for more opinions from more people all the time, which can have unanticipated and unwelcome consequences.

"In the twenty-four-hour news cycle, the political moment seems to trump any sense of history," added Graham. "I guess what we're losing in the Senate is a sense of history and perspective. The intense pressures of the twenty-four-hour news cycle don't allow one to reflect very well about who we are and what we're doing . . . [As a result], you're no longer the most deliberative body in the world. You're just an extension of the political moment."

This new-media environment reinforces hyper-partisanship in Washington, because the new media generally aim at smaller audiences than the old. Talk radio and cable television are not trying to attract people from different points on the political spectrum, as the three networks and the major newspapers did when they had a virtual monopoly on news dissemination. Instead, they target one end or the other of that spectrum by offering programming that reinforces the opinions that viewers or listeners already hold. This so-called "narrowcasting" is the secret of Rush Limbaugh's success, and of the success of Fox News and MSNBC as well. Conservative programs on talk radio and cable television have bigger audiences than liberal ones—perhaps because, as surveys show, there are more self-identified conservatives than liberals, perhaps because, unlike liberals, conservatives feel that the mainstream media does not serve them properly. Limbaugh surely entertains his listeners, but that contributes to the problem.

The new media seek to capture audiences by presenting news as entertainment and politics as sports—a kind of "PSPN" alongside ESPN. The USA Network has a slogan that refers to the offbeat stars of its comedies and dramas: "Characters welcome." That could be the slogan of cable news and talk radio as well. They offer the public outsize, quirky, passionate, controversial personalities. Not for them the dry, on-the-one-hand-and-on-the-other style of discourse. Unfortunately for the country, such a measured, dispassionate, sometimes even boring approach is the appropriate one for the complicated issues of public policy that will determine the American future. Aiming as they do to entertain, the new media thrive on conflict. Indeed, the programs they present often bear more than a passing resemblance to professional wrestling, with stock heroes and villains, exaggerated feuds, and, since the programs are explicitly either liberal or conservative, a predetermined outcome. At times, all that's missing are the Tarzan outfits and fake body slams.

This is not a useful model for public debate on the serious issues the country now faces. As Jon Stewart put it in an interview with Rachel Maddow on MSNBC (November 11, 2010): "The problem with the twenty-four-hour news cycle is it's built for a particular thing—9/11. Other than that, there really isn't twenty-four hours of stuff to talk about in the same way. The problem is, how do you keep people watching it? O.J.'s not going to kill someone every day. So that's gone. So what do you have to do? You have to elevate the passion of everything else that happens that might even be somewhat mundane—and elevate it to the extent that this is breaking news . . . You begin to lose any meaning of what breaking news means."

Cable news does not exist in order to bridge the partisan divide but rather to thrive on it, feed it, and inflame it. Those who watch cable news shows and listen to talk radio learn that the people on the other side of that divide are foolish, hypocritical, and sometimes wicked—not that the problems the country faces are complicated, difficult, and urgent.

The new-media outlets have relatively small audiences. In 2010, prime-time programs on Fox averaged about two million viewers (although some programs had as many as three million), and the numbers for MSNBC and CNN were even smaller: 764,000 and 591,000, respectively. Most blogs and websites attract a trickle of visitors at best. Yet they help to shape our public life because they matter a great deal to our public officials.

In sports, when a player is frustrated, distracted, and confused by an opponent to the point that he performs badly, the opponent is said to be "in his head." Similarly, the new media are "in the heads" of American politicians. All the elected officials with whom we spoke for this book—without exception, Republican and Democrat alike—said that talk radio, cable television, and the Internet exercised substantial influence on how they did their jobs. It prompted them either to say things in more pointed ways to get attention or to spend time and energy reacting to things said about them. "Did you see what that blogger said about me?" is how a lot of sentences begin in Washington these days. Again, in some cases the greater scrutiny on politicians, on how they spend their time and money and on what they say in one place as compared with what they say in another, is an asset for democracy. This makes elected officials, and everyone else, more accountable.

Sometimes, though, it can be a distraction, or worse. On balance, we think the impact of the new media is positive, but its downside is not negligible.

It can instantly purvey both misinformation and corrections to the misinformation. Put up a lie or a mistaken fact and the Internet will both spread it and correct it at lightning speed. The problem, though, is that the falsehood often draws much more attention than the correction, and the sites that spread falsehoods are different from the sites that correct them, so the corrections often don't reach the right people.

Senator Bennett told us that during his unsuccessful 2010 campaign for renomination he encountered people who roundly criticized him for positions that he had never taken. He was accused, for example, of supporting the Obama health-care plan, when he had in fact outspokenly opposed it—and made this clear on his official website, where he posted his own innovative alternative. When he asked his constituents where they had gotten their mistaken beliefs, they usually replied, "The Internet"— meaning the far-right-wing sites that had become their sources of news.

"I lost the campaign on Facebook, YouTube, all of the rest of that," Bennett told us as his staff cleared out his Senate office in December 2010. "I couldn't penetrate it. It was saturated with Glenn Beck. Glenn Beck is on television every day. The Glenn Beck groupies pick out pieces that they love, and then it's all over, as they say. It goes viral. That's where [the Utah state Republican delegates who voted in the primary] got their information. They didn't get it from *The New York Times*."

Bennett told us that an old friend wrote to him out of the blue to ask why he was pushing a constitutional amendment providing that "every member of Congress, after one term, gets full pay for life [and] every member of Congress has a gold-plated medical plan for which they do not pay." The friend, said Bennett, had apparently heard some such thing from Glenn Beck and shared it with everyone on his Christmas card list—including Bennett. So the message to voters, said Bennett, was "Throw them all out—they raised their salaries while they are cutting Social Security benefits to pay for it."

How did Bennett respond? He and his wife sat down at the computer and wrote the following reply: "Dear X: Thanks for sending me this to give me an opportunity to comment. Number one, we have frozen our salaries; number two, the Social Security thing is set by law; number three, I wish that it were so that I got full salary for the rest of my life just for serving one term; we do not have a gold-plated health care plan—we have exactly the same as any other federal employee."

And to that voter's credit, said Bennett, he got a response. The voter sent the following note out to his Christmas card list: "Senator Bennett has been our friend for a long time, and he set the record straight, and I want everybody to know that these are the facts."

The correction had little effect. Repeatedly during the campaign voters came up to him at rallies, Bennett said, and grilled him: "'You voted for ObamaCare.' 'No, I didn't.' 'Yes, you did. I read it on the Internet.' 'You voted for ObamaCare.' 'You voted for the stimulus.' 'You voted for TARP.' I said, 'Look, I am the guy who changed the proposed law from $700 billion to two tranches of $350 billion, because I wanted to see if it worked before I voted for the second, and I voted against the second $350 billion because of the way the first $350 billion was headed.' 'No, no, you wasted $700 billion. Glenn Beck told me so.'" That is character assassination masquerading as news. Democratic colleagues are getting the same treatment from some left-wing websites, said Bennett. "Nobody pays the least bit of attention to CBS News anymore. If Walter Cronkite were to be resurrected, nobody would hire him, let alone listen to him."

The political consequences of the new media landscape that Bennett describes, along with hyper-partisanship and the power of special interests, are paralyzing the American political system. The paralysis-induced failure to address adequately the country's four major challenges is, in turn, pushing America toward a grim future. That future, which we will inherit in the absence of major political change, is already visible on the shores of the Pacific Ocean.

California, Here We Come

Once upon a time, both the United States of America and the state of California were the envy of the world. Each was favored by geography with fertile soil and abundant natural resources. Each developed the institutions and customs that made it a prosperous, creative, exciting place. Each became a fast-growing land of opportunity, both a model for others and a magnet for people from elsewhere, who flocked there by the millions.

So glowing was each one's reputation that each became associated, in the public mind, with the most precious of all metals. California was the Golden State from the time, in the middle of the nineteenth century, when large deposits of gold were discovered there, triggering the first of many waves of immigration. In that same era, among European Jews, for whom the New World was their hoped-for destination, America was known as *die goldene medina*—"the golden land." In the most remote and provincial pockets of Europe, the legend that America's streets were actually paved with gold was half believed.

The American dream reached its peak in California. The historian Kevin Starr entitled his multivolume history of the Golden State *Americans and the California Dream*; an early study of the quintessential California institution, the film industry, called it "the Dream Factory"; the slogan of Disneyland, which opened outside Los Angeles in 1955, is "Where Dreams Come True"; and a 1965 hit by the Mamas and the Papas (ranked as number 89 on *Rolling Stone* magazine's list of the top 500 songs of all time) was called "California Dreamin'." It was written while the group was living in New York.

In the twentieth century California became the America of America, as admired and respected (with a touch of resentment and jealousy thrown in) by the other states of the union as the United States itself was by the other countries of the world. The American public-private formula for prosperity—education, infrastructure, immigration, research and development, and a business-friendly economic climate with appropriate regulation—reached its zenith in California, which became the favored location of that characteristically American business, venture capitalism.

As the home, as well, to forward-looking industries such as electronics and aerospace, to Hollywood and Silicon Valley, California was where Americans could see the future. For decades what they saw was inspiring.

Now it is chilling.

At the end of the first decade of the twenty-first century, the state was suffering from an unemployment rate of 12.5 percent, considerably higher than the very high (9 percent) national average. Its fiscal condition was dire: the state budget deficit exceeded $25 billion, fully 25 percent of total public expenditure. (At 10 percent, the federal budget deficit of that year was considered catastrophically high; and states are required by law to balance their budgets.)

Moreover, California faced future yearly deficits estimated at $20 billion or more and pension obligations of perhaps $500 billion. San Diego, the state's second-largest city and the eighth largest in the United States, with almost 1.4 million people, teetered on the brink of bankruptcy. Meredith Whitney, one of the few financial analysts to predict the subprime-mortgage debacle, rated California's financial condition as the worst among the fifteen largest U.S. states. Whitney's report (described in Bloomberg News, September 29, 2010) "rates the states by four criteria: economy, fiscal health, housing and taxes . . . 'The similarities between the states and the banks are extreme to the extent that states have been spending dramatically and are leveraged dramatically,' Whitney said. 'Municipal debt has doubled since 2000. Spending has grown way faster than revenues.'"

Public education—think Berkeley—was once the jewel in California's crown and the key to its prosperity. By 2011, however, the state's primary and secondary schools, as measured by the test scores of their students, were among the country's weakest, and its system of higher education, which once set the standard for the rest of the country, even the world, had to raise tuition sharply, provoking protests from students on several campuses.

On March 23, 2011, the *San Francisco Chronicle* summarized what was happening to state's higher education system:

> About 10,000 students will be turned away, and an untold number of employees will lose their jobs next fall across California State University's 23 campuses. That was the grim news Tuesday out of Long Beach, where CSU trustees discussed how the university that serves more than 400,000 students will shrink amid devastating budget news from the state. "We're facing the worst financial situation the CSU has ever had," said Trustee Bill Hauck, chairman of the university system's finance committee.

While California's population has continued to grow, approaching forty million, the growth no longer comes from internal migration from other parts of the United States. In fact, more people now choose to leave California each year than move there from other states, an unthinkable trend during the Golden State's golden era. If it has not died, the California dream is now on life support.

There is more than one reason for this. The end of the Cold War reduced the size of America's defense industry, many of whose firms were located in the state. California is home to more immigrants, many of whom enter the United States illegally, than any other state, straining its public facilities. Its crazy-quilt governmental system, in which public referenda can tie the hands of the legislature and override, or complicate, an already complicated state constitution, makes it difficult to govern even in the best of times.

The state's basic failure, however, has been a political one. *Its problems require collective action to solve.* That can only come through the political system, but California's political system has not coped with the challenges the state faces. Californians, of course, know this. An article by Bill Whalen in *The Weekly Standard* (December 27, 2010) reported that "according to the Public Policy Institute of California, only 13 percent of voters approve of the two branches of state government's working arrangement. Only 2 percent of Californians trust the state to always do right. Just 3 percent have a great deal of faith in Sacramento's decision-making process."

We cite California's present condition because it is an all-too-plausible harbinger of America's future. The political failures of the Golden State and of the United States are much too close for comfort. Like the national political system, California's politics are polarized along partisan lines to such an extent that the state has become virtually ungovernable. Democrats and Republicans have such radically different public philosophies, and have become so hostile to each other, that they have not been able to find mutually acceptable solutions to the state's most basic problems of education, taxation, health, infrastructure, prisons, and pensions. For example, California's conservative anti-tax activists have set the gold standard for holding down property taxes ever since a freeze of sorts was voted in by state residents in 1978—along with handcuffs that require a two-thirds vote by both houses of the state legislature to enact any new taxes.

At the same time, though, politics in California, like national politics, operates under the sway of powerful special interests, whose donations to candidates for public office and lobbying of public officials tend to aggravate rather than resolve the state's problems. California's public employees' unions, for example, are particularly adept at winning benefits for their members: a Sacramento fire-truck driver earns a salary of $144,000 per year in a county where the average annual wage is about $52,000. Firefighters should be well paid, but there have to be some limits. When you combine powerful public employee unions with powerful anti-tax activists and little willingness to compromise in one state, it spells "bankruptcy."

There's an old Navajo saying that if we don't turn around now, we just might get where we're going. If we as a country don't find a way to overcome hyper-partisanship and super-empowered special interests, we too may get where we're going—to the place at which California has already arrived. That will be us.

THIRTEEN

Devaluation

As we peer into society's future, we—you and I, and our government—
must avoid the impulse to live only for today, plundering, for our own ease
and convenience, the precious resources of tomorrow. We cannot mortgage the material assets of our grandchildren without risking the loss also
of their political and spiritual heritage.

—President Dwight D. Eisenhower's Farewell Address,
January 19, 1961

On November 26, 2010, *The New York Times* ran an unusual article—
the advice of a dying man. It was the life story of Gordon Murray, a
former bond salesman for Goldman Sachs who became a managing director at both Lehman Brothers and Credit Suisse First Boston. He had
recently decided to cease all treatment for his glioblastoma, a type of
brain cancer, but rather than live out his days going through his bucket
list, the story noted, "he hunkered down in his tiny home office here
and channeled whatever remaining energy he could muster into a slim
paperback. It's called *The Investment Answer,* and he wrote it with his
friend and financial adviser Daniel Goldie to explain investing in
a handful of simple steps." What struck us was the line—a red line,
really—that Murray drew between the old Wall Street where he began
his career back in the 1970s and the Wall Street that eventually blew up
in 2008. The story noted that Murray "got a lot of second chances thanks
to an affluent background and basketball prowess. He eventually landed
at Goldman Sachs, long before many people looked askance at anyone

who worked there. 'Our word was our bond, and good ethics was good business,' he said of his Wall Street career. 'That got replaced by liar loans and 'I hope I'm gone by the time this thing blows up.' ' "

It is hard to find a more concise and accurate description of something else that happened with the end of the Cold War and the passing of the baton from the Greatest Generation to the baby boom generation: an erosion of important, traditional American values that long underpinned our public and commercial life.

This decline in values has done as much as political hyper-partisanship to undermine our ability to address our great challenges and revive our formula for prosperity. This decline did not happen overnight. It occurred gradually, little by little, almost imperceptibly beneath the surface of daily events, like the geological process known as continental drift that, over millions of years, divided the Earth's surface into its separate landmasses. Because it happened in an incremental way, we didn't notice it—until the subprime crisis in 2008 showed just how far we had drifted from some of the bedrock values that used to be us.

Here again, the passage from one generation to another has made a large and, from the point of view of the country's future, unfortunate difference. Although the Great Depression ended in 1940, World War II concluded in 1945, and the most dangerous moments of the Cold War had passed by the mid-1960s, those searing historical traumas lived on in the memories and consciousness of the men and women who had lived through them. It forged their collective identity as not only the Greatest Generation but also "the prudent generation." The press mocked President George H. W. Bush for using the word "prudent" so often, but it was a favorite word of many members of his generation—and for good reason. They had encountered more than one black swan—the one-in-a-million kind of disruption that can capsize the whole world and turn rich into poor, the settled into refugees, the carefree civilian into the battle-scarred soldier, and the eternal optimist into the cautious investor. Taken together, their life experiences made that generation prudent, inclined toward collective action, and comfortable with government and expert authority.

As the Harvard political philosopher Michael J. Sandel put it, our parents' generation came of age at a time "when we took the importance of government for granted—when world events made obvious the importance of government and collective action on behalf of the public good. The shared premise was that the public realm mattered and that government action was a necessary instrument of the public good. The debate was over how much and to what extent."

Collective action on behalf of the public good, after all, had been necessary for survival, and it was by fighting the Depression, winning World War II, and containing the Soviet Union—by doing big, hard things together—that the Greatest Generation achieved remarkable success.

As the Cold War ended and that generation started retiring, it was replaced in positions of leadership by the baby boom generation (to which we, the authors, belong): the cohort of seventy-eight million Americans born between 1946 and 1964. We have to admit that the conduct of our own generation, in contrast to that of our parents, has been more than a little selfish, pampered, and, at times, reckless and irresponsible.

Unscathed by great disruptions, unburdened by the necessity of great sacrifice, unpressured by the daily effort of confronting a huge global predator—and, in addition, hurried and besotted by new technologies and electronic markets that have encouraged short-term thinking—the baby boom generation has in too many cases displayed too little fiscal prudence, too much political partisanship, and too short a sense of history to engage in the collective nation-building at home that America badly needs today.

A well-functioning political system must be rooted in something deeper than itself: a culture, which is most vividly expressed through certain values. We believe that as the boomer generation has assumed a dominant place in American society, the country has strayed from three of the core values on which American greatness depended in the past.

The first of these changes involves a shift from long-term investment and delayed gratification, which were characteristic of the Greatest Generation, to short-term gratification and get-it-now-while-you-can thinking, which alas is typical of the baby boom generation.

The second change is the loss of confidence in our institutions and in the authority of their leaders across the society. Related to this is a shift in how this society sees people in authority, whether politicians or scientific experts—a shift from healthy skepticism to cynical suspicion of everything and everyone. This shift makes generating the kind of collective action we need to solve our big problems and update our traditional formula for prosperity that much more difficult.

The third shift in values is a weakening of our sense of shared national purpose, which propelled us in—and was reinforced by—the struggle against fascism in World War II and against communism in the Cold War. As we have emphasized, although the Cold War had its dangers and excesses, and although no one should wish for its return, it did bring one benefit, whose importance becomes all the clearer in hindsight: It fostered a feeling of American solidarity, a shared sense of the national interest, as well as a seriousness about governance, which could rally the country to do important and constructive things at home and abroad.

Every one of us has a friend who looked great in high school, maybe even quarterbacked the football team, but over the years put on more and more weight, so that at the high school reunion, when he walked through the door at the hotel, everyone smiled politely while muttering under his or her breath, "Wow, he really let himself go." That was America after the end of the Cold War: lots more gadgets, and much bigger houses, but so much of it bought with liar loans, bailouts, stimulus, cheap credit, and more tax cuts with money borrowed from China and from the next generation. We really did let ourselves go . . .

"Don't pretend we didn't see this coming for a long, long time, the writer Kurt Andersen observed of this era in a *Time* magazine article (March 26, 2009), which he later turned into a book called *Reset: How This Crisis Can Restore Our Values and Renew America*.

In the early 1980s, around the time Ronald Reagan became President and Wall Street's great modern bull market began, we started gambling (and winning!) and thinking magically. From 1980 to 2007, the median price of a new American home quadrupled. The Dow Jones industrial average climbed from 803 in the summer of 1982 to 14,165 in the fall of 2007. From the beginning of the '80s through 2007, the share of disposable income that each household spent servicing its mortgage and consumer debt increased 35%. Back in 1982, the average household saved 11% of its disposable income. By 2007 that number was less than 1%. The same zeitgeist made gambling ubiqui-

tous: until the late '80s, only Nevada and New Jersey had ca-
sinos, but now 12 states do, and 48 have some form of legalized
betting. It's as if we decided that Mardi Gras and Christmas are
so much fun, we ought to make them a year-round way of life.

This is not the place to undertake a comprehensive review of all the
norms that have underpinned American society. Nor do we believe that
the core values responsible for American greatness over the decades
have disappeared. To the contrary, we are confident that they can be
revived. They do, however, need reviving.

Jerry Maguire

The first shift, from deferred to instant gratification, from a long-term to
a short-term perspective, has been described by Dov Seidman, the CEO
of LRN, whose book *How* explores how values issues play out in the
business world. In Seidman's view, two competing kinds of values ani-
mate business, government, leadership, individual behavior, and relationships. He calls them "situational values" and "sustainable values."

Relationships propelled by situational values, he says, involve calcu-
lations about what is available in the here and now. "They are all about
exploiting short-term opportunities rather than consistently living the
principles that create long-term success. They are all about what we *can*
and *cannot* do in any given situation."

Sustainable values, by contrast, are "all about what we *should* and
should not do in all situations." As such, they literally sustain relationships over the long term. Sustainable values, according to Seidman, are
the "values that connect us deeply as humans, such as transparency, integrity, honesty, truth, shared responsibility, and hope." They are therefore "all about how—not how much . . . Situational values push us
toward the strategy of becoming 'too big to fail.' Sustainable values inspire us to pursue the strategy of becoming 'too sustainable to fail,'" by
building enduring relationships. As the collapse of major Wall Street
banks such as Bear Stearns and Lehman Brothers has demonstrated,
Seidman explains, "What makes an institution sustainable is not the
scale and size it reaches but how it does its business—how it relates to its

employees, shareholders, customers, suppliers, the environment, society, and future generations."

Just how far Wall Street drifted into situational values came out in some of the congressional hearings about the causes of the 2008 subprime crisis. On April 27, 2010, Senator Carl Levin (a Democrat from Michigan) questioned the Goldman Sachs CFO David Viniar about e-mails in which Goldman bankers described bonds they were selling to their customers as "crap."

> Sen. Levin: And when you heard that your employees in these e-mails, in looking at these deals, said God what a shitty deal, God what a piece of crap, did you feel anything?
> Viniar: I think that's very unfortunate to have on e-mail.
> Sen. Levin: Are you . . . ?
> (*Laughter*)
> Viniar: And very unfortunate.
> Sen. Levin: On e-mail? How about feeling that way?
> Viniar: I think it's very unfortunate for anyone to have said that in any form.

Even with Senator Levin's prodding, Viniar seemed not to realize that the problem was *what* was said, and the rank cynicism behind it, not the fact that it was put in an e-mail that became public. Goldman had fallen into such situational behaviors—just sell any piece of junk, just get the deal done—that it was ready to injure its own customers. That is about as far from sustainable behavior as one can imagine for an investment bank, and even when it was exposed, the firm's chief financial officer didn't get it.

In his book, Seidman highlights the 1996 movie *Jerry Maguire*, one of the main themes of which is the conflict between situational and sustainable values. The title character is a big-time, self-centered sports agent who has a sudden moral awakening one night and writes a new "mission statement" for his firm. It proposes that he and the other agents in the firm restructure their business and reduce the number of their clients while better serving the clients they keep. In essence, his message is: Let's be in it for the long haul and for the right reasons in the right way—let's behave less situationally and more sustainably.

Maguire, played by Tom Cruise, stuffs a copy of the new statement in the mailbox of everyone in his firm. The next morning, when he walks into the office, he receives a standing ovation from fellow agents, bookkeepers, and secretaries. His boss, Bob Sugar, played by Jay Mohr, who is grinning broadly, joining in the applause, and giving Maguire a thumbs-up, is asked by another senior colleague, "How long do you give him?" Sugar answers out of the side of his mouth, "Hmmm, a week." Sure enough, within a week Maguire is fired by Sugar, and his former co-workers move in quickly to strip him of all his clients. His career is devoured by the very situational values he was decrying.

Seidman notes that the film revolves around a series of personal relationships in which the characters wrestle with the choice between the philosophy of "Just do it!" (just do whatever the situation allows) and the philosophy of "Just do it right" (think and act sustainably).

For instance, after being booted from his firm, Maguire thinks he has been able to hold on to one big client, a college star, to represent—the prospective number-one National Football League draft choice Frank Cushman, played by Jerry O'Connell. When Maguire goes down South to visit Cush and his father, Matt, played by Beau Bridges, at their small-town home, they make an ostentatious handshake deal and the father says that a written contract confirming that Jerry represents his son isn't necessary. "My word is stronger than oak," Matt tells Jerry. A few weeks later, though, at the NFL draft, Sugar swoops in and steals Cush away from Maguire, simply because in that situation he was able to engineer a better deal, or so he claimed. And anyway, Cush and Maguire had no contract, *only* a handshake. Maguire confronts Matt and tells him how disappointed he is.

"I'm still sort of moved by your 'My word is stronger than oak' thing," Maguire seethes.

At that point, Maguire is left with one employee ready to work for him, the sweetly sincere secretary Dorothy Boyd, played by Renée Zellweger, who is swept off her feet by Jerry's sustainable-values pitch, and one athlete ready to stick with Maguire, the demandingly sincere football player Rod Tidwell, played by Cuba Gooding Jr. Tidwell, for all his focus on money, is also bound to Maguire by something intangible, something, well, sustainable. Tidwell and Boyd represent the opposite of Cush and Sugar—loyalty in the face of hardship. There is no more sustainable value than that. This contrasts with opportunism in the face of hardship. There is nothing more situational than that.

Jerry Maguire became one of the top-grossing films of all time because, Seidman argues, "it struck a chord in people tired of cutting corners. We were in the 'Just Do It' decade. The world was accelerating rapidly and 'Just Do It,' the advertising slogan of the sports shoe manufacturer Nike, captured the self-centered zeitgeist of the decade." It was the decade when Nike's most famous representative, Michael Jordan, turned professional basketball from a contest of cooperative, closely integrated five-man teams into a stage for individual athletic virtuosity. The spirit of the age also infected business. Managers, Seidman said, under pressure "to answer the short-term demands of an increasingly insistent capital market, looked for shortcuts and easy solutions, managing for the here and now in ways that often neglected long-term goals."

In the decade after the release of the film, the drift from sustainable to situational values helped to trigger America's worst economic crisis since the Great Depression. From Wall Street to Main Street, far too many Americans abandoned the save-and-invest mentality of their Depression-era parents for what became the prevailing ethos of the day, which bankers call IBG/YBG: Get whatever you can now and either "I'll be gone" before the bill comes due or "you'll be gone" before you really have to pay the piper.

This was at the heart of the subprime-mortgage mess. The mortgage broker who first sold a family a subprime mortgage and then passed it off to a bigger financial institution, such as Fannie Mae or Citibank, knew that he would be "gone" if and when the family buying the mortgage defaulted. No problem—his firm would no longer own the mortgage: Fannie Mae or some investment bank in Iceland would own it. So there was no risk for him personally in signing up high-risk home buyers who were sometimes actually encouraged to lie about their incomes—or lack of them. The broker told the family assuming the mortgage that the same was true for them: If they couldn't meet the monthly payments when they started kicking in, no problem. Just walk away from the property—"you'll be gone"—or sell it for a profit because, as we all "knew" at the time, housing prices would keep going up forever. They would never go down.

The rating agencies, whose fees and incomes depended on how many of these subprime mortgage bonds they got to rate, had an incentive to give them high ratings so they would sell more easily, leading more investment houses and banks to want to use their rating services. And if those bonds blew up, well, said the raters, IBG—"I'll be gone." The investment banks had a great incentive to bundle more and more mortgages into bonds and sell them all around the world because the commissions were huge and, as long as they didn't hold too many on their own balance sheets, if they blew up, who cared? IBG—"I'll be gone." IBG and YBG, the essence of situational thinking, became the order of the day, while sustainable thinking—"I will behave as if I will always be here to be held accountable"—went out the window. No one summed up this attitude better than former Citigroup CEO Charles Prince, who told the *Financial Times* (July 9, 2007) just weeks before the credit markets entered their subprime death spiral, "As long as the music is playing, you've got to get up and dance." And when that situational music was playing, far too many Americans, from Wall Street to Main Street, got up and danced.

What started in the 1980s with home entertainment systems for nothing down and nothing to pay for thirty days reached its ultimate conclusion in the Terrible Twos: the American dream—a house and yard—for nothing down and nothing to pay for two years. When in our history was the American dream ever so cheap? Never, and as things turned out, it was not so cheap this time, either. It all turned out to be an expensive illusion.

Seidman argues that this was all possible because we created, first in our own minds and then in our actions, two different worlds in which we operated. He illustrates the point with a reference to the scene in *The Godfather* in which Sal Tessio, having plotted the assassination of Michael Corleone, the head of the Corleone crime family, is discovered and sent off to be killed himself. Before his execution, Tessio asks Tom Hagen, the family's trusted adviser, to tell Michael that he had not been planning a personal act of vengeance. "Tell Mike it was only business. I always liked him."

We did the same thing, according to Seidman. "We created a separate sphere where we could behave situationally. The business world became that sphere. All those subprime mortgages—they were 'only business.' The idea was that there was an amoral space where as long as you were not breaking the law, your only responsibility was to 'shareholder value and pursuit of profit.'"

The damage inflicted by the rise of situational over sustainable values has affected public life as well. The short-term, me-first, never-mind-the-future attitude that did so much harm to the country's financial system also obstructs the necessary responses to America's major national challenges. Reinvesting in our formula for greatness—in education, infrastructure, and research and development to assure continuing economic growth and a rising standard of living—making broadly shared short-term sacrifices to reduce the federal budget deficit so that future generations are not burdened with huge debts, and cutting back carbon emissions today to mitigate climate change in the years ahead, all qualify as sustainable policies. The baby boom generation, in thrall to the situational approach to the world, has failed to undertake them.

Delaware governor Jack Markell spelled out the negative consequences of the shift from the Greatest Generation's sustainable outlook to the boomers' emphasis on the short term: "People acted as though they forgot that we owed at least as much to the next generation as to the current one. Lots of politicians argued that cutting taxes was the right thing to do because it gives people money back that actually belongs to them. What they weren't saying, but should have, is that absent spending cuts that nobody wants to make, what we're really doing is borrowing from our kids to give to the current generation. Not very responsible. Instead of investing for the long term, we focused too much on what will impact the next poll and the next election. Businesses have similar problems when they focus too much on the next quarter. They fail to make the investments they need for long-term prosperity and eventually they die. Government follows this pattern to the peril of all of us."

We now have day-thinking politicians trying to regulate day-trading bankers, all covered by people Tweeting, blogging, or commenting on cable TV moments later. When the two powerful forces of technology and markets converge in a way that encourages or even forces everyone to think situationally, it is hard to expect that the society and political system will produce sustainable thinking and outcomes. Everything gets *shortened*—from the time you are prepared to hold a stock, to the time it takes to form an opinion or fire off a comment, to the time you devote to studying any subject, to the length of time you should take amassing a savings before you buy your own home. When there is no time to think sustainably, it is not surprising that we see so many people acting situationally.

The Decline of Authority

At a Tea Party rally in Colorado in October 2010, the *Financial Times* reported (October 25, 2010), one of the speakers had this to say: "I am not an expert in anything. But look where the so-called 'experts' have got us. They are a bunch of liars, crooks, and thieves." A national poll taken that month found that faced with a congressional contest between someone with experience in the job and a candidate without it, people preferred a novice by 48 to 23 percent. Perhaps this can be chalked up to business—or politics—as usual in the United States. Politicians as a group have seldom enjoyed high popularity in America, 2010 was a year when many voters were angry, and there is a national tradition, especially when times are hard, of wanting to "throw the rascals out" of office—all of them.

These days, however, experience and expertise in other areas don't command much respect, either. In the fall of 2010, Tom met Professor Nicholas Comerford, a soil scientist at the University of Florida and the 2010 president of the Soil Science Society of America, who told him this story: "I have ten acres of land and decided to plant some blueberries this year. There is a Florida cattleman I know, from an old family from the South, who is now in his eighties. His kids won't let him raise cattle anymore so he went into blueberries instead. I went to pick up some blueberry plants from him to plant on my own land and we got to talking about things. The subject of climate change came up, and he said to me, 'I don't believe any of that climate change stuff.' And I said, 'Well, we probably disagree on that, but if you like I could tell you what my views are and why I believe in it.' And he said, 'No, I'm happy with my opinions.' Great guy, salt of the earth, but just not interested."

Skepticism of expert opinion is always appropriate: It is in fact at the heart of the scientific method. Indeed, a measure of skepticism about *all* opinions, especially one's own, is healthy. But in the ever more complicated world we are living in, the professional judgments of experts are, in the end, indispensable. The details of technical and scientific fields lie beyond the easy comprehension of almost all nonspecialists. Such details are like foreign languages, and the rest of us have to rely on experts to translate for us. Otherwise, like travelers in a country whose language we don't know, we will get hopelessly lost. This is especially true at a time when we have to make drastic cuts in our national, state, and local budgets. We should not simply reduce these budgets across the board. We should do so with a strategy informed by expertise on the world in which we are living and the requirements for thriving in it.

It isn't just scientists and those regarded as experts who suffer from a lack of credibility. People in positions of authority everywhere have less influence than in the past. In the landscape of American education it is generally acknowledged that the country's colleges and universities stand out, continuing to lead the world. Yet even at this level teachers suffer from a shortage of authority, which makes it hard for them to do their jobs.

Commenting on a book on deficiencies in student learning on American college campuses in *The Chronicle of Higher Education*, Thomas Benton, the pen name of a professor of English, wrote:

> It has become difficult to give students honest feedback. The slightest criticisms have to be cushioned by a warm blanket of praise and encouragement to avoid provoking oppositional defiance or complete breakdowns . . . Increasingly, time-pressured college teachers ask themselves, "What grade will ensure no complaint from the student, or worse, a quasi-legal battle over whether the instructions for an assignment were clear enough?"

Indeed, Americans have little confidence in virtually every institution, a poll sponsored by the Associated Press and the National Constitution Center reported in September 2010. The scientific community, for example, commanded the confidence of only 30 percent of the respondents and organized religion of only 18 percent, and they outranked all but two of the total of eighteen institutions listed—those two being the military and small business. This augurs badly for the task of meeting the major challenges our country faces because our institutions, including but not limited to the federal government, are crucial for the collective action that is required in each case. If the public doesn't trust these institutions, they can't be effective. Where the nation's institutions are concerned—especially government—a healthy, necessary skepticism has given way to corrosive cynicism. The late senator Daniel Patrick Moynihan once said that "everyone is entitled to his own opinion, but not his own facts." Yet more and more, especially in American public life, rumors, allegations, and assertions that are simply untrue pass as facts.

On November, 4, 2010, Tom got a taste of how all of this can filter down and affect the way real people see the world. After giving a lecture that day at Indiana University, he turned on the television in the evening and saw Anderson Cooper on CNN discussing a report that President Obama's ongoing trip to India and Asia was costing U.S. taxpayers $200 million a day—about $2 billion for the entire trip—and would involve redeploying thirty-four navy ships. Cooper was impelled to check out the story because the evening before on his program, Representative Michele Bachmann, a Republican from Minnesota, asked where she thought deep cuts in the federal budget would take place now that the Republicans had won Congress on a budget-cutting platform, had said this: "I think we know that just within a day or so the president of the United States will be taking a trip over to India that is expected to cost the taxpayers $200 million a day. He's taking 2,000 people with him. He'll be renting over 870 rooms in India, and these are five-star hotel rooms at the Taj Mahal Palace Hotel. This is the kind of over-the-top spending. It's a very small example."

The next night on his program, drawing on research by the website Factcheck.org and on his own CNN team's reporting, Cooper reconstructed the origins of the story. It had started with a comment by "an alleged Indian provincial official," from the Indian state of Maharashtra, "reported by India's Press Trust, their equivalent of our AP or Reuters. I say 'alleged' provincial official," Cooper went on, "because we have no idea who this person is, no name was given . . . It was an anonymous quote . . . Some reporter in India wrote this article with this figure in it. No proof was given; no follow-up reporting was done . . . The Indian article was picked up by the Drudge Report and other sites online, and it quickly made its way into conservative talk radio." Well-known talk-show hosts Rush Limbaugh, Glenn Beck, and Michael Savage—all with sizable listening audiences—repeated and elaborated on it, seemingly without making any independent efforts to check its veracity with the White House.

While for security reasons the White House ordinarily does not comment on the logistics of presidential trips, in this case it made a partial exception. White House press secretary Robert Gibbs said, "I am not going to go into how much it costs to protect the president, [but this trip] is comparable to when President Clinton and when President Bush traveled abroad. This trip doesn't cost $200 million a day." Geoff Morrell, the Pentagon press secretary, said, "I will take the liberty this time of dismissing as absolutely absurd this notion that somehow we were deploying 10 percent of the navy and some thirty-four ships and an aircraft carrier in support of the president's trip to Asia. That's just comical. Nothing close to that is being done." Cooper noted that President Clinton's 1998 trip to Africa—with 1,300 people and of roughly similar duration—cost, according to the Government Accounting Office and adjusted for inflation, "about $5.2 million a day."

The next morning Tom held a breakfast discussion with Indiana University honors students—their best and brightest. "I came in, grabbed a bagel, sat down at a table, and several students joined me," Tom recalled. "The first thing—*I mean the first thing*—the first student asked me was: 'Did you hear that Obama's trip to India is costing $200 million a day?' It was depressing. I explained to him that Anderson Cooper had debunked the whole thing on his show the night before—that it all started with an unnamed provincial official in India. The student listened politely, but did not really seem convinced."

As for Bachmann, she announced that she was running for president in 2012.

While the false report about a presidential trip is a graphic but not terribly important example of robust misinformation, other mistaken beliefs have the potential to do serious harm to the country. A poll taken by the centrist Democratic group Third Way in the summer of 2010 revealed that "three quarters of those polled said they believed that the budget could be balanced without raising taxes," *Washington Post* columnist Ruth Marcus reported (November 13, 2010). "The same number said the budget could be balanced without touching Social Security and

Medicare." If most Americans continue to believe these things, it will be impossible even to start a serious public conversation about reducing the federal deficits, much less actually reduce them.

As the old saying goes, "It ain't what you don't know that gets you into trouble. It's what you know for sure that just ain't so."

Service Envy

The third imperiled value is the sense that America is one nation, a single community to which all of us belong and in whose fate we all share. Such a sentiment is what motivates the kind of voluntary, short-term sacrifices necessary to bring the budget into balance, take out insurance against climate change on behalf of the next generation, and pay for the investments needed to renew the American formula for economic growth.

Today, where public policy is concerned, more and more we are encouraged to think of ourselves as partisans—liberals or conservatives, or members of groups into which the census divides us that are entitled to special consideration, or as individuals with specific economic interests to advance. Of course, we are all of those things, but in the past we also thought of ourselves as, first and foremost, citizens of the United States. Americans: That used to be us.

The new information technology has helped to erode this particular value. With hundreds of television channels in every cable package and millions of websites that anyone with an Internet connection can visit, our national attention is far more fragmented than it once was. In today's media world we have far more choices than ever before, but also much less common information. And with the new electronic technology that we all use, while communication is much easier, we spend more time alone—texting while walking down the street, eyes down, and listening to an iPod all the while.

During the Cold War era, especially in its early years when memories of World War II were fresh, national unity and the readiness to make sacrifices when and where necessary seemed to most everyone to be matters of national survival. As the Princeton historian Daniel T. Rodgers put it in his book *Age of Fracture*, "Of all the dangers against which presidents spoke after 1945, none called out stronger rhetorical effort than a weakening of public resolve. In the standing tension between 'our common labor as a nation' (as Eisenhower put it) and the temptations of a purely private life, Cold War presidents spoke for the imperatives of public life."

As we moved from a nation of citizens to a nation of shareholders and "netizens," the willingness of presidents to speak about and uphold the imperatives and responsibilities of public life became rare. After the terrorist attacks on the World Trade Center and the Pentagon—when the whole country was ready to address those responsibilities—President Bush vowed to go after the terrorists, and essentially left it at that. He never rallied Americans to even the most simple, necessary, and obvious collective action—to free ourselves from our bondage to imported oil, for example, by using less gasoline and paying more for it through a gasoline "patriot tax."

We occasionally attend Washington Wizards basketball games together. There often comes a point in the game when a spotlight shines on an upper-deck box at center court, where wounded Iraq and Afghan war veterans from Bethesda Naval Hospital and other institutions are seated, some in wheelchairs, some visibly wounded or missing limbs. Everyone in the crowd invariably stands and applauds them. That is commendable. But we suspect there is more behind that applause than the wish to show support for wounded warriors. We believe it also derives from the fact that the U.S. military has become the carrier of the traditional values that have become diluted in much of the rest of America—and people miss that. What are those values? They include not only the military's unabashed love of country and a sense of duty to serve it—and if necessary make the ultimate sacrifice. They include as well the fact that in the military, authority and expertise are still respected, although they have to be earned (and are occasionally flouted). The military at its best still takes the long view and can act collectively in pursuit of big goals.

The armed forces have become, in Michael J. Sandel's words, "the last repository of civic idealism and sacrifice for the sake of the common good. We have outsourced and confined to the military a concentrated expression of the civic ideals and patriotism that should be shared by all American citizens."

In a sense, the military has become disconnected from mainstream

America and is instead a kind of museum of the values that made America a great country. We like to visit this museum and express our appreciation for what is exhibited there, but then we return to our own lives, which have nothing to do with what we've just seen.

We have also outsourced sacrifice. If World War II was "the good war," and the Korean War "the forgotten war," and Vietnam "the controversial war," the conflict that began with the attacks of September 11, 2001, and has sent U.S. troops to Afghanistan and Iraq for nearly a decade can be called "the 1 percent war." The troops deployed to these combat zones and their immediate families make up less than 1 percent of the population of the United States. The rest of us contribute nothing. We won't even increase our taxes, even through a surcharge on gasoline, to pay for these wars. So we end up asking 1 percent of the country to make the ultimate sacrifice and the other 99 percent to make no sacrifice at all.

Consider what Dana Perino, then the Bush White House's press secretary, said when she was asked (in October 2007) about a proposal by some congressional Democrats to levy a surtax to pay for the Iraq war. "We've always known that Democrats seem to revert to type, and they are willing to raise taxes on just about anything," she answered. And if taxes were raised to pay for the war, Perino added, "does anyone seriously believe that the Democrats are going to end these new taxes that they're asking the American people to pay at a time when it's not necessary to pay them? I just think it's completely fiscally irresponsible."

Asking Americans to pay for a war with a tax hike used to be us. Now it is considered a fiscally irresponsible act of partisanship. Robert Hormats, formerly an investment banker and currently the undersecretary of state for economic affairs, is the author of *The Price of Liberty*, a book about how America has paid for its wars since 1776. He explains: "In every major war we have fought in the nineteenth and twentieth centuries, Americans have been asked to pay higher taxes—and nonessential programs have been cut—to support the military effort." The wars in Iraq and Afghanistan were the first time this has not happened. Remarkably, *we actually lowered taxes.*

"It is sad to see how difficult it is for politicians today to ask people to do anything other than enhance their economic well-being," remarked Timothy Shriver, the chairman of the Special Olympics. "I still see this enormous hunger for public purpose—people wanting to be part of something bigger than themselves, people volunteering to help others, looking for ways to join in solving big problems. But our political leaders won't channel all this goodwill into national purpose and I don't understand why." Too often, what has filled this political vacuum is anger. "People have fallen into blaming each other," Shriver added. We are hungry, and instead of going out and finding fresh food—finding big hard things to do together, like nation-building our own country—"we are eating ourselves."

That did not used to be us. Indeed, when we talked to Tim, his father, Sargent Shriver—who helped President Kennedy create the Peace Corps in 1961 and became its first director—had just died, and Tim had been reflecting a lot about his father's life and that of his generation.

"The other day," Tim mused, "I came across something my dad wrote. He said, 'When we started the Peace Corps, we realized that we were risking everything.' I thought, Why was the Peace Corps a risk? But that is how they saw it. They felt that they were risking their professional reputations and careers, risking the credibility of the president of the United States, risking young people's lives and the country's reputation in the middle of the Cold War, on an idea that to many seemed foolish. The idea of risk is so tied to the idea of greatness—you cannot be great without risking yourself."

That idea of taking big risks for big gains, to do big things that would be truly sustainable, for us and for others, said Shriver, "is gone from our public life now. Now, it is all about split the difference, triangulate, and just get me 51 percent."

His father's generation, said Shriver, had a lofty view of the power of political leaders—not that they should run your life, or just build huge bureaucracies, or just cut your taxes, either. The leader's role was to enlist and enable and inspire Americans—average citizens, businesses, churches, universities, artists, and more—to do big things in the world to help others. "My dad actually thought that if we created a program like the Peace Corps that would offer young Americans the chance to work for nothing, live in adverse conditions, help others, and build relationships, everyone would want to do that. They actually thought everyone would want to work for nothing to help poor people and, in the process, help themselves."

They actually thought, Shriver added, "that Americans all didn't just want to file their taxes—that people wanted to give to their country, they didn't just want to get from it. They want to be part of something larger—to believe in ideas that can change the course of their lives and even history itself."

These were our parents, concluded Shriver; surely we are not that different from them. Surely we have it in us to be their heirs in values as well as material things. And surely it is well past time we started proving it.

PART V

REDISCOVERING AMERICA

FOURTEEN

They Just Didn't Get the Word

Of thee I sing, baby,
Summer, autumn, winter, spring, baby!
Shining star and inspiration,
Worthy of a mighty nation—
Of thee I sing!

—George and Ira Gershwin

We began this book with the declaration that we are optimists about America, but frustrated optimists. Readers who have come this far can be forgiven for asking, "We understand now why you're frustrated, but how can you still be optimistic?" The short answer is that we stand on our heads a lot.

It is easy to be an optimist about America if you stand on your head, because the country looks so much better, and is so much more inspiring, when viewed from the bottom up rather than from the top down. When you look at the country that way you see that the spirit of the Greatest Generation has not died. It is true, as Timothy Shriver suggested, that our politicians are now guilty of the soft bigotry of low expectations when it comes to summoning the American people to do big hard things together. But what is inspiring, and what is the basis for our optimism, is the number of people and small groups who are summoning themselves with their own trumpets.

That is why, although much of this book has dwelled on our weaknesses, this chapter will dwell on our strengths, which in fact have much deeper roots and are more relevant than ever to the world in which we're living. America's greatest strength is the fact that wave after wave of people still either come to this country or come of age in this country eager to try something new, or spark something extra, undeterred by obstacles, hard times, money shortages, or weak-kneed politicians. Indeed, what keeps us optimistic about America is the seemingly endless number of people who come here or live here who *just didn't get the word*.

They didn't get the word that we're supposed to be depressed or in a recession or unloved by the rest of the world. They didn't get the word that new immigrants are supposed to wait their turn, college dropouts are supposed to flip hamburgers, and people of color are supposed to go to the back of the bus. Instead, they just get on with it—whatever "it" is. For all our ailments as a country today, our society and economy are still the most open in the world, where individuals with the spark of an idea, the gumption to protest, or the passion to succeed can still get up, walk out the door, and chase a rainbow, lead a crusade, start a school, or open a business. "Show me an obstacle and I will show you an opportunity" is still the motto of many, many Americans, be they business entrepreneurs or civic and charitable entrepreneurs. So Rosa Parks just got on that bus and took her seat; so new immigrants just went out and started 25 percent of the new companies in Silicon Valley in the last decade; so college dropouts named Steve Jobs, Michael Dell, Bill Gates, and Mark Zuckerberg just got up and created four of the biggest companies in the world. So, when all seemed lost in the Iraq war, the U.S. military carried out a surge, not a retreat, because, as one of the officers involved told Tom, "We were just too dumb to quit." It was never in the plan, but none of them got the word.

Through his reporting, Tom has had a chance to meet and interview some of these Americans who just didn't get the word, *who are just too dumb to quit*, in the very best and most complimentary sense of that phrase. They range from soldiers and sailors, to teachers and inventors, to civil-society organizers, to small-business entrepreneurs. When you hear their voices you will understand why, if we were to draw a picture of America today, it would depict the space shuttle taking off. It would show enormous thrust coming from below, pushing the shuttle upward through the clouds. In our case, that thrust is coming from all the Americans who didn't get the word. Unfortunately, though, right now, our booster rocket—the American political system—is cracked and leaking energy. And the pilots in the cockpit—politicians in Washington, D.C.— are fighting over the flight plan. As a result, we can't generate the escape velocity we need to get to the moon or beyond. So, yes, we must repair that booster rocket, and the pilots must agree on a flight plan. But have no doubt that if and when they do, America's natural thrust coming from below is still powerful enough, if harnessed, to take us to any galaxy.

Here are profiles of some Americans who did not get the word, along with a discussion of how our government can function as a more effective booster rocket to help the entrepreneurs among them to expand their businesses and create more jobs.

Far Too Dumb to Quit

In July 2009, Tom followed along with Admiral Mike Mullen, the chairman of the Joint Chiefs of Staff, on his trip to Afghanistan. One of their first stops was Camp Leatherneck, in Helmand Province in southern Afghanistan. This is the most dangerous part of the country. It's where mafia and mullah meet—the place where the Taliban harvest the poppies that get turned into the heroin that funds their insurgency. After President Obama announced the more than doubling of U.S. troops in Afghanistan, the first group of fresh marines deployed to the country landed at Camp Leatherneck. It was 115 degrees in the sun the day Tom covered Admiral Mullen's visit, a day that began with the chairman addressing all the soldiers in the camp in a makeshift theater.

"Let me see a show of hands," Mullen began, "how many of you are on your first deployment?" A couple of dozen hands went up. "Second deployment?" More hands went up. "Third deployment?" Still lots of hands were raised. "Fourth deployment?" A good dozen hands went up. "Fifth deployment?" Still a few hands shot up. "Sixth deployment?" One hand went up. Admiral Mullen asked the soldier to step forward to shake his hand and have a picture taken with him.

Watching the scene, Tom recalled, "I could only shake my head in wonder: What have we done to deserve such people?" As in all such big gatherings of U.S. troops, you could be sure there were mothers who had left their husbands and children for a year. There were soldiers who came back to the fight after being injured. There were infantrymen who first signed up after 9/11 simply because they thought it was their duty to defend their country. These soldiers are a reminder that the spirit of sacrifice for the nation is not dead in America, even if it could use some bolstering. Never have so many asked so much of so few—and never have those few delivered so much for so many and asked for so little in return.

Ride, Mister?

Tom was attending the Energy and Resources Institute climate conference in New Delhi in February 2009, when during the afternoon session two young American women—along with one of their mothers—propositioned him. Well, not exactly propositioned, but they did propose an excursion. "Hey, Mr. Friedman," they asked, "would you like to take a little spin around New Delhi in our car?"

Tom replied that he had heard that line before. Ah, they answered, but you haven't seen this car before. It's a plug-in electric car that is also powered by rooftop solar panels. The two young women, recent Yale graduates, had just driven it all over India in a "climate caravan" to highlight the solutions to global warming being developed by Indian companies, communities, campuses, and innovators, as well as to inspire others to take action. They asked Tom if he wanted to drive, but he had visions of being stopped by the police for driving on solar power without a license and ending up in a New Delhi jail. Not to worry, they told him. Indian policemen had been stopping them all across India. First they would ask to see driver's licenses, then they would inquire about how the green car's solar roof managed to provide 10 percent of its mileage—and then they would try to buy the car.

They headed off down Panchsheel Marg, one of New Delhi's main streets, with Caroline Howe, then twenty-three, a mechanical engineer on leave from the Yale School of Forestry and Environmental Studies, at the wheel and her colleague in this endeavor, Alexis Ringwald, a Fulbright scholar who was then studying in India and is now a solar entrepreneur, sitting in the back. Young Americans like them can be found literally all over the world today. They obviously did not get the word and they are unabashedly optimistic that if something they strongly believe in is not happening, it is because they're not doing it.

Howe and Ringwald joined with Kartikeya Singh, who was then starting the Indian Youth Climate Network (IYCN) to connect young climate leaders in India, a country coming under increasing global pressure to manage its carbon footprint. "India is full of climate innovators, but they are so spread out across this huge country that many people don't get to see that these solutions are working right now," Howe explained. "We wanted to find a way to bring people together around existing solutions to inspire more action and more innovation. There's no time left just to talk about the problem."

Howe and Ringwald thought the best way to do that might be a climate-solutions road tour, using modified electric cars from India's Reva Electric Car Company, whose CEO Ringwald knew. They persuaded him to donate three of his cars and to retrofit them with batteries that could travel ninety miles on a single six-hour charge, and to include a solar roof that would extend them farther.

Between January 1 and February 5, 2009, they drove the cars on a 2,100-mile trip from Chennai to New Delhi, stopping in fifteen cities and dozens of villages, training Indian students to start their own climate action programs and filming twenty videos of India's top homegrown energy innovations, which they posted on YouTube. They also brought along a solar-powered rock band, plus a luggage truck that ran on plant oil extracted from jatropha and pongamia, plants locally grown on wasteland. A Bollywood dance group joined at different stops, and a Czech who learned about their trip on YouTube took part with his truck that ran on vegetable-oil waste.

Deepa Gupta, twenty-one, a co-founder of IYCN, told the *Hindustan Times* that the trip opened her eyes to just how many indigenous energy solutions were budding in India, "like organic farming in Andhra Pradesh, or using neem and garlic as pesticides, or the kind of recycling in slums, such as Dharavi. We saw things already in place, like the Gadhia solar plant in Valsad, Gujarat, where steam is used for cooking and you can feed almost 50,000 people in one go." At Rajpipla, Gujarat, when they stopped at a local prince's palace to recharge their cars, they discovered that his business was cultivating worms and selling them as eco-friendly alternatives to chemical fertilizers.

"Why did this tour happen?" asked Ringwald. "Why this mad, insane plan to travel across India in a caravan of solar electric cars and jatropha trucks with solar music, art, dance, and a potent message for climate solutions? Well . . . the world needs crazy ideas to change things, because the conventional way of thinking is not working anymore."

Howe and Ringwald's adventure is just one small piece of evidence that the spirit of enterprise, innovation, and adventure that have done so much to make America what it is today is alive and well among its youth—even 10,000 miles away.

America's All-Girl Navy

In October 2005, Tom spent a couple of days on the USS *Chosin*, a guided-missile cruiser patrolling the northern end of the Persian Gulf, where it protected the main export terminal for all the oil that is pumped in the southern half of Iraq. The terminal is about ten miles into the gulf, inside Iraqi waters, but only a few hundred yards from Iranian waters. Iraqi fishermen and the Iranian Revolutionary Guard Corps in speedboats have to be regularly shooed away by the U.S. Navy when they get too close to the pumping station.

The first morning he was aboard ship, Tom recalled, he woke up at 5:00 a.m. in a tiny guest bunk, splashed some soap and water on his face, and went out to walk laps around the deck just as the sun was coming up. As he did, his mind kept coming back to the extraordinary contrast between the political culture of the U.S. Navy and the political culture of both the Iraqis on land and the Arab and Iranian fishermen in the Persian Gulf. Iraq is a multiethnic society, but one without a melting pot. For decades it had to be held together by a dictator's iron fist. And now, as we see, Iraqis are still trying to find a way for Kurds, Shiites, and Sunnis to live together peacefully, but without that iron fist. When the Iraqi navy dropped Tom off on the *Chosin*, two things struck him. One was the diversity of the U.S. Navy—blacks, whites, Hispanics, Christians, Jews, atheists, Muslims, all working together, bound by a shared idea, not by coercion. The Iraqi navy, by contrast, is all male and almost all of them are Shiite Muslims. As Mustapha Ahansal, a Moroccan American sailor who acted as the *Chosin*'s Arabic translator when its commandos boarded ships in the gulf to look for pirates or terrorists, told Tom, "The first time I boarded a boat we had six or seven people—one Hispanic, one black person, a white person, maybe a woman in our unit. [The Iraqi] sailors said to me, 'I thought all Americans were white.' Then one of them asked me, 'Are you in the military?' It shocks them, actually. They never knew that such a world exists, because they have their own problems. I was talking to one of their higher-ups in [the Iraqi] coast guard and he said, 'It is amazing how you guys can be so many religions, ethnic groups, and still make this thing work and be the best in the world. And here we are fighting north and south, and we are all cousins and brothers.'"

"The other thing that struck me," Tom recalled, "was that a disproportionate number of the *Chosin*'s officers were women, so you heard women's voices all day long giving orders over the ship's loudspeaker and radio. And because the local Arab fishermen also hear this chatter, many of them probably thought the *Chosin* was an all-female ship." The 110-foot U.S. Coast Guard cutter *Monomoy*, alongside the *Chosin*, had a female deputy captain, who often led the landing parties that inspected boats in the gulf. One of the navy's fast patrol boats, also alongside the *Chosin*, had a female captain. "Being a female boarding officer is a huge asset because they are so curious they want to talk to us more, so we can learn more things," said Reyna Hernandez, the twenty-four-year-old executive officer of the *Monomoy*.

Nagga Haizlip is an Iranian American sailor who served as the *Chosin*'s English-Farsi translator when it confronted boats from Iran's Revolutionary Guards. Dressed in navy fatigues, she told Tom, "If I call [the Iranians] on bridge-to-bridge radio, they will not want to talk to me. They will say, 'I want to speak to a man.'" As for the Iranian fishermen, she said, "They don't understand I am actually in the U.S. Navy. That surprises them. It is different from their culture. They ask how do people get along [on the *Chosin*] and how do they live together. They are curious."

They're curious because they can see that this diversity clearly doesn't detract from our military might. It is actually a vital source of our strength, although one that we often take for granted.

Teach for America

What can you say about Wendy Kopp, the founder of Teach for America (TFA), other than that she absolutely, positively did not come even remotely close to getting the word? Kopp's great insight was recognizing that many others in her generation hadn't, either.

In 1989 she wrote her senior thesis at Princeton about an idea she had for college graduates, including those from the most prestigious universities in America. She conceived of a program where graduates would take a five-week summer crash course in the basics of education and then spend the next two years teaching in the most challenging and poorest public schools in the country.

At Princeton that year, Kopp recalled, "Everyone was thinking that all we want to do is make money, and I was descending into a funk. I had applied to every two-year program—McKinsey, Morgan Stanley, Procter & Gamble, and Bain & Company. But I was also looking for other things. I had no passion to do something with corporations. I was looking for what I could do to make a real difference. I was convinced that I was not alone. I felt I was like thousands of people. I didn't know one person who was going to these Wall Street firms who really wanted to do that. I had been focused on education. So one day I realized that no one was recruiting anyone to teach in high-poverty communities as they were [recruiting people] to go to Wall Street."

Kopp was certain, even though she had no proof, that America's education problem "was solvable if we just made it our generation's priority." She had an intuition that if Princeton graduates went to the Mississippi Delta and discovered how many fifth graders there were reading on a first-grade level, they would be as outraged about that injustice as their parents had been about "separate but equal" education, and would want to make changing that condition their cause. If that happened, she thought, Teach for America could spawn "a generation of new leaders who would work together for the rest of their lives to affect the fundamental changes needed to truly solve America's education problem. That was my insight in the beginning."

It took a while to prove, but Kopp's intuition turned out to be correct, and then some. "At first," she recalled, "everyone I met said, 'This is a great idea, but college students will never do this.' People would actually start laughing when I told them the idea. Back in the summer of 1989, after I graduated from college, when I showed the list of the 100 colleges where we were going to recruit, the human resources director of the L.A. school district said to me, 'You get me 500 students from Stanford who want to teach in my public schools and I will hire all 500 of them.' So we spread flyers under doors [at these colleges] and 2,500 applied in the first year—in response to a one-page flyer that basically said we need real leaders in our generation to address the education problem in our country. I just think there is an inclination to serve, and we needed to give people viable paths to act on this inclination. In the first decade we were getting 3,000 to 4,000 applications a year with just flyers and posters."

Kopp was confident that her organization had the capacity to grow faster and bigger but knew it needed to recruit with something more than flyers. So she developed teams of recruiters and TFA grads who went out on campuses, told of their own experiences, identified students with leadership potential, and urged them to try out. It worked.

"Last year we had 46,000 applicants and 4,500 were accepted," said Kopp. The number of applications in 2010 increased 32 percent over 2009, a huge jump even with a slumping economy. About 40 percent of African American seniors at Harvard applied for TFA, and at both Harvard and Yale nearly 20 percent of the entire senior classes applied. More than 25 percent of all Spelman College seniors applied. At 130 colleges and universities more than 5 percent of the senior class applied, including big schools such as Michigan and Wisconsin. That is some of that thrust coming up from below.

Kopp said that of all the TFA grads, about one-third stay on as teachers, one-third stay in education, and one-third go on to other things. Not all education experts support the program, because it puts the least experienced teachers in the most challenging classrooms. It will take more time to determine how much of a difference TFA teachers are making in the lives of children, but the organization is clearly spawning some of the leaders that Kopp hoped for. Michelle Rhee, the former chancellor of the Washington, D.C., schools, and Michael Johnston, the Colorado state senator who spearheaded the Colorado education reform, are both TFA alums.

"People are ready to be called upon to serve and make a difference," said Kopp. "The energy is there. It is just all about finding it and tapping into it . . . We now even have adults applying."

There is something Teach for America has taught us all: Many, many Americans, including the most academically accomplished, are still eager to help solve the country's hardest problems, if we create effective frameworks for them to do so. Many young people today are much more motivated by "Show me the significance" than they are by "Show me the money."

Tianjin Again

While the military protects our country and Teach for America recruits people to work in the places most relevant to our future prosperity—our schools—neither does what is essential to sustain the American dream in the future: create thriving businesses and well-paying jobs. Fortunately, though, America's private sector is also full of people who didn't get the word. Although the government doesn't always make it easy for them, luckily many of them are too dumb to quit. Here are the stories of two.

While Tom was standing in the lunch line at the Tianjin convention center in September 2010, an American man approached him, eager to share the story of his energy start-up. He was the kind of person you meet at such conferences, who are invariably full of ideas, Tom recalled. "They all start by saying, 'Can I just take a minute and tell you about my invention? You see, I have this duck that paddles a wheel that blows up a balloon that issues methane that turns a turbine . . .'" Some of these ideas seem a little wacky, but what they show is how alive America is, how full of people eager to start things. The man who approached him in Tianjin had a real gleam in his eye, so Tom decided to schedule a lunch with him. His name was Mike Biddle, and he definitely did not get the word.

Biddle's story captures so much of what is right about America today, so much of what is wrong, and so much of what we have to do collectively to thrive in the world we invented. Biddle is the founder of MBA Polymers, which has invented processes for separating plastic from piles of junked computers, appliances, and cars, and then recycling it all into pellets to make new plastic while using less than 10 percent of the energy required to make virgin plastic from crude oil. Biddle calls it "aboveground mining." In the last four years, his company has mined about 150 million pounds of new plastic from old plastic. Biddle's seed money for the research on which his enterprise is based, which took seven years to develop, came from American taxpayers through federal research grants and private investors. Yet today only his tiny headquarters are in the United States. His factories are located in Austria, China, and Britain. "I employ 25 people in California and 250 overseas," he says.

He would like to have a factory in America that would justify all those research grants, but that would require an appropriate energy bill. Why? Americans collect for recycling only about 25 percent of the plastic bottles they use for consumption. However, most of those used bottles—and nearly all the rest of our used plastics—either end up in landfills or are put out to bid. The highest bidders ship them overseas, mostly to China, where they get recycled into new plastics. In China, however, they often get recycled with crude, low-tech processes that damage the ecosystem and put workers' safety at risk. Getting people to recycle regularly, and on a large scale, is a hassle. To overcome that, the European Union, Japan, Taiwan, and South Korea—and prospectively China in 2011—have enacted producer-responsibility laws. These laws require anything with a cord or battery—from an electric toothbrush, to a cell phone, to a laptop, to a washing machine—to be collected and recycled, under responsible environmental health and safety standards, at the manufacturers' expense. These laws give Biddle and his process the assured source of the raw plastic junk he needs at a reasonable price—in Europe and Asia. (Because recyclers now compete in these countries for junk, the cost to the manufacturers for collecting it is steadily falling, so they don't object to the law.)

"I am in the EU and China because the aboveground plastic mines are there or are being created there," said Biddle, who won *The Economist*'s 2010 Innovation Award for Energy and the Environment. "We are leading the way in China. The Chinese government gives tours of our facility in Guangzhou . . . I am not in the U.S. The potential mines in America are hands-down the biggest in the world, but there is no national collection law that gives me the scale of raw material we need to make our process economically viable here."

Biddle had enough money to hire one lobbyist to try to persuade Congress to copy the nationwide recycling regulations that Europe and Japan already have in place and China is drafting. The proposed

2010 clean-energy bill would have similarly required anything with a battery or cord to be recycled at the manufacturer's expense, but, in the end, there was no bill. It could not garner anything close to a majority in the Senate. So we Americans educated Biddle, we subsidized his technical breakthroughs, and now workers in other countries will get the jobs we paid to create.

"I am a Green and very much a free-market guy," said Biddle. "My bible is Ayn Rand. It is really hard for me to lobby for legislation [in America]. It is just not in my nature. But I cannot do my business if the rules aren't fair. I can beat anybody, and so can any American entrepreneur, if we have the same playing field. We've had oil subsidies because we thought it was important to have our own domestic oil supply; we have farm subsidies to be assured of our own food supply. Well, what about for technology? To get a technology launched we need the market-shaping rules. I don't want a subsidy. I want the market shaped the right way by laws, so that Americans will want to adopt this new technology that we invented . . . We all say we want high tech. Well, then create regulations and standards that will enable our high-tech innovators to create the jobs here."

Biddle paused for a moment. "Sometimes I feel like I have lost my country. It is just not that exciting to be an American right now. I come back and nothing works, and I have all this stuff in my way and I can't do business here. I find myself always on planes doing business in other countries—*because they get it*. If I took those hundred hours I have spent in D.C. lobbying and spent them in China lobbying Chinese officials, I have this feeling they would have listened. But [in D.C.], it is like talking to a brick wall." How can we be pessimists about a country that in the depth of the Great Recession produces a Mike Biddle—and all those like him who did not get the word? But how can we not be frustrated by a country that produces a Mike Biddle but then doesn't put in place the laws and regulations that will enable him to locate and expand his business here?

Buffalo Bob

There is one more person who obviously did not get the word whom we'd like to introduce. His firm is the oldest manufacturer in continuous op-

eration in Buffalo, New York. His name is Robert Stevenson. In an era
when most manufacturing has moved out of Buffalo—to the South, to
Mexico, or to China—Eastman Machine Company, founded in 1888 by
Stevenson's great-grandfather Charles Stevenson, keeps humming along.
It is now a fifth-generation family business. Remaining alive and profitable as a small manufacturer—115 employees, $30 million a year—is not
easy. Every year it requires Stevenson to become a little nimbler, a little
more global, a little more innovative, a little more automated, and a
little bit faster—as well as a little bit hungrier for some precisely targeted
government help. His story shows why it is important that we remain a
manufacturing country and what it takes both to inspire new ideas and
to turn them into decent-paying manufacturing jobs *in America*.

Eastman today is the world's largest manufacturer of fabric-cutting
machinery and the software that manages it. The firm makes machines
that can cut virtually any kind of cloth fabric, composite, or synthetic
material—from designer dresses, to Kevlar vests, to the carbon-graphite
materials that go into building NASCAR racing vehicles, to the fiber-
glass and composite panels from which the blades of wind turbines are
made.

Who goes into such a business? Great-grandpa—sort of. Eastman
started out making small electric machines to cut through cloth for
sweatshops to make into dresses, pants, and shirts. Its original customers
were low-margin businesses that depended on cheap labor, which meant
that Eastman had to keep its labor costs down as well, but its workers
were unionized. As globalization and the IT revolution opened more
labor markets, Stevenson and his father had to decide whether to keep
manufacturing in Buffalo and, if so, how to do that with unionized
workers. "We realized back in the 1980s that we could have commodity
parts made anywhere, but we decided that we were going to assemble
the machines and manufacture critical parts in the U.S.," he told us.
"And we have a United Auto Workers union! We had to convince the
union workers over the years that the concept of one man, one machine,
could not be sustained, since all machines today are computer controlled. The worker is the enabler of the machines, but he is not the
machine. He sets the specs, loads and unloads things, but the machine
runs itself. For us, the big breakthrough was getting our union to agree
that one man could run more than one machine. So if that worker
makes $18 an hour and runs four machines, that comes down to $4.50 an

hour per machine, and that makes us very competitive. It was a contin-uing education process for us and our union, but they got it."

That process was not always a smooth one. "Working with our union, UAW Local 936, has not always been a serene relationship," said Stevenson. "We have fought and negotiated hard with them and in the past thirty-five years endured two strikes. However, my standing prin-ciple was that we as a company would be committed to remain in Buf-falo, and we would be committed to maintaining and employing as many manufacturing jobs as we could. Fortunately, enough union mem-bers understood, and we now have a great relationship. It would at times have been easier for us to give up and move the company, or give in and lose the company. However, the key issue again was letting the employ-ees know that while they may not agree sometimes with our strategic decisions, we always operate under the principle that our community is important."

Not only is his company five generations old, but members of the families of some of Eastman's employees have worked for it for that long as well. "When I started working for my father after graduating from Yale in 1973," Stevenson explained, "he put me to work in the factory in our service department. After a few months he asked me to come to his office and wanted to know how things were going. I told him in the language of the shop, that things were going good, but at times we had some 'fucking problems' and that we couldn't get those 'fucking parts' out of production fast enough. He looked at me and responded, 'I paid for a Yale education so you can talk like that?' The point is that the fac-tory environment is very different from the front office. But the ability to speak the language of your environment is a must. Connecting with people and understanding where they are coming from is critical. And yes, we did solve that 'fucking' issue and get parts moving faster." And they did solve their labor problems as well.

After labor relations, the second big challenge Stevenson faced as he took over the company from his father was reinventing it for the hyper-connected world. It was quickly apparent to him that doing all they ever did would not ensure all they ever got. The barriers to entry into the fabric-cutting business were too low with China in the game. The fabric-cutting business that he inherited was becoming a commodity, so he redefined "fabrics."

"We reinvented ourselves by building machines that enabled us to get into markets beyond cutting cloth for apparel and upholstered furniture," he explained. "Now we sell into the aerospace industry," because airplanes and wings are now made of woven carbon-graphite fibers. "We sell to the wind industry, because the turbines are also made of high-tech fibers. We sell to the auto industry." The company set about inventing, in collaboration with hired programmers, a new generation of software for improved continuous cutting and motion control over all automated cutting systems.

Still, the world kept getting flatter and the competition from China kept increasing. "Up until 2001, we were nearly vertically integrated: we manufactured most of our products right here in our Buffalo factory," said Stevenson. "We brought in the forging and the raw material; we cut the metal, stamped the parts, formed the parts, and assembled them into finished products." But because of price pressures from globalization, from China, and from China's brazen piracy, Eastman decided that to improve its profit margins it simply had to subcontract some functions to lower-cost countries.

"In the 1980s we felt we needed to be more global," he explained, "so my brother Wade and I formed our own company in Hong Kong to distribute our products in Asia and China. That gave us an entry into China. We've since established a factory in China, in Ningbo [about an hour southwest of Shanghai], which opened in 2004. The original reason was that they started to pirate our cloth-cutting machines. It was just outrageous. Our company is named 'Eastman,' so they called their copy of our machine the 'Westman.' It was that brazen. They just completely copied our machine. I am a small company. I can't afford always to be taking these guys to court. For the Chinese, there is no such thing as piracy. We had the guys there who copied us actually congratulate us on making such a nice machine! And then the Chinese government put a 37 percent tariff on my real machines so I could not export them there. So we said, 'Okay, we will just establish our own factory in China and we will use Chinese-made parts and copy our own machines and sell into the China market'—and because they like American-made products, they want the quality, they buy from us."

But Stevenson will not move his main production line to China with his most advanced machines. "If I have a commodity part that can be made cheaper in China, I will source that to China. If you want to sell globally, you have to source globally" and take advantage of all the cost-saving possibilities that are out there. But ultimately, says Stevenson, the world still thinks highly of "American-made" and he continues to manufacture the parts and assemble his advanced machines in Buffalo.

In today's hyper-competitive marketplace, he added, "speed wins. It is not the biggest companies that always win but the fastest. Adaptability and responsiveness to your customers and your employees will ultimately win the battles."

That is his company's "extra." It is not just the three C's—creating, communicating, and collaborating—that he is putting to work. He and his employees, he says, are always looking to forge sustainable relationships with their customers by treating each one as an artisan would—as a customer seeking a product tailored to a set of specific needs. That's his competitive advantage as a little guy.

"We pride ourselves on getting information out the same day that it is requested, parts shipped, machines repaired, and the like," Stevenson says. "We don't seek to be the largest. We like knowing our customers. We think we can be very competitive in areas where the customer wants a relationship. People still call up and say, 'I want to speak to Robert.'" The successful CEO today, he elaborates, must listen to his employees and make sure that he has enlisted every one of them as inventors as well. About half of Eastman's 115 employees are blue-collar, the rest white-collar. Precisely because he knows how valuable his line workers are as innovators, Stevenson says he is worried about the future.

"We have a lot of workers in their late fifties," he explains, "and our concern is: How are we going to replace them? Because a factory job is not something people aspire to anymore. There is this concept that you have to go college and not become a blue-collar worker. We pay health care, pensions, all the holidays, and $18 to $22 an hour. I think it is going to be a major issue for this country in the next few years. Our biggest problem is finding factory workers who are going to replace this group of men and women in their fifties who started with us."

That is especially a problem, he explained, because blue-collar work is not what it used to be. On the shop floor, as is the case everywhere else, average is over.

"We look for a guy who can think for himself a little bit, not like before," said Stevenson. "We sell an $80,000 to $150,000 computer-controlled cutter, and it has a software program that helps the customer design parts. So when we hire these young guys, I tell them, 'You are the face of the company. The customer just spent a lot of money and he expects you to know all that there is to know about this machine.'" That means not only that the Eastman employee must be familiar with what the customer's business is, but he must also understand how any machine can be tweaked for the customer. "So our guy has to be able to do a little engineering on the spot, sometimes even a little sourcing over at the local Home Depot to get exactly what the customer needs," said Stevenson. "We found that guys who are the most successful are ex-military guys, because they have been forced to do the same thing out in the field. In the old days the union guy said, 'My job is to polish the fork, not shine the spoon.' We cannot afford to have one man, one job anymore. We need adaptive abilities. So what we are looking for are people who have the ability to say, 'Today I may be wiring something, tomorrow I am running a machine, and the third day I am assembling . . .' I was looking at an advertisement that we created in the mid-1990s. The tagline reads: 'We sell solutions, not machines.'"

Stevenson offers firsthand testimony about the importance of keeping manufacturing in this country in order to produce innovation and sustain the American dream. If we don't have people touching the products, we won't have people improving those products and inventing new ones.

"Innovation comes in small steps most of the time, not giant leaps," he explained. "We don't look for the silver bullet that will transform our product line but rather for incremental improvements. Many times our new products or improvements come from customer requests or from our field guys who see an issue and then suggest how to resolve it. For example, a customer wondered why we couldn't marry a laser cutting head to our regular knife cutting head to create a dual-purpose machine. The request went to one of our field engineers. He adapted a design and, voilà, it worked, and now we have a new product line that is taking off. Listening and then acting was the key."

For all of these reasons, said Stevenson, the role of CEO has changed dramatically since his great-grandfather's day. The term "boss" remains, but that is where the similarity ends.

"The role of the CEO now is not to dictate but to empower," he explained. "Because today you just can't have all the answers anymore. I don't know everything . . . The power of the people is immense—if you can challenge them and get your people working toward a common goal. I set the goal and show the road and say, 'How you drive on that is up to you . . .' I think that the old picture of the head of the company who says 'It is my way or the highway' doesn't work anymore. There is no such thing as 'your way' anymore. There is a global way, and there are a lot of cultures that do things equally well and sometimes better. If we don't understand that and incorporate those ideas into our business, we are going to fail because we will become insular."

Stevenson is chairman of the Board of Trustees of Medaille College, and not only out of community spirit. Because his own company has limited funding for research and development, he depends on collaborations with the local universities to help solve problems that can keep his company at the cutting edge of technology. "What can help small businesses like ours is the ability to gather 'intellectual capital' from the local state colleges that our tax dollars support. We have the ability to manufacture, sell, and distribute. We have the know-how to penetrate foreign markets. What we don't always have is access to the latest technologies that are being developed in universities today." Stevenson says if Americans can learn how better to "tap that knowledge and create the synergy between small business and the educational institutions, we will create such energy that manufacturing will come roaring back."

A Hand Up, Not a Handout

American manufacturing has been doing a lot more roaring than most Americans realize. Since the 1890s, America has been the world's largest maker of manufactured goods. Only in 2010 did China overtake us, producing just over $1 trillion in 2010, when we produced just under $1 trillion. So we're hardly out of the blue-collar manufacturing business.

In some ways our manufacturing "problem" is that we're too adept at it. According to a 2011 report by IHS Global Insight, the economic analysis firm, the U.S. still far surpasses China in productivity, with

11.5 million American factory workers producing roughly the same value of goods as 100 million Chinese workers. That is a real positive. Because of the high level of American productivity—the result of well-trained workers leveraging more and more advanced machines, robots, and software—the value created by the average American worker is much greater than that created by an average Chinese worker, which means that an American worker can still earn far more than a Chinese worker. Rather than mass-producing relatively low-value goods, which just creates a lot of low-paying, low-skilled jobs, American manufacturing is properly focused on high-paying, high-productivity factories that make such things as aircraft, medical and scientific equipment, control systems, and specialized industrial machinery and chemicals.

In 2009, the average American manufacturing worker earned $74,447, including benefits, according to the National Association of Manufacturers. Wages alone totaled about $63,000. As long as we keep improving productivity, we can keep paying blue-collar workers decent wages.

But the drive for greater productivity requires replacing human labor with more and more sophisticated machines, operated by higher- and higher-skilled workers. Therefore, if we want not only to keep advanced manufacturing in America, but to expand it—so that there will be more good blue-collar jobs for future generations—we need more people starting companies in America that manufacture things and more existing manufacturers continuing to produce in America or others coming here from abroad to do so.

According to the Bureau of Labor Statistics, the size of typical new businesses in America has been steadily declining as companies take advantage of technology and networking to do more things with fewer people. In 2000, the average new firm had 7.7 employees. By 2010, that number had fallen to 5.5.

That is why stimulating and attracting and keeping start-ups is so important. As Robert Litan, who heads research for the Kauffman Foundation, notes: "Between 1980 and 2005, virtually all net new jobs created in the United States were created by firms that were five years old or less. That is about forty million jobs."

As we said earlier, economics is win-win. Companies today can and should take advantage of the whole globe to design, manufacture, and sell their goods and services. But not everyone will win equally, and as the world gets increasingly hyper-connected, we must make sure that American workers have access to the education, tools, and start-ups they will need to win their share. That requires something that America has long lacked—a comprehensive twenty-first-century jobs strategy.

Every good strategy starts with a vision of where you ultimately want to go. Our vision for America is simple—but not modest. We want America to be for the whole world what Florida's Cape Canaveral was for America's space program—a launching pad where innovators and entrepreneurs the world over want to locate all or part of their operations because our workforce is so productive; our infrastructure and Internet bandwidth are so advanced; our openness to talent from anywhere second to none; our funding for basic research so generous; our rule of law, patent protection, and investment- and manufacturing-friendly tax code superior to what can be found in any other country; and our openness to collaboration unparalleled—all because we have updated and expanded our formula for success.

We want America to be *the place* to dream something, design something, start something, collaborate with others on something, and manufacture something—in an age in which every link in that chain can now be done in so many places. No one should ever have to say "I am moving from America to Singapore because it is more hospitable to innovation and entrepreneurship."

Just the opposite should be true. "You will know you're successful," said PV Kannan, the India outsourcing entrepreneur, "if new companies in China and Brazil and India say, 'We want to move our headquarters to America because that is the best place in the world to do business.'"

That's the goal—so how do we get there? The country needs a job-creation strategy based on the world in which we are actually living. Historically, Americans have not wanted their government to single out particular firms for special treatment or particular industries for taxpayer-funded subsidies. The U.S. government doesn't pick winners. It lets the market do that.

Generally, we think that approach is correct. We oppose corporate handouts. But we do favor hand-ups—ways in which every local and state government and the federal government can give a hand up to en-

trepreneurs who want to start new businesses in America and manufacture here—and then let the market sort the businesses out. Just assuming
that a rising economic tide alone will bring in more blue-collar jobs—
as we are doing now—is not a smart strategy. It is not a strategy at all.

"While a robust economic recovery is a foundation for job growth,
a cyclical rebound in GDP growth alone is unlikely to put enough
Americans back to work," McKinsey & Company analysts observed in a
June 2011 study entitled *An Economy That Works: Job Creation and
America's Future.* "Job creation must become a national priority, not a
by-product of other policy decisions." McKinsey's report concludes that
a job-creation strategy has to include a variety of initiatives, which
echoed what we heard from policymakers and entrepreneurs: addressing
the growing mismatch between the needs of employers and the skills
American workers get in school and in the job market; finding ways to
make globalization a better source of job creation in the United States;
stimulating innovation and new company start-ups; and simplifying regulatory procedures that create obstacles to job creation.

Listening to politicians browbeat employers for not hiring more
American workers, you wouldn't know that there is a need to harmonize
what people are studying in school with what the workplace is looking
for in the way of skills. McKinsey noted that "despite rising educational
attainment and $18 billion spent annually by the federal government on
job training, employers say they cannot find workers with specific skills.
Meanwhile, students lack a clear picture of which jobs to prepare themselves for."

McKinsey found that 30 percent of the companies it surveyed said
they have had positions open for six months or longer because they
could not find the right people for them, and nearly two-thirds reported
that they routinely have openings that are difficult to fill. At the high
end of the labor market, the most difficult occupational categories to fill
were in science and engineering, followed by those in computer programming and information technology. Next are jobs for statisticians
and mathematicians who can manage new "big data" systems that use
vast amounts of information to drive a range of business activities. But
"skill shortages are not just confined to Ph.D. engineers, scientists, and
computer programmers," McKinsey found. "Our interviews reveal a
broad set of fields at all levels of education—welders, nursing aides,

nutritionists, and nuclear technicians—in which employers cannot find qualified workers." For that reason, McKinsey argued that American business needs to become more involved "in developing curricula in community colleges and vocational schools, and a national jobs database would provide the basis for informed decisions about majors and training programs."

You hear this complaint in every major city. "We see it right here in Kansas City with the local engineering and manufacturing firms," said Robert Litan. "A lot of them are facing huge retirements in their labor force, and they can't replace [those workers]. Where are the kids who will come in who know this stuff?"

In that spirit, we, the authors, our tongues partly in cheek, offer one specific proposal: a tax of $15,000 a year on the tuition for law school or business school, combined with a $15,000-a-year tuition subsidy for students pursuing graduate degrees in engineering, science, or other specific vocational studies. Somehow we have to find a way to get our best and brightest back to starting companies that make things that improve people's lives and away from devising complicated financial products for Wall Street to make money from money. As Vivek Wadhwa, the expert on business and immigration, likes to say, "Friends don't let friends get into finance."

As for harnessing globalization to drive investment in America, the McKinsey study argued that "despite the recent financial crisis, the global economy is booming and American companies have mostly adapted and thrived in it. However, the same cannot be said for American workers. The United States needs a national conversation on how to ensure that its workers—not only its companies—win 'market share' in the growing global marketplace." One idea is to seek out more foreign direct investment in the United States to finance brand-new start-ups, not just to buy existing firms. America should present itself as the world's biggest and safest emerging market, and we could underline that, McKinsey suggested, by creating a special "business visa" that makes it painless for potential investors to come scout, purchase, and negotiate with businesses in America. Why leave that to China? We should be looking for ways to give incentives to companies that have outsourced work to India or China—where wages have been rising in the biggest markets—to bring it back onshore. With today's high-speed telecommunication networks, it can be just as efficient and almost as cheap (without any language issues) to locate a call center in Bangor, Maine, as it is to go to Bangalore, India. With a rising global middle class, tourism is another industry that has huge room to grow in America, and is a big employer. As McKinsey notes, foreign visits to America fell from 26 million in 2000 to 18 million in 2003 before recovering to 24 million in 2009. That is a lot of hotels, amusement parks, transport vehicles, and restaurants not built, and a lot of service jobs lost.

Any jobs strategy also has to include leveraging the balance sheets of state and local governments to stimulate more start-ups. " Innovation, new industries and new company creation are essential for strong demand growth and job creation," McKinsey noted. "An important first step will be to restart the flow of financing to start-ups and growing young companies."

Jennifer Granholm, who served as governor of Michigan from 2003 to 2010, has been a pioneer in this activity. "In Asia, government is not the enemy, and we can't afford to treat it that way here," Granholm told us. "We have to make targeted smart investments that leverage private money going into competitively emerging companies"—in what are clearly going to be strategic industries. "If we don't have the policies that create both the supply and demand for advanced manufacturing here, we are going to be a has-been country," she added. "We are playing on a global playing field today. The board has enlarged so much. You cannot just cut taxes to fix all the problems."

For industries such as clean energy, surely the next great global industry, said Granholm, "we need a federal policy that creates a national market and gives predictability to investors and manufacturers, to be confident that their output can and will be sold here." This involves not picking winners but planting seeds. In 2009, the federal government created a competition for start-up grants—$2.4 billion worth—for electric battery and storage companies. Through that process, seventeen Michigan-based start-ups won grants, which the state of Michigan then augmented with smaller stipends.

"This enabled them to get off the ground and attract private capital," said Granholm. "It also enabled us to build an entire battery cluster in Michigan, with the whole supply chain. It led to $5 billion worth of investment from the private sector and 63,000 jobs. None of this would have happened without federal policy. We could never have done it as a state alone. States don't have the resources in tough economic times. We are not picking winners. Those companies will now live or die on their own, but we helped them get started. They are not looking for giveaways. They just need access to capital to get started. Every Asian country is doing this . . . The electric car is going to be a trillion-dollar industry. It is going to be the most technologically advanced mass-produced product in the world."

The electric car will resemble an iPad on wheels. It will spin off a huge applications industry as well, Granholm added. "So we have to decide: Are we going to be in that industry or not? If we are, we need to seed that garden and get these plants growing here—otherwise they will grow somewhere else."

These incentives do matter, especially times of slow growth. Paul Otellini, the CEO of Intel, told us that barely a month goes by without some country's leader contacting him and offering the likes of $1 billion in tax credits and other incentives if he will open an Intel plant and create jobs in that country. "I can build a factory anywhere on earth but here and get a $1 billion discount," said Otellini. "If we said that we are going to put in place a policy whereby we will give five years of federal and state tax relief to anyone on earth, American or foreign, who puts up a factory in a U.S. state that creates jobs—and we will only start taxing you five years from now—it costs the country nothing." The jobs and taxes would not have existed without the factory, and five years down the road the factory and its jobs will be producing tax revenue and creating other jobs for local suppliers, truckers, restaurants, lawyers, accountants, and barbers for years.

K. R. Sridhar, the principal co-founder of Bloom Energy, which employs 1,000 workers in California plants making a fuel-cell technology that helps power Google and other Silicon Valley firms, knows a lot about the trials and tribulation of innovating and manufacturing in America. The most important thing that government can do to help accelerate the development of new technologies and industries, he says, is to use its buying power and standards-setting power to help budding manufacturers get across what he calls "the second valley of death."

This is an important but little understood problem in start-up manufacturing. In the lexicon of Silicon Valley, "the valley of death" refers to the point at which someone has invented something that works beautifully in a laboratory but is still unproven as a product that can become commercially viable and offer customers economic value. The difficulty of getting inventors across that first valley of death is why God created venture capitalists. They build a team, fund it, and show that whatever the invention is, "you can do it outside the lab," explained Sridhar. "That is where the maximum risk is and that is where the maximum return is. The government should not be involved there with taxpayer money."

Many of the bits-and-bytes companies (i.e., software, services, or dot-coms) that manage to get across the first valley of death then proceed to "manufacture" their products in the least-cost, highest-productivity locations in the world. Because those products can be digitized, the work assembling them can be done anywhere at relatively low cost. So the jobs these bits-and-bytes innovators create are not very "sticky," says Sridhar. Companies such as Facebook (2,000 employees) and Twitter (400 employees) "create a lot of wealth but not a lot of jobs."

That is usually not the case with new inventions that involve bending metal—such as fuel cells for cars or the big electric cutting tools that Eastman makes. These require big investments in factories and production equipment—things that cannot easily be moved. These companies typically have a "second valley of death" that they have to cross before they reach profitability, and here state and local governments and the federal government can play important roles, without picking winners.

"Let's say that you have proven the value proposition for your product—you are across the first valley of death," said Sridhar. In order to get your business to take off and gain market share, "you need scale manufacturing, because the cost of a new technology will only come down with scale manufacturing." And if you have scale manufacturing, you will also get access to more investors and better bank loans, which you need in order to drive and expand your business.

What government can do to help manufacturers achieve this kind of scale is shape the market. It can do that with tax holidays and cheap capital for the building of plants, of the kind Intel and Governor Granholm suggested. It can do that by offering to be the first buyer of a proven product—energy-efficient windows for government offices, solar water heaters for the military, electric cars for the post office. Or it can do that by creating legislation that raises standards—the way Mike Biddle proposed for recycling plastics—which immediately creates scale demand for a new American-made technology.

With start-up manufacturing, said Sridhar, the big question is always "Who is going to buy those first 5,000 cell phones that will actually cost more than landlines" but the sale of which is crucial to bringing down the price? "That is the second valley of death, where governments can help." Once a manufacturer has achieved those economies of scale, the factory he has built, the machines he has invested in, and the jobs he has created become "very sticky," added Sridhar. It is very costly to move those jobs—and the suppliers and service providers that grow up around them—to another country.

Finally, any jobs strategy has to involve the government clearing "the path for investing and hiring," the McKinsey report argued. "Uncertainty over the direction of regulation—and the time and expense required to comply with current regulation—has made companies hesitant to invest. Speeding the resolution of investment decisions, too often delayed by overlapping or conflicting environmental and land use regulations or by their unnecessarily slow application, is critical. 'Plug and play' enterprise zones—pre-approved for most zoning and environmental permits—could cut in half the time to bring a new plant online. Another critical obstacle to job growth is the backlog at the U.S. Patent Office, where it can take more than 3 years to get approval . . . The United States still scores well on the World Bank's Doing Business survey, but it has slipped in some key areas, falling to number 27— behind Thailand and Saudi Arabia—on ease of getting a construction permit."

We need regulations and we need standards; they are essential to a properly functioning economy and to give innovators incentives to achieve higher and higher levels of performance. But more attention has to be paid to making these standards clear and easy to address, with one-stop shopping, and to pruning constantly those that are obsolete. Said Sridhar: "Countries that are open for business will assign you an official who is your one point of contact to work with you and the local government to make what you need to happen, happen—whether it is a road or utility connection or a some other permit." Sridhar said he is obviously ready to abide by all the laws on the books, "but if I do, I don't want to still get tied up in [local red tape and lawsuits] in a way that bogs down my ability to start my operations."

Regulatory and tax uncertainty is a silent job killer. "I don't care what society decides about the level of taxes and health-care costs, but I need to know exactly what they are going to be for the next five years," concluded Sridhar. "Because when you invest in a factory you have to know exactly how long it is going to take to recoup your capital."

Fortunately, more and more of the fifty U.S. states are getting this message. For instance, Delaware's governor, Jack Markell, said that when he was recruiting the start-up electric car company Fisker Automotive to locate its factory in an abandoned General Motors plant in Delaware, he saw it as part of his job "to understand their business better than anyone else." When the Fisker team visited, Markell assembled the state's entire congressional delegation, the state leadership from himself on down, and the county leadership to join him in enticing them to Delaware. He called Ellen Kullman, the CEO of DuPont, and persuaded her to commit to buying a certain number of Fisker electric cars and to partner with the start-up on paint for its vehicles. Then Markell topped it all off with a $21.5 million five-year no-interest loan that converts to a grant if Fisker creates a certain level of jobs and other milestones in his state. "I made a personal commitment to buy the first car off the line, and the head of our economic development office is buying the second one," said Markell. "You want to reduce the friction and make it impossible for them to go somewhere else."

The larger point is this: We cannot ride on our reputation from the last century, or on the sort of public-private partnership we had then, to get through the new century. If we are going to generate the number of decent-paying jobs we need, we need a jobs strategy in line with global best practices. That strategy will almost certainly have to involve more government investment and incentives in generating start-ups than Republicans have traditionally favored, and it will almost certainly require more public assistance and incentives to corporations than Democrats have traditionally favored. That is what it means to update our formula for prosperity—melding ideas from the left and the right with the new and the old. We need a hybrid approach that takes the best of both parties.

"Waiting for the U.S. job market to correct itself and clinging to the solutions of the past will not hasten the return to full employment or set the stage for sustained job creation in the years to come," the McKinsey study concluded. "To create the jobs that America needs to continue growing and remain competitive, leaders in government, business, and education will have to be creative—and willing to consider solutions they have not tried before. Workers themselves will need to acquire the right skills and adapt to a future of lifelong learning and new ways of working. As Peter Drucker warned, 'The greatest danger in times of turbulence is not the turbulence; it is to act with yesterday's logic.'"

Hope in the American Dream

Byron Auguste, the management consultant who specializes in education and social issues and has been an important guide for us, summed up where America finds itself today in a March 5, 2011, speech to the Harvard Business School community: "We face some big challenges right now, short term and long term," he observed. "But if the goal is to have the most prosperous and dynamic economy ten years, twenty years, fifty years from now, I'd rather be us than anyone else. Compared with the other rich countries, we have youth, openness, dynamism, the best minds from around the world, enormous human capital, the deepest capital markets, unparalleled institutions of innovation, and a market no global businesses can ignore. Compared to the big developing countries, we have high social trust, low corruption, an historic link between effort and achievement, and democracy, as messy as it sometimes is.

"These issues are very personal for me," added Auguste, whose parents grew up in the Caribbean, "and they inform the work I do both at McKinsey and in Hope Street Group [a nonprofit group of professionals and entrepreneurs who promote innovative policies to expand the American middle class]. My parents came to this country when I was a toddler, in 1970. My father worked as a factory shipping supervisor, and my mother made $6,000 a year as an architectural assistant. They bought a little brick house for $28,000 near 7 Mile Road in central Detroit. They saved enough money, and felt secure enough, that my dad quit his factory job and went back to school to become a computer programmer. He changed jobs and we moved to Arizona, where I attended pretty good public schools and won college scholarships. At every step, the institutions and values of this country made a difference, gave us a chance, and made our progress possible. But that American dream can't be taken for granted. I visited my old neighborhood in Detroit a few years back. Our clean little brick house sat in a derelict block, with no middle class in sight and atrocious local public schools. People doing work my parents did often can't afford to buy a home in a safe neighborhood. Many can't take the chance to change jobs or go back to school, as my father did, for fear of losing health coverage, which costs far more now than then. The jobs that got my parents started in the 1970s now face much more intense and global competition. This isn't a reason to despair; but it *is* a reason to act differently—to reform our institutions and strengthen our shared values."

Acting differently will require putting in place a different set of incentives for our political leadership, to loosen the grip of extreme polarization and powerful special interests on our public policies. That, in turn, will require a shock to the system. It could come from the market or Mother Nature or the middle of the political spectrum. We vote for the one from the middle, and the next chapter explains why and how it might come about.

FIFTEEN

Shock Therapy

Alexis de Tocqueville was a French aristocrat, born in 1805, who visited the United States in 1831 and 1832 with the intention of studying its prisons. In 1835 he published *Democracy in America*, based on his travels and investigations. Of all the thousands of books written about this country, Tocqueville's remains one of the best, with insights into American society, American values, American institutions, and the American national character that remain valid and relevant 175 years later.

Suppose that Tocqueville, with his intellectual gifts and powers of analysis, had been born in, say, 1970. His aristocratic background would have had no bearing on his career. He probably would have gone to one of France's elite schools but might not have taken part in French politics, as the original Tocqueville did. Nor would he necessarily have joined, and risen in, the country's national bureaucracy, as men of his caliber did for much of the twentieth century but did less frequently at that century's end. Instead, he might well have continued his education abroad. He might have studied history at an English university, spent a few years in Asia, earned a degree from Harvard or Stanford business school, and then done what many people with a cosmopolitan background and analytical gifts did at the end of the twentieth century and the beginning of the twenty-first: join an international consulting firm.

Suppose, further, that that firm was commissioned by a large multinational corporation to prepare, under Tocqueville's direction, an assessment of the United States as a place in which to invest and to do business in the second decade of the twenty-first century and beyond. The report that emerged from that assessment would be the work of many hands, filled with charts, graphs, statistics, and PowerPoint presentations. Tocqueville himself would likely write the conclusion, based on his own travels, conversations, and ruminations. We think it might read something like this:

Twenty years ago, even ten years ago, a report such as this one would never have been commissioned. The United States was the best country in the world for business of any kind, the one with the largest and most open market, the most transparent legal system with the strongest property rights, the biggest and most efficient financial system, the most modern infrastructure, and the most dynamic ongoing research and development in almost every field. It was a magnet for capital and talent. No company of any size, indeed no company that merely aspired to international growth, could afford not to operate there, and none needed a consultant to tell it that.

Now, alas, things are different. Over the past decade especially, America has changed, and not for the better. The country still has many of its major and distinctive economic strengths, but worrying signs of stagnation, and even decline, have begun to appear. Unemployment remains stubbornly high even though the Great Recession of 2007–2009 has officially ended and productivity is at record levels. The federal budget deficit keeps rising, without a credible long-term plan to bring it truly under control. Consumption of foreign oil keeps rising as well, also without any strategy for reducing it. American students consistently score lower on international achievement tests than their age-mates in other countries. The country's roads are crowded, its public transportation systems are decaying, its bridges occasionally collapse. Major American firms are moving research-and-development facilities outside the United States. Low-skilled immigrants arrive in the country illegally in large numbers, while America fails to take steps to attract and keep the best-educated and most energetic people from abroad, the kind who have founded and built so many high-tech enterprises. The national debate is consumed by absurd distractions, such as establishing beyond a doubt that the president was born in the United States, or increasingly partisan social issues, such as abortion, with scant time and attention paid to discussing the fundamental changes in the world in which Americans are living and the need to adjust to them.

Americans understand that something is amiss, and they worry about it. Polls show growing pessimism among them about their country's future. I myself have limited faith in these surveys. For gauging the mood of a society polls are, in my opinion, a poor substitute for firsthand and in-depth observation. With all due respect to my number-crunching associates, anthropologists are more reliable guides to a society than statisticians. But the conversations I have engaged in across America in the course of compiling this report—with old friends, new acquaintances, and American colleagues—paint the same picture as do the data in these surveys. The people with whom I have spoken share a gnawing fear that their country is slipping and that the characteristically American promise that the future will be better than the past will not be kept. Those who are fortunate enough not to have to worry about their own jobs and their own economic futures are worried about the future of the country as a whole. They are right to worry, but they are not the only people with cause for concern.

The future of the United States has important implications for your company, of course. You will have to decide, on the basis of your assessment of that future, how much to invest in the country, how many people to station there, and the volume of sales in the American market on which you can count in the years ahead. The American economic future obviously matters a great deal to Americans as well: It will largely determine their personal wealth and security.

What happens in and to the United States has a far wider significance, however, of which everyone who has a stake in the global economy should be mindful. This is the country most responsible for organizing and sustaining the international economic system in which the present era of globalization has flourished. Its economic and military strength have underpinned the vast expansion of cross-border trade and investment during the last six decades, and especially the last two. America is in our era what the historian Plutarch said Rome was in ancient times, "an anchor to the floating world." Weaken that anchor and the world will drift in directions we cannot foresee and probably will not like. A declining America will be bad for business—all business, including yours.

Let me be clear: The country's traditional strengths have not disappeared. American society is as vibrant as ever. As I traveled the country, I encountered, as I always do, impressive local businesses, creative teachers, active civic organizations, and visionary leaders. Yet all of that energy and talent is not adding up to the national vitality that the world has come to expect.

What is needed to revitalize the United States—to reverse the worrisome trends, harness all its grassroots energy, spur economic growth, restore the national morale, and assure American global leadership into the next decade and beyond? The answer may surprise you, for it is the same kind of answer our firm gave you twenty years ago when you asked us what we thought were the preconditions for investing in the former Soviet Union and other postcommunist emerging markets. Do you remember our answer? It was "shock therapy."

Yes, you read that correctly. American politics are stuck, and it now seems to be in need of the kind of jolt that economists and consultants recommended for the country that America defeated in the Cold War, and on occasion for other emerging markets beset with severe economic problems.

It is not hard to see why. Neither of America's two major parties seems able to address in serious fashion the challenges the country confronts. Their political philosophies are worlds apart, and neither outlook is suitable for the present moment. The Democrats act as if government is the solution to all of America's difficulties; the Republicans act as if government is the cause of all of them. The Democrats behave as if virtually every program the government created in the twentieth century is perfect and cannot be changed in any way; the Republicans seek to send the country back to the nineteenth century, before any of those programs existed. Neither approach will give the country the policies it needs to succeed in the decades to come.

In fact, the parties have reversed their historical positions. A generation ago Democrats stood for progressive change. Now they defend every federal program as if each were sacred. They have become the most conservative force in American politics. The term "reactionary liberalism" is not a contradiction in terms; it is an accurate description of the Democrats' approach to governance. The Republicans used to be the conservatives in the original, genuine, European sense, opposed to sudden, rapid shifts in public policy and prudent when it came to public finances. Now they are the party of fiscal radicalism and recklessness, cutting taxes without reducing spending and thereby pushing the United States ever deeper into debt. The two parties are, however, united on two things—unfortunately.

Neither has the courage to take the necessary serious steps to address the dangerously high budget deficits: reduce spending on the main entitlement programs (Social Security and Medicare), raise taxes, and invest in the programs on which economic success depends. And neither has the courage to reduce America's, and therefore the world's, ruinous dependence on oil by raising the price of gasoline.

I know what you are thinking. When operating in emerging markets, your business usually seeks political stability. Indeed, the very stability and predictability of its politics were always major assets for the United States. Now, in our view, they have become liabilities.

To forestall American decline now requires a certain kind of political instability. The country needs to refocus its attention on what is important and unblock its clogged channels of government. Neither will happen if present trends continue. Business as usual in American politics is a recipe for national decline. George Voinovich, a retiring senator from the Republican Party, made the point dramatically in 2010, when he said of the Congress in which he was completing his second term, "I think we have to blow up the place."

That was, of course, a deliberate exaggeration. The American political system does not need blowing up, but it does need shaking up. For patients with certain kinds of mental illnesses, psychiatrists once routinely prescribed the application of an electrical stimulus, which was known as "shock therapy." The same term, as we said, was used to describe sharp and blunt changes of economic policy, usually designed to stop rampant inflation in emerging markets or postcommunist states. This is what America now needs—but not in the economic realm. It needs political shock therapy.

Your investment decisions about the United States should depend on whether you believe it will get the political shock therapy it requires. You are entitled to know my opinion on this question. On balance, I am bullish on America. I am cautiously optimistic that the country will rally, as it has so often in the past, to meet the challenges it confronts. But I confess that I am not sure of this. What I do know, and this is my concluding point, is that the future of America itself and, I believe, the future of the world as well rest on the answer to that question.

Respectfully submitted,
A. de Tocqueville

Why Shock Therapy?

What kind of shock therapy to the American political system is needed, and from where might it come? Tocqueville lived in an age of revolution. He was born a few years after the greatest of all of them, the French Revolution of 1789, and lived through two others, in 1830 and 1848. Nothing of that sort is in store for the United States. Nor does the country need fundamental changes to its system of government, a system that has served it well for more than two centuries and has proven equal to the task of coping with a series of major challenges. The problem for modern America is not that it has the wrong political system but rather that the eminently serviceable political system it does have is not functioning properly. And to get it to function properly is going to require a shock—like giving smelling salts to revive a person who has fainted or jump-starting a car with a dead battery. Such a shock could come from a number of places: from outside the country by some external foe, from a devastating global economic crisis, from Mother Nature, from a grass-roots movement within the country, or from the top of the political system itself.

We hope that it will come from within—from a combination of grassroots and high politics. We mean by this a serious independent presidential candidate. We agree with Senator Voinovich: We think it is time, figuratively speaking, to blow the place up.

Our political system is stuck. It is under the sway of powerful special interests that work for policies that are at best irrelevant to and at worst counterproductive for the urgent present and future needs of the United States. The two parties are so sharply polarized that they are incapable of arriving at the deep, ideologically painful compromises that major initiatives, of the kind required to meet the major challenges America faces, will require.

Moreover, as we have tried to demonstrate, these pathologies of our political system have deep roots. They are the products of broad historical and social trends in American society. The net effect of these powerful forces has been to create a set of perverse political incentives for avoiding rather than addressing our major challenges.

Democrats are right that the government must make investments in—that is, spend money on—education and infrastructure if the United

States is to succeed in a globalized economy in which sophisticated information technology is spreading ever more rapidly. Republicans are right that the engine of national economic advance will have to be the private sector and that the government must tailor its policies to encourage and enable private innovation and entrepreneurship. But both parties are wrong to assure Americans that taxes will never rise, as Republicans do, and that the benefits they have been promised will never be cut, as Democrats do.

In other words, to adapt to the new world and the major new challenges it has thrown at us, it is not enough to find a sliver of common ground between left and right. The country must move, in political terms, "to higher ground," as Don Baer, the former communications director in the Clinton administration, put it—higher ground on which it can make the changes that will sustain the American dream and American global leadership into the next decade and the next generation.

As the former Republican congressman from South Carolina Bob Inglis told us, what we need today is "a hybrid politics" that would replace grudging compromise between two hostile ideologies with a creative synthesis. "We need to take the strengths of both parties and use them to the benefit of the country," said Inglis. "Democrats tend to concentrate on fairness. Republicans excel at building meritocracies. The truth is, Americans want and need both. We want and need the wealth that meritocracies can create, but we also want and need fairness so that the little guy doesn't get squashed by the big guy. Hybrid politicians—aware of the external threats that we face together—would welcome the improvements that their counterparts could offer."

To put it another way, the United States needs a politics of the "radical center." This may sound like a contradiction in terms, but it isn't. The policies necessary to meet America's challenges are centrist in that they fall, on the left-right political spectrum, somewhere in the considerable space between what have become mainstream Democratic and mainstream Republican positions. People in the middle—centrists—are often called "moderates," implying that they are lukewarm about everything. But they need not be weak-willed people who wish to befriend everybody, offend nobody, and change nothing. The policies we need are also radical because they involve far more substantial changes in the current ways of doing things than Democrats or Republicans are on course to propose. Especially on the federal budget, the two major parties act as tenacious guardians of the status quo, but the status quo does not give the country the tools necessary to make the present century, like the previous two, an era of American prosperity.

To get to that higher ground, to be able both to articulate a program of the radical center and then to generate a mandate for it, we need to overcome or change the perverse political incentives that now keep such ideas and candidates promoting them on the fringe. How can we do that?

In theory, either party could nominate a presidential candidate who, once elected, would embrace a program of the radical center. In practice, though, such a "Trojan horse" candidacy is highly unlikely. Once elected, a president does not become a free agent. He or she enters office with obligations to those whose support put him or her in the White House and therefore cannot simply jettison the promises that attracted that support in the first place. The most loyal supporters tend to be the most ideologically polarized members of the candidate's own party, who are the most zealous guardians of its doctrinal orthodoxies. Nor can a president rely on personal popularity to enact an agenda of the radical center. To do this, charisma is not enough, as two recent examples demonstrate. Arnold Schwarzenegger entered the governor's mansion in California under unusual circumstances, having won a special election and with widespread goodwill and the advantage of a powerful and widely known public image. He tried to adopt policies to stop his state's downward economic spiral, but largely failed. He made his share of political mistakes, but in the end it was the entrenched power of the two major parties that thwarted him.

Similarly, Barack Obama won the presidency promising a new era of cooperation in American public life, but his first two years reproduced the partisan rancor of his predecessor's time in office. He did inherit an economic disaster that demanded immediate attention, and the attention his administration paid to shoring up the economy used up much of the political capital he brought to office. But he devoted his remaining capital to expanding health-care coverage. That was certainly a worthy goal and one that had an almost religious significance to his own political party but, as enacted, it is unclear how much it will do to equip the United States to meet the challenges we face.

"Change We Can Believe In" proved to be an effective campaign slogan but not a useful guideline for governing. Obama did not seek a mandate for the radical centrist agenda that would enable Americans to thrive in the world in which they were living, and so, when he began his presidency, he did not have one.

The only way around all these ideological and structural obstacles is a third-party or independent candidate, who can not only articulate a hybrid politics that addresses our major challenges and restores our formula for success but—and it is a huge but—does this in a way that enough Americans find so compelling that they are willing to leave their respective Democratic and Republican camps and join hands in the radical center. Only that could change a political system that rewards our politicians for postponing hard decisions and blaming the other party rather than making those decisions.

In business and politics, people respond to incentives, and when the incentives are perverse, people behave perversely. Move the cheese, move the mouse; keep the cheese where it is and the mouse doesn't move. We need to change those incentives before the market or Mother Nature does it for us. We need to move the cheese, and only a compelling third-party candidate, with a compelling hybrid politics, can do that.

A Third Way to a New Way

A third-party or independent presidential candidacy might seem, at first glance, an odd way to administer the needed shock to the American political system. After all, in the history of the American republic no third-party candidate has ever been elected president. In fact, third-party candidates have rarely been elected to any office. Since the Republicans replaced the Whigs in 1854 and joined the Democrats as one of the country's two major political parties, the two of them have had a stranglehold on American politics. They have managed to maintain it for more than a century and a half for several powerful reasons.

To compete with them, a third party must get on the ballot, and that is not easy. Each state has its own election laws, and the Democrats and Republicans in the state legislatures who write these laws have deliberately made access to the ballot difficult almost everywhere. California is once again the extreme example: to get on the presidential ballot a candidate who is not a Democrat or a Republican must gather 1.1 million valid signatures, which usually requires at least 1.6 million total signatures. Collecting them one at a time outside a supermarket or in a mall, which is how it is usually done, is not easy.

Moreover, victory in an election for virtually every American office, including the presidency, goes to the candidate with the most votes. This means that candidates are often elected with less than 50 percent of the votes and candidates and parties that finish second or lower get nothing. This single-member, plurality, district system differs from electoral systems based on proportional representation, in which parties earn the number of places in the legislature that is proportional to their share of the overall vote. A third party can reasonably aspire to a share of political power in a system of proportional representation, but not in the United States.

American voters often develop an allegiance to one or the other of the two major parties—they come to identify with the Republicans or the Democrats—which makes it emotionally trying for them to cast a ballot for any other party. New York Mets fans don't become New York Yankees fans just because the Mets have one or two bad seasons. The same is true in politics. Party loyalty reinforces the Republican and Democratic duopoly, as does the fact that they have dominated the American political system for so long. Also, the nation's political history has been, on the whole, and with the notable exception of the Civil War, a successful one, so Americans have acquired a respect for the idea of a two-party system. Although political parties are not mentioned in the Constitution, the belief that there should be two and only two of them has achieved quasi-constitutional status—that is, an arrangement with which it is unwise to tamper—in the eyes of many voters.

The failure of challengers to the Democrats and Republicans has become self-fulfilling: Because third parties do not win elections, voters expect them not to win and thus do not vote for them so as not to waste their votes. This calculation, a major reason for the weakness of third parties (and thus the strength of the Republicans and Democrats), can, however, be seriously mistaken. A vote for a third-party presidential candidate can be an effective way to change the direction of American national policy—and that is the strategy we are advocating.

A third party succeeds not by winning elections but by affecting the agenda of the party that does win. A third party—or what became far more common in the twentieth century, an independent candidate leading a party that does not outlast the candidacy—can affect the agenda of the two major parties by drawing an appreciable number of votes. By doing so, it demonstrates the existence of a bloc of voters uncommitted to either major party. Since the core business of both Democrats and Republicans is the winning of elections, each has a fundamental interest in attracting as many voters as possible. That means that one or the other will move to co-opt the supporters of any independent candidate by embracing whatever the candidate stood for that earned their support—provided that support is substantial. Historically, the two major parties have been like large retail stores that seek as many customers as possible by offering a wide variety of items—in the case of the parties a wide variety of policies. Like such stores, Republicans and Democrats have been willing and, within limits, able to add to their offerings whatever their customers—that is, voters—have wanted. Once the large stores begin to carry the products customers want, the smaller establishments close their doors.

So it is with third parties. The historian Richard Hofstadter compared third parties to bees: After they sting, they die. While third parties and the proprietors of the small businesses suffer from this process, voters and customers do not. To the contrary, they get what they want.

We would like to see the emergence of a very big bee that can sting both parties in a way they can neither ignore nor shrug off. When an independent presidential candidate makes a strong showing, the dynamics of the two-party system impel the major parties to capture his or her voters, if at all possible. In this way those voters can exert greater influence over the policies of the victorious candidate than do the voters who actually supported the candidate in the election. This has happened three times in the twentieth century.

In 1968, the former Alabama governor George Wallace won five Deep South states and captured just over 13.5 percent of the popular vote, mainly but not exclusively from Southern states, where he won 34.3 percent, in a presidential election in which the Republican Richard Nixon narrowly defeated the Democrat Hubert Humphrey, gaining 43.4 percent of all ballots to Humphrey's 42.7 percent. Wallace ran as an opponent of the civil rights laws passed between 1963 and 1965. During those years the United States experienced a revolution in race relations. Wallace offered himself to the public as a counterrevolutionary.

He also placed on the national agenda other issues that, although having racial overtones, were not exclusively racial in character and persisted as national concerns for the next two decades. One was support for "law and order," a reaction to the civil disturbances in a number of American cities, such as Los Angeles and Detroit, between 1965 and 1968. Another was populist hostility to the federal government and what he and others came to see as America's liberal establishment. Wallace advertised his scorn for such people, whom he called "pointy-headed intellectuals who can't park a bicycle straight." In different ways, both Jimmy Carter and Ronald Reagan took up his anti-Washington theme, and it helped both of them get elected president, in 1976 and 1980, respectively.

The Wallace campaign also had a more immediate impact—on public policy rather than on the style of presidential campaigning. During and after the campaign, Nixon made a concerted effort to win the favor of Wallace voters, an effort that became known as his "Southern strategy." He appointed an official, lodged in the White House, with special responsibility for protecting that region's interests. He made a point of his opposition to the compulsory busing of schoolchildren to achieve racial balance within school districts, which federal courts had ordered in a number of states, not all of them in the South. The Nixon administration might not have pursued all the policies that many Wallace voters wanted—it did not seriously attempt to repeal the major civil rights laws—but those voters could see that the administration for which they had not voted had adopted at least some of the policies, and attitudes, of the candidate whom they had supported.

Almost a quarter century later another independent candidate, H. Ross Perot, who had made a fortune in the data-processing business, did even better in a presidential election. In 1992, he won 18.9 percent of the popular vote in a three-way contest with the Republican incumbent, George H. W. Bush, who polled 37.5 percent, and the Democratic challenger, Governor Bill Clinton of Arkansas, who won with 43 percent.

Perot's principal campaign issue was the danger posed by the federal budget deficits the country was running, which were, in fact, more modest than today's. Like Nixon, once in office Clinton moved to try to capture Perot voters by addressing the issue that had motivated them to support an independent candidate. His first major policy proposal was a program designed to reduce the deficit by $500 billion over five years through tax increases and spending cuts. By the end of his second term as president, the United States had a budget surplus for the first time in several decades. The Democratic senator Russ Feingold of Wisconsin, who was elected to the Senate for the first time in 1992, told us that for the deficit reduction that followed "the impetus came from Perot." A vote for Perot, far from being wasted, helped to achieve what his voters most wanted.

The influential twentieth-century independent presidential candidacy that is perhaps most relevant to the conditions of the second decade of the twenty-first century is the one most distant in time: Theodore Roosevelt's 1912 effort to regain the presidency. Roosevelt had been president from 1901 to 1909 as a Republican. In 1912 he ran as a Progressive against his handpicked Republican successor in the White House, William Howard Taft, and the Democratic governor of New Jersey, Woodrow Wilson, who was elected. Roosevelt won 27.4 percent of the popular vote; he carried six states and so earned eighty-eight electoral votes. Wilson won 41.8 percent, while Taft, the incumbent, polled a mere 23.2 percent.

The Progressives were an established party when Roosevelt accepted their nomination, but so closely identified did the campaign become with the personality of the candidate that, after he proclaimed himself as "healthy as a bull moose," his third party became known as the Bull Moose Party. Personal motives undoubtedly contributed to Roosevelt's decision to run in that year. His ego was large enough that it was said of him that he wanted to be "the bride at every wedding, the baby at every christening and the corpse at every funeral." But he also undertook his independent candidacy to promote measures that he regarded as vital for America's future. He believed that Taft had done too little to carry forward the reform agenda that he had devised as president to deal with the challenges to the country of the new world that the Industrial Revolution had created. The growth of factories and cities, Roosevelt was convinced, required adjustments as sweeping as those America must now make to cope with the challenges of globalization and the IT revolution.

In 1912, the Bull Moose platform included proposals for such measures as the direct election of senators, direct primaries to choose candidates, women's suffrage, the regulation of business, a minimum wage, an eight-hour workday and a six-day workweek, unemployment insurance, and old-age pensions. All of these were ultimately enacted. During the campaign, Wilson tried to co-opt Roosevelt voters by declaring that, like the former president, he too opposed the large business monopolies known as trusts.

The first two years of the Wilson presidency resembled Roosevelt's vision of the office. Unlike Taft but like Roosevelt, Wilson made the executive branch an active agent of reform. Unlike William Jennings Bryan, the 1908 Democratic presidential candidate, but again like Roosevelt, Wilson acted as a progressive reformer, not an agrarian populist. He steered through Congress progressive legislation of the kind Roosevelt had championed, such as the establishment of the Federal Trade Commission and child labor laws. Roosevelt had a profound impact on the public policy of the United States when serving as its president, but he also changed the course of American history through his subsequent role as an unsuccessful third-party presidential candidate.

If the goal of the Bull Moose campaign of 1912, the Wallace campaign of 1968, and the Perot campaign of 1992 was to make the candidate the president of the United States, each of them failed. Insofar as the voters who supported these independent candidacies wanted to send a message to one or both of the major parties to pay more attention to particular issues, however, the three campaigns can be judged successful.

Could an independent campaign achieve similar success in the years to come? Specifically, could our kind of independent candidate, one who advocates a comprehensive revitalization of the traditional American formula for economic growth and serious steps to reduce the federal budget deficit, reform the tax code, and wean the country from fossil fuels, attract enough support to persuade Republicans or Democrats, or both, to make these policies their own? There are good reasons to believe that the time is ripe for this.

Recall that the extreme polarization of American politics has made the two major parties less representative of the country as a whole than ever before. Neither party expresses the preferences of a large slice of the electorate. The number of voters who register as independents has grown steadily over the decades and is now roughly the same size as the number who identify themselves with either of the two major parties. In fact, a Pew poll taken in October 2010 found that more voters identified themselves as independents (37 percent) than as Democrats (31 percent) or Republicans (29 percent). In this sense the United States already has a three-party system, but the third party—the radical center—has no formal platform or political leaders representing it.

Polls consistently show a high level of discontent with the direction of the country. A Pew survey at the end of 2010, to give just one of many examples that could be cited, found a staggering 72 percent of respondents dissatisfied with national conditions. Americans also hold the two major parties in low esteem. A *Washington Post*–ABC News poll taken in September 2010 reported that only 34 percent of the respondents said that Democratic candidates deserved reelection that year, and only 31 percent said that Republicans did—this in a year when Republicans went on to win a sweeping victory in midterm elections. A June 2010 poll conducted by Ipsos Public Affairs, an independent movement to create a more open presidential election, found that 71 percent of respondents said they would like to see more than just the Democratic and Republican Parties represented on the presidential ballot.

Yet another sign of the public dissatisfaction with politics and government on which an independent candidate could capitalize is the pattern of voting in the last three national elections. Each has been what political scientists call a "wave" election, with the electorate swinging unusually sharply in one direction or the other. In 2006, the Democrats won thirty new seats in the House of Representatives and six in the Senate, gaining control of both bodies. In 2008, they won the presidency, twenty-four additional seats in the House, and eight in the Senate. In 2010, the electorate shifted even more sharply in the other direction, with the Republicans gaining control of the House by picking up sixty-three seats and winning six in the Senate as well. This is the behavior of an electorate—especially its independent voters, who tilted sharply to the Democrats in 2008 and just as sharply to the Republicans in 2010—searching for an approach to governance that, as of the 2010 election, it had not found.

The electoral success of the Tea Party movement in 2010 also suggests that the moment for another influential independent presidential candidacy may have arrived. Arising from the nation's grass roots and outside the formal structures of the two major parties, its members organized themselves to express their opposition to the size of government in general and the size of the federal deficit in particular. Underlying their discontent, interviews with its members suggest, was a broad anxiety about the future of the country. In view of the large and so far unmet challenges America faces, such anxiety is warranted—although to meet the challenges will require not only the fiscal prudence that Tea Partyers demand but also activist government in selected areas—education, infrastructure, research and development—of the kind their ranks do not view favorably. The Tea Party might more aptly be called the Tea Kettle Party, as Tom has quipped, because its main effect has been to let off steam. It has not offered a coherent program—an engine—to harness that steam to move the country in the directions in which it needs to go.

In the 2010 election, Tea Party adherents supported the Republican Party, but as much because this was the obvious way to register dissatisfaction with the course of public policy—since the Democrats controlled both the White House and Congress—as because they had confidence that the Republicans could or would fix the things they regarded as broken. Many of those who counted themselves members of or sympathizers with the movement called themselves political independents. Many of those who identified with the Republicans might well be willing at least to entertain seriously supporting an independent presidential candidate. On balance, therefore, the rise of the Tea Party movement counts as further evidence that the time is once again ripe for an independent candidacy that can administer a shock to the American political system and compel serious attention to the challenges the country confronts.

Since a national presidential campaign is expensive and an independent candidate cannot draw on the money normally available to major-party candidates, access to resources matters as well. Two wealthy supporters of Roosevelt financed much of his 1912 campaign. Perot had enough wealth of his own to fund his campaign himself. He spent an estimated $75 million on it.

But at the same time, modern information technology provides tools that were not available to Perot, let alone Wallace or Roosevelt, for over-coming some of the barriers to a successful independent presidential candidacy—specifically the raising of money and the dissemination of the candidate's message. The presidential campaigns of former Vermont governor Howard Dean in 2004 and of Texas representative Ron Paul and especially Illinois senator Barack Obama in 2008, coming from dif-ferent parts of the political spectrum, demonstrated that it is possible to raise impressive sums of campaign money in small individual contrib-utions from many people through the Internet. The Internet and the social media such as Facebook and Twitter also provide channels for making known a candidate's program that can serve as alternatives to established news organizations and that cost far less to use than buying television time for campaign commercials. By employing these chan-nels a candidate can both raise money and save money.

When one sees how the Internet has leveled hierarchies and broken up monopolies everywhere, it is hard to believe that it will not have a substantial impact on the last big duopoly in America—the two-party system. That system has changed remarkably little since the nineteenth century, but we do not believe that, in the hyper-connected world, it can continue to resist change. The year 2012 might well be the moment when the Internet does to the two-party system what Amazon.com did for books and iTunes did for music—dramatically broaden both access and choices.

Imagine

It is impossible to know in advance how much support such a third party representing the radical center with a compelling candidacy could at-tract. It is entirely possible that polling on the subject before such a party and candidate emerge will understate its potential. Most Americans, after all, pay little attention to politics most of the time. The peak of na-tional attention comes during our quadrennial presidential elections. A presidential election therefore offers an opportunity that is not other-wise available to educate and persuade voters. We believe the country is more open than ever to considering a serious independent candidate who can tap into the broad anxiety among Americans about their country's future by explaining the challenges it faces and proposing a hybrid politics to meet those challenges. We would have no problem if a prominent Democrat or Republican should decide to bolt his or her party and become that candidate. Whoever it might be, if he or she is a serious person, we believe that such a candidate could do as well as Ross Perot did in 1992 and even conceivably as well as Theodore Roosevelt did in 1912. The only way to find out how such a candidacy would fare is to launch one.

Matt Miller, the McKinsey consultant who writes for *The Washington Post*, penned a column (November 11, 2010) in which he tried to imagine a Sunday talk show that included a serious third-party candidate:

> Last Sunday, for example, you could see Christiane Amanpour chafing, with reason, at the fiscal nonsense emanating from [Republicans] Rand Paul and Mike Pence. This isn't meant as a partisan remark—on another week the host would justly bristle at Democratic bunk . . .
>
> How are the parties able to get away with this?
>
> Because there's a missing chair.
>
> Rerun that Sunday show tape, but now suppose there's a third "official" voice. "Mark Johnson from The Third Party," the host says, "what do you make of it?"
>
> "Actually, Republicans and Democrats aren't giving you an honest picture," Johnson says. "The truth is that once the economy's back on track, taxes are going to rise in the years ahead no matter which party is in power, because we're retiring the baby boomers. That means we'll double the number of people on Social Security and Medicare. We've already got trillions in unfunded promises in these programs. Even if we trim their growth, and cut other spending, which we need to do, the math doesn't work at current levels of taxation. And we can't borrow the whole boomers' retirement from China. So the idea that we can keep overall taxes where they are now, let alone cut them, is a Republican hoax.
>
> "But Democrats are kidding you when they make it sound like we can solve the problem by taxing a few people at the top. The truth is that to pay for the boomers' retirement, taxes will have to go up some on everyone. But there's also good news—

if we're smart about it, and change the way we tax ourselves, we can pay for the boomers and still keep the economy humming. That's the conversation we need to have. Here's the kind of tax reform it would take . . ."

"If you find this missing voice appealing—and can imagine it weighing in across the hundred issues where both parties are in cahoots today to deny reality," Miller concluded, "then you understand why we need a third political party."

Picking up on Miller's version of a talk show, imagine a televised presidential debate in which an independent candidate seriously committed to deficit reduction took part along with the Democratic and Republican candidates—just as Ross Perot shared the stage with George H. W. Bush and Bill Clinton in the 1992 debates. The third candidate would challenge the two parties' typical, mealymouthed evasions on the most urgent issue of the day—the budget—by beginning this way:

"What are you two talking about? It is absurd to talk about budget numbers without starting the conversation with far more important questions: What world are we living in? What are the new requirements of this world for educating our people and building our country? It is easy to spend without a strategy for the future, but it is lethal to cut without such a strategy. Let me tell you how I see the world we are living in today—a world, by the way, that we invented—and then connect the picture I have drawn with the spending I would cut, the taxes I would raise, and the new investments I would insist on making."

The two major-party candidates would either have to offer comparably serious descriptions of the world and link them to their budget plans or risk appearing cowardly, ignorant, deluded, or duplicitous—or all four—in the eyes of the tens of millions of voters who were watching.

Beyond taking part in the debates and the campaign, ideally an independent presidential candidate would change the national conversation altogether—in a way that could move the nation toward the measures necessary to secure the American dream and sustain American power in the world. To do so, though, he or she would have to do on the stump what we suggested for that TV debate. At every stop, such a candidate would begin by raising and answering, candidly and in detail, that most important of all questions for public policy: What world are we living in?

Presidential candidates, like presidents, have a bully pulpit. To move America in the right direction, a candidate would have to use it to educate the American people about the four major challenges they confront—globalization, the IT revolution, deficits and debt, and energy and the environment—and to outline the responses necessary to secure their future in this hyper-connected world. In particular—to paraphrase the political analyst William Galston, a senior fellow at the Brookings Institution—a third-party candidate would have to tell the public not only why the Democratic and Republican approaches to our major challenges are "unacceptable," but also why the status quo in each case is "unsustainable"—and therefore why a credible third approach is both vital and unavoidable. It is shocking how little teaching of that kind America's elected leaders have done over the last decade.

As in the TV debate, the independent presidential candidate who can give the political system a constructive shock would then offer at each campaign stop a strategy to meet these challenges: raising more revenue through increasing taxes, including energy taxes; reducing expenditures by cutting government programs, including popular, beneficial programs such as Social Security, Medicare, and defense; and investing more money in education, infrastructure, and research and development in order to upgrade the nation's traditional formula for economic success. The candidate would have to make it clear that the three must go together—cutting spending, raising revenue, and investing in the formula. All are necessary. None can be left out. A governing program including only one or two of the three will not be fair, politically viable, or effective in dealing with America's challenges or opportunities. The combination of taxing, cutting, and investing is mandatory in the short term to achieve what must be America's primary policy goal in the long term—the economic growth to fulfill every American's individual and national aspirations. The candidate America needs would demonstrate his or her seriousness about doing what the country needs by spelling out *with specificity* which taxes would rise, which programs would shrink, and where investments would be made and why they would be transformative for education, infrastructure, and investing—rather than falling back, as presidential candidates tend to do, on generalities and platitudes.

Finally, an effective third-party candidate would bring something else to the campaign—inspiration. Leadership involves more than honestly describing hard choices and specific policies. Leadership also involves the ability to get people up out of their seats. Americans do not want to be just "okay." They want to be great. They want ours to be and remain a great country. A successful third-party candidate would be one who persuaded them that we have all the natural advantages to be great in the coming decades—by reclaiming our position as the world's best launching pad, the place to which the most energetic and creative people from around the world want to come to start things, share things, build things, design things, and invent things. That is the foundation for American greatness. We have the raw materials to build that foundation. What is needed is the right leadership and collective action.

We have no doubt that Americans will sacrifice when summoned to do so by a leader with a credible plan that apportions the burdens equitably and that has as its goal not simply balancing the budget but sustaining American greatness.

An independent presidential candidate who did all these things—describing, more vividly and accurately than the two major parties have yet done, the world in which its citizens are living and are destined to live in this century; prescribing the policies that will make it possible for Americans to thrive in that world and for America to exercise global influence in this century, as they did in the last one; and galvanizing the country to adopt these policies—could provide the shock therapy we need.

It may be a long shot, but it's the best shot we have. Sticking with the status quo, by contrast, is a sure thing—a sure pathway to decline.

We fully understand the math working against any third party. We know that such a candidate is very unlikely to win. But we also know that the more honest, plausible, and inspiring he or she is, the better the Democratic and Republican candidates will have to be. And, at a minimum, if our kind of third-party candidate did well, he or she would do to the established candidates what Theodore Roosevelt, George Wallace, and Ross Perot did in 1912, 1968, and 1992—force them to adopt and implement parts of the third-party agenda. In that case, the independent candidate would have given the American political system what it so badly needs—a shock compelling serious attention to the issues on which the country's future depends.

Such a candidate would have the same impact as a philanthropist, improving the lives of other people after he or she is gone. Philanthropists' bequests do change the world for the better, and an independent presidential candidacy can change America—and therefore the world—for the better as well.

Of such a candidacy two things may be said with some confidence: First, it would not win the presidency. Second, over the long term it would probably have a greater impact on the course of American history than the person who did.

SIXTEEN

Rediscovering America

But does it have a happy ending?"

That is the question our friends asked us whenever we told them the title of the book we were writing. Our answer was always the same: We can write a happy ending, but it is up to the country—to all of us—to determine whether it is fiction or nonfiction.

One thing we know for sure: The path to a happy ending begins with the awareness that something is wrong, that changes are necessary, and that we the people have to be the agents of those changes. At some level Americans do understand this. The anxiety about China's rise is one sign of a justified and, if it can be channeled properly, ultimately healthy concern about the state of the nation. Here is another: In 2009 and 2010 President Obama's Republican critics accused him of denying America's history and status as an "exceptional" country. The charge stemmed from an overseas news conference in which, asked whether he believed in the concept, he replied, "I believe in American exceptionalism, just as I suspect the Brits believe in British exceptionalism and the Greeks believe in Greek exceptionalism." (He then went on to list some of the features that, in his view, make America exceptional.)

The idea of exceptionalism, as used by scholars, refers to the ways that America has differed historically from the countries of Europe: the fact that it was founded on a set of ideas; that it lacked a hierarchical social order with a hereditary aristocracy at the top; that the Europeans who settled North America did so in a huge, sparsely populated territory; and that it attracted immigrants from all over the world. In political discourse the term has come to have a celebratory as well as an analytical meaning. It refers to what makes America special: its wealth, its power, the economic opportunity it has provided for its citizens, and the example of liberty and prosperity that it has set for the rest of the world.

The fuss over exceptionalism was in one sense a normal episode in American politics, an effort by one party to portray the other as disconnected from basic American values and traditions, of the kind that began with the fierce political battles between Alexander Hamilton's Federalists and Thomas Jefferson's Democratic-Republicans. But it also tapped into the national undercurrent of unease about the country and its future, the concern that the American dream is slipping beyond the reach of the next generation. Alas, such fears are all too justified.

The debate about exceptionalism reminds us of a story attributed to Abraham Lincoln. He asked, "If you call a horse's tail a leg, how many legs does a horse have?" And he responded to his own question in this way: "The answer is four, because calling a horse's tail a leg doesn't make it one."

Similarly, declaring that America is exceptional—that is, special—doesn't make it so. Exceptional, meaning exceptionally wealthy, powerful, and dynamic, is not a distinction that is bestowed and then lasts forever, like an honorary degree from a university. It has to be earned continually, like a baseball player's batting average. Too often in recent years, though, we have treated "American exceptionalism" as just another entitlement—just another thing we get to enjoy without paying for. Those days are over. America's exceptionalism is now in play. It is not an entitlement. It is not a defined benefit. To retain the exceptional status that Americans rightly value but wrongly assume is automatically ours, the country must respond effectively to its four great twenty-first-century challenges—the ones posed by globalization, the IT revolution, our large and growing deficits, and our pattern of energy consumption. Unfortunately, not enough Americans seem to understand the first two and too many want to deny the necessity of addressing the second two. The first two we need to look at so much more closely, and the other two we have to stop looking away from so insistently.

The stakes are exceptionally high. For Americans, whether the United States masters these challenges will determine their country's future rate of economic growth, on which will depend the continuation of the best features of their society: opportunity, mobility, and social harmony. These are now at risk, as a single, glaring, ominous statistic makes clear: In the first decade of the twenty-first century, the majority of American households made no economic gains at all.

For the rest of the world, the stakes are just as high, perhaps even higher. Consider a list of some of the major events in world affairs at the end of 2010 and the beginning of 2011. In November 2010, a website called WikiLeaks began releasing more than 250,000 classified diplomatic cables of the American government, some of them embarrassing to it and to the governments of other countries, cables that had apparently been supplied by a single low-ranking member of the American armed forces who had obtained access to them.

In December 2010, China went to extraordinary lengths to disrupt the Nobel Peace Prize ceremony for one of its citizens, Liu Xiaobo, a democracy advocate serving an eleven-year prison sentence for "inciting subversion of state power." Under pressure from Beijing, eighteen countries boycotted the event. In the first months of 2011, pro-freedom uprisings erupted around the Arab and Muslim world—in Tunisia, Egypt, Bahrain, Libya, Yemen, and Syria. In March 2011, the largest earthquake in the recorded history of Japan set off a tsunami that killed more than 22,000 people and devastated entire towns in the northeast part of the country. The tremor and the floods that followed led to dangerous breakdowns in nuclear reactors in the path of the tsunami.

There is an acronym that business consultants use to describe moments like these: VUCA, meaning "volatility, unpredictability, complexity, and ambiguity." We are going through a period of history with a very high VUCA rating. The world is turbulent because it has multiple sources of turbulence: bullying governments, such as China's; repressed and angry societies, such as those in the Arab world; the forces of nature, which are, as ever, powerful and unpredictable, as the devastation in Japan reminded us; and lone individuals, such as the source of the WikiLeaks cables, empowered—indeed super-empowered—by two of the defining trends of our era: globalization and the IT revolution.

In this unstable world, the United States stands out as both a beacon and a supplier of stability. Americans sometimes underestimate the importance, and the value, of American power for other countries. (It doesn't help that other countries are not routinely lavish, or even public, in their appreciation for what the United States does in the world, even when they do appreciate it.)

Americans also sometimes misunderstand their country's power. Those on the left often do not fully understand its constructive uses, concentrating instead on the occasional abuses that always attend the exercise of power. Those on the right often do not fully understand its sources—that American power is not simply a matter of will but of means, and those means need to be constantly renewed and refreshed, which depends on our successfully meeting the country's major domestic challenges. The world we grew up in was a world in which America had a lot of leverage. Indeed, it was a world shaped a certain way because we had the leverage to shape it that way. That is precisely what we are losing. We cannot make ourselves safer abroad unless we change our behavior at home. But our politics rarely connects those two dots anymore. If we want to shape the world, we have to be serious about American strength, and if we want to be serious about American strength, we need to be serious about the sources of American strength—our formula for greatness.

On this matter, we mince no words: A world shaped by a strong America—strong enough to provide political, economic, and moral leadership—will never be a perfect world, but it will be a better world than any alternative we can envision.

In fact, the United States provides to the world many of the services that governments furnish to the societies they govern. With a weakened America, one that has failed to rise to the challenges it confronts and has therefore become less wealthy and less confident, the world will likely enjoy less governance, which will make it more disorderly and less prosperous. In that case, everyone, not just Americans, will suffer.

Will the United States meet its major challenges and thus sustain the American dream for future generations and preserve the country's large and constructive global role? Again, we are ultimately optimistic in our response to this question.

For one thing, whatever the pathologies of the American political system, American society retains the characteristics that made the United States exceptional among the countries of the world; the country remains full of people who have not gotten the word. In general, if you were to design a country ideally suited to flourish in the world we are living in, it would look more like the United States than any other. In a world in which individual creativity is becoming ever more important, America supports individual achievement and celebrates the quirky. In a world in which technological change and creative destruction take place at warp speed, requiring maximal economic flexibility, the American economy is as flexible as any on the planet. In a world in which transparent, reliable institutions, and especially the rule of law, are more important than ever for risk-taking and innovation, the United States has an outstanding legal environment. In an age in which even the cleverest inventors and entrepreneurs have to try and fail, sometimes repeatedly, before finding the business equivalent of a mother lode, the American business culture understands that failure is often the necessary condition for success.

The other reason for our optimism about America's future is that over the course of its history the United States has rarely failed to meet major challenges. It is in fact our failure to meet major challenges that is unusual—or, one might say, "exceptional." When tested, from the days of the revolution in the eighteenth century to the drawn-out Cold War struggle in the twentieth, America and Americans have found ways to excel. The country's past supplies fertile grounds for optimism about its future. That is one reason that we have given a book about that future a backward-looking title. A country that steps up to the challenges that it faces and masters them is the country that used to be us.

In fact, the key to a successful future is to draw on features of American history that made the country successful in the past: understanding, as we have before, the world in which we are living; renovating our traditional public-private formula to spur economic growth; and removing, perhaps through a method that has worked in the past, the political obstacles that stand in the way of the collective efforts the country needs.

Alexis de Tocqueville originated the idea of American exceptionalism in *Democracy in America*. What he found exceptional was precisely Americans' concentration on the here and now, on their actual circumstances, rather than on abstract or theoretical considerations. "A thousand special causes," he wrote, "have singularly concurred to fix the mind of the American upon purely practical objects. His passions, his wants, his education, and everything about him seem to unite in drawing the native of the United States earthward."

Over the last two decades, this changed. As a country, and as a political system, we lost our characteristic focus on the world we are living in. We misinterpreted the end of the Cold War, failing to recognize that it was not only a great global victory but also the beginning of a great global transformation, one that made the world in some ways more demanding for Americans than it had been during the decades of conflict with communism. We missed the very turn that we, more than any other nation, helped to bring about.

It is hard not to see a parallel between America and IBM, one of the country's iconic companies, which is celebrating its centennial in 2011. America's history has been one of continual reinvention—and so has IBM's. It started out making clocks, scales, cheese slicers, and the like. After generations leading the market in punch-card tabulators, in the early 1960s its boss bet the company on the mainframe computer, and wound up dominating that business. Then, twenty years later, IBM essentially invented the personal computer.

Nevertheless, despite this history of embracing the future and shucking the past, IBM didn't understand the implications of its own creation. It invested too much for too long in the mainframe. Its financial and management models were based on things remaining as they had been, not as they were becoming. It treated the PC as a niche product. And those mistakes nearly brought down the whole company.

How did IBM lose sight of the world it invented? Listen carefully to the answer of Samuel Palmisano, IBM's current chairman and CEO, when we asked him that question: "You spend more time arguing amongst yourselves over a shrinking pie than looking to the future," said Palmisano, and so "you miss the big turn" that you have entered, even a turn that your own company invented. "We missed the PC. It isn't like we didn't have the technology," he explained. "We invented the PC, but we missed what it really was. At the time, everybody [at IBM] thought it was just kind of a neat little personal productivity tool. But instead it became a new platform. And we missed it."

When you start thinking of other departments and colleagues in your own company as the opposition—instead of focusing on the other companies against which you must compete—you have lost touch with the world in which you are living. When you come to see your exceptionalism as permanent, you set yourself up to wind up less than exceptional. This can be lethal for a company—and a country. America's political parties today strayed, said Palmisano, "because they have focused on themselves" more than on the priorities of the country as a whole.

Under the leadership first of Louis Gerstner and then of Palmisano, IBM got back on track by relentlessly scrutinizing itself and the world in which it was operating. By doing so, it mastered the next big change in technology, which was networking—the hyper-connecting of the world in which the principal platform is no longer the PC but rather billions of interconnected smartphones, sensors, computers, and servers. IBM bet that in such a world the most lucrative business would involve sifting and analyzing all the data being generated and using all that information to advise customers on how to get the most out of their individual businesses. IBM found a new core competency and scaled it. In the process, it reconnected with its history of continual reinvention.

The same can be true of America. It is obvious now what our core competency is. We have greater potential than any other country to thrive in the future by becoming the world's most attractive launching pad—the place where everyone wants to come to work, invent, collaborate, or start something new in order to get the most out of the new hyper-connected world.

America, of course, not only underappreciated the world it invented, it also overinterpreted the events of September 11, 2001. It devoted more attention, political capital, and resources than were warranted to the threat of terrorism, serious though it was and is. While pursuing the worthy but not vital goals of nation-building in Afghanistan and Iraq, we recklessly pumped up our annual deficits and cumulative national debt to new and dangerous heights, and pumped out more and more greenhouse gases, heedless of the potentially devastating consequences.

The first task for Americans, with the Terrible Twos behind us, is to focus on the nature of the world in which we are living and the most important challenges it presents to us. Unless we do this, we will adapt no better to the new era that began with the end of the Cold War than the dinosaurs did in adapting to the world that sudden changes in the environment created for them.

As we have argued, the key to doing so is updating—renovating— America's traditional, and historically successful, formula for enlisting the government in selected ways to help foster a dynamic private sector. Of the five parts of that formula—education, infrastructure, immigration, research and development, and regulation—we have devoted the most attention in the preceding pages to education. In this century, education is the foundation of economic strength and American economic strength is the foundation of the country's vital, indispensable role in the world. The Duke of Wellington, the conqueror of Napoleon, once asserted that the Battle of Waterloo—the decisive engagement with the French leader, fought in 1815—was won "on the playing fields of Eton," an exclusive British private school in which the nation's elite was trained. In the same spirit, one could argue that the stability and prosperity of the twenty-first-century international order will be maintained—or lost—in the classrooms of America's public schools.

The other four parts of our formula are in no less need of upgrading if America is to continue to thrive. While infrastructure has underpinned economic activity since the time of the Roman Empire and its impressive roads and aqueducts, research and development has become vital only in modern times, and its value is growing. Economic growth in the United States will increasingly come from innovation, and innovation is more and more the product of both incremental advances and decisive breakthroughs in science and technology, which funding for research and development supports.

America also needs to adjust its policies on immigration to the needs of the world we are living in. Just as important as resolving the status of the estimated twelve million people who have entered the country illegally is making it easier for talented foreigners to come to, and remain in, the United States. Foreign-born engineers, scientists, and entrepreneurs have made huge contributions to the American economy over the last quarter century and can make even larger contributions in the decades to come—if we let them. Finally, the regulations that govern American business need modernization. The trick in imposing them is to strike the appropriate balance between, on the one hand, rules that are too numerous and constricting, which discourage risk-taking, and, on the other, regulations insufficiently strict to prevent damaging "externalities" and excesses.

If we want to preserve the American dream for future generations, we must understand that the guidance we need cannot be found by simply rereading the Constitution, or proclaiming our exceptionalism at higher and higher decibel levels. The secret of our success has always been combining an understanding of the world in which we were living with the updating of the American formula in order to adapt to the circumstances of the time, even when this required overcoming political differences and doing big, hard things together.

Colonel Mark Mykleby spent twenty-four years in the Marine Corps as an aviator and a special strategic assistant to the chairman of the Joint Chiefs of Staff. In his last year at the Pentagon, Mykleby co-authored with Captain Wayne Porter, of the U.S. Navy, "A National Strategic Narrative," a paper about how to fix America, with an emphasis on sustainable values, which they published under the pseudonym "Mr. Y," a historical tip of the hat to the alias of "X" used by George Kennan in his *Foreign Affairs* article. Just before retiring in 2011, Mykleby, a friend of Tom's, shared this thought with us: "At no time in our history have our national challenges been as complex and long-term as those we face today. But the most salient trait of our time is not the threats posed by terrorists, an anemic economy, or climate change. It's our inability to respond coherently and effectively to obvious problems before they become crises . . . If we can't even have an 'adult' conversation, how will we fulfill the promise of and our obligation to the Preamble of our Constitution—to 'secure the Blessings of Liberty to ourselves and our Posterity'?"

How indeed?

Maybe the best way for us to answer that vital question is by ending this book where we began: We don't need to imitate China. And China's fate, whatever it is, will not determine ours. What we need is not novel or foreign. What we need instead is to understand our own history. We need to adapt the formula, the priorities, and the practices that are embedded in that history and in our culture. We need to reconnect with the values and ideals that made the American dream so compelling for so many generations of Americans, as well as for so many millions of people across the globe.

That is all part of our past. That used to be us. And because that used to be us, it can be again. That is why, today, the history books we need to read are our own and the country we need to rediscover is America.

ACKNOWLEDGMENTS

INDEX

Acknowledgments

We have benefited enormously from the many people who took time to share their thoughts with us about America's future. Byron Auguste, Michael Barber, Curtis Carlson, Susan Engel, Hal Harvey, Craig Mundie, Joe Romm, and last but certainly not least, Dov Seidman, all deserve our special thanks for not only contributing their ideas but also reading portions of the manuscript for us.

In addition, we want to thank, for sharing their time and insights, Peter Ackerman, Léo Apotheker, Don Baer, Evan Bayh, Robert Bennett, Mike Biddle, Joel Cawley, Alan Cohen, Martin Dempsey, Larry Diamond, John Doerr, Arne Duncan, Russ Feingold, Joel Finkelstein, Jeff Garten, Bill Gates, Lindsey Graham, Jennifer Granholm, Jeffrey Immelt, Bob Inglis, Michael Johnston, PV Kannan, Andy Karsner, David Kennedy, Wendy Kopp, Alan Kotz, Ellen Kullman, Ray Lane, Jeffrey Lesk, Michael Maniates, Jack Markell, Stan McChrystal, Ernie Moniz, Mike Murphy, Paul Otellini, Sam Palmisano, Raghuram Rajan, Kasim Reed, Ken Rogoff, Diane Rosenberg, David Rothkopf, Michael Sandel, Dan Simpkins, Alan Simpson, Brad Smith, K. R. Sridhar, Robert Stevenson, Joe Stiglitz, David Stockman, Subra Suresh, Jerry Tarde, Marc Tucker, Chuck Vest, James R. Vivian, Tony Wagner, David Walker, and Randi Weingarten.

Tom also wants to thank his bosses, Arthur Sulzberger Jr., the chairman of the Board of the New York Times Company, and Andy Rosenthal, the editorial page editor, for making possible the leave he needed to work on this book. That leave coincided with the "Arab Spring," and, thanks to Arthur and Andy, Tom was able to move back and forth from book-writing to column-writing as events dictated.

Our literary agent, Esther Newberg, as always, contributed her ideas as well as her business prowess and we benefited from both.

Our assistants, Gwenn Gorman of *The New York Times* and Kelley J. Kornell of The Johns Hopkins University School of Advanced International Studies, were invaluable in keeping the trains running on time as we each maintained our day jobs while writing this book.

This is Tom's sixth book with Farrar, Straus and Giroux and Michael's first, and it would not have been possible without the vision of FSG's best-in-the-business president and publisher, Jonathan Galassi, and his team: Jeff Seroy, Sarita Varma, Debra Helfand, Susan Goldfarb, Jonathan Lippincott, and Jill Priluck.

A special mention, though, goes to this book's FSG editor, Paul Elie. His devotion to our project and contribution to every page is deeply appreciated by us both. He has been a real partner. For any would-be author at FSG, just three words of advice: "Ask for Paul."

Finally, as we note in the dedication, this book benefited enormously from two other people closer to home: Tom's wife, Ann Friedman, who, besides teaching school, edited the manuscript, and Michael's wife, Anne Mandelbaum, who not only gave us her wise counsel and support, but also asked during one of our phone conversations the most important question of all: "Why don't you two write a book about all this?"

Index

A NOTE ABOUT THE AUTHORS

Thomas L. Friedman is a three-time recipient of the Pulitzer Prize for his work with *The New York Times* and is the author of five bestselling books, including *The World Is Flat* (2005). Michael Mandelbaum, the Christian A. Herter Professor and Director of American Foreign Policy at The Johns Hopkins University School of Advanced International Studies, is the author or co-author of twelve books, including *The Ideas That Conquered the World: Peace, Democracy, and Free Markets in the Twenty-first Century* (2002).